Pittsburgh Series in Composition, Literacy, and Culture

Pre/Text
The First Decade

Victor J. Vitanza, Editor

UNIVERSITY OF PITTSBURGH PRESS
Pittsburgh and London

Published by the University of Pittsburgh Press, Pittsburgh, Pa. 15260
Copyright © 1993, University of Pittsburgh Press
All rights reserved
Manufactured in the United States of America
Printed on acid-free paper

Library of Congress Cataloging-in-Publication Data

Pre/Text : the first decade / Victor J. Vitanza, editor.
    p.   cm. — (Pittsburgh series in composition, literacy, and culture)
    Collection of ten articles which previously appeared in Pre/Text and a new "A retrospective and two prospectives."
    Includes "Contents of volumes 1–10" of Pre/Text.
    ISBN 0-8229-3763-8. — ISBN 0-8229-5513-X (pbk.)
    1. Rhetoric. [1. Pre/Text.]   I. Vitanza, Victor J.
II. Pre/Text.   III. Series.
P301.P684   1993
808—dc20   93-1007
                                                          CIP

A CIP catalogue record for this book is available from the British Library.
Eurospan, London

. . . for the 49 readers

Contents

Acknowledgments   ix

A Retrospective and Two Prospectives   xi

1. Rewording the Rhetoric of Composition
   Paul Kameen   3

2. The Dance of Discourse
   Louise Wetherbee Phelps   31

3. Cognition, Convention, and Certainty
   Patricia Bizzell   65

4. Rhetoric in the American College Curriculum
   S. Michael Halloran   93

5. The Rhetor as *Eiron*
   C. Jan Swearingen   117

6. Thomas De Quincey in a Revisionist Rhetoric
   William Covino   163

7. The Writing of Scientific Non-Fiction
   Charles Bazerman   181

8. Neo-Romanticism and the History of Rhetoric
   Sharon Crowley   217

9. The History of Rhetoric and The Rhetoric of History
   John Schilb   237

10. Toward a Sophistic Historiography
    Susan C. Jarratt   263

    Afterwords
       David Bartholomae   287
       Steven Mailloux   299

    Contents of Volumes 1–10   315

    Notes on Contributors   321

Acknowledgments

There are far too many people to acknowledge and to thank; I will mention a few of the many, beginning at what was the "beginning" as I have come to understand it:

I thank and acknowledge my immigrant grandparents, who set sail from the country of rhetoric to come to this country of opportunity: Vito and Mary Vitanza (Piano di Grecci, Sicily) and Frank and Lillie Ditta (Corleone, Sicily). I thank my parents: Joe and Paula Vitanza (Houston, Texas), who inspired me with a sense of ambition, difference, and community.

I thank others, recently more involved in the development of *PRE/TEXT:* Richard Young and the National Endowment for the Humanities (who provided the opportune moment); and nine NEH Fellows, especially Sharon Bassett (who helped me dream about *P/T*) and Jim Berlin (who was especially supportive); the administration and my colleagues at Eastern Illinois University, especially the former president Daniel E. Marvin, Jr., and the chair of English, James Quivey, and my colleagues Roger Whitlow and Donald Dolton; the administration and my colleagues at the University of Texas at Arlington, especially Thomas Porter and Emory Estes.

Moreover, I would like most especially to thank my various graduate assistants: at EIU, Michael Gress and Susan Morris; at UTA, Jane Smith-Broyles, Lynn Worsham, Lorie Goodman Batson, Michelle Ballif, and Diane Mowery. Each of them, some more than others, contributed beyond what could or should be expected. Without them, nothing.

I would like to thank the authors who have contributed to *P/T;* the photographers and cartoonists; the production crew and typesetters (at EIU, David Reed and Donna Wolke; at UTA, Dorothy Estes, Connie Carver, Susan Darovich, and most recently Robert Cook); and of course the printing crews (especially Bill Foster).

I would like to thank my wife, Toni Vitanza, for her help and support.

Finally, I would like to thank Jean Ferguson Carr, David Bartholomae, and the staff of the University of Pittsburgh Press.

A Retrospective and Two Prospectives

A Retrospective

> "Fools had ne'er less wit in a year,
> For wise men are grown foppish,
> And know not how their wits to wear,
> Their manners are so apish."
> — The Fool (*King Lear*)

> The ambivalence of writing [or editing] is such that it can be considered both an act and an interpretative process that follows after an act with which it cannot coincide. As such, it both affirms and denies its own nature or specificity.
> — Paul de Man

> The artist [or publisher] can . . . become "subversive" by merely singing, in all innocence, of respite by the Mississippi. It takes no heroism, or even awareness, for him to contribute his part in this "revolution."
> — Kenneth Burke

"De Beginnibus"   It was easier to start the journal *PRE/TEXT* than it is to write an account of its first decade. Ignorance can encourage us to act without any reservations whatsoever, while experience can and often does make it impossible for us to ignore the possibility of failure or of making a fool of ourselves. Hesitation never entered my mind. Nor did the appropriateness of my taking on this venture. (I had absolutely no standing in the field of rhetoric and composition, or for that matter in any other field.) It was naiveté and a certain-but-apparently-uncertain recklessness — some might say and, in fact, did say — that were behind the inception of and perhaps even the motives of *PRE/TEXT*.

Today, however, in respect to writing this retrospective, it's for me a different story altogether: it's with self-conscious awkwardness and trepidation that I — or a part of me — approach this task. (The self-consciously mischievous, perverse part, to be sure, is still very much at work here.) It's not a problem of evaluating the journal: whether *PRE/TEXT* has been a brilliant success or a miserable (or magnificent) failure or, at worst, simply mediocre must be left to those writing their own retrospectives and to future reviewers and historians. My concern, instead, is with a "history" of the journal's inception and its constant attempts at reconception. My concern is with Proteus. Therefore, a caveat: I do not intend—as the genre of the introduction or retrospective might lead some readers to expect or even to demand—to "introduce" each of the "authors" and their ten articles reprinted here. In other words, I do not wish to be the readers' reader. Nor do I wish to be the readers' prefacer, that is, their liar. I wish, instead, to be the readers' perverse "fool." As we proceed, all this perhaps might become somewhat more unclearly clear.

In preparing for this my brief account, I read the personal notebook that I started in the fall of 1979 and continued through 1982. I read through numerous letters that I had carefully filed away—ten years' worth. And I recalled many particular conversations with various members of the editorial board, with colleagues, with friends and antifriends, and with acquaintances. My conclusion is, and most likely will remain, that the story—or at least, the particular stories that *desire* to be told here—*cannot be told.* Yes, they cannot be told! (I would, you see, also not only frustrate the readers' expectations in dis/respect to genre, but I would further perversely arouse their expectations. I would write a story, given my pretext, by exclaiming that it cannot be told. After all is said and undone, what other kind of writing is there!)

There is, to be sure, a double bind here. Allow me to explain further. The problem, quite ironically, is about *appropriateness.* For the story to be told, I would have to engage in large quantities of what we often refer to as "academic gossip." (I do remember once, however, writing Ross Winterowd, asking him if he would like to be *P/T*'s West Coast "gossip columnist," or as I put it, "the Hedda Hopper of the western world of rhetoric and composition." Ross wrote back and quite properly declined.) For the story to be told, dear readers, I would have to give my account of many of the early "receptions" of the journal, when it was being initially thought through and after its first couple of volumes appeared. (These were extremely tough times, for the new profession was into what depth psychology would call deep denial of anything pretextual. So you see, the profession and I were made for each other.) But let's suppose that I were to tell (further rationalize) *the* story—the story as I experienced it—and submitted it to the University of Pittsburgh Press. What would happen is that its outside reviewers would say, and its editors would agree, that "You can't say this and we can't publish that." Therefore, find some other way to say what desires to be said. Hence, indirection.

I do recall and can vaguely report on, in the form of a representative anecdote, having been slipped a note (let us repeat, a slip of a note) at the 1981 College Composition and Communication Conference, by one of our second-generation, revered colleagues, telling me how disgusted she was by the inaugural volume: specifically, how unreadable it was, how it was devoted to self-aggrandizement; but at the same time, how she, nonetheless, had enjoyed two articles in it.

I had a double private response: I was simultaneously disappointed (the roller coaster plummeted) and perversely elated (the roller coaster ascended). She thought: *Ambivalence.* I thought: *How rhetorical!* With this "event," the word *pretext* — like a free-floating signifier — took on radically different meanings. (But, of course, there were other such "events.")

The inauguration of a journal is a major event in any discipline or field. But journals are started by either "proper" organizations or "proper" names. (An Aristotelian profession would settle for nothing less.) *PRE/TEXT* was started with or by neither. From the beginning — wittingly and unwittingly — *inappropriateness* became the journal's guiding principle. *PRE/TEXT,* or *P/T,* eventually recognized that it had donned the mask of (a) P. T. Barnum. (Or I should more accurately say, at least, that such a recognition encouraged *P/T* to attempt on occasions to wear — as it still attempts to wear — such a mask.) *P/T* attempted not only to be different from "organized" and "institutionalized" journals but also different within its own issues. It desired to commission and publish manuscripts that other journals in the field did not or would not (think of) publish(ing). It attempted to be a "troublemaker."

P/T's table of contents, therefore, radically shifted on occasion from the expected to the unexpected, the appropriate to the inappropriate. (It's best that way with genres, whether "introductions" or a "table of contents.") Also its mocking ads, its covers, its giving awards for the worst, but by far still the best, article in *P/T,* its denouncements of particular manuscripts or even special issues that it had published — all stood in playful, perhaps tasteless, juxtaposition to the discipline of rhetoric and composition and its publishing/editing conventions.

P/T. A three-ring circus. Concessions. And then, a sideshow with freaks. And then, again, a flock of chickens, celebrating KB's and PT's "human barnyard." (In other words, everything for the potentially perverse family of rhetorics.) But this agenda, this act, this "program," is difficult, if not downright impossible, to maintain. Freaks even get tenure (or plucked) or get partially appropriated/co-opted or simply become "the new thing." And then, because of imitation, eventually become "the old thing." And then discarded. *P/T,* nonetheless, has been dedicated (and will continue to be) to the avant-garde, to the principle of searching for newer beginnings or, better put, for *new audiences. New ethoi.* And *new paraTheories.*

New Audiences. P/T has been dedicated to those people and ideas that have been, heretofore, "excluded." Such as those who are the "inappropriate." And why? So that they might be "included" — thereby ever widening and dispersing the field of rhetorics and possible audiences. For a simple (and silly) example, I recall a member of the field of composition complaining to me that she had sent a manuscript to *College Composition and Communication* but that it had been rejected because it was "too theoretical." In the returned manuscript, she said, the word *epistemology* had been circled and a question mark had been placed in the margin. (Oh, how I laughed, and she, too.) In the 1970s and 1980s, the field of composition could be very conservative, and hence the members of the Conference and the readers of *CCC* were kept (editorially) conservative. (Of course, the battle for conservatism continues today even in dis/respect to *College English*. One simply has to read the letters complaining about the articles being published. Such a battle is, of course, inevitable and necessary. And besides, without it, there could be no pretext.)

But *P/T*'s push for discovering and inventing and including new audiences was wider than simply addressing the conservatism of rhetoric and composition teachers, historians, and theorists who find their home in English departments; its push was also for the other conservatism to be found abundantly in speech-communication departments, though *P/T* has included frightfully few authors from speech and has fewer subscribers in that field. (Philosophy, anthropology, and classics follow even further behind.)

New Ethoi. If *P/T* on occasion reached for new audiences, it also (ever) reached for the possibilities of new *ethoi,* new masks and ethics, in relation to languages, rhetorics, and writing and speaking. It's not only that *ethos* and ethic of *P/T* Barnum but also those of Lenny Bruce, Elmer Fudd, Candy Barr, Favorinus, Yorick, Trotsky, Antonin Artaud, Diogenes of Sinope, Mickey Mouse, Bertha Papenheim, and far too many excluded Others. Jean Baudrillard says: "Disneyland is presented as imaginary in order to make us believe that the rest is real, when in fact all of Los Angeles and the America surrounding it are no longer real."[1] I have thought: "*PRE/TEXT* is presented as imaginary in dis/order to make all of us in the profession(s) of rhetoric and composition believe that the other journals and publications are real, when in fact all of them and our profession(s) surrounding them are no longer real, or ethical, in relation to writing (speaking, thinking, reading) and its teaching."

New ParaTheories. Peter Sloterdijk has written: "In laughter, all theory is anticipated."[2] I recalled: "As Nietzsche wrote, 'Objections, digressions, gay mistrust, the delight in mockery are signs of health: everything unconditional belongs in pathology.'" When I was my most pompous and mocking, I thought: "As Voltaire said, 'The Editor is playing to an

Introduction xv

audience that has forgotten how to laugh.'" My sense, however, is that our profession does not wish to laugh; it demands seriousness, for how else — I hear so many of its members claim — can we be a discipline? Discipline = no laughter. Disciplines, like genres and high theory (itself), exclude. We know that we — those of us who, nonetheless, identify with the College Composition and Communication Conference — have become a discipline when we have created our own outsiders. (Lest there be some serious misunderstanding, this should all be good for a laugh, that is, a symptomatic pretext. You see, CCCC *is* my home, but I would make it uncanny!)

These excluded are what *P/T* (bar none) has reached for. It is easier to reach than to grasp. Much that is in *P/T,* by today's standards and perhaps those of the eighties, is conservative, or is written in normal discourse for a normal audience and for an (apparently) normal field. Yes, *P/T* could not keep, in the midst of it all, from being conservative. But — I have to stress — it was so easy to be outlandish and to upset particular members of the field. To actually make them angry. To have them demonstrate quite publicly how intolerant they can be. I remember that when the first brochure stated that *P/T* would be willing to publish "anonymous" articles, someone in our profession was outraged. (See, it is a question of academic genres with their proper editorial conventions.) How simple it is to upset the status quo. To test the field for tolerance. Perhaps that is what *P/T* has been about. If rhetoric can conserve, it can also upset stasis, as Richard Ohmann taught me and many of us when he was the editor of *College English.*

Some More Beginnings   Thus far, I have unabashedly spoken of apparent beginnings, or origins. I am well aware — sophistically and philosophically so — that there are only pitfalls when thinking in terms of origins as well as prefaces or introductions or taxonomies. I am intermittently a poststructuralist, a postmodernist, a Nietzschean, and a Sophist. Such are my predispositions. I am consequently aware that for every person who has been associated with *P/T,* there's a different story of origins, or influences; there are different representative anecdotes. They have their stories and anecdotes. And I have mine. (This will become more self-evident as you, dear reader, begin to study the ten articles and the "afterthoughts" that follow them. I hope that you find them as amusing as I have.)

Looking through my 1979-1982 notebook and rummaging through my mind, I have come upon the following scattered "beginnings." In lieu of a "coherent story," I give both appropriately and inappropriately these following passages and recollections in the form of a truncated "chronicle."

xvi   Introduction

- When born, I was delivered by Dr. G. Suttle Ham. (I have the documents to prove this one, just as Tristram has his novel.)
- When an undergraduate in the sixties, I was the editor of a little magazine at the University of Houston called *Harvest*. I remember going through the magazine's exchange file and finding numerous copies (from volume 1, 1957, to 1962) of *The Evergreen Review,* which later spawned Grove Press. It was this journal and this press that first influenced me to be a publisher and an editor. (For those not familiar with the review and the press, it is important to know that both introduced many of the important literary avant-garde of this century to American audiences, such writers as Jean-Paul Sartre, Samuel Beckett, Jack Kerouac, Allen Ginsberg, William S. Burroughs, Ho Chi Minh, and Susan Sontag.)

Moreover, at the same time at Houston, I met Robert Bonazzi, a fellow student, who had been "excluded" from being an editor for *Harvest,* but had independently started a little magazine of his own that he called *The Fly's Eye*. Bonazzi went on to start and develop yet another new and more exciting magazine called *Latitudes,* and then eventually he started Latitudes Press. He has been an inspiration to me.

- In 1975, I wrote my doctoral dissertation, "The Dialectic of Perverseness in the Major Works of Edgar Allan Poe."
- In 1978-1979, I was a National Endowment for the Humanities Fellow, along with nine other post-docs, in residence at Carnegie Mellon University in Pittsburgh.[3] We were all working with Richard Young, who in part created the conditions for the possibilities of *P/T*. Two days a week in the mornings, Young introduced us to classical and modern rhetorical invention (and Linda Flower and John Hayes unofficially introduced us to empirical research into the composing process). Other days of the week and during the evenings, however, some of us read a number of poststructuralist texts, which were not getting any play—though they desired to play—in the journals of our field. From these reading experiences, we eventually began to think of the necessity for a new journal.
- In 1978, Charles Kneupper introduced me to Richard McKeon's article on rhetoric as architechtonic productive arts.[4] (McKeon's nostalgic, neo-Aristotelian vision of rhetoric subsequently and explicitly informed the objectives of the journal from 1980 to 1986.)
- In 1978, Sharon Bassett introduced me to Paul Feyerabend's *Against Method: Outline for an Anarchistic Theory of Knowledge*. She first pointed out to me that the subject index included "rhetoric, 1-309." (Feyerabend's sense of humor and play and his view of sophistic rhetorics became a counterbalance to McKeon's neo-Aristotelianism. Feyer-

abend gave *P/T* a sophistic concept of [writing for an] audience. In the acknowledgment, he mentions the occasion for his book:

> This essay is the first part of a book on rationalism that was to be written by Imre Lakatos and myself. I was to attack the rationalist position, Imre was to restate and to defend it, making mincemeat of me in the process. Taken together, the two parts were supposed to give an account of our long debate concerning these matters that had started in 1964, had continued, in letters, lectures, telephone calls, papers, almost to the last day of Imre's life and had become a natural part of my daily routine. The origin explains the style of the essay: it is a long and rather personal letter to Imre and every wicked phrase it contains was written in anticipation of an even more wicked reply from the recipient. It is also clear that as it stands the book is sadly incomplete. It lacks the most important part; the reply of the person to whom it is addressed.[5]

Both professionally and personally, this passage has become both figurative and literal.)

• In the spring of 1979, several of the NEH Fellows met Samuel Ijsseling at a Heidegger conference at Duquesne University, Pittsburgh. He told us of his *Philosophy and Rhetoric in Conflict.* (He eventually agreed, quite graciously, to be *P/T*'s European associate editor. Paul Feyerabend also eventually agreed to serve [symbolically] on the editorial board.)

• In the spring of 1979, I talked with the NEH Fellows about the possibilities of a journal, and talked with others who visited CMU and others at the University of Pittsburgh. (It is, indeed, especially fitting that this volume is published by the University of Pittsburgh Press.) When the NEH seminar came to an end and we all packed up to go our separate ways, I announced that *I was going to start a journal.* The response was "yes, that's a good idea." After all, who would or could believe what would eventually happen? At most, it was suggested by someone that this "journal" might be a simple mimeographed newsletter to be circulated among the NEH Fellows and their friends.

• In the fall of 1979, after returning to Eastern Illinois University, I designed a brochure announcing the new journal and had it printed. It was distributed by members of the editorial board at the 1980 College Composition and Communication Conference. We got 150 subscribers. Individual subscriptions were $6.00; institutions, $8.00. *P/T* was in business, but could not pay the bills. And the bills have to be paid!

• In the fall of 1980, I applied to the dean of the graduate school for an Academic Needs Assessment Grant and received it, the monies of which partially paid for the first double issue.

• The first volume (Spring/Fall 1980), with a publication order of 250 copies, appeared in 1981. The cover photo, by Linda Smogor, was of a new building rising out of ruins. (This double issue has never been surpassed. In my estimation, it has been the only successful issue of *P/T.* Where else was there to go? This is the problem of the avant-garde, or at least a call for the avant-garde. As editor and publisher, I [or we] have never been able to surpass this issue! In an allegorical article on cookery and recipes, I wrote of breaking rules concerning taste: "Jello and tuna together *is* anarchy.")

With this first volume, I set the following editorial policy: "These objectives are only initial, general guidelines. Instead of having standing objectives, the editors and advisory board hope, expect, and wish to foster the view that the kinds of articles published in *P/T* will determine the kind of journal(s) and objectives *P/T* will evolve into and have from issue to issue. The editors have made it their standing policy, however, to be less receptive to conventional academic articles with clearly stated theses that involve no risk and that especially lead to a sense of closure and that have as their main goal to analyze the logic of theories and finally to prove or refute them. The editorial board will be more receptive, instead, to the kind of open-ended speculative discourse found in exploratory articles, progress reports, and working papers. Hence the title and term 'pre/text.' The board will also be receptive to prospective contributors who wish to publish their pre/texts under a 'pseudonym' or 'anonymously,' and will likewise be receptive to suggestions for any other unorthodox formats, guidelines, or procedures that will enhance success in the inter-disciplinary study of rhetoric and in communications between the journal's subscribers and contributors" (5–6).

• After the inaugural volume appeared, Edward Corbett was the first member of our profession (to my knowledge) to become openly supportive of *P/T*. (Professor Corbett continued to be supportive in a number of invaluable ways.)

• In 1981, *P/T* established a standing "special interest group" with the College Composition and Communication Conference, and discussed—greatly with the help of Sam Watson, Jr.—Michael Polanyi and the importance of his work to rhetoric and composition. (Under the name of *"PRE/TEXT:* A Forum for the Inter-Disciplinary Study of Rhetoric," the group has included other discussions on such topics as "revisionary histories of rhetoric," "how philosophy can help us," "women in the profession of composition," "can the virtue/*areté* of writing be taught?"

Introduction   xix

"the problem of the ethical subject," and "Jacques Lacan and writing." Some of these became "projects" to be published in *P/T*.)

• In 1982, I moved to the University of Texas at Arlington, and *P/T* became a quarterly. (The subscription price jumped to $12.00 and then eventually to $15.00.)

• Well into 1985, *P/T* had very few subscribers, though seemingly everyone was reading it. (Its status has been "underground.") Hence, "a cover story" for the exact (embarrassing) number of subscribers was eventually dreamed up: "49 *PRE/TEXT* readers can't be wrong." (*P/T* continued to be published from a year to a year and a half behind the calendar. Money problems!)

• In 1983, a reviewer in an article in *College English* on journals in the discipline of rhetoric and composition relegated *P/T* (along with *Philosophy and Rhetoric*) to a footnote, essentially dismissing it as not relevant to the field. Similarly, in 1989, at an executive committee meeting of the College Composition and Communication Conference, there was an attempt, in agenda item IX.A.1, to exclude *P/T,* once again, from being recognized as contributing to the field of rhetoric and composition. (Under discussion was the giving of awards for the best articles published yearly in each journal in the field.) The agenda item was voted down.

• In 1985, I was advised by a contributor that an editor's job was to keep authors from making fools of themselves. I, perversely, began to think: "Why not [continue to] let particular authors make *fools* of themselves? After all," I reasoned, "it's simply a matter of what kind of *fool* we want to be." (I have learned much from Papa KB.)

• In 1987, the subtitle of *P/T* was changed from "An Inter-Disciplinary Journal of Rhetoric" to "A Journal of Rhetorical Theory." (José Harari says: "the imaginary functions as the pre-text of theory.")[6] Moreover, the "objectives" were dropped from the inside front page. (The changes signaled both a movement away from the McKeon influence—that is, from neo-Aristotelianism—and a willingness to further embrace ever imaginary Feyerabendisms—that is, playing the game of theory "without criteria.")

• In 1987, James Berlin—a member of the editorial board and, therefore, somewhat prejudiced—began to refer to *P/T* as "the *Critical Inquiry* of rhetoric and composition." (And I kept thinking that *Critical Inquiry* was the *PRE/TEXT* of critical and literary theory!) As I said, we have our perverse, separate stories.

• In 1989, Robert Connors, not a member of the editorial board, graciously stated at a historiography conference (at UTA) that Victor, with some of his colleagues, started *P/T* because what they wanted to say needed a forum. (Not unlike the editors of *Critical Inquiry* [Chicago] and *South Atlantic Quarterly* [Duke], they/"we" published our own works. Hence, the infamous 1987 historiography double issue.)

• In 1990, John Schilb suggested to me that a retrospective of *P/T* be attempted. I wrote a letter to the editorial board concerning this matter. Eventually I was surprised to receive a letter from Jean Ferguson Carr and David Bartholomae (editors of the Pittsburgh Series in Composition, Literacy, and Culture) saying that they were interested in publishing the volume. (Evidently, "you *can* go home again.")

The editorial board helped select the ten articles to be included in this retrospective. The articles, it was understood, were *not* to be selected as "the best of *P/T*." (The selection was made "without criteria.")[7]

• In 1990, after the College Composition and Communication Conference, I received a letter claiming that I (along with my cartoonist Dick Collier, who draws my ideas) had plagiarized the pencil-to-a-rose concept that is a standing design for the cover of *Rhetoric Review*. The author of the letter—allegedly the "author" of the design—had seen a *P/T* ad with a similar design on it, which had appeared also previously on the *P/T* cover of volume 9, no. 1-2, but in the form of the same pencil metamorphosizing into a "chicken claw." The letter was not at all humorous, for it stated that I ought to acknowledge (publicly repent) this theft to the profession!

Well, it was clear to me that the author of the letter knew nothing about *P/T* and also was humor impaired. I began to feel like the editor/publisher of *The National Enquirer* but without a stable of attorneys. I discussed the matter with my friend and colleague, Theresa Enos. We both laughed. I finally wrote a letter to the author of the letter explaining that *P/T* Barnum (aka Barnone) was "into" fun, and in this case, "into" making parodies of the other journals in the field and that Theresa and I had previously worked this one out and that we laughed and hoped that she might laugh as well. I also tried to explain the "brilliance" behind my idea of the chicken claw as a countertheory of the composing process. And I tried to explain other things. Evidently, the matter has been dropped. (But the mischievousness continued, with "The Burpean Corner," which first appeared in volume 10, no. 1-2.)

• In 1990, on *60 Minutes,* the then editor of *Vanity Fair,* Tina Brown, was asked what were her guidelines, or her secret, for a successful issue of the magazine. She said that each issue had to have something "tasteless" in it. (I realized, then, that I had been living in the future anterior.)

Now, I guess that this characterization—un/namely, my use of the word *tasteless*—needs some serious explaining, for the readers of the manuscript for the University of Pittsburgh Press questioned me concerning this point. For starters, I can explain, as Brown did, that on at least one page of each issue there must be something that does not belong, something that demonstrates downright poor taste, something that the genre or issue of a "scholarly" publication demands to be excluded. (This *tasteless* something would be like, you see, mixing tuna and jello on the same plate.)

Or I can explain that *tasteless* means that in at least every issue there should be one article/essay that the profession has not yet developed a taste for, but which I would attempt, as an editor, to get the discipline, nonetheless, to begin to acquire a taste for. Editing and publishing, in this case, then, is like feeding something different to guests who insist on only their unquestioned taste for boiled meat and potatoes. Do you catch my drift?

• In 1992 (July 27), I received the two readers' reports for this retrospective (as I mention above) and I began to see, once ever again, that *P/T* has only, if fortunate, "49 Readers," and that these two readers, how un/fortunate, were not among the number. (I jest?) One reader wrote: "Why is the history of an editorship given primacy over the development of substance, or non development of it if he [VV] thinks that the better course?" Because I am not an editor for *College Composition and Communication* but for myself. Similarly, the other reader suggested that I make a "Wordsearch [to] minimize redundant references to 'me.' Can VV keep the sense of humor but focus on the journal? (This is an editorial, not an existential, question—I hope.)" No, I do not, cannot, separate my (various) selves from the journal, any more than I can separate substance from style.

Both readers suggested that I rewrite my retrospectus so that what I have to say might introduce new graduate students to our field, "English Studies." I have already introduced new students by saying that Disneyland is to Los Angeles as *PRE/TEXT* is to the field of rhetoric and composition.

Finally—and most disturbingly—both readers (so much for *homologia*) were "down" not only on my retrospective but also (and more so) on Steven Mailloux's afterword. One writes: "Nothing suggests that [Mailloux] has taken seriously [!] either the essays or an historian's responsibility [!] to select and arrange to make sense—even several kinds of sense—of a decade of the journal. . . . [T]his afterword trivializes subversion into mere aimlessness [!]. It also trivializes the journal, which deserves better [!]."

Recalling lines from *King Lear*, I don't know if I should don the mask of the "bitter fool" or "sweet fool."

Two Prospectives

A View   What will have *P/T* become during the next decade? In part, this question has to do with the kinds of articles/essays that I would like to publish. (I say "in part" because a publication is composed of more than just articles. It is composed of its pretexts as well. Our field, along with its editors and subscribers, has failed to acknowledge this point and its rhetorical implications. Hence, my wisecrack earlier about Disneyland. And about tastelessness.)

As a member of a panel of editors scheduled by the Research Network at the 1990 College Composition and Communication Conference, I was asked what kinds of manuscripts I was interested in receiving. My answer, which might serve well for this prospective, was/is that I don't know, but that my attitude toward what I want is "proleptic." In other words, I will have known when I see it. I added, however, that it's easy to say what I don't want, which is specifically what every other journal is publishing.

Having referred to this past statement, however, I am still intrigued with the future, while guardedly concerned about any future of an illusion.

Two new possibilities on the horizon for *P/T* are, first, the inclusion of what I have referred to as "re/inter/views" (which are described in the Fore/word to volume 10, no. 1-2); it's very important that our colleagues be encouraged, as a collective, to read widely and to encounter the authors that they read, especially in published exchanges. Hence, the idea of combining reviews and interviews in what I have labelled "re/inter/views." A second possibility for *P/T* is the eventual inauguration of *P/T* Press, with the publication of a book each year. This latter possibility will be difficult to achieve but worth attempting. These, then, are two new possibilities, but it needs to be stressed that *P/T* will remain the same in its differences with THE DISCIPLINE of rhetoric in general.

I would like *P/T* to continue to place into diaspora any attempt by our field — which I broadly define as anyone interested in language and (mis)communication — to define (or to limit) itself to *being* either a discipline or a metadiscipline or, if possible, both. *P/T*, therefore, will continue in its efforts to guard this *question of being,* that is, to guard the question concerning the limits of the field. And how? One possible way, as stated previously in the retrospective, is to "include" what any movement toward totalization or systemization might demand "to exclude." (And to systematize is, indeed, to exclude.)

As I said and as I cannot repeat enough, the discipline of rhetoric is conservative while denying the possibilities of being (perpetually, laughingly) revolutionary. If it does speak of revolution or of change, it speaks seriously. *P/T*, therefore, will continue to attempt to enact what it is to be *homo rhetoricus* as opposed to *homo seriosus*. (Richard Lanham in the first two chapters of *The Motives of Eloquence* [hereafter, referred to as *ME*][8] has made this distinction brilliantly.) The movement toward seriousness, toward systemization or a "unified field," toward (alleged strategic) feminine essences, toward consensus and collaboration and *homologia* (cooking together), toward a total(izing) lack of tolerance, say, in style, is getting worse and worse in our discipline. In fact, there is an ever growing movement toward being *a*rhetorical itself. (At the 1990 Research Network at the CCCC, a member of our profession stood up and said that "for *the health* of our discipline, we should exclude anyone who wants to talk about Foucault"! Such a movement, *P/T* will stand *against*.)

Having looked to the future (via the past), however, *P/T* — it must also be stressed — will continue to include the dispossessed of the profession. To paraphrase Gilles Deleuze and Félix Guattari, in rhetoric there is only desire and the social. *P/T* will continue to make the social ever wider, dispersing it, by adding greater levels of what desires to be said, but heretofore has been only silenced.

During the past decade, *P/T* added those writers and thinkers (as Robert Connors has said) for whom there was no place in the field. Today, however, many of these people have gone on to become major voices, in great part, because of *P/T*. (I perversely see this as terribly unfortunate; for it was never the intention of P. T. to make Stars for the field! Success, indeed, is its own failure.) Therefore, given the language game of avant-garde art, the language game of the future anterior, these major voices must drop out of *P/T,* and in their place new-but-yet-unknown voices (both music and noise) must be found and then heard. As editor, I would be Schönberg, with a twelve-tone system. And a lot of discordance.

And I would finally add that the social conscience of *P/T* — but with still greater levels of desire — must continue to be elevated. To this end, or newer beginning, I now turn to Jim, who became the associate editor in 1990.

Victor J. Vitanza

Another View   The ultimate triumph of any political coalition is achieved when its customary manner of articulating its position is established as natural, normal, obvious, and self-evident discourse, the language best suited to discussing the genuinely important issues in any debate. Henceforth, arguments for any position counter to the authorized version of things-as-in-themselves-they-really-are must be presented, to be taken seriously, within the terms of this natural, normal, and obvious discourse. The "clear and plain language" so insisted upon today by those within and outside of the academy is simply the assertion of a frame, a margin, to restrict and contain the discussion of opposing viewpoints. If you must speak, dissidents are told, you must use my language, the terms I immediately understand. (But of course the positions offered by the opposition often cannot be enunciated within the terms of this dominant discourse, terms that have come to represent "common sense" — the interpretation that immediately occurs to anyone who is apprehending experience within the perspective inscribed in "clear and plain language." Another way of characterizing this situation is to assert that a political group achieves hegemony when it succeeds in convincing a majority (or at least a majority of those with power) that its manner of discoursing is the path to truth, while its various opponents' characteristic modes are "mere rhetoric." Rhetoric then becomes a term for illusions and distortions and even lies, to be regarded as the discredited jargon of the enemies of truth.

This sort of exchange was demonstrated time and again in the efforts of President George Bush and his administration to characterize opponents to their policy of exterminating Iraqis during the Persian Gulf War as practitioners of propaganda or "mere rhetoric." The allied forces, Bush and his spokespersons assured us, were "liberating Kuwait" by "surgical strikes" with "smart bombs," focusing on "strategic military targets" in Baghdad. The unconscionable murder of thousands of civilians was described as mere "collateral damage." The most painful part of watching the reports of that war in the U.S. media and the press was the eager and willing complicity of reporters in the efforts of government officials to construct this sanitized, monologic version of the unfolding events of this ugly war. It is not just that those in power were attempting to manage the news: this is as American as apple pie or criminal fraud among bank managers and defense contractors. What was genuinely disturbing was that those who were most immediately being managed, our media representatives, seemed to have become helpless to resist. This was most obvious in the questions they asked, questions articulated within the reassuring rhetoric of the militaristic government officials they were interrogating. Only one rhetoric — one mode of talking and writing — was permissible, and so only one version of events was allowed. And in its clarity and plainness and comfort ("smart bomb" video displays on television never endanger people, only "military installations"), this rhetoric effectively obscured the bloody and cruel suffering and death that were being visited on innocent civilians in the name of truth, freedom, democracy, and the American way.[9]

PRE/TEXT makes people angry. Despite the number of subscribers who look forward to its arrival with keen relish, I suspect that a larger group considers it only because conscientious research makes it necessary.

I have in fact encountered a surprisingly large number of scholars of sane mind who are frankly appalled by *PRE/TEXT*'s . . . I struggle for a word . . . existence. It is not simply that the journal has no comforting party line: the same can be said for any number of journals not nearly so controversial. It is instead, I think, *P/T*'s unique commitment to oppose all party lines, dedicating itself to the continual disruption of all complacency, all discourses of comfort and consolation. The journal from its start has been devoted to dissonance and subversion, refusing to support any single faction or constituency. (I remember Victor Vitanza — or the V.V. Project, as Kenneth Burke once characterized him — suffering pangs of doubt at CCCC in Dallas in 1981 as a disparate array of individuals managed to overcome their natural tact and reticence in order to apprise him of the garbage he had foisted on the world in the first issue.) It seems to me that V.V. has designed each number so that it is certain to offend someone, if not (and this by now is its tacit aim) everyone, everywhere. (I have even heard it denounced by people whose careers it unquestionably furthered.) The purpose of the journal has been shaped in opposition from the start, and, the furies willing, it will continue to follow this disruptive and deviant path.

PRE/TEXT's subversiveness is particularly important at this time. Rhetoric, alas, has become respectable as a discipline. Offering a subject of study, methods for pursuing this study, and graduate programs for creating specialists in its methods, it has found a space in the sacred groves of the university. When listing the disciplines that are to be included in the interdisciplinary work of cultural studies, for example, discussants commonly include rhetoric. Similarly, the indexes of books on literary theory or historiography or postmodern philosophy reveal the role that rhetoric is now given in serious intellectual concerns. It was, of course, not always so. When V.V. founded *P/T* in 1980, rhetoric figured in popular discourse only as the contrary of truth (indeed, as today) and in university departments as the devalorized opposite of literary texts (English), of empirical investigation (communication), and of the pursuit of rational truth (philosophy). *P/T* was of course a part of the general activity that accompanied the displacement of these invidious oppositions, and, more important, it has had a role in the continuous effort to disrupt and displace them. And this, I would argue, is the future of *P/T* (at last I get to it), as it has been its past.

The return of rhetoric as a legitimate domain of investigation has been an interdisciplinary affair. As English and communication and philosophy have taken the rhetorical turn, so have history and sociology and psychology and economics and even, wonder to behold, the "hard sciences" of physics and biology. *P/T* will continue to be a place for workers in these (and other) diverse disciplines to present their work.

Statements that are occasionally too hot to be handled by journals dedicated to normal discourse, or business as usual, will continue to find a sympathetic audience in *P/T*. Of course, these essays will remain disruptive, disrespectful, and destructive of complacency in keeping with the highest (some would say the lowest) standards of the journal.

While *PRE/TEXT* will continue to serve those who cannot find a hearing elsewhere, it will also provide an equally exceptional service for those who work in the more traditional domains of rhetoric—in English, communication, and philosophy departments. It is especially important that *P/T* maintain its challenge to these fields, particularly now that they have become so comfortably situated in previously hostile territory. The strongest impulse of academic disciplines is to serve their members' material interests, that is, to devise methods to capture a good share of the rewards provided by academic institutions. (Given the institutional corruptions of higher education in its predilection for simple counting games in evaluating the value of a scholar's work, this is not unexpected, but I will leave this matter for another time.) The result is that normal discourse in a field of study will usually gravitate toward the safe and cozy—for example, toward distinctions that finally do not make much difference in the practical affairs of a society. Against this impulse, *P/T* will remain a forum for "abnormal discourse," for statements that challenge "what everybody knows." (I am obviously using Richard Rorty's distinction between "normal" and "abnormal" discourse, but I mean by it an activity more contestatory and subversive than he in his political innocence can tolerate.) *P/T* will continue to be oppositional, finding no place to rest secure, dedicated to the position that no position can be final and irrefutable (except of course for this originary one, a contradiction with which *P/T* can live). This does not mean, I hasten to add, that its contributors will not take stances or that they will be constantly changing their minds (although the latter is neither unlikely nor to be regretted). It does mean that *P/T* essays in their collective force will constantly interrogate and problematize each other, jostling their fellows into indeterminacies and new, less assured and settled stances.

PRE/TEXT is a forum where we can all get together to disagree, establishing relationships, as V.V. and I have done, on mutual and heartfelt disrespect. (I could never be troubled to argue with a position or person I did not genuinely dislike at least part of the time. It is out of scorn that worthwhile differences are discovered. Without rancor there is no rose.) I see a tendency in rhetorical studies to retreat into the camp of one's own affiliation—the crowd of *Rhetorica* or *Philosophy and Rhetoric* or *College Composition and Communication* or *Quarterly Journal of Speech*, or of whatever journal happens to applaud one's perspective. I do not wish to disparage these or other journals in rhetoric, some

Introduction xxvii

of which have generously included my own work. Nor do I wish to suggest that they generate no disagreement: they certainly do. Only *P/T*, however, creates a clash that cuts across all affiliations, collecting the entire range of differences and generating a battle of all against all. This fracas is saved from sheer nihilism, furthermore, in revealing and creating new alliances and disalliances, however temporary, opening up new possibilities for a richer, more complex discourse.

This brings me back to rhetoric and the war against Iraq. The central role of rhetoric in human affairs has never been more apparent. When the Bush administration denied rhetoric in the name of truth, freedom, democracy, and the American way, it reminded us that all terms are rhetorical, especially such apparently transparent ones as these. These designations themselves are finally terrains of ideological battle in a quest to determine who will decide what their meanings will be. During Desert Storm, according to the currently hegemonic discourse, truth, freedom, democracy, and the American way demanded support for the systematic destruction of a people and their way of life, complete with war reparations afterward. While our generals told us that our mission was to liberate Kuwait, our forces were around the clock undertaking horrifying bombing sorties into Iraq. An Associated Press news release for March 1, 1991, estimated that "collateral damage" had ended the lives of 20,000 Iraqi civilians; the final tally of military casualties was, of course, even higher. Meanwhile, those of us for whom truth, freedom, democracy, and the American way mean something else searched the media and the popular press for someone to offer an oppositional definition — any oppositional definition. Instead, citizens in huge numbers, following the lead of their elected officials in Congress, willingly, eagerly, relinquished their right to protest the actions of the Bush administration and were furious with those of us who refused to join them in this political self-immolation.

I do not wish to say that *PRE/TEXT* is somehow come to save us from our flirtations with fascism. I do think, however, that this journal provides us with a model for democratic discourse that can be instructive, particularly since, as I said before, it operates at the intersection of so many different ongoing debates and debaters involved in the teaching and practice of rhetoric. Rhetoric after all is what is being threatened today in the political arena, both as an activity and, at the University of Texas at Austin, as a field of study. *P/T* has no political program, and some of my leftist friends would dismiss it precisely on that score. It has published an issue on Barbara Herrnstein Smith (vol. 10, nos. 3-4); one on Expressive Writing, edited by Peter Elbow (vol. 11, nos. 1-2); another on Marxism and Rhetoric, edited by John Trimbur and me (vol. 13, no. 1-2); and one on Queer Rhetoric, edited by Margaret

Morrison (vol. 13, nos. 3–4). But all these disparate voices are presented precisely because taken together they offer a rich set of alternatives, conflicts, and antagonisms. Of equal importance, these materials are put forth under the aegis of V.V., the deconstructive demon whose own work tacitly reminds us that these formulations, despite their best intentions, are inadvertently endorsing exclusions and margins and gaps and contradictions. There is no center—safe and secure—to *P/T,* as there is no safe and secure center to truth, freedom, democracy, and the American way. These formulations are rhetorical constructs which must be deconstructed and reconstructed, displaced and refigured, continually, probing their consequences for the material practices of our everyday lives. Now that rhetoric is back on the academic agenda, perhaps diplomacy, the art of rhetoric at its best, has a chance to challenge war, the refusal of rhetoric in the final desperate quest for certainty and closure—human annihilation.

James A. Berlin

Notes

1. Jean Baudrillard, *Selected Writings,* ed. Mark Poster (Stanford, Calif.: Stanford Univ. Press, 1988), pp. 171–72.

2. Peter Sloterdijk, *Critique of Cynical Reason,* trans. Michael Eldred (Minneapolis: Univ. of Minnesota Press, 1987), p. 42.

3. They were Sharon Bassett, James A. Berlin, Lisa Ede, David Fractenberg, Bob Inkster, Sam Watson, Jr., Vickie Winkler, and the late William Nelson and Charles W. Kneupper.

4. Richard McKeon, "The Uses of Rhetoric in a Technological Age: Architectonic Productive Arts," in *The Prospects of Rhetoric,* ed. Lloyd F. Bitzer and Edwin Black (New York: Prentice-Hall, 1971), pp. 44–63.

5. Paul Feyerabend, *Against Method: Outline for an Anarchistic Theory of Knowledge* (London: Verson, 1975), p. 7. There's another passage from *Against Method* that has been influential. It speaks of the future anterior and prolepsis: "by incorporation into a language of the future, which means *that one must have to argue with unexplained terms and to use sentences for which no clear rules of usage are as yet available.* Just as a child who starts using words without yet understanding them, who adds more and more uncomprehended linguistic fragments to his playful activity, discovers the sense-giving principle only after he has been active in this way for a long time—the activity being a necessary presupposition of the final blossoming forth of sense—in the very same way the inventor of a new world view (and the philosopher of science who tries to understand his procedure) must be able to talk nonsense until the amount of nonsense created by him and his friends is big enough to give sense to all its parts (256–57; Feyerabend's emphasis).

6. José Harari, *Scenarios of the Imaginary* (Ithaca, N.Y.: Cornell Univ. Press, 1987), p. 17.

7. In this case, I say this with tongue in cheek.

8. Richard A. Lanham, *The Motives of Eloquence* (New Haven, Conn.: Yale Univ. Press, 1976). In 1985, Jim Berlin told me that someone in the field asked him: "Do you know about this new journal *PRE/TEXT?*" Jim's response: "Of course, *c'est moi!*" Yes, P/T (Barnum, barnone) celebrates so-called self-aggrandizement! It would make a virtue of it. Read the "afterthoughts" by some of the contributors to this volume and again there are ample examples of further self-celebration.

9. This was written during the first days of the Persian Gulf War. At the time of this editorial revision, some two years later, Bush in the last hours of his presidency, continued his policy of mass destruction with the renewed bombing of Baghdad. President-elect Clinton offered his unequivocal support.

Pre/Text
The First Decade

1 : REWORDING THE RHETORIC OF COMPOSITION

Paul J. Kameen
Carnegie-Mellon University

> Strange philosophies have arisen upon the supposition that everything which is known to us figures in thought as a discursive communicable proposition.
>
> —S. K. Langer

EXPLORING TEXTS

There are dozens, perhaps hundreds of composition textbooks currently on the market. Yet selecting one for a course is most often a frustrating and unforgiving process of sifting the adequate from the unacceptable, of groping, guessing, and compromising. When confronting this seemingly chaotic array of approaches competing for our attention it is important for us to remember that a composition textbook is not simply a pedagogical device for enabling students to improve their writing; it is also a definition of what writing is and what writing is for, a kind of argument whose surface rhetoric depends on a broad web of meta-rhetorical assumptions, both epistemological and linguistic. These assumptions determine the shapes each argument can and will assume. Only by exploring texts on this level can we begin to find an orderly procedure for distinguishing various methods and for evaluating their relative merits.

From this vantage point a myriad of possibilities yields to an initial order. For there are three major foci around which most composition textbooks constellate, with each group depending on a different epistemic base for initiating discourse. These bases are (1) in the realm of forms, with particular emphasis on the abstract modes of thought that organize knowledge and discourse; (2) in the inner precincts of the self, with particular emphasis on experiential writing and authentic voices; and (3) in the domain of audience, with particular emphasis on writing as a heuristically-enabled, information-processing behavior.

On the broadest level, each of these categories is both created and bounded by certain metaphoric conceptions of the "universe of discourse" within which writing can take place. Each inscribes itself within various sets of dichotomies—thought/feeling, form/content, expression/communication, self/audience, etc.—which constrain its field of inquiry. These pairs, usually conceived as polar opposites rather than as dialectical contraries, constitute the channels along which that approach issues. On a more concrete level, each is both created and bounded by the very particular metaphors that function as analogies for the writing process. One such metaphor is the word "exploration," which serves as a powerful symptomatic emblem of implicit assumptions concerning the nature and purpose of composition.

Thus, metaphors exert a double pressure on any definition of the writing process. Yet despite the nominal concessions that the above approaches make to the exploratory function of language-as-metaphor, each relegates language to a subordinate status in relation to some other, essentially nonverbal base for invention. And each leaves its own metaphors largely unquestioned and unexamined. This exclusion of language as a possible site for creative invention precludes the best avenue for restoring a dialectical relationship among the binary concepts that metaphorically impinge on our theories. It also makes it difficult to take self-conscious advantage of the particular metaphors, like exploration, that weave their epistemological designs into the surfaces of our texts.

I will in the course of my own exploration sketch out a few lines along which we might move toward a conception of language as a metaphor that resolves the apparent contradictions out of which current theories of composition seem to issue and around which they seem to congregate. I will turn most often to Coleridge to sustain and elaborate this counterpoint. I choose him not because he best illustrates the alternative that interests me, though he does that quite well, but because his rhetoric is one of the most widely misunderstood of all those that hover over the current landscape of composition theory.

Most textbooks currently in print ground their epistemological priorities in formalistic relationships between thinking and writing. This category of form-based texts includes all of those "current-traditional"[1] rhetorics and readers sub-divided according to classical patterns of discourse or traditional modes of analysis. I will look in detail at Frank D'Angelo's *Process and Thought in Composition*,[2] primarily because it is so forthright and enthusiastic about its biases in this direction. As D'Angelo says:

> each of us to a certain extent must follow certain lines of development in our thinking because the mind is organized according to certain

principles. It recognizes temporal, spatial, logical and psychological principles and relationships in the universe. . . . Principles of composition . . . are *ways of knowing* (*Textbook,* p. 42, italics his)

And later:

Paradigms, at least the kind that we will be concerned with, represent *patterns of thought* that give your writing a sense of direction and provide you with a formal means of ordering your ideas. (*Textbook,* p. 70, italics his)

The epistemological premises of D'Angelo's approach are quite clear: "Thinking" is a way of knowing inscribed within a finite and specifiable set of formal cognitive processes whose products are "ideas": "Every time you analyze, classify, exemplify, enumerate, compare, contrast, or discern cause and effect relationships, you are inventing ideas" (*Textbook,* p. 42). Through its formal structures the mind invents ideas; only thereafter does, or can, one write. Thus a radical form-content distinction is central to D'Angelo's system: "The concept of structure is our model of understanding, and it is not inaccurate to separate the idea of structure from the concept of content."[3] For D'Angelo this distinction is not simply a useful one, but one that is necessarily pre-requisite because it is genetically pre-determined:

the structural properties which underlie our mental operations must be genetically inherited. In generating discourse, the individual uses this underlying, abstract structure as a base. Then he supports this structure by filling in the details from the universe of discourse around him. (*Theory,* p. 26)

One could not ask for a starker demarcation between form and content, and the use of the narrative indicator "then" clearly separates thinking from writing not only modally but temporally. D'Angelo's claim that "one of the tasks of the rhetorician is to relate the structure of thought to the structure of discourse" (*Theory,* p. 16) must, then, be specious; for discourse is merely a repetition of innate structures of thought "filled in" with details. The only relational devices which D'Angelo proposes are syntagmatic analysis (which seeks patterns of linear sequence) and paradigmatic analysis (which seeks patterns of "dynamic organizational processes" [*Textbook,* p. 73]), both of which are simply tools for discovering implicit forms in what one reads or has written.

Such an explanation of the writing process has serious consequences on the level of intention. That thoughts can exist whole and conscious

6 *Paul Kameen*

in some pre-verbal realm suggests that a writer begins with a clearly afore-thought intention which language can then be used to represent. A century of debate about intentions and intentional fallacies among literary critics, not to mention the influence of phenomenological philosophies, may not have dismissed this representational notion of language from our discourse. But it should at least cause us to look carefully at D'Angelo's ontology of mind.

To be sure, when language is diminished to purely functional flesh on a form, it is difficult to see any ways in which writing can be exploratory. D'Angelo does, in fact, use the word only rarely and off-handedly. He says, for instance, that the formal categories of thought "give rise to certain questions that enable you to explore a general subject to get ideas for writing" (*Textbook,* p. 57). Exploration, like thinking, proceeds in the abstract, non-verbal realm of forms and produces "ideas," again presumably pure structures of thought that can be fleshed out with words. Writing has become here something of an after-thought (in both senses of the word); and only if it is properly prepared for on the intentional level of ideas and forms can it proceed toward its resolution in a text of organized details.

Writing is thereby reduced to a formulaic elaboration of a chosen (or assigned) pattern that pre-constitutes the text that can be produced. There are, of course, a variety of recent alternate views which redeem language as a mode of invention. But I will, as I promised, restrict my discussion to Coleridge, who, in his effort to counter certain misreadings of Plato and Bacon, argues generally against deductive formalisms. As Coleridge says:

> They both saw that there could be no hope of any fruitful and secure method, while forms merely subjective were presumed as the true and proper moulds of objective truth.[4]

What fascinates Coleridge in both Plato and Bacon, despite serious reservations in the latter case, is their concern for developing "the science of method" (p. 361), the purpose of which is "not so much to establish any particular truth, as to remove the obstacles, the continuance of which is preclusive of all truth" (p. 357). Coledridge recommends a sort of self-conscious philosophical experimentation in which induction is guided by "the forethoughtful query" (p. 361). Thus for Coleridge "an idea is an experiment proposed, an experiment is an idea realized" (p. 362). Such experiments are by definition rhetorical and can occur only through the meditational power of language itself. Like Plato, Coleridge recommends that systems which depend on radical form-content distinctions be "re-signed, as their proper trade, to the sophists" (p. 357).[5]

Between the mid-sixties and mid-seventies there was a shift away from textbooks with a formalistic agenda and toward approaches whose epistemologies were grounded in an experiential model of writing. Authenticity, expression, voice, and particularly "self" are the passwords into this arena, and many of the values associated with this mode of teaching writing are, or more properly *seem to be,* derived from the rhetoric of Romanticism that I have just counterposed against D'Angelo. I have chosen as the exemplar of this approach James E. Miller and Stephen Judy's *Writing in Reality,*[6] because it represents a boadly based devotion to the concept of self-discovery as the motive for writing and depends heavily on the familiar vocabulary associated with this notion of discourse. In addition, and this will become useful later, it illustrates a rhetoric that the "new rhetoricians" characterize pejoratively as "vitalistic," or in Ross Winterowd's terse expression, "the looky-feely-smelly" approach to composition.[7]

Miller and Judy begin their argument with a direct assault on formalistic procedures for teaching writing:

> a student who has received exclusive training in so-called practical forms may, ironically, be limited in the ability to write those forms successfully, limited by the very narrowness of the experience. . . . [But] if you engage in a variety of imaginative writing experiences and if that engagement is personally satisfying, we think you will have enormously extended both your powers over the written word . . . and deepened your sense of self. (p. 8)

Despite this initial indication that they will keep invention at least partially in the field of language, a theme that recurs throughout the text, their argument collapses around the claustrophobic "sense of self" that concludes this passage. Language becomes something that one assumes "power over" in order to render the egocentric self.

"Each self," they tell us, "is the center of a universe. If we believe what our senses seem to tell us, the entire world is arranged around us to be apprehended by us" (p. 52). Writing, moreover, "constitutes the discovery of the self" (p. 30), and the writer must "follow the injunction to 'let the self go on paper'" (p. 40), in order to reach the ultimate goal which is to *"seek out the truth and unravel the snarled web of* [his] *motivations"* (p. 12, italics theirs). Writing then not only begins but ends in an entirely self-contained world of subjective experience.

Miller and Judy have delivered the writer out of the bondage of formal structures which D'Angelo imposes over intentionality. Yet they have delivered him into an equally confining world wherein the motivation to write must arise mysteriously from "inner sources" (p. 5). There is not then a great deal that we can actually *teach* about writing; for as Miller and Judy inform the student in their introduction, "we feel no need to teach you about language. . . . You have the language; our aim is to help you release and control it" (p. 5). The implication is that the proper role of the instructor is simply to provide students with occasions for discourse and that they in turn will "participate more actively, directly, and consciously in that creation of the self which is the major challenge of existence" (p. 45).

This challenge is to be met by "the processes of the imagination," which "remain shrouded in mystery" (p. 6). But for Miller and Judy to think imaginatively is simply "to see things from a fresh point of view, to treat all experience, as Breton suggests, as if it is 'strange'" (pp. 72–73).[8] Breton's recommendation to make things "strange" is here reduced to seeing things from "a fresh point of view," thereby stripping off the self-transcendent possibilities that are inherent in his conception of surrealism and transmuting language into a medium that merely extends and amplifies the range of our own solipsism. To the extent that truly imaginative exploration remains possible, it is confined entirely to the enclave of the inner self.

Though the word "exploration" appears over and over again in this text, the underlying assumption about its principal function is clearly stated in the introduction: "people develop control over words as they use language for exploration of inner worlds" (p. 5). We have here not an alternative to D'Angelo's diminution of language, but a simple obverse. Language remains for Miller and Judy a representational flesh for the forms that the self molds for it to fill. The writer "controls" words by appropriating them to his "inner world." There is even, later in the book, a full retreat to a formalism that, ill-defined as it might be, D'Angelo would applaud:

> there are a *variety* of forms that can be explored [or exploited] to publicize an idea . . . [and] much of the day-to-day writing in which we engage provides opportunity for genuine exploration and learning — discovering and rediscovering things about ourselves and our universe. (p. 23)

The simultaneous yokings of exploration with both exploitation and learning suggest the confused anti-formal yet representational epistemology that constitutes the sub-structure of their argument. The exploratory imagination has, again, been reduced to fleshing out forms or dis-covering "things."

Coleridge provides a refreshing and rigorous alternative to these hermetically sealed conceptions of the knowing mind. For Coleridge, the imagination makes possible not simply the self, but a truly dialectical relationship between self and world:

> In a self-conscious and thence reflecting being, no instinct can exist without engendering the belief of an object corresponding to it, either present or future, real or capable of being realized; . . . in every act of conscious perception, we at once identify our being with that world without us, and yet place ourselves in contradistinction to that world. . . . So universally has this conviction leavened the very substance of discourse; that there is no language on earth in which a man can abjure it as a prejudice, without employing terms and conjunctions that suppose its reality. (p. 365)

Imagination is therefore a self-transcending function of mind that establishes and maintains a balance between inner and outer, subject and object, self and nature. The interpenetrations among these seemingly incommensurable worlds are dynamic and transubstantial, a dialectic for which language is both the instrument and expression.

Coleridge does, of course, draw a sharp distinction between "nature" and "self," object and subject. But for him "in all acts of positive knowledge there is required a reciprocal concurrence of both, namely of the conscious being and of that which is in itself unconscious."[9] The self, therefore, cannot expropriate or subjugate the world. For "during the act of knowledge itself, the objective and subjective are so instantly united that we cannot determine to which of the two the priority belongs" (BL, p. 145). "Self-consciousness is not," Coleridge goes on, "a kind of *being* but a kind of *knowing*" (BL, p. 155). And what the self knows is the simultaneity of the attentive subject with the object it attends to. Most experience-based approaches to composition forsake this balancing of self and world, accomplished through language, in favor of a purely self-expressive discourse. It is such reductive misstatements of Romantic theory that the "new" classical rhetoricians call "vitalism," wrongly attributing it to Coleridge.

Such extreme self-based models have, as one might expect, excited equally extreme opposition, particularly from the "new rhetorics," which conceive of discourse not as an expression arising from the self but as a message focused toward an audience. These rhetorics are allied around a commitment to audience-based discourse, process models of composition, heuristic procedures for invention, and a general antagonism toward "vitalism."

As Richard Young explains this last issue:

> Vitalist assumptions, which have dominated our thinking about the composing process since Coleridge, appear to be inconsistent with the rational processes and formal procedures required by an art of invention. Vitalism leads to a view of writing ability as a knack and a repudiation of the possibility of teaching the composing process; composition tends to dwindle into an art of editing.[10]

What Coleridge himself says, though, is this:

> Method, therefore, becomes natural to the mind which has been accustomed to contemplate not things only, or for their own sake alone, but likewise and chiefly the relations of things, either their relations to each other, or to the observer, or to the state and apprehensions of the hearers. (p. 343)

Far from suggesting that we depend on knacks or inspiration, Coleridge recommends a methodology by which we reflect phenomenologically on the relations that exist among all aspects of the writing process: world, self, and other. In addition, he goes on:

> Where the habit of method is present and effective, things the most remote and diverse in time and place, and outward circumstance, are brought into mental contiguity and succession, the more striking as the less expected. (p. 347)

Thus his method is not only for integrating diverse materials but for creative invention itself.

Let us put aside this reference to Coleridge, who has really nothing to do with recent "vitalist" models of the composing process. What we have then is not a battle between imagination "shrouded in mystery" and cognition available to empirical study but a quarrel between process and product based approaches to writing. Because vitalistic approaches seem to be product oriented (this is certainly untrue, even unthinkable, for Coleridge), the new rhetorics focus on the "composing process."[11]

One of the most systematic of such "process models" of composing is problem-solving, and I will use Linda Flower's *Problem-solving Strategies for Writing* as a representative example of this approach.[12] Flower's system depends immediately on certain self-proclaimed assumptions about writing as a way of knowing. First among these is the belief that writing is motivated by the perception of problems (Flower grounds her definition of "problem" in a felt sense of unresolved conflict) which, by linguistic intervention, can be solved. This problem/solution paradigm is introduced with the metaphor of writing as a goal-directed be-

Rewording the Rhetoric of Composition 11

havior, a way of getting "from A to B." The implied assumption is that a writer can confidently know, at least in all the ways that matter, where he begins (point A) and where he needs to end (point B). Thus, though the path may vary, the teleological nature of the task is prescribed, and the medium of language has value principally as the pathway between intention and effect, both of which can be distinguished clearly from the product that the text represents. We come to know, in short, by setting clear goals and using the available tools (in this case language) for reaching them.

Evident here is the powerful reverse-analogical effect of the computer on the modes of text production which problem-solving recommends. The writer, like a data bank, contains in his memory bits of information which certain mental processes, like programs, can assemble into networks. These formal processes, governed toward a goal by the assignment of a particular problem space, fill their slots with the appropriate information, the result of which is a "solution." What all of this ignores is that computers and their programs are man-made and alterably designed for particular purposes: to solve mechanical or tedious or time-consuming problems of information manipulation and distribution. The inevitable consequences of this metaphor-transformed-into-fact is the confinement of writing to a similar domain of "solvable problems," tasks for which writing is only occasionally needed. Writing, in fact, is best suited to those human problems which have no specifiable solution, even an ill-defined one, and for which the word "problem" creates more confusion than it clears up.[13]

To move most efficiently between the A-B poles of the writing process certain heuristics are recommended. These include brainstorming ("jotting down thoughts in whatever order they come"), WIRMI ("What I Really Mean Is"), notation techniques ("flow charts, trees, brackets, boxes, arrows, etc."), and "satisficing" ("Take the first acceptable solution or alternative instead of searching for the very best one") (p. 3.5). These heuristics constitute Flower's arsenal for invention, their strengths enhanced by the rhetorical context within which they are placed. For Flower posits only four alternative strategies to the ones she recommends: trial and error ("the almost random way the writer keeps trying to combine words and phrases in the hope that one version will finally sound acceptable"), the top-down strategy ("When this method works, it produces a final product in one efficient pass through"), words looking for an idea "([the writer] has let the momentum of language itself direct composition and lead her down the garden path"), and inspiration ("the words seem to flow unbidden and the first draft is the final one") (pp. 3.3–3.8). These are, of course, widely used, and effective, composing strategies, reduced here to an almost cartoonish simplicity for the sake of a stark contrast with the heuristics presented as their alternatives. That the above definitions are derived from analyzing the protocols of writers who are faring poorly at their tasks leaves them all the more questionable.

The same technique is used later in the book to distinguish writer- from reader-based prose — to the latter's advantage since problem-solving depends on audience-basing to distinguish itself from its vitalistic competitors.[14] Writer-based, or what I have earlier called self-based prose, is in Flower's view characterized by "what psychologists call 'egocentrism.' . . . We see it all the time in young children who happily carry on a one sided conversation or a spirited but highly elliptical monologue about what they are doing" (p. 6.25).

To redeem the egocentric garble of self-based prose the writer must perform what Flower calls a "Difference Analysis . . . the first step [of which] is to make a mental chart gauging the distances between you and the reader in three main areas: Knowledge, Attitude and Needs" (p. 6.1). These differences are scaled upward in three categories: "Like Me," "Some Difference," or "Large Difference" (p. 6.1). By thus outlining a gridded difference scale between himself and his reader, a writer transmutes his hermetic self-based prose into clear, information-laden communication with his audience. There is of course a great deal to recommend in a strategy that seeks to avoid the problems associated with writing-only-for-oneself. But this one places an oppressively onerous burden of prediction and specification on the writer. That our knowledge and needs can be clearly distinguished from one another, let alone from someone else's, is by itself problematic. But that either of them can be precisely differentiated from the attitudes that organize, motivate and support them is, simply, an indefensible assumption. This becomes clear when we consider Flower's suggestions for applying the difference scale to attitudes:

> When we say a person has knowledge, we usually refer to their conscious awareness of explicit facts and clearly defined concepts. This kind of knowledge can be easily written down or told to someone else. However, much of what we "know" is not held in this formal, explicit way. Instead it is held as an image, a loose cluster of associations. For instance, my image of lakes as places to live and vacation is made up of many childhood memories and experiences. . . . [The] most salient or powerful parts of my image, which strongly color my whole attitude towards living on lakes, are thoughts of cloudy skies, long rainy days, and feeling generally cold and damp. By contrast, one of my best friends has a very different cluster of associations, and his image is best char-

acterized by thoughts of sun, swimming, sailing and happily sitting on the end of a dock. Needless to say, we communicate on the subject of visiting a lake only with some difficulty. (p. 6.2)

To begin with, these images, as Flower admits, are themselves a form of "knowledge," and they are, as she implies, originally engendered by the extent to which needs and expectations are or are not satisfied. If, as Flower suggests, writers must take fully into account such image-based attitudinal differences between themselves and their audiences, then the writing task is not simplified but made insuperably complex. Even in the most intimate relationships a writer cannot anticipate every eccentric attitudinal construction a reader might apply over his text. To try to do so would be paralyzing. Flower has simply cast writers out of the egocentric spaces of their own experiences and into the equally "elliptical" egocentric spaces of their readers' "inner selves."

I began my analysis of problem-solving with some attention to the notion of "problems" themselves. Let me return briefly to that terrain to consider the types of exploration that this approach allows or recommends. As Flower explains:

> Every problem has what we could call its own problem space. This space contains all the aspects of the problem: its causes, its parts, all of the possible solutions you could invent, and all possible ways to get to those solutions. . . .
> It often helps to think of this problem space as if it were a rather large uncharted territory. The first thing you as a writer need to do is explore this territory. (p. 4.1)

This seems a plausible, if arguable, geographical metaphor — until its definition is fully extended within the framework of assumptions I have just plotted. For, as Flower goes on, "exploration" means to "know your rhetorical problem before you start writing and polishing those sentences that are supposed to solve it" (p. 4.1). We return here to that remarkably stark, but characteristic, division of the stages of the writing process that problem-solving posits: One must first "know" one's problem, as if examining all the causes, parts, possible solutions, and paths to those solutions were a fairly simple matter. Then one writes the sentences that might solve it. Then one polishes those sentences until they do solve it. One might ask how this model could be seen as metaphorically coincident with exploration. That becomes clear when Flower explains that a "major difference between good writers and poor writers is in how they explore or *represent* their problem to themselves" (p. 4.1, italics hers).

The identity of exploration (an active, process metaphor) with representation (a static, formal metaphor) is symptomatic of problem-solving's chronic reliance on a formalistic epistemology and a mimetic conception of language. The writer holds and knows "problem spaces" in his consciousness, redacts them into plans, then fleshes out those plans with sentences that can be polished until the problem is solved.

All of this depends, of course, on a definition of information as bits of data available to memory and ultimately independent of the value-shaping, manufacturing mind that redeems in some sense, skewed as it might be, the self-based models of composing. That we would conceive of language and writing as a behavior utterly freed from the ethical and moral imperatives upon which we so obviously depend for the motives and the consequences of our discourse is a great sacrifice to make for a few heuristics, most of which are already available in the vocabularies of other, less formulaic, approaches for teaching writing.

In each of these approaches, radically different, contradictory even, as they might at first seem, the same end has been reached: the subordination of language to the service of something that supersedes it, whether that be our own thoughts, our own feelings, or the thoughts and feelings of our readers. These retreats to representational notions of language, for which words are harnessed to report, record or present some other, more important and distinctly separate reality, are not only unacceptable but unnecessary. For discourse is not grounded in forms or experience or audience; it engages all of these elements simultaneously. And the locus of this synthesis is the text itself, which both enacts and creates our intentions, our voices and our audiences. As Coleridge suggests, writing is neither process nor product, it is both in the continual act of becoming one another; writing is neither self nor world, it is both in the continual act of becoming one another; writing is neither information nor expression, it is both in the continual act of becoming one another. Writing is, most simply, the potential of language being explored under the mutual guidance of writer and reader. It is work and play with words. What we need to restore to our textbooks is a recognition that invention can take place not only at the site of form or self or audience but, encompassing all of these, through the metaphoric power of language, on the locus of the text itself.

Languaging

I have talked a lot thus far about exploring. Let me explore a little, then, in a meditative fashion, the conception of language I have hinted at. I begin with a passage from Martin Heidegger's "Building Dwelling Thinking":

Dwelling and building are related as end and means. However as long as this is all we have in mind, we take dwelling and building as two separate activities, an idea that has something correct in it. Yet at the same time by the means-end schema we block our view of the essential relations. For building is not merely a means and a way toward a dwelling—to build is in itself already to dwell. Who tells us this? Who gives us a standard at all by which we can take the measure of the nature of dwelling and building?

It is language that tells us about the nature of a thing, provided that we respect language's own nature. In the meantime, to be sure, there rages round the earth an unbridled yet clever talking, writing and broadcasting of spoken words. Man acts as though *he* were the shaper and master of language, while in fact *language* remains the master of man. Perhaps it is before all else man's subversion of *this* relation of dominance that drives his nature into alienation. That we retain a concern for care in speaking is all to the good, but it is of no help to us as long as language still serves us even then only as a means of expression. Among all the appeals that we human beings, on our part, can help to be voiced, language is the highest and everywhere the first.[15]

— "to build is in itself already to dwell": To begin to write, to begin to think about writing, to think about thinking, to think about, to perform any of these basic acts is already to have begun a composition; and the arena of this composition is language. A text *means* the instant it is initiated. It begins to issue toward itself out of these first seeds, which are language. To build a text is not then to master language but to yield to it, to let it guide meanings toward fruition. Language is not cloth for intentions abstractly conceived. Language conceives intentions and nurtures them into texts. Language is in this sense itself a "forethoughtful query" which invites certain responses, responses that do not waft in fully fleshed on the breath of inspiration, but issue forth from the dwelling of the query. And that dwelling is language. As Werner Heisenberg points out, even "natural science does not simply describe and explain nature; it is part of the interplay between nature and ourselves; it describes nature as exposed to our method of questioning."[16] Nature responds to the questions that we ask it. To build is already to dwell.

— "It is language that tells us about the nature of a thing": We do not know a thing first and then employ language to render it. Language shapes what we know, is what we know, is what we are, as we begin to build toward a dwelling of words that allows meaning to gather in the text. Meaning arises from language, not vice-versa. To create, to build, a text is to allow meaning to emerge from the inherent "logic" of language. This is not in the least to say that one writes by letting words flow onto paper without work or care. Quite the contrary. The previously noted analogies of exploration with exploitation and representation illustrate what can happen when the logic of language is *not* allowed to make meaning clear, when words in fact subvert one another and in contradiction banish meaning from its dwelling in the text. Words have, via their buried roots, a metaphoric logic that both enlarges and constrains their meanings. To use language carefully is to respect the domain that such invested meanings have both opened and inscribed. No writer, of course, can be perfectly aware of, absolutely attentive to, every word in this text (I'm certain I have misused hundreds here, and have had my own thoughts thereby misled in hundreds of ways of which I remain unaware.). But to ignore *all* the words in a text, to write as if language were one-dimensional, perfectly transparent gloss for our thoughts, is to risk finding the "nature of a thing" only by accident or chance. And the odds are heavily against it.

— "Man acts as though *he* were the shaper and master of language, while in fact *language* remains the master of man. Perhaps it is before all else man's subversion of *this* relation of dominance that drives his nature into alienation": As long as language is held subservient to something other than itself, as it is in each of the approaches I have earlier described, then the writer will be alien to his text; he will not dwell there because he is not building a place for himself to dwell. If the writer is alien to his text, so also will his reader be. And in at least two crucial ways, so also will be meaning. The first of these arises when the built text is closed to the dwelling of language-as-metaphor. Language thereby shrinks to a transparent facade which is, paradoxically, opaque to interpretative exploration. Verbal richness, "style," is absent, which, again paradoxically, obstructs entry for the reader. The second arises from the first. To dwell in language is to dwell in a "world"—to *be* "in that domain to which everything belongs" (p. 145). To subjugate language is therefore to subjugate every other aspect of the text—self, other and world; to cease to listen attentively to what language "tells us about the nature of a thing." This is, to be sure, a profoundly ideological issue, and Heidegger explores it more fully than I shall. But that writing of the sort I am groping toward here engages issues of value, often on a grand scale, I have already admitted. And it is only via this route that man's alienation can be relieved. For only when man begins to act as though *language* is the shaper and master of that domain to which everything belongs will he discover that he himself remains the master of the language that he dwells in.

— "It is of no help to us as long as language still serves us even then only as a means of expression": Language constitutes worlds; it is intimate to our knowing. It does not simply "express" the self by asserting inner experiences into the presence of others; it does not simply communicate information by translating it from one place to another by means of codified "expressions"; it does not simply represent across an unbridged chasm referents that are out of its domain. Language is not a tool to express something else with; it is what is expressed. I find some help here, from what may seem an unlikely source, in Alfred North Whitehead's essay, "Expression."[17] His is an extraordinarily subtle and complex definition: simply put, and on the most basic level, to exist is to express. But in relation to verbal rhetoric the issues are fairly clear. Expression is "the activity of finitude impressing itself on its environment"; it is "essentially individual" in that it makes possible the "diffusion" of "novel" meanings and understandings (pp. 28-29). But expression can never be entirely eccentric and hermetic when language is its vehicle; for language is the "systemization of expression" (p. 48). Language, therefore, is innately public in that at least on the level of grammar and denotation it is commonly shared by all members of any given linguistic community. Verbal expression is mediate; it provides for individual, private meanings to be cast into public, available texts. By definition, speaker and listener are engaged in a mutual dialectic; one presupposes the other. Language preserves the commonality of speaker and listener, making meaningful discourse possible, without leveling off the range of difference that a human individual requires if he is to say something original. Language thus conceived is in its essence metaphoric; it provides for the intimate communion of "self" with "nature," "speaker" with "hearer." Words thus conceived are not signs that refer univocally to objects; they are evocative of meanings. And meanings are *made* at the intersections of self and nature, speaker and listener, constituting both at the moment of their making.

—"Among all the appeals that we human beings, on our part, can help to be voiced, language is the highest and everywhere the first": Language is an appeal, it moves toward, speaks to, approaches, and is never finally there. To presume that language is material for which we build an image of our thoughts is to cut it off permanently from that for which it is always striving: an appeal that we help to be voiced. Language opens worlds, texts, invested with meanings; it is our access to the intimacy of engagement and assent. Language is metaphoric just here—it appeals through our voice for convergences of worlds; it unites us to worlds that appeal for, and to, our knowing. Without this mediation of language as maker and shaper, self and text remain alien to one another; writer and reader have no common arena for intercourse; rhetoric is reduced to craft, persuasion to technique. We become "sophists," using language to manipulate in the guise of informing, indoctrinate in the guise of convincing, threaten in the guise of debating. Language is what we know, it is how we know, it is why we know. It is a way of touching, and teaching, as we think. It is the highest appeal that we can help to be voiced. As Heidegger reminds us:

> Thinking our way from the temple of Being, we have an intimation of what they dare who are sometimes more daring than the Beings of beings. They dare the precinct of Being. They dare language. All beings — objects of consciousness and things of the heart, men who impose themselves and men who are more daring — all beings, each in its own way, are *qua* beings in the precinct of language. This is why the return from the realm of objects and their representation into the inner-most region of the heart's space can be accomplished, if anywhere, *only in this precinct.* (p. 132)

Renaming the Imagination

In order to restore language as a functionally creative element in acts of composition, it is necessary to begin to specify those mental processes through which language enacts expression. These processes are best organized under the aegis of a concept that has long been a commonplace in the lexicon of rhetoric: imagination.[18] Imagination is, admittedly, a term that rhetoricians seldom use these days without some evident embarrassment about its anachronistic clang in conversations about subskills, heuristics, models, data and testability. This temerity is understandable, given the current aversion to concepts that resist quantification. And imagination is particularly unwelcome because of the abuses it fostered during its own recent stint as a rhetorical buzzword. I would like, though, to initiate an exploratory dialogue, to question some of our conceptions of this concept, to approach imagination along a few relevant tangents, all in the hope of renovating the term enough to make it serviceable again. My motive is not that of an antiquarian seeking to preserve an historical monument for aesthetic reasons. I believe that we need the term, for it allows us to say some things about thinking, knowing, and writing that are otherwise almost unsayable.

Let me begin on familiar turf, with a brief look at the term that has effectively replaced imagination as the key word for creative thinking in the vocabulary of current composition theory: invention. That this label is any less prone to the confusion of multiple definition, the ambiguity, that plagues "imagination" is arguable. But it does stand somewhere along the route toward the functional definition I am seeking.

Invention covers a broad range of discovery procedures in the various camps of the "new rhetoric," though it is almost always used to mean those ways of knowing that ultimately provide the writer with material for his text. For the problem-solver, invention results from the use of heuristic devices for generating information (generally through recovery from long-term memory). For the tagmemicist, invention involves the application of an epistemological grid for discovering what one does (or does not, but can) know about the subject-topic. Other examples include Burke's pentad[19] and Berke's 20 questions.[20]

In each of these cases prescribed strategies direct a search motivated by a need for content that applies to the rhetorical situation. The result of an effective search is the body of information required to make the text. The writer then forms this material into a coherent, working whole adapted to the requirements of his immediate audience. With the exception perhaps of the last example, these searching strategies are generally presented in contrast to classical or formal approaches to content development (the former depending on taxonomies of "topoi" and the latter on standard "modes of analysis.") Young illustrates this essential difference with a passage from Bacon's *Advancement of Learning:*

> The invention of speech or argument is not properly an invention: for to invent is to discover that we know not, and not to recover or re-summon that which we already know. . . . Nevertheless, because we do account it a Chase as well of deer in an inclosed park as in a forest at large, and that it hath already obtained the name, let it be called invention.

Young's interpretation of this distinction seems to pivot on the "Chase" analogy at the heart of this passage. Classical invention, it implies, does not enable the discovery of the previously unknown but only summons up the already known. Modern invention, on the other hand, provides for the methodical acquisition of new knowledge in a given context.[21]

The chase "of deer in an inclosed park" is an accurate (and devastating) characterization of rigidly formalistic approaches to writing. But let us examine the proposed alternative. While there is no guarantee that the hunter will easily find a deer in the open woods, he does have a very clear idea of what he is searching for, he can make and execute plans to find it, and it is the only thing he *will* find given the goal-directed framework that pre-constitutes his search. It is on this point that invention and imagination part company. For the imagination is more like an explorer than a chaser; its mission is not to find a pre-designated something, but to discover the best of what is there to find, to creatively shape that which fills the needs of his "forethoughtful query." That may, in fact, be a deer; and it may not.

This is not to say that the imagination is entirely unfettered by any practical constraints. Far from it, as Coleridge makes clear time after time. For him imaginative thinking involves purposive (but not goal-directed) forays into the unknown. And such events are guided by the rhetorical relations that maintain among the various aspects of the process—nature, self, and audience—as they intersect in the act of composition. Coleridge's "method" is designed not only to enhance creative thinking, but also to initiate it.

Invention, therefore, is a fairly mechanical "special case" of creative thought that imagination absorbs into its broader systems. This supercession is suggested in Coleridge's distinction between the "secondary imagination" and "fancy":

> [The secondary imagination] dissolves, diffuses, dissipates, in order to re-create; or where this process is rendered impossible, yet still, at all events, it struggles to idealize and to unify. . . .
> Fancy, on the contrary, has no other counters to play with but fixities and definites. The fancy is indeed no other than a mode of memory emancipated from the order of time and space; and blended with, and modified by that empirical phaenomenon of the will which we express by the word *choice*. (BL, p. 167)

Imagination is, as I indicated earlier, guided by method, and methodological thinking is directed by the will, a kind of induction shaped by constitutive intentionality. Fancy, on the other hand, is implemented through choice, the mechanical expression of will when its mission is the routine selection of the most appropriate one from the available many. Will is synthetic: it establishes intentional relations, unifies incommensurable worlds, makes new meanings possible. Choice is integrative: it orders units, selects meanings, assembles groups. In a parallel way, imagination shapes wholes, asserts forms, constitutes meanings; fancy arranges wholes, discovers forms, constructs meanings. The difference between these two fundamental ways of knowing seems to have been for Coleridge something like that between an original metaphor being made and a dead metaphor being used. Modern rhetorical theories do, of course, claim that invention can accomplish more than Coleridge provides for fancy. But even if invention is elevated from a subset of imaginative thinking, its function remains relatively mechanical by comparison. This is made evident in several modern theories of mind. I will consider as an example Susanne Langer, who shares Coleridge's conception of creative knowing, but seeks the sort of balance of contraries I have just described.

Langer both admits and respects a way of human knowing that does not yield to easy analysis, proof, or quantitative definition; a way of knowing that functions as a whole-making conceptual and perceptual system. This "non-discursive" mode of mind depends on "insight" as its principle instrument of apprehension. Its more accessible counterpart is the "discursive" mode, whose principal instrument is logical thought. These two modes are complementary (in very nearly the sense that Neils Bohr formulated for quantum mechanics); they constitute incommensurable epistemic systems and express themselves through different types of symbolization. Yet despite these obvious differences, Langer posits their ultimate inseparability on a phenomenal level:

> The two types of symbolism which I call respectively "discursive" and "intensive," are so different that they are supposed to be apprehended by different faculties. But as a matter of fact they are both present in almost every act of cognition. Just as it is futile to divide the mental life into sense, emotion, reason, and other separately functioning motives, so it is bootless to dichotomize knowledge into intellect and intuition, one of which excludes the other.[22]

Langer ascribes this synthetic power of mind to "understanding," and laments the "peculiar poverty of the conventional language" (p. 163) in the face of such experience. Coleridge, of course, attributes this power solely to imagination, and language is the primary instrument by which that power can be both enacted and expressed. Coleridge's enthusiasm, admirably contagious as it is, may need to be tempered a bit; language may be only awkwardly adapted to the expression of certain mental events. But we needn't retreat to the vocabulary of silence that seems occasionally to tempt Langer. "Conventional language" is impoverished because we have cut it off from its role as a functional metaphor and domesticated it almost entirely into the service of discursive thinking. Even metaphor itself has been rooted up and replanted into the various boxes we now call "tropes," thereby consigning it to a purely ornamental role in acts of expression.

Langer and Coleridge do differ somewhat in the role they ascribe to verbal language; but they share the same epistemology: to know is to interpret; to interpret is to make meaning; and to make meaning is to recognize on the phenomenal level the unity and integrity of the creative human experience—even though we can know our knowledge on the discursive level only in terms of polar opposites. Language, then, both creates and bounds the field of our discourse; it does not represent but occasions the junctures of thought with thing, self with other. It is in that sense, as Coleridge and Langer, Heidegger and Whitehead recognize, an instrument rather than a record of creative thought. To deny it that role, either philosophically or pedagogically, is certainly to impoverish it almost beyond redemption.

Like philosophers of mind, psychologists have recently been puzzling toward a fuller understanding of the less accessible, "imaginative" ways of human knowing. This trend is well illustrated in Silvano Arieti's research into creativity, reported in *Creativity: The Magic Synthesis*.[23] "Imagination" and "fancy" are a cumbersome pair of terms in this arena also. But they are not entirely alien, in that depth psychology has long recognized a similar dialectic of knowing and has appropriated a companionable set of dual concepts: the "primary" and "secondary" processes originally distinguished and defined by Freud.

The primary processes are inherently non-discursive, essentially private ways of knowing that find expression through intensive symbolizations. Freud focused his attention almost exclusively on dreams; but this mode of inner expression, Arieti suggests, by no means exhausts the realm of possible vehicles that the primary processes can utilize. Secondary processes are, like Langer's discursive mode, those ways of knowing shared broadly across a language community, usually acquired through acculturation. Arieti, in order to take fuller advantage of the seminal possibilities of Freud's insight, has developed an alternate pair of concepts that accentuate a different aspect of the original distinction. His contrast is between "logical" and "paleological" thinking:

> In secondary-process thinking and in standard Aristotelian logic, a class is a collection of objects to which a concept applies. . . . But in paleological or primary-process thinking, a class is a collection of objects that have a predicate or part in common . . . and become identical and equivalent by virtue of this common part or predicate. (p. 71)

These categories are reminiscent of Lev Vygotsky's distinction between complex thinking, which like Arieti he associates with primitive, mythic, "participatory" ways of shaping the world, and conceptual thinking, the currency of culture.[24]

Arieti's main goal in making this distinction is to differentiate both of these ways of knowing from a third, intermediate, mode of mind, which he calls "the tertiary process":

> The concept of the tertiary process does not exist in Freudian theory. Freud has the great merit of having stressed the importance of the psychic reality as something to be distinguished from the reality of the external world. But he insisted that the two realities must remain distinguished, lest psychic reality be used as an escape from external reality. . . . However, when we deal with the problem of creativity, a different prospect is desirable. The tertiary process, with specific mechanisms and forms, blends the two worlds of mind and matter, and, in many cases, the ra-

tional with the irrational. Instead of rejecting the primitive . . . the creative mind integrates it with normal logical processes in what seems a "magic" synthesis from which the new, the unexpected, the desirable emerge. (pp. 12-13)

When purely paleological thinking is verbally expressed its chief characteristic is opacity, "a loss of diminution of the socially established semantic value" (pp. 81-82). When purely logical thinking is transformed into language the opposite occurs — the private is entirely absorbed into the public. In either case the dialectic necessary to creativity remains unsynthesized. Arieti makes such synthesis possible by naming a new way of knowing, which he calls "amorphous cognition," whose principal agent is the "endocept." Endocepts are neither percepts nor concepts; they reside neither in the inaccessible realm of the unconscious, the repository of paleological thinking and its intensive symbols, nor among the commonly shared cognitive processes that make culture possible. But as dispositions "to feel, to act, to think" (p. 55), they mediate between these two domains, and in that role provide the mechanism for original thought. Such acts of "concrete universalization" result when an endocept is finally embodied in a form. The creative work issues "from a reservoir of unpredictable and incommensurable imagination, and also form an understanding that seems incommensurable and unpredictable because it derives from the potentially infinite symbolic process of man" (p. 186).

While Coleridge's definition of imagination has, in current composition theory, been consigned to the realm of paleological thought ("primitive," "mysterious," "unknowable," etc.), it is in fact far more appropriate to situate it in Arieti's endoceptual domain. Coleridge had a good deal more respect for "primitive" modes of thought than he did for the most mundane version of conceptual thinking, fancy. And his conception of the imagination does have a good deal to do with the non-discursive process of mind. But it does not reside in anything like Freud's version of the unconscious. One can see this immediately in Coleridge's definition of the primary imagination as "the living power and prime agent of all human perception, and as a repetition in the finite mind of the eternal act of creation in the infinite I AM!" (BL, p. 167). This, of course, is an apotheosis of perception and not of dreaming. The active eye both posits and constitutes the outer world, in the *manner* of a creating god, if not in effect. Coleridge's notebooks are filled with illustrations of the essential function of emotion, feeling, in this act of organic shaping.

For Arieti, creativity depends on the synthesis of competing modes of thought. It requires that both paleological and logical ways of knowing coalesce, through endoceptual intention and under the conscious guidance of a directing and selecting will, into new and unexpected wholes. These are precisely the roles that Coleridge ascribed to the imagination and its motive principle, the will.

Arieti's research raises a host of speculative possibilities, both for philosophers of mind and for psychologists. One of the more important of these seems to be identifying the structures that provide for the interpenetrations of primary and secondary processes, despite their apparent surface incommensurability. For two such seemingly disparate realms to coalesce into seamless wholes—and that is what happens when both perception and conception are creative—they must share some common formative processes. It may in fact be the case that the secondary processes are simply highly stylized structural ways of knowing generalized over a long stretch of human history out of the far less rigid formative strategies of paleological thinking. And the imagination may be nothing more—or less—than the agent of that transformation and the vital route of concourse between these two fundamental modes of mind.

Both Vygotsky and Piaget suggest that such a process is repeated on a very small scale in the development from infancy to adulthood. There are, their research indicates, very powerful, if not so obvious, formative structures inherent in the "primitive" mind that allow even the youngest child to begin to shape his world into meaningful wholes. Freud, of course, concentrated his attention only on a few of the unconscious manifestations of such processes, and he treats only two in any detail (displacement and condensation). I suspect, though, along with Arieti, that there are many other similar processes of differentation, constellation, and formation that operate "non-discursively" not only in perception but in conception. And it could well be these that human reason has formalized into the secondary processes of discursive thinking that constitute the armature of culture. If that is the case, it is through the mediate power of what I have named imagination, and through its principal instrument, language-as-metaphor, that this transformation has been accomplished. To abide by any rhetoric, then, that dismisses this creative potential, either by trivializing it or by ignoring it, is not only to misconstrue what language is for, but also to fail to appreciate what we as human beings really are.[25]

NOTES

1. See Richard Young, "Paradigms and Problems: Needed Research in Rhetorical Invention," *Research on Composing: Points of Departure*, eds. Charles R. Cooper and Lee Odell (Urbana, Ill: National Council of Teachers of English, 1978), pp. 29–48; and James A. Berlin and Robert P. Inkster, "Current-Traditional Rhetoric: Paradigm and Practice," *Freshman English News,* 8, No. 3

(Winter 1980), 1-4, 13-14, for a complete discussion of the definition and significance of this term.

2. Frank J. D'Angelo, *Process and Thought in Composition* (Cambridge, Mass.: Winthrop, 1980). Hereafter cited as *Textbook*. See Charles Yarnoff, "Contemporary Theories of Invention in the Rhetorical Tradition," *College English*, 41, No. 5 (January 1980) for a somewhat different analysis of D'Angelo's rhetoric. Other textbooks which rely on similar form-based assumptions about the composing process are Michael E. Adelstein and Jean G. Pival, *The Writing Commitment* (New York: Harcourt, 1980); Billie Andrew Inman and Ruth Gardner, *Aspects of Composition* (New York: Harcourt, 1979); Louise Rorabacher and George Dunbar, *Assignments in Exposition* (New York: Harper, 1979); J. Karl Nicholas and James R. Nicholl, *Rhetorical Models for Effective Writing* (Cambridge, Mass: Winthrop, 1978).

3. Frank J. D'Angelo, *A Conceptual Theory of Rhetoric* (Cambridge, Mass.: Winthrop, 1975), p. 9. Hereafter cited as *Theory*.

4. S. T. Coleridge, "On Method," from *The Friend*, Second Section, Essays IV to XI, reprinted in *The Portable Coleridge*, ed. I. A. Richards (New York: Viking, 1950), p. 362. All otherwise undesignated references to Coleridge are from this essay.

5. See James A. Berlin, "The Rhetoric of Romanticism: The Case for Coleridge," *Rhetoric Society Quarterly*, 10, No. 2 (1980), 62-74.

6. James E. Miller and Stephen N. Judy, *Writing in Reality* (New York: Harper, 1978). This book has its roots in Miller's *Word, Self, Reality: the Rhetoric of the Imagination* (New York: Dodd, Mead, 1972). Other textbooks which rely on similar self-based assumptions about the composing process are William E. Coles, *The Plural I: The Teaching of Writing* (New York: Holt, Rinehart and Winston, 1978); see also Coles' *Composing as a Self-Creating Process* (Hayden, 1974); James M. Mellard and James C. Wilcox, *The Authentic Writer: English Rhetoric and Composition* (Lexington, Mass.: Heath, 1977); William Nichols, ed., *Writing from Experience* (New York: Harcourt, 1975).

7. W. Ross Winterowd, ed., *Contemporary Rhetoric* (New York: Harcourt, 1975), p. 39.

8. This sentence refers to an earlier excerpt from Breton's first "Surrealist Manifesto" (1924): "If your experience isn't strange to you, it's false." Not even in this radically subjective early definition of surrealism was Breton willing to sacrifice world to self, and in "What is Surrealism" (1936, reprinted in *Paths to the Present*, Eugen Weber, ed. [New York: Dodd, Mead, 1966], pp. 254-79), he takes great pains to demonstrate the self-transcendence that surrealism requires.

9. Samuel Taylor Coleridge, *Biographia Literaria*, ed. George Watson (New York: Dutton, 1965), p. 145. Hereafter cited as BL.

10. Richard Young, "Invention: a Topographical Survey," in *Teaching Composition: 10 Bibliographic Essays*, ed. Gary Tate (Fort Worth: Texas Christian Univ. Press, 1976), pp. 20-21. This interpretation of Coleridge, and the use of the term "vitalism" — which originates in biology — is derived from an unpublished dissertation (Hal Rivers Weidner, *Three Models of Rhetoric: Traditional, Mechanical and Vital*, University of Michigan, 1975), which Young credits without quoting in "Paradigms and Problems" (see above). Weidner posits the causal

link between Coleridge and "vitalism" with an argument more often based on a presumption of what Coleridge said than on an interpretation of actual texts. I am reluctant to explore his argument in depth because it remains in the peculiar semi-public realm of dissertation publication. But its influence is, through others, becoming so widespread — its conclusions cited as if they were facts — that a thorough critique may well be in order soon.

11. Most of these process models of composition are reactions not only against "vitalism" but also against the severity of form-content distinctions inherent in formalistic rhetorics. Yet most of them are, in the end, vulnerable to the same objections, largely because of their dependence on a positive epistemology. In the case of tagmemics, for example, "Kenneth Pike argues that 'certain universal invariants underlie all human experience as characteristics of rationality itself.' These invariants function as axioms in tagmemic invention" (Richard Young, "Invention: A Topographical Survey," above, pp. 30–31. See also Richard E. Young, Alton L. Becker, Kenneth L. Pike, *Rhetoric: Discovery and Change* [New York: Harcourt, 1970], for a complete exposition of tagmemic rhetoric). The key words here, of course, are "universal" and "invariant." While the tagmemic grid derived from these axioms is more dynamic and flexible than are D'Angelo's forms, it is in fact a similar map of the mind enforcing a form-content distinction that pre-constitutes any space upon which it operates. Thus, the difference between "process" — as the new rhetoricians use it — and "method" — as Coleridge uses it — is a significant one. "Processes" are formal, hierarchical procedures for inquiry; they cannot function without content, but they can be specified and taught as content-independent "heuristics" that lead to "solutions" of rhetorical "problems." "Method," on the other hand, is a dialogical procedure, the shape of which is content-dependent and cannot be precisely prescribed in formal terms; and it is ultimately related to "truth" as both the motive for and the consequence of effective rhetorical inquiry. In the most general terms, then process models emerge from a philosophical ambience imbued with Aristotelian and positivistic assumptions about human knowing; method models emerge from a philosophical ambience imbued with Platonic and phenomenological assumptions about human knowing. The former is essentially hierarchical, the latter essentially dialectical.

12. Linda Flower, *Problem-solving Strategies for Writing* (Pittsburgh: Carnegie-Mellon Univ., 1978). This book is currently available only in this in-house version; Harcourt, Brace has contracted to publish a market text in 1980. There are not as yet a large number of textbooks which rely heavily on audience-based assumptions about the writing process. Some examples are Maxine Hairston, *A Contemporary Rhetoric* (Boston: Houghton, 1978); Thomas E. Pearsall and Donald H. Cunningham, *How to Write for the World of Work* (New York: Holt, 1978). There are also several textbooks which define writing as essentially purposive in nature (e.g., James M. McCrimmon, *Writing with a Purpose* [Boston: Houghton, 1980]). This approach shares many of the epistemological assumptions that govern audience-based conceptions of discourse.

The term "problem-solving" originates in cognitive psychology and has recently been employed more narrowly in artificial intelligence research. For a "definitive presentation of the information processing approach to human cognitive processes" (flyleaf), see Allen Newell and Herbert A. Simon, *Human Problem Solving* (Englewood Cliffs, N.J.: Prentice-Hall, 1972). For background on problem-solving as it has been applied to composition theory, see Janice Lauer, "Heuristics and Composition," *Contemporary Rhetoric* (see fn. 7, above); and the entire issue of *College English,* 33, No. 6 (March 1972), especially Richard L. Larson's "Problem-solving, Composing and Liberal Education," pp. 628–35; and selected articles in *College English,* 39, No. 4 (December 1977), especially Linda S. Flower and John R. Hayes, "Problem-Solving Strategies and the Writing Process," pp. 449–61.

13. See W.B. Gallie, "Essentially Contested Concepts," reprinted in *The Importance of Language,* ed. Max Black (Englewood Cliffs, N.J.: Prentice-Hall, 1962).

14. This preoccupation with audience as the guiding force in discourse has its deepest roots, of course, in classical rhetoric. But the theories of composition I am discussing seem to derive their framework in this regard from two primary sources: (1) Ch. Perelman and L. Olbrechts-Tyteca, *The New Rhetoric* (Notre Dame: Univ. of Notre Dame Press, 1969), originally published in 1958. Perelman and Olbrechts-Tyteca devote a significant portion of their compendious study of contemporary rhetorical strategies to the delineation of the "three kinds" of audience-awareness relevant to acts of composition. As they explain, "the first such audience consists of the whole of mankind, or at least, of all normal adults; we shall refer to it as the *universal audience.* The second consists of the single *interlocutor* whom the speaker addresses in a dialogue. The third is the *subject himself* when he deliberates or gives himself reason for his actions" (p. 30). That these categories are significantly different from those implicit in formal and experiential models of the composing process is arguable. (2) Carl Rogers, whose strategies for client-centering therapeutic relationships have been transmitted into the rhetorical mainstream by Young, Becker, and Pike (see above) via Anatol Rapaport, *Fights, Games and Debates* (Ann Arbor: Univ. of Michigan Press, 1961). Rogers' techniques are clearly useful for certain kinds of helping relationships in which mutual trust is already presumed (e.g., between friends), or in professional diadic relationships in which mutual trust is implicitly contracted for. But they are only awkwardly adapted to most other rhetorical situations, particularly those which involve balanced opponents competing for the assent of a larger, uncommitted audience. In addition, in my view, which is based on some training in counseling procedures, the Rogerian approach cannot be easily reduced to technique. It works well only when the proffered empathy and trust are genuine and are *perceived* as genuine. Thus it intimately engages issues of character and personality interaction.

For a comprehensive summary statement of the need for audience-based discourse see Ruth Mitchell and Mary Taylor, "The Integrating Perspective: An Audience-Response Model for Writing," *College English,* 41, No. 3 (November 1979), 247–71.

15. Martin Heidegger, *Poetry, Language and Thought,* trans., Albert Hofstadter (New York: Colophon, 1971), p. 146.

16. Werner Heisenberg, *Physics and Philosophy: The Revolution in Modern Science* (New York: Harper, 1958), p. 81.

17. A. N. Whitehead, *Modes of Thought* (New York: Macmillan, 1938).

18. Mary Warnock, in *Imagination* (Los Angeles: Univ. of California Press, 1976), traces the development of philosophical interest in the imagination, from the early empiricists and Kant, through the Romantics, to a variety of recent phenomenologists.

19. See Kenneth Burke, *A Grammar of Motives* (New York: Prentice-Hall, 1945), and *A Rhetoric of Motives* (New York: Prentice-Hall, 1950).

20. See Jacqueline Berke, *Twenty Questions for the Writer: A Practical Rhetoric* (New York: Harcourt, 1975).

21. See above, "Invention: A Topographical Survey," p. 38, and Richard E. Young and Alton L. Becker, "Toward a Modern Theory of Rhetoric: A Tagmemic Contribution," *Contemporary Rhetoric*, ed. W. Ross Winterowd (New York: Harcourt, 1975), p. 132. The passage cited in both essays is from Francis Bacon, *Works of Francis Bacon*, eds. James Spedding, Robert Leslie Ellis, Douglas Denon Heath (New York: Hurd and Houghton, 1869, Vol. VI), pp. 268-69.

22. Susanne K. Langer, *The Practice of Philosophy* (Cambridge: Harvard Univ. Press, 1930), pp. 164-65.

23. Silvano Arieti, *Creativity: The Magic Synthesis* (New York: Basic Books, 1976).

24. Lev Vygotsky, *Thought and Language*, trans. E. Hanfmann and C. Vakar (Cambridge, Mass.: MIT Press, 1962), originally published in 1934.

25. I would like to thank Ann Berthoff and my fellow NEH summer seminarians for their contributions and responses to the third section of this paper, "Renaming the Imagination," and would like to thank the National Endowment for the Humanities for the summer grant that allowed me to research the topic. My special thanks to Steve and Jean Carr for intellectual enrichment and technical assistance throughout the process of composing, revising, and text-editing this manuscript.

AFTERTHOUGHTS

"Rewording the Rhetoric of Composition" was my first foray into the public realm of composition theory. I had been teaching and thinking about composition for a number of years, first as a part-timer, then on a series of one-year terminals, as was common for new faculty in the mid-1970s. "Composition" was less a disciplinary matrix for research and publication — though the framework for that was beginning to emerge — than the pedagogical dues one was expected to pay to earn a way into the more reputable work of teaching, and writing about, literature. This bias in the economy of the profession had seemed to me, almost from my first moment in a classroom as a TA in 1972, to be irritatingly elitist, a microcosm of what had gone slowly wrong with academe over the preceding twenty years. That's at least how I thought of it then, flush with a sense of mission that came partly from my own personal background and agenda, partly just from naiveté. I simply couldn't endorse the arcane, almost arbitrary distinctions the discipline was then enforcing (and in large measure still is) among the various kinds of writing and reading — creative, critical, expository, whatever — that constituted its domain. I had, after all, been writing poetry for years before I went to graduate school to study literature and criticism and I wanted to continue. And beyond that, almost embarrassedly, at least among my young colleagues, I found myself wanting to teach composition as well, enjoying the challenge of a pedagogical task that seemed to leave others so burdened, bilious, bored.

In short, my own vision of the discipline was quite at odds with the conventional hierarchies of English studies in the seventies. But it took extraordinary circumstances to bring these smoldering disaffections finally to flame. In 1979, steeled and wearied from several years of fierce, and from my point of view failed, infighting in my department, my career on the verge of what looked more and more like permanent "termination," I decided finally just to write what I wanted to write — not so much a "groundbreaking" as a ground-clearing piece, something that would allow me to go on as a composition "theorist" in a way that excited and satisfied me, in a way that maintained integrity with my various other interests and ambitions, if and when I happened to land another job. I did. And I have gone on. Nothing I've written and published since, though, can rival in my mind the passion, and the stakes, that I associate with "Rewording," which forged my professional identity and defined both my prospects and their limits in unusual ways.

The piece was turned down by the other major disciplinary journals. I sent it tentatively off to PRE/TEXT, a new journal. Some courage, maybe. Or desperation. Probably a little of both: I was hardly a marquee name in the profession. But there it is in vol. I, no. 1. Ten years hence I'm still not sure quite how to evaluate it. But as I read the opening paragraph again, for the first time in years, I think: I like this. It is what I wanted to say: the instruments and practices that constitute our pedagogies and, to be even more particular, the daily life of our classrooms, are ideologically "hot" in ways that we cannot afford to ignore. We need to reflect, ourselves, and put our students in a position to reflect, on exactly that aspect of our enterprise. Not to recognize such an obligation, and to act with some sense of urgency, and agency, on behalf of that recognition, is to forsake the most frequent and immediate opportunities we have to exercise our professional authority. I think I knew that long before I wrote the article, as I believe anyone who takes teaching seriously knows it. But I had no method, no system, no context, for working it out in practice. That was the work I did for myself in "Rewording."

In the first year or two after the article was published I had several colleagues from small and community colleges approach me at CCCC to say that the article had helped them with their work in almost exactly the same ways that its writing had helped me. They were not, at least then, publishing articles in *College English* or *College Composition and Communication*. They were teachers trying to teach their four or five sections of composition every semester responsibly and well. I am immensely grateful still for the sense of accomplishment and pride, during an otherwise difficult time, that those few remarks offered me.

As for the rest of the article: At the time I wrote "Rewording" I was especially concerned about the emerging audience-based theories of composition. These approaches, as I saw it, were premising themselves on largely unreflected-upon, and highly arguable, assumptions about all manner of things, from the concept of the "reader" all the way to the relationship between the academy and the "real" worlds of business, government. I took, and have continued to take, sharp issue with all of that, trying to knock a few dents in that Juggernaut. And there is Heidegger in the middle of it all. Odd. I wanted to experiment with a less sequential, more meditative format and discourse. I'd do it differently these days, but I like the attempt. and I'd do the argument on imagination differently, too. Poststructuralism simply voids many of my manners of speaking. But I don't "disagree with" what I've said, especially about Coleridge, who seemed to me then to have been too long abused by misreading, or, more likely, no reading at all. My critiques of the several textbooks I chose are, I know, harsh. I had qualms about that at the time. But I believed then, when I was just learning how to grapple with the problems and practices of teaching, as I believe now from my position as director of a major composition program, training and supervising large cadres of graduate students and part-time faculty, that those who are defining the terms of our workplaces, in journals, at conferences, and especially in the textbooks that thousands of less empowered colleagues, working marginally, irregularly, and very, very hard, are asking their students to buy, those who are making a living at it (sort of), or sometimes much more than that, ought to demand nothing but the best from one another. To ask less, for me at least, would be a disservice to this earlier version of myself, the one who had the gumption and the gall to imagine that from the edge of the left margin he could, in fact, "reword the rhetoric of composition." That is a person who—despite his excesses and faults, despite all that has intervened for better and for worse in the interim decade, or will from here on—that is a person I want very much to stay on good, working terms with.

2 : THE DANCE OF DISCOURSE: A DYNAMIC, RELATIVISTIC VIEW OF STRUCTURE

Louise Wetherbee Phelps
University of Southern California

Since the turn of the twentieth century a new physics has radically, deeply, and indelibly changed our beliefs about physical reality and human knowledge of the physical world. Quantum mechanics and relativity describe the universe as a cosmic dance of energy patterns that is understood, and indeed constituted as we know it, through our interaction with it. This new framework for understanding the physical world invites a corresponding revolution in our concept of understanding symbolic realities, specifically the structures of meaning in written discourse. When the modern view of physical reality is extended to the symbolic realities of texts, it transforms the structure of prose into an illusion of the dance of discourse created by our participation in it. In this paper I seek to develop such a dynamic, relativistic view of discourse structure for composition and suggest its relevance to our models and representations of structure in the teachings of writing.

The issues I address are philosophical, not technical. They generate questions like this: What is being structured in written discourse? From what perspectives do we interpret structure? In what time frames is discourse structure constituted? What role do we play, as writers and readers, in constituting it? Questions, on the other hand, about how in the instrumental sense—how writers and readers construct or reconstruct specific structures, how texts express and elicit them—are not asked here: they await transformation of the ontological and epistemological framework that organizes research and teaching in the emergent discipline of composition.[1]

A point of entry to any conceptual framework is through its terminology. In Kenneth Burke's formulation, any nomenclature, whether deliberately chosen or spontaneous, acts as a "terministic screen" through which reality is selectively perceived. It screens or filters first, by its power to redirect the attention into certain channels rather than others; and more deeply, by defining the range of what is possible and what is problematic.[2] In the case of composition theory, the contemporary scene is dominated by a powerful terministic screen presented as an *antithetical pair* around which value polarizes. This pair, which organizes our perception and conception of discourse structure along with much else, is "process" and "product."

Briefly, "process" refers to writing as a productive activity to which are attached the positive values of speech (as both thought and human action) and art (the creation of a symbol). "Product" characterizes texts as the artifacts or meaningful forms resulting from a writer's composing process. For reasons that will become clear, both the logic of this conception of writing and the historical circumstances in which it was formulated make text as product a reductive concept with highly negative connotations. This characterization of texts places strong constraints on a concept of discourse structure, which must ground itself in ideas of texts and their meanings.

The antithesis in composition between process and product was explicitly formulated as a symbolic weapon in the revolt of the 1960s against a failed teaching tradition. It was intended to make a contrast between a teaching practice preoccupied by textual objects, rules, and conventions and a projected dynamic pedagogy that would focus on the psychology of writers' composing processes. It succeeded in reversing the value structure of composition pedagogy and, by opening a new field of questions and topics, in reconstituting the field as a research discipline. What it did not do was lay bare the sources of that antithesis in the teaching tradition itself, nor the connections between it and currents of thought in twentieth century language studies. This fact may help to explain why composition, so long a highly unself-conscious field, remains relatively impervious to recent changes in attitudes toward texts within sister disciplines such as literary theory, and why I have chosen here to invoke modern physics instead as a source of insight about our notions of discourse structure.

One unobserved point within recent composition theory is that the process/product opposition restates a very general, fundamental polarity between process and structure that underlies the modern study of symbolism in general and language in particular, and has motivated many of its controversies. During most of this century—until about ten years ago—structure has been the dominant and favored term. The polarity received early and classic expression in two closely related distinctions made by the French linguist Saussure, between *langue* and *parole,* synchrony and diachrony.[3]

In Saussure's vocabulary *langue* is the abstract system of language structure that underlies individual acts of speaking *(parole)*. For the purpose of analyzing the relations within this system the linguist considers it synchronically, along the "axis of simultaneities," where all its elements coexist timelessly in a given state. Diachronic analysis deals with the "axis of successions" along which things change over time; thus it is concerned with language history and use. Most of Saussure's influential interpreters have read him as giving not only methodological but ontological priority to structure, thought as an abstract, relatively stable, well-ordered, and self-contained, over process or event, the transient, personally idiosyncratic phenomena of actual speech acts. This priority correlates with an emphasis on the synchronic or simultaneous perspective over the linear, temporal, diachronic one.

When these structuralist notions are applied to literature the text becomes the object of study that corresponds to langue, and calls for synchronic analysis. The text tends to assimilate to itself the characteristics of language, including structure, autonomy, and inherent, self-contained meaning independent of the particular reader and context. Particularly if it is nonpoetic prose, as in the texts of the composition class, the text appears to be governed and produced by the rules of *langue*.[4] Given such a conception of the text, discourse structure becomes an empirical property of a nonliterary ("expository") text which can be abstracted objectively and reported by readers reliably and consistently, in part because it has been fixed into the text by a writer from a mental or written outline.

In the teaching tradition these objectivist conceptions of text, textuality, meaning, and discourse structure were not well-articulated theoretical constructs. The structuralist influence was not scholarly, but cultural (and thus the historical variations and subtleties of actual structuralist positions are largely irrelevant to composition). Through composition teachers trained primarily in literature, structuralist ideas filtered indirectly into the composition texts and classroom, where they met and reinforced the still powerful intrinsic formalism of the New Critics. Since they did not come through scholarly channels and were not perceived as fitting into theories, these concepts received little critical attention and were absorbed and used in vague, selective, and contradictory ways. As has frequently been pointed out with respect to the traditional teaching paradigm in composition, such concepts constituted a body of received, tacit wisdom which managed to make overall sense to people in pragmatic terms, partly through sheer familiarity, until the whole was challenged and opened to critical examination in the 1960s. As far as discourse structure is concerned, the prevailing concept of text and its structure was (and is) expressed pragmatically by such notions and practices as outlining, the five paragraph essay, the classification of paragraph types, the interpretation of all these as rules for creating structure, and the "correcting" of texts by teachers.

Objectivist conceptions of texts and their meanings are now under sharp attack across a broad spectrum of fields concerned with symbols, where movements toward a constructivist, interactionist, context-dependent view of language are gathering force and converging. We may picture these currents of thought in linguistics, literary theory and criticism, cognitive science, philosophy, rhetoric, ethnography of communication, and other human sciences as representing a comprehensive redirection of interest, attention, and value from the structure to the event pole of the polarity, from symbols and symbolic structures in themselves to acts of symbolizing in social contexts. In the case of texts and their interpretation, that shift translates into such ideas and emphases as these (shared to some degree by an astonishingly diverse and multidisciplinary group of thinkers): the reader as constructor, creator, or major contributor to textual meaning; the dissolution of texts as static objects; the principle of the indeterminacy of meaning; the radical dependence of meaning on scene or context; the importance of structures of expectation; notions of implicit dialogue; the significance to understood meaning of what is not there; the historicality of interpretation.

The reversal of polarity in composition appears to fit neatly into this picture, but it has remained curiously isolated from parallel developments in other fields. The change embodied in the foregrounding of the composing process was experienced within the field as a purely local phenomenon. Numerous descriptions of "paradigm shift" make no mention of external influences; the motive for change is located in researchers' and teachers' recognition of discrepancies between actual writing behavior and the recommendations and practices of the textbooks and classroom, along with their dissatisfaction with the progress of research in the field. The egocentricity of a field pulling itself up by its bootstraps, trying to transform a teaching practice into an art and a science of composition, is understandable. It is harder to explain how an objectivist attutide toward texts could survive intact the overthrow of the value system in which it was embedded, or why the dynamics of "process" were not extended to the text and its interpretation as in other disciplines, especially since compositionists are generally aware of this move in such fields as literary theory and reading theory.

Two reasons, at least, suggest themselves: the paradox of the terminological pair, and the strategy of compartmentalization. In a terminological opposition, one pair is defined and given its positive value by contrast to the other, the negative or absence of those values. The second term must be so construed as to play this role with reference to a specific issue or question which the polarity addresses. In composition the polarity of structure and event was framed as a solution to a pedagogical crisis in which the issue was how to teach writing, and success was defined as an individual's ability to produce a good text. In that context the polarity of process and product served to devalue teaching based on judgments of finished texts as compared with teaching aimed at helping students with the task of production. But this opposition was quickly reinterpreted as a description of the psychology of "making" texts in which the composing process acquired intrinsic value. It is this limitation to a psychological framework (as opposed to a transactive one) which locked the compositionists into a conception of text as product. The narrowing of the event of discourse to the writer's process of making a symbol required the made symbol or product as its opposite. To that notion of product were attached all the negative associations of teaching based on texts. Texts became even more quintessentially objects — inanimate, static, self-contained, and rigidly organized — by comparison with the vital, creative, temporal, subjective, fluid, open-ended features of composing.

The strategy of compartmentalization reinforces this paradox. The process/product opposition is itself compartmentalizing, in that it separates the text from the historical process of production, and writing from reading. As a result, theorists can tolerate severe dissonances in their belief systems about texts, structures, writing, and reading, for instance adopting the objective, empirical approach to the study of discourse structure in student writing and model expository prose, a radically subjective point of view in literary criticism, and a constructivist position about the psycholinguistics of reading, distributing approaches, techniques, and attitudes acquired from other fields into the appropriate boxes. This compartmentalization has effectively protected a traditional conception of discourse structure from the more dynamic, relativistic views of language use put forth in such other fields.

It is claimed that the reorientation of composition from product to process effected a paradigmatic change. I do not think so, despite its profound and dramatic impact. The dichotomization of process and product, the psychological, writer-centered interpretation of process, the ironic way these preserve and heighten an objectivist characterization of texts and their structures — all these suggest rather a transitional stage leading to a genuinely new paradigm, as yet only dimly perceived. The essence of the underlying paradigm that still controls our view of symbolic realities (especially in practice) rests not in the way the polarity is construed, but in the dualism itself, in the ontological split and its implications for a theory of knowledge or an epistemology of the text. We may recognize the new paradigm when we find it (if that is not a contradiction in terms, since paradigms are made up of precisely those assumptions which remain tacit, unrecognized and unexamined) by its power to reintegrate texts into a dynamic of discourse.

In this essay I suggest that one way out of the trap in which we find ourselves is to recognize our conflicts as a local expression of the confrontation between two epistemologies: on the one hand, the world view of western classical science inherited from Newton and Descartes, and on the other, the new physics as it has developed in the twentieth century from relativity theory and quantum theory. Let me expand this comparison briefly.

There are two strands to the notion of objective description which arises from the Cartesian division of the world into mind and matter, or subject and object. The more basic, I think, and the less obvious is the immutability of reality in both its subjective and objective aspects. The very possibility of consistent and repeatable observation depends on the conception of both subjects and objects as stable, determinate wholes which do not significantly change over the interval of observation. That is, they are treated for the purposes of description as fixed states rather than dynamic processes. A static perspective on the observer and observed is closely linked to the second strand of this notion, the absolute ontological independence of objects from the consciousness and situation of individual observers. The ability of the human observer to perceive and describe reality directly and without mediation is taken for granted, as is the observer's accuracy, lack of prejudice, technical skills of observation, and canonical perspective.

These are the same assumptions that underlie the opposition of structure and process in the context of symbolic realities, and which specifically govern the practice in composition of describing the meaning structures of texts. But it is exactly these assumptions that have been shattered by the new physics. From relativity theory and quantum theory emerges a new physics embedded in a radically different metaphysics, which must ultimately transform the understanding of symbolic as well as physical reality. The new metaphysics transcends these dichotomies by merging subject and object, structure and process in a play of energies whose patterns are realized as objects precisely through our temporal interplay with them. I propose to explore the implications of this dynamic, relativistic world view for a conception of structure as process in written discourse. Throughout my discussion I will be drawing my characterization of this new world view largely from two lucid books written as introductions for the layman: *The Tao of Physics,* by Fritjof Capra, and *The Dancing Wu Li Masters: An Overview of the New Physics,* by Gary Zukav. Both authors emphasize the convergence of this view of the universe with that of Eastern mysticism, where the structure of physical reality emerges from a cosmic dance of creation and destruction through the interaction of observer and observed. First, however, I would like to consider how a conception of discourse as dance is motivated from within the field of composition itself.

Problems of Practice

Because composition now draws information constantly from fields where interactionist epistemologies have been and are being articulated, it might be expected to change its outlook on symbolic realities through their influence, despite the retarding forces I have described. I think, however, this will happen only to the degree that these attitudes or views are perceived as meeting an existing need for reconceptualization. There are indeed powerful internal forces at work to motivate a new view of discourse structure (embedded in a larger transformation of the philosophical framework of the field that is beyond the scope of this paper).[5] These forces are pragmatic, arising from the strain on composition practice caused by the identification of more and more problems in teaching and analysis that cannot be solved through a traditional conception of discourse structure. As these tensions gradually erode the old paradigm from within, they also functionally anticipate a new one, defined by what it must do and explain. From this point of view modern physics appears as a solution to the problem posed by the inadequacies of the current conception of structure, because its principle of the dance fits the criteria we arrive at empirically for a new one.

To understand the deficiencies of the present view of discourse structure in composition, we must examine how this largely tacit concept is institutionalized in teaching practice. (The scattered theoretical discussions of form in composition, though interesting and suggestive, are not at all illuminating about the underlying conceptual agreements embodied in our use of the term "discourse structure" in both teaching and research. An example is the debate over paragraph structure, which never addresses these concerns.)[6] To get at this concept, it is easiest to start by establishing its reference, which can then become the common ground between the traditional concept and the revised one I will propose. In philosophical terminology, the reference of a term is its power to point to some environmental fact in our common experience. What concrete fact of experience, then, are people pointing to when they "refer" to the structure of a given text?

This is an extraordinarily difficult question to answer. In one sense, the reference of the term "structure" here *is* the text, as a symbolic construct that embodies an organized meaning. But people separate, or abstract, the organization of discourse as meaning from its specific form as a verbal object, as shown by their ability to restate or summarize that meaning in different language. In this sense, when they speak of structure they are referring to a mental experience. To define the reference of "discourse structure" as the text does not get us anywhere. How, then, are we going to specify reference to a mental experience?

Fortunately, the reference of the term discourse structure has objective correlates other than the full text. Not only can people reconstruct meanings as different full texts, but they can represent them in a special way that highlights structure, which I call making *discourse maps*. The most homely and common example is the traditional Roman numeral outline and its looser variants. If you ask people to describe (in the sense of *indicate* or *point to*) the structure of a text, most of them will make a rough outline using some numbered system, linear order down the page, with indentation. What they are doing is abstracting the meaning or content of the text and recasting it in a form intended to bring out its principles of organization, its plot, how it is put together. A discourse map is any representation of textual meaning that renders the organization, i.e., structure, of the discourse more vivid to the senses and mind by condensing meaning elements and arranging them in a spatial array that reveals their relations. Among the more exotic examples (rarely taught in the composition classroom, but used frequently by both discourse researchers and ordinary people) are trees, flow graphs, networks, and matrices.[7]

The common use of some form of traditional outline for nonfiction texts suggests that it is a relatively direct and complete, if not perfect, representation of a mental experience of discourse structure. It thus supplies us with an ostensive definition of structure as a set of features that characterize textual meanings. First, there are three features that are rendered iconically: division into elements, indicated by numbering and lettering; linear order of experience, by numbering and vertical space; and hierarchy, by indentation. The elements are of course specified by condensed language ("topics" or sentences). Relations among the elements, insofar as these cannot be expressed by order or hierarchy, are more or less clearly named; importance, for example, could be expressed by subordination or position in climactic order, whereas contrast, cause-effect, and problem-solution relations would have to be named. (Without modification, traditional outlines cannot express the latter iconically, though other discourse mapping techniques can.) Finally, the physical boundaries of the outline, often confined to one page, mark off the meaning unit represented there as relatively self-contained and, through its organization, a whole greater than the sum of its parts. Except in its entirety, the outline cannot directly express this integrity of the meaning, but often tries to evoke it indirectly by code language highly saturated or resonant with meanings, such as a title, main-topic phrase, or thesis statement.

The outline plays an important part in institutionalizing and reinforcing a static model of discourse structure, in which we view meaning as an object contained in the text, accessible to an "objective" description, capable of spatialization and thus open to simultaneous comprehension of all its parts. This static model represents an interpretation of the features of structure I have described, and of our relation to what is being structured. It is the narrowness of this interpretation I want to question, not the features themselves, which are stated generally enough to characterize many complex systems. This interpretation is not a direct consequence of the nature of an outline as an icon, i.e., visual scheme, but arises in our use of it. Although the outline as a spatial array does allow static, synchronic interpretation, it also has a linear (vertical) dimension which could represent the reader's time. Outlines and other discourse maps could also be used in sets to represent the development of a meaning structure over the writer's time in composing, or variations in the interpretation of structure according to the perspective of the observer. Indeed, when we actually observe students working on papers in a classroom or writing lab setting over an interval of days or weeks, they often produce a series of representations—lists, notes, outlines, drafts—that objectify stages in the evolution of structure toward its characteristic discursive form in the final text. Thus an outline is not inherently incompatible with a dynamic, relativistic concept of discourse structure; it simply reflects our inability to think in such terms within the dominant objective paradigm.

The descriptive inadequacy of a model of discourse structure based on this paradigm can easily be observed in a classroom setting because of the problems it creates in teaching writing. I have already implied one, its inability to account for the evolution of structure through what I like to call shadow texts, or shadows of the text: all the various pre/textual and textual writings that lead up to a finished text, especially when the composing act is extended. The static model is functionally ahistorical because it is applies only to full, final texts. In addition, the model does not recognize fragmentary or partial structure where meanings have acquired only some of the structural features of discourse and may lack others, such as order; so it cannot handle pre-textual structure even if we try to apply it historically.

There is a corresponding weakness in a static model with respect to reading: its inability to account for the construing of structure in the reader's mind over time. There are two kinds of "time" here during which reading is experienced as an event, namely as a series of cognitive acts felt as responses to another person's speech act. The first is the time of a single reading or "read-through" from beginning to end. This time and what happens during it are under intensive investigation by scientists interested in the process of language comprehension. The second time, which has received less attention, is the span during which a reader peruses a text more than once, often in separate time periods, and perhaps with aids such as notetaking, intensive study of some sections, and so on. The latter experience leads toward a more synchronic grasp of meaning, with all its elements and relations experienced simultaneously. Both these dimensions are necessary to understanding the processes by which readers comprehend, remember meanings, and perform thought operations such as comparison and criticism on the meaning structures of texts.

The inability to cope with structure as it develops over these different time frames is one aspect of the most profound defect in a static model of written discourse structure. This is the fact that it cannot connect text as a symbolic object to the event of discourse. Written discourse is patently a communication transaction involving experiences by writer and readers that are life events for both. When the text is detached from both composing acts and correlative reading acts and transformed into an autonomous, context-free object in which meaning has somehow been fixed as "content," there is no way to explain its participation as a mediating element in the felt event of communication initiated by the writer and consummated uniquely by each successful reading act. The text and the acts of the discourse event become ontologically incompatible within a static concept of discourse structure.

Finally, a static model is unable to account for simultaneously valid interpretations of what is being structured, which would be experienced by a single writer or reader as alternating perspectives. There seem to be several ways to "see" the meaning of a text; for example, one might take a particular text rhetorically (pragmatically) as a series of logical and emotional appeals, or semantically as a set of assertions. Many factors determine a choice of perspective, among them motive, immediate situational context, cultural setting, stage of writing or reading, and knowledge and beliefs of the observer, but the event nature of discourse makes certain perspectives more immediate or natural, directing our energies into one or another channel of interpretation.

The needs discovered in teaching based on the current model lead us to state the following criteria for a new conception of structure in written discourse. First, it must be dynamic, accounting for change and development in a structure over time, both as it is composed and as it is read. Second, it must be relativistic or perspectival, allowing interpretation to vary with alternate perspectives or gestalts of meaning according to contextual factors. Third, it must account for the constitution or reconstitution of structure as a process in which the observer plays an interactive role as participant in a communication event. The next section will consider the correspondence of these criteria to the principles of modern physics.

THE WORLD VIEW OF THE NEW PHYSICS

As the demands for a new concept of structure originally develop in relation to practical tasks, they present themselves as separate and independent problems. If we solve them in any sense, our solutions are ad hoc and incoherent because we lack the philosophical framework to connect them.[8] Thus, we may argue in one context for examining and teaching discourse structure over composing time, and in another for the possibility of semantic or pragmatic perspectives on what is being structured, and in yet another for the mediating function of the text, without ever exploring the logical and psychological interdependence of these ideas. The view of knowledge and reality expressed by modern physics (which corresponds to that of Eastern philosophies) gives coherence to these disconnected observations and conclusions about structure by giving us an epistemology in which two principles are organically related. The first is the basic event-nature of the universe in which objects (as structures of forms) are constituted interactively from the energy of flux (i.e., structure *is* process). The second principle is the identity of the dancer with the dance: the significance of perspective to all knowledge, and thus the participation of the observer in the reality observed. These principles correspond almost exactly to the criteria for a concept of discourse structure that are empirically motivated by composition practice, and lead us independently to a dynamic, relativistic view of discourse, its structure, and our knowledge of these as writers and readers.

No matter where we start in the new physics, it leads us (as Gary Zukav puts it) back to ourselves.[9] A number of independent discoveries converge to emphasize the creative role of human consciousness in constituting reality as the phenomenal world of everyday experience and the more sophisticated perceptual world of the scientist. Among the most important are relativity theory and, in quantum theory, Bohr's principle of complementarity (as aspect of the Copenhagen interpretation of quantum mechanics) and Heisenberg's uncertainty principle. Although I share the ignorance of most non-physicists about these concepts, with the help of Capra and Zukav I think we can understand how radically they have changed scientists' views about our knowledge of reality.

Each of these ideas or theories recognizes in a different way the significance of perspective to understanding. From there it is a short step to seeing observers first as participants in the reality they observe, and then as creators of it. (The process is not solipsistic, but intersubjective: that is, the world as we know it is a collective creation of human consciousness, not a dream of the individual.) Einstein was the first to radically undermine the Cartesian-Newtonian paradigm. His relativity theory showed that the geometry of space and time is not inherent in nature but a construct of the human mind. Einstein discovered that all measurements of time and space depend on the observer's frame of reference—that is, they are relative rather than absolute. Events appear different to observers in different co-ordinate systems. Zukav tells us:

> Einstein's revolutionary insight was that events which are simultaneous for one observer may occur at different times for another observer depending upon their relative motion. Put another way, two events, one of which occurs before the other as seen from the frame of reference of one observer, may occur at the same time when seen from the frame of reference of another observer. . . . In other words, "sooner," "later," and "simultaneous" are local terms. They have no meaning in the universe at large unless they are tied down to a specific frame of reference.[10]

Since there is no privileged (motionless) frame of reference known to us, the relativity of measurements means that both space and time themselves are relative concepts rather than absolute properties of reality, "merely elements of the language a particular observer uses for his description of the phenomena."[11] Nor are space and time independent, as in the Newtonian model; they form the four-dimensional continuum of space-time.

Although in a relativistic framework space-time measurements, and thus knowledge of an object, are dependent on the point of view of the observer, this is not quite the same as saying that the observer constitutes the object. Quantum theory takes us this further step, blurring the ontological distinction between subject and object. The initial conditions postulated in quantum theory may seem at first to maintain the distinction, for the theory begins by dividing the physical world into the observed system and the observing system.[12] (The observing system includes not only the scientist doing the experiment, but the entire physical context of the observed system.) Quantum theory describes the observed systems in terms of probabilities, or tendencies for sub-atomic particles to exist or atomic events to occur. But these tendencies are actualized by the process of observation: in other words, the observer actually constitutes the observed reality by his interaction with it.

Capra makes the following analysis of observation in atomic physics.[13] The process of observation involves first isolating a particle by means of the preparation process and allowing it to travel unobserved (thus undisturbed by processes of preparation or measurement) over some physical distance, where it is then observed through the process of measurement. As Capra points out, this analysis makes the particle an artifact of the observation process: "the particle constitutes an intermediate system connecting the processes A and B and has meaning only in this context: not as an isolated entity, but as an interconnection between the processes of preparation and measurement."[14] Since one can only approximate the "isolation" of the particle (from the rest of the universe) in the interval between preparation and measurement, the "particle" itself as a distinct physical entity is an idealization or abstraction from a seamless unity. Zukav calls it a "correlation": "All that exists by itself is an unbroken wholeness that presents itself to us as webs (more patterns) of relations. Individual entities are idealizations which are correlations made by us."[15]

The concept that particles are correlations created as objects through the process of observation is only one of several features of quantum theory that undermine the Cartesian split between objective, independent reality and an observing subject. The Heisenberg uncertainty principle describes the limits of our possible knowledge about subatomic nature. Heisenberg showed that we cannot in principle know at the same time both the position and momentum of an individual subatomic particle such as an electron, because in trying to measure its properties we change them. (We can locate or indirectly "see" an electron using gamma rays, but the energy of gamma rays knocks the electron out of orbit and changes its momentum unpredictably. Less energetic rays, for example light, have too long a wave length to "see" such a small thing as an electron.)[16] Furthermore, as Zukav points out, since particles are *defined* in terms of their position and momentum, we can never see them as they "really are" but only as we choose to see them.[17]

Bohr's principle of complementarity deals with the problem of perspective in yet a different way. He formulated this principle to explain the wave-particle duality of light, later discovered to apply literally to all physical phenomena. Light exhibits wave-like properties in some contexts and particle-like behavior in others. This fact presents the quantum paradox, since these behaviors or properties are mutually exclusive: something cannot be both wave-like and particle-like at the same time. Essentially Bohr resolved this paradox by accepting it. He said that these contradictory views are both right, and both are necessary for a complete understanding of the phenomenon of light. Since we cannot understand light both ways simultaneously, which property light reveals is decided by our choice of experiment. This means, however, that we are not observing properties of light itself, but of our interaction with light. Since light is constituted through our observations of it, its reality is dependent on such interactions with human consciousness (and for that matter we ourselves exist by virtue of these interactions).[18]

Although there are disagreements among physicists over the philosophical interpretation of quantum theory, the common element in such interpretations is an interactive conception of the relation between ourselves and reality. In a world where we ourselves are integral elements in a web of energy patterns, there is no such thing as an independent observer, physicist John Wheeler suggests:

> Nothing is more important about the quantum principle than this, that it destroys the concept of the world as "sitting out there," with the observer safely separated from it by a 20 centimeter slab of plate glass. Even to observe so miniscule an object as an electron, he must shatter the glass. He must reach in. He must install his chosen measuring equipment. It is up to him to decide whether he shall measure position or momentum. To install the equipment to measure the one prevents and excludes his installing the equipment to measure the other. Moreover, the measurement changes the state of the electron. The universe will never afterwards be the same. To describe what has happened, one has to cross out that old word "observer" and put in its place the new word "participator." In some strange sense the universe is a participatory universe.[19]

The redefinition of the observer as participant in a cosmic web of patterns is closely connected to a redefinition of reality as basically event (temporal flux or dance) and only derivatively — in transient illusions — object (or state). The connection emerges with particular clarity in S-matrix theory, the most successful attempt so far to combine quantum theory and relativity theory in a quantum-relativistic description of subatomic particles. S-matrix theory applies to hadrons, which are particles held together by strong interactions (the nuclear force which binds the nucleus). According to Capra,

> The important new concept in S-matrix theory is the shift of emphasis from objects to events; its basic concern is not with the particles, but with their reactions. Such a shift from objects to events is required both by quantum theory and by relativity theory. On the one hand, quantum theory has made it clear that a subatomic particle can only be understood as a manifestation of the interaction between various processes of measurement. It is not an isolated object but rather an occurrence, or event, which interconnects other events in a particular way. . . . Relativity theory, on the other hand, has forced us to conceive of particles in terms of space-time: as four-dimensional patterns, as processes rather than objects. The S-matrix approach combines both of these viewpoints.[20]

The Dance of Discourse 45

In S-matrix theory an individual hadron (particle) is defined as a transitory state in a network of reactions, a local condensation or concentration of a quantum field. According to Capra "the structure of a hadron . . . is not understood as a definite arrangement of constituent parts, but is given by all sets of particles which may interact with one another to form the hadron under consideration."[21] Structure or form in the physically experienced world is thus defined dynamically as the tendency or probability for certain reactions to occur, whereby the energy of the atomic patterns manifests itself as mass, or particles. "Subatomic particles are dynamic patterns which have a space aspect and a time aspect. Their space aspect makes them appear as objects with a certain mass, their time aspect as processes involving the equivalent energy."[22] These tendencies are governed by conservation laws that allow energy to flow only through certain reaction channels, corresponding to quantum numbers. Thus structure does not emerge arbitrarily from the matrix of the dancing energy patterns, even though it is defined in terms of processes rather than stable objects.

Both Zukav and Capra frequently use the metaphor of a cosmic dance, drawn from Hindu mythology, to emphasize that the universe as described by modern physics is in essence event, or "patterns of organic energy," as "Wu Li" (the Chinese word for physics) is translated. Structure as an aspect of processes is the orderliness of the cosmic dance; as an aspect of objects it is constituted by the intentionality of human consciousness, simultaneously directed toward and participating in this dance. Capra paints the following picture of reality as a Heraclitan flux, undergoing constant movement, change, and transformation:

> The exploration of the subatomic world in the twentieth century has revealed the intrinsically dynamic nature of matter. It has shown that the constituents of atoms, the subatomic particles, are dynamic patterns which do not exist as isolated entities, but as integral parts of an inseparable network of interactions. These interactions involve a ceaseless flow of energy manifesting itself as the exchange of particles; a dynamic interplay in which particles are created and destroyed without and in a continual variation of energy patterns. The particle interactions give rise to the stable structures which build up the material world, which again do not remain static, but oscillate in rhythmic movements. The whole universe is thus engaged in endless motion and activity; in a continual cosmic dance of energy.[23]

In the next section I will describe a dynamic, relativistic view of discourse structure in accord with both the needs demonstrated by teaching practice in composition and the epistemological principles laid down in the new physics. The fundamental reality we will be dealing with is written discourse as a communication event, the dance of discourse. Discourse structure will be treated as an organization of this experience which may be interpreted by participants from various perspectives, called *gestalts*. Observers trying to describe structure (for example, discourse analysts or teacher-editors) are always necessarily participants in the communication event. As event, structure develops within a time frame. Because of the nature of inscription, which separates discourse participants in time-space, we will take into account various experiential times: two historical times, those of the full writing and reading acts, which may involve repeated passes through a text and its pre/texts; and the virtual time associated with the speech act performed by the text and experienced in any pass through it.

Structure as Process

The basic premise for the conception of discourse structure I will consider now is that all discourse, spoken or written, is an event in the life processes of individuals. In Paul Ricoeur's words, "discourse has an act as its mode of presence."[24] The minimal speech event incorporates two reciprocal acts, an overt productive act by a speaker and a covert receptive act by one or more listeners. In writing, this speech event is somehow inscribed in a text. Let us consider now exactly what this premise means, drawing both on Ricoeur's rich work in hermeneutics, or theory of interpretation, and on speech act theory as developed by John Searle and others from the work of J. L. Austin.

Ricoeur's characterization of discourse as event is made in the context of his effort to resolve dialectically the structure/process polarity as posed by structural linguistics. He thus develops his definition in terms of a contrast between discourse as *parole,* or individual act of speaking, and *langue,* language as system.[25] Discourse as event differs from language as system in a number of important traits. First, speech acts are actual, therefore temporal, whereas systems of signs are virtual, therefore a-temporal. Second, they are creative (always producing new sentences), therefore infinite, whereas the language system is a finite, closed set of signs. Third, discourse as event has both reference to the world and self-reference, to the participants in the event, their discourse acts, and their immediate situational context. Signs considered within the semiotic system (i.e., not in use) do not refer or self-refer; rather they have a differential value. That is, they are formally defined by their difference, their opposition to other units in the system. In Ricoeur's view, these characteristics of discourse as event give it an ontological priority over the system.

Inscription does not change the fact that discourse is an event — it still involves two or more individuals performing reciprocal, interdependent acts in a real world. But it does greatly change the way all these traits of speech and events are realized. Most of the differences arise from the separation of the two component acts of the discourse event in time-space, which is made possible by the mediating function of the inscribed symbols. Structural features laid down in the text must organize the dance of cognitive energies between writer and reader so as to constitute the complete discourse event.

One major effect of inscription is to divide and complicate the simple time frame that is in speech shared by speaker and listener. The productive and the receptive acts acquire the potential to be greatly stretched out — over days, weeks, or more. In the case of writing, structure takes on a historical dimension through its gradual evolution (sometimes radical transformation) over composing time. It is often possible to actually observe the life history of a discourse structure and to study the forces shaping it as it passes through pre/textual representations, drafts, and revisions. Ironically, the drawing out of reading time through re-reading and study (that is, repetition) has the opposite effect of enabling a synchronic understanding of the text as a simultaneous network of elements and relations — a meaning-object.

Distinct from the historical times of the actual, indefinitely prolonged writing and reading activities is an internal discourse time frame in which the speech act is performed and taken up. This time frame is virtual in the discourse, and actualized uniquely by each reader. To understand what this virtuality means, we must consider what happens when a speech act is inscribed in the text. The writer composes a speech act *as* text, which means that he invests in the text his own power to perform a speech act. To do so he creates a persona, a speaker-in-the-text, who performs a speech act invented and authorized by himself and directed toward imagined readers. The time frame of this speech act, though lived by the writer in any sustained thinking or writing through it, is shaped to fit the cognitive processes of the anticipated comprehender. The virtual speaker and act, including its time frame, must be activated by the reader's comprehension in order to consummate the speech event.

The complexities of the virtual speech act and the reciprocal reader's act of comprehension are crucial in determining the possible interpretations of discourse structure. The virtual speech act created by a writer (as distinct from the writer's act of composing) has two dimensions, which I will call *conceptual* and *rhetorical*. These are not distinct acts, but aspects of one act that I am abstracting for purposes of discussion. They correspond roughly to the terms "referential" (sometimes "semantic") and "pragmatic" respectively, used by many linguists and philosophers to describe two major functions of language; and also to John Searle's distinction, with respect to speech acts at the sentence level, between a propositional act (what I say) and an illocutionary act (what I do in saying).[26] The conceptual or reflective act, as a function of the whole discourse, is a train of thought that progressively develops a conception of the world. Such an act of thought must be directed at, or operate upon, something construed as an object. The object in this case is a selected set of facts of experience treated in the discourse as given. In nonfiction discourse the speech act operating on this act progressively produces an interpreted object that is identified with the real world, of which interlocuters are presumed to share an overlapping experience confirmed by a common language. In its subjective aspect, we may call this interpretation, in Kenneth Boulding's term, an *image* of the world, meaning that it is the picture of the world (knowledge, beliefs, attitudes) held by the writer as an individual.[27]

In the rhetorical function of the discourse act, a writer addresses this reflective train of thought (and the conception of the world it produces) to an audience, giving the whole conceptual act a certain communicative (or illocutionary) point and force. In this aspect the discourse is an investment of self into a conception, a commitment to it in social terms and for social purposes; and it invites the reader to take up this commitment as intended.

The reader's act has two aspects also, but only one is fully inscribed and therefore significantly structured by the text. This is what I will call the *allocutionary* act, adopting a term used somewhat ambiguously by Ricoeur.[28] By this I mean what Austin calls "uptake"—the reader's comprehension of the speech act as intended in its conceptual and rhetorical dimensions, which should ideally correspond exactly to that speech act as laid down in the text. Contemporary research on language comprehension, which studies this receptive act under the name "discourse processing," shows it to be enormously complex, constructive, and inferential, though closely guided by the text. Terry Winograd, an artificial intelligence specialist interested in modeling language use on computers, describes the text from this point of view as a "concrete trace" of the reader's comprehension processes. "In language . . . a comprehender begins with a perceptual object that was designed with the explicit intent that someone would analyze it. The speaker designs a sentence anticipating how the hearer will interpret it, and the hearer interprets it in the light of hypotheses about the intent of the speaker.[29]

The allocutionary act, or processing level of the reader's act, contrasts to the *perlocutionary* act in the degree to which it is a structured part of the discourse event as mediated by the text. The perlocutionary act, as I define it, is that aspect of a reader's response that escapes detailed inscription: it is invited, stimulated, or opened up by the text, but not closely controlled by it. For example, it includes sustained emotional effects and their consequences in (the reader's) action; the logical extension of an argument or world beyond what is articulated in the text; or comparison and evaluation. Perlocutionary effects in this sense belong broadly to the sphere called "rhetoric," where expression and comprehension expand into a dialogue between reader and text that is only vaguely anticipated in the writer's original intention.

Ricoeur gives an interesting sketch of the ways different aspects of speech events are inscribed, and how fully. He concludes that the propositional act is quite fully exteriorized in the sentence, through the grammar of the language. The illocutionary act in speech depends somewhat more on gesture and prosody, but it can also be fixed in writing through grammatical paradigms, as can the interlocuters themselves (through self-reference) and their immediate contexts of writing, speaking, reading, within situations and worlds. (These are expressed through deictic features which point to the environment: for instance, tense, definite articles, demonstrative pronouns. For example, "I" as both writer and projected speaker of a text can speak of "you" the reader, of "now" and "later" in the discourse time, of "this" or "that" which I just spoke of.) However, Ricoeur says:

> Without a doubt we must concede that the perlocutionary act is the least inscribable aspect of discourse and that by preference it characterizes spoken language. But the perlocutionary action is precisely what is the least discourse in discourse. It is the discourse as stimulus. It acts, not by my interlocuter's recognition of my intention, but sort of energetically, by direct influence upon the emotions and the affective dispositions. Thus the propositional act, the illocutionary force, and the perlocutionary action are apt, in a decreasing order, for intentional exteriorization which makes inscription in writing possible.[30]

Not all, then, of the actual experiences of the discourse event by writers and readers can be inscribed. What is inscribed, and therefore, strongly structured through the text, are the essential aspects of the discourse as communication. The general form of this structure has been described earlier as a set of structural features (division into elements, order, hierarchy, and so on.) The question, then, is how these features apply to or organize the discourse event as experienced by writers and readers. Another way to ask the question is this: how does the nature of the inscribed discourse event determine in what ways structural features are interpreted to form wholes? I suggest that from this description of event we can derive certain gestalts, or perspectives on structure, that are natural for writers and readers to take. These are not different readings of the textual meaning in the sense that literary critics may disagree over the character of Hamlet. Rather they are alternate complementary views of the same structural features that may be taken by the same or different readers, views which are strongly associated with context and purpose. These perspectives allow us to understand the same structure as dynamic process or static object, act (pragmatic) or world (referential) or image (belief set), meaning or language, just as the wave-particle duality allows to understand light in two complementary aspects.

The notion of gestalts as perspectives on structure was introduced in the context of linguistic analysis by George Lakoff, to solve a problem presented by the description of sentence structure in terms of transformational derivations.[31] It has been established that transformational derivations do not accurately describe the way people actually construct (or comprehend) sentences in real time. They are an attempt to account for conflicting or at least different interpretations of the structure of a sentence, interpretations which we clearly need to make in order to understand sentences. The metaphor of depth or levels is used to account for such conflicts, and these levels are projected onto stages in an ordered derivation, with the deepest level corresponding to the earliest stage. Regardless of linguists' protests that they do not mean derivations to describe performance, "derivations" clearly force us to think of different systems of information as structural alternatives that replace one another in linear succession. What this means, says Lakoff, is that with respect to the structural features of sentences "Generative grammar does not allow for apparently conflicting analyses both to be right from different viewpoints."[32] He thus suggests eliminating derivations in favor of describing sentences in terms of the intersection of simultaneous gestalts, by means of which sentences can interrelate different kinds of information. (I would add that though gestalts are simultaneous in one sense, only one can be focal for a given person at a given time while writing or reading, the others functioning tacitly.)

This proposal makes a great deal of sense in the linguistic context, but may not mean much to someone who is not familiar with the various linguistic perspectives Lakoff gives as examples of possible gestalts (for example, GRAMMATICAL, UNDERSTOOD ROLE, PHONOLOGICAL).[33] Without that knowledge, perhaps even with it, the whole idea seems highly abstract and vague, and the analogy with discourse structure hard to make. In general, though we are very familiar with the notion of multiple perspectives on phenomena in everyday life, it seems

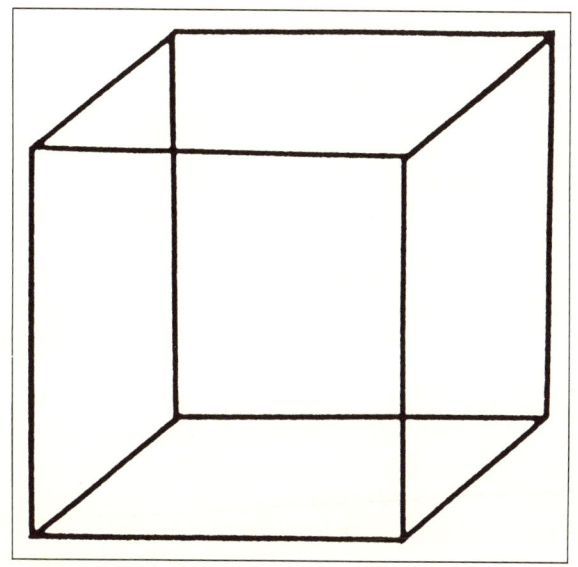

Figure 1. Necker Cube

much harder to apply this idea to a symbolic reality like the structure of meanings in a text. For this reason, it may help to consider a simpler, physical case of multiple viewpoints, namely the visual perception of multi-stable phenomena, where abstract line drawings can be perceived in two or more variations. These have been discussed from a phenomenological point of view by Don Ihde in his book *Experimental Phenomenology*.[34]

When people first look at an abstract line drawing such as the famous Necker cube, they "see" the drawing immediately in one or another variation (see Figure 1). The drawing appears to them as this or that. This appearance is a gestalt, in which the lines structure a particular whole. In the case of the Necker cube, there seem to be two natural perspectives, each producing a different visual interpretation. Ihde calls them the rearward and the forward three-dimensional aspects, or gestalts. In one, we see from above, looking down on the top of a box projecting toward us from right (back) to left (front). In the second, we see from below the bottom of a box projecting toward us from left (back) to right (front). These gestalts are mutually exclusive interpretations of the lines as structuring one or another whole; let us say Box 1 or Box 2. However, it is relatively easy to shift from one perspective to another. Most people do so spontaneously and can easily learn to do so at will.

Deliberately seeing the cube two ways, and moving back and forth between them, takes the viewer from literal-mindedness, in which he sees reality as having only one ("normal") aspect, toward polymorphic-mindedness, the ability to fluently shift perspectives on reality. Ihde shows that by practice in phenomenological methods of deconstruction and reconstruction viewers can greatly expand the number of variations they see in a multi-stable figure.[35] These variants are not limitless nor idiosyncratic to the viewer; they are systematic topographical possibilities that follow from the essential nature or givenness of the phenomenon.

A perceptual gestalt is from the point of view of the perceiver a comprehensive interpretation of the object that excludes other, simultaneously focal understandings of its structure. Anything that does not fit this interpretation (for example, an unmotivated line in the Necker cube) becomes a nonstructural detail that fades into the background like static in a radio broadcast or a stray pencil mark on a typed page. But the experience of polymorphic variation instructs us that any spontaneous perceptual gestalt represents only one mode of presence of the object. When gestalts lose their sedimented perceptual inevitability, they come to be felt as complementary ontological possibilities in the figure corresponding to epistemological possibilities in our minds. These simultaneous possibilities for gestalts can be projected into time as alternate realities, each acquiring greater richness and depth through the viewer's tacit awareness of the others. We have arrived by another path at Bohr's principle of complementarity.

In the deliberately simplified example of abstract figures, naive seeing produces a very limited set of "natural" gestalts (in the case of the Necker cube, two). It is not so easy to identify certain gestalts as natural for viewing texts—natural in the sense of being spontaneously taken up by the discourser without effort or will. For one thing, with texts we are not talking about a single person's private mental experience of seeing an object, but about a highly complex social event involving two participants whose activities mutually define, determine, and affect one another. Inscription complicates the matter further by creating roles for real participants to play (and exchange), and by opening the abstract event laid down in the text to unknown numbers of reading partners. Furthermore, the experience of a discourse event through the mediating text changes its condition from spontaneity to deliberation, making possible planning for the writer and repeated readings and study for the reader. Under these conditions a discourser may take up gestalts purposefully; and even if not, there is no reason to suppose that an initial gestalt will endure or even dominate the whole experience of writing or reading.

On the other hand, there is not unlimited or arbitrary variability to interpretations of written discourse as structured, any more than with the line figure. Gestalts flow first from the basic nature of written discourse as human event, specifically one in which symbols are instrumental to human transactions. Any analysis of symbolic action, such as Kenneth Burke's pentad, the communication triangle, or Roman Jakobson's analysis of discourse functions, yields essentially the same elements, presumably reflecting basic structures in human consciousness of events: participants, their roles, their actions, objects and instrumentalities, and situational context or background for the event. (Grammar reveals the same underlying structures.)

Gestalts of discourse structure arise through the foregrounding or focusing of attention by participants on one or another of these basic elements in discourse events under the special conditions of inscription. For example, following my own analysis of the inscribed discourse event I could develop at least these ways of experiencing the text (each open to both participants):

1. the text as a *voice* enacting a symbolic action on behalf of a writer
2. the text as a *world,* accepted as corresponding to the "real world" the discourser knows and believes in
3. the text as *image* or set of beliefs held by the speaker about a common world, to be weighed against those of others
4. the text as a *trace* of the process of comprehension, a set of cues that correspond to a planned sequence of cognitive events
5. the text as a *conventionalized discourse situation* with a historically sedimented generic structure (reflecting frames for understanding types of speech events)
6. the text as a *linguistic object* obeying rules of a grammar, conventions for inscription, customs of usage.

The text may be said to structure each of these experiences or gestalts through its cues to structural features like global conception, division, ordering, hierarchy, and internal relationships among ideas.

These gestalts represent broad channels along which attention naturally flows to constitute structure, though they are not equally salient under all circumstances for all participants. They can be observed in practice: for example, in the way outlines are filled in with topics and sentences, the terms in which writers and readers talk about and edit drafts in classroom workshops, and the way people summarize texts such as news articles to one another in everyday conversation. But at the same time, gestalts can be multiplied indefinitely by abstracting elements differently from the event matrix as well as by narrowing the field of view. Discourse structure emerges from the dance of discourse as one thing or another—the progress of a metaphor, the clashing of positive and negative lines of force, alternating voices in a conversation—by virtue of the attention of the dancer. Like other aspects of cognitive processing, the attention of a reader is subject to textual cuing; but it is too volatile and too fluid over a period of time to be consistently controlled. And both writers' and readers' attention follow naturally the course set by their purposes, even if they do not deliberately take up different gestalts.

In the natural attitude, a discourser grasps symbols as meaning, and it requires a special and "unnatural" effort in speech to concentrate on symbols that for their own sake, though we do this often enough (for example, noticing a grammatical slip in someone's speech, or hearing an unintentional pun). But it is natural in written discourse to alienate oneself or, in Ricoeur's term, to distanciate oneself from the event to consider the textual object instrumentally and perhaps analytically, because one of the functions of inscription is to permit objectification of the event in various aspects for different purposes, especially those related to the possibility of craft and skill in writing and reading. In fact, this objectification can apply to the "meaning" in event (i.e., what is done, what is said, what is felt) as well as to the text as a linguistic artifact, instrument of conception and communication.

Structural gestalts are not, then, abstract entities residing in texts, but correlations made by us, just as are subatomic particles. They are experientially a function of attention or focus as the mind plays over the empirical possibilities afforded by the text (perhaps deliberately inscribed by the writer) and its situational context. Since human attention fluctuates constantly over any period of lived time, and writing and reading takes real time, it follows that any discourse gestalt, or more accurately the text understood through a gestalt, is properly described as transient and illusory, like the correlations of the physicist which momentarily realize energy as mass, or particles. It is likely that discoursers drift in and out of structural gestalts in the course of composing and interpreting texts, to a considerable degree without conscious control or volition. We need to explore deeply, through such methods as phenomenological inquiry and protocol analysis, exactly how changing interpretations of structure come into being and what their function is in the craft of writing or careful reading, especially within the composing acts of the classroom which involve the interactions of student writers, peer editors, and teachers.

This essay performs a polymorphic variation at a higher level than those we might ask of student writers and readers or even of teachers looking at particular texts. It asks that we as a profession step back from and deconstruct our sedimented conception of discourse structure, to carry out a reconstruction. In that reconstruction, discourse is essentially dance, event, or pattern of symbolic energies in which the discourser participates, ordered or structured with the aid of cues laid down by the writer in the text for himself and the reader. The aspects in which this structure and what is structured appear to us are a function of how we relate ourselves to the event as we experience it and contemplate our experiences through objectification.

I do not intend to take up at any length here the implications for either research or teaching practice of such a dynamic, relativistic view of structure. Many of them are implicit in my discussion of problems of practice in the old paradigm, which defined what a new conception of discourse structure must do or explain. For example, it is now possible to treat the entire set of inscriptions preceding a final text as the same object (or event) in different stages of its history. Such a view calls among other things for the diversification of techniques for discourse mapping to fit the needs of both writers and readers (especially critical readers such as student writers, peer editors, and teachers) during composing. Indeed, competing descriptions of structure, which are usually closely associated with a representational scheme (for instance, the cube suggested by Ellen Nold and Brent Davis for analyzing paragraphs),[36] can now be seen as complementary, correlating to one or another focus suitable for some purpose and stage in writing and reading activities or in subsequent analysis. Other research tasks and teaching strategies are suggested by the concept of gestalts and the question of their function to writers and readers. Surely it would behoove teachers to develop, and learn to teach, techniques for systematic free variation of perspectives which could be selectively taken up during composing and editing by themselves and others working with student writers on pre/texts and texts. For example, the gestalt which sees a text as a trace of reading processes is a useful perspective for discussing and evaluating transitional cues in drafts.

In the end, though, it is emphatically not the purpose of this essay to prescribe practice or even give advice, but to change conceptions, from which changes in attitude necessarily follow, and hence changes in ways of understanding and acting in situations. If some of us have professed something like a dynamic, relativistic view of structure, or at least been quick to repudiate a static one, few if any composition professionals have really believed it enough to act on it. (Imagine a teacher picking up a student theme — not a literary text — and reading it with a consciousness of her role as participant in a dance of symbolic energies which the text attempts to structure ... or treating a scribbled list as the first manifestation of an emerging structure to be realized in a future text.) If we do come to take seriously an interactive view of written discourse and its structure, composition teaching and research will operate in a new world as unstable and exciting as that of early twentieth-century physics,

56 *Louise Wetherbee Phelps*

which Zukav describes as "a picture of chaos beneath order,"[37] and of which Heisenberg wrote: " . . . the demand for change in the thought pattern may engender the feeling that the ground is to be pulled from under one's feet."[38]

NOTES

1. I have avoided the term "rhetoric" here because I am specifically concerned with concepts that have characterized the teaching of nonfiction writing in American universities, as expressed in school textbooks and pedagogical practices. For this, "rhetoric" is too inclusive a term, though we might speak more narrowly of something like a "compositional rhetoric": that is, the theory of communication through written symbols that was implicit in earlier composition teaching and is now being explicitly formulated and revised in theoretical studies and empirical research.

2. Kenneth Burke, "Terministic Screens," *Language as Symbolic Action: Essays on Life, Literature, and Method* (Berkeley: Univ. of California Press, 1968).

3. Ferdinand de Saussure, *Course in General Linguistics,* ed. Charles Bally and Albert Sechehaye in collaboration with Albert Riedlinger, trans. Wade Baskin (New York: McGraw-Hill, 1959).

4. See Mary Louise Pratt's discussion of this illegitimate metaphor in *Toward a Speech Act Theory of Literary Discourse* (Bloomington: Indiana Univ. Press, 1977), pp. 3-37.

5. These larger issues are discussed in Louise Wetherbee Phelps, *Composition in a New Key,* unpublished ms., 1980.

6. See the bibliographical essay on "Structure and Form in Non-Fiction Prose" by Richard Larson, in *Teaching Composition: Ten Bibliographical Essays,* ed. Gary Tate (Fort Worth: Texas Christian Univ., 1976), pp. 45-71.

7. See Thomas G. Sticht, "Comprehending Reading at Work," in *Cognitive Processes in Comprehension,* ed. Marcel Adam Just and Patricia A. Carpenter (Hillsdale, N.J.: Erlbaum, 1977), pp. 221-46, for a study of representational schemes used in solving logical problems.

8. I am speaking here from practical experience, having worked for some years to develop a dynamic model of discourse structure for teaching. Although I arrived at most of the principles described here, I could not make them coherent with one another until reading about modern physics provided an overall principle of integration, symbolized here by the metaphor of the dance.

9. Gary Zukav, *The Dancing Wu Li Masters: An Overview of the New Physics* (New York: Morrow, 1979), p. 136.

10. Zukav, p. 168.

11. Fritjof Capra, *The Tao of Physics: An Exploration of the Parallels Between Modern Physics and Eastern Mysticism* (Boulder: Shambhala, 1975), p. 63.

12. Zukav, p. 93.

13. Capra, pp. 134-37. This is the Copenhagen interpretation of quantum

mechanics, which is not accepted by all physicists. However, other interpretations are even wilder and farther from common sense; and all agree on the creative role of the observer. See Zukav's discussion of these philosophical issues with respect to the actualizing of the Schroedinger Wave Equation, pp. 96-110.

14. Capra, p. 135.
15. Zukav, pp. 95-96.
16. Zukav, pp. 133-34.
17. Zukav, p. 135.
18. Zukav, pp. 116-18.
19. J. A. Wheeler, in *The Physicist's Conception of Nature,* ed. J. Mehra (D. Reidel, Dordrecht-Holland, 1973), p. 244, quoted in Capra, p. 141.
20. Capra, p. 264.
21. Capra, p. 266.
22. Capra, p. 203.
23. Capra, p. 225.
24. Paul Ricoeur, "Structure, Word, Event," trans. Robert Sweeney, *Philosophy Today,* 12 (1968), 114-29; rpt. in *The Philosophy of Paul Ricoeur: An Anthology of His Work,* ed. Charles E. Reagan and David Stewart (Boston: Beacon Press, 1978), p. 114.
25. In addition to "Structure, Word, Event," see Ricoeur's "Creativity in Language," trans. David Pellauer, *Philosophy Today,* 17 (1973), 97-111; rpt. in *The Philosophy of Paul Ricoeur,* pp. 120-33; "The Hermeneutical Function of Distanciation," *Philosophy Today,* 17 (1973), 129-41; and *Interpretation Theory: Discourse and the Surplus of Meaning* (Fort Worth: Texas Christian Univ. Press, 1976). Primary sources for speech act theory are J. L. Austin, *How to Do Things with Words* (Cambridge: Harvard Univ. Press, 1962); and John R. Searle, *Speech Acts: An Essay in the Philosophy of Language* (Cambridge: Cambridge Univ. Press, 1969).
26. Searle, pp. 22-30. Austin originally established this distinction in slightly different terms and without the very general application that Searle and later theorists give it.
27. Kenneth Boulding, *The Image* (1956; rpt. Ann Arbor: Univ. of Michigan Press, Ann Arbor Paperbacks, 1961).
28. Ricoeur, *Interpretation Theory,* p. 14. The usage of terms in speech act theory and its applications varies idiosyncratically and confusingly from one author to the next. I am departing from classical speech act theory in attributing some components of the total speech event (which there are considered part of the speaker's act) to the reader. In this respect I agree with W. Ross Winterowd's analysis of speech acts in Dorothy Augustine and W. Ross Winterowd, "Intention and Response: Speech Acts and the Sources of Composition," unpublished ms. But our terminology is different; what he calls perlocutionary act I have called allocutionary, in order to preserve Austin's original sense of perlocution as the consequences *following* from consummation of intention in the reception of a speech act.
29. Terry Winograd, "A Framework for Understanding Discourse," in *Cognitive Processes in Comprehension,* p. 67.
30. Ricoeur, "Distanciation," pp. 132-33.

31. George Lakoff, "Linguistic Gestalts," *Papers from the 13th Regional Meeting, Chicago Linguistic Society* (April, 1977), 236–87.

32. Lakoff, p. 246.

33. Lakoff, p. 263.

34. Don Ihde, *Experimental Phenomenology: An Introduction* (New York: Putnam, Capricorn Books, 1977).

35. With effort I've been able to achieve twenty-nine variations of the Necker cube, five of them suggested by Ihde. Here they are: (1) Box 1 (forward); (2) Box 2 (rearward); (3) an insect centered on a hexagonal two-dimensional surface; a cut gem seen (4) from outside and above looking down on its facets and (5) from inside below looking up at them; a table positioned on a square floor from twelve different angles, six forward and six rearward (6 through 17); two open books facing each other and touching edges, from eight angles (18–25); three-dimensional stickman (26) and three two-dimensional stickmen with arms and legs in different positions (27–29).

36. Ellen W. Nold and Brent E. Davis, "The Discourse Matrix," *College Composition and Communication,* 31 (1980), 141–52.

37. Zukav, p. 213.

38. Werner Heisenberg, *Across the Frontiers* (New York: Harper, 1974), p. 162, quoted in Zukav, p. 211.

A version of this essay appears in *Composition as a Human Science* (New York: Oxford Univ. Press, 1988).

Takes, Fixes, and Uptake

I'd almost forgotten how I relish teaching writing in that focused, intense way that started in the Cleveland State Writing Lab. I was a director then, too, but there was more teaching time. In those years—1973 to 1977—I did a lot of close reading of shadow texts . . . whatever language the students brought us: the assignment questions they had turned into text; lists, notes, outlines; whatever we wrote down together as we talked one-on-one. Several times a week I planned workshops where students would read such texts with me and the author. That's where, and when, "Dance" was born.

At Syracuse, I've stolen time from administration to co-teach some of our undergraduate "writing studios," but mostly it's been graduate (or postgraduate) courses for our studio teachers, who are professional writing instructors and graduate assistants. But this fall I figured out how to teach writing and teach our teachers—in a graduate writing studio. It's actually an excuse for a workshop on our own professional or academic writing. The first thing I did was ask the class to (re)read "Dance" with me. We started with correspondences.[1]

> Dear Fellow Writers,
> As I imagined I would be, I am at a loss to comment on this essay. That's why I need your help! There seem two directions I could take. [Like Cyrano's nose.] Narcissistic: place it in relation to my own writing, to life themes, to the motives that led me to write it and the ways it led into other writing and so on. Intertextual: look outward, connect it to other work in the field. The problem is, that seems to me to be the job of readers. Once I published the essay, I let go of it. Like all writers, what I wanted was for readers to teach me something by their readings; I wanted them to appropriate and build on it.

Ironies emerged: writing a retrospective on "Dance" — an essay on how readers and disciplines intersubjectively create textual and institutional meanings over time — in the absence of substantive response from the composition community. Dancing with myself. Reading with my friends in profoundly local ways (specific to our teaching community) a work populated with extradisciplinary voices and seeking — for itself, for composition — the contexts, cultural resonances, conversations, and dances of a broad public discourse.[2]

TAKE 1

> HENRY: Last semester, looking for information about discourse theory, I encountered two books: Timothy Crusius's *Discourse: Critique and Synthesis of Major Theories* (1989) and Diana MacDonell's *Theories of Discourse: An Introduction* (1986). Crucius recognized as major theories only those in the Anglo-American vein . . . MacDonell only the French socialist theorists. Nothing could have made clearer how differing discoursers see even discourse differently. Louise has a third take on discourse through physics theory and Ricoeur. . . .

It's more striking to me now how much the text indwells a linguistic and text-linguistic gestalt of discourse . . . that fact historicizes "Dance" and its take on discourse for me. New gestalts have become salient, bringing into focus cultural and political understandings of discourse as activity. But that's a loss as well as a gain, exploiting the fullest potential in the social-symbolic analogy to the cosmic "dance" but displacing to the horizon the insights gained by foregrounding its structural, interpersonal, and pedagogical interpretation.

HENRY: which led me back to a qualification in her preface: In postmodern culture the writer reads what she needs in order to think, to make sense, not in order to know what is fashionable. There can be no canon of theory, any more than of literature" (*Composition as a Human Science,* xii).[3] I think of Eliot's idea of the individual tradition. This notion that one thinks and writes along a self-constructed genealogy of other thinkers is something I am curious about. How does such a genealogy play out against the sum of knowledge in a field? What if the genealogy is considered too idiosyncratic? Has anyone recognized this as a conscious style of proceeding, and does it have consequences when juxtaposed with other styles? . . . Was this risky for Louise?

LOUISE: Compared to Carolyn Miller [writing in the same Pre/Text issue] I lacked a disciplinary matrix, having just emerged from a graduate education invented by myself, in isolation from the field as a personally experienced community and knowing it primarily as a body of texts. (The other articles in the issue come from different discourses and don't really speak directly to one another. It must have been quite disorienting for the readers!) I had extreme difficulty fictionalizing my audience . . . placing myself . . . because I wasn't arguing an issue that was already being argued — I was trying to convince the field it had a neglected or unrecognized problem. Carolyn talks about (and models) how writing addresses a "public" and what it assumes about them. Most of which, I couldn't.

CHARLIE: Did the article's reception confirm, contradict, or complicate her notion of the audience she was writing for? Did the article do what she thought it would do — stimulate the kinds of discussion she hoped for, provoke the kinds of response she intended? Does she think she knows how people were affected by the article? A discussion along these lines might have some implications for the conditions of postmodern scholarship.

TAKE 2

DAVID: The essay responds to a real problem, acknowledging and enacting the feminist practice of grounding action and investigation in the specific concerns raised by a real, ineluctable difficulty of doing something for someone (responding well to students' papers is a deep pragmatic impetus in this essay).

I can trace in my own texts, from their source in the practice of the Writing Lab, the trajectory by which I searched for theoretical conceptions to solve this teaching problem, and then used them to generate practical activity.[4] The problem was, how do I, as teacher-reader, grasp structure as it evolves concretely between minds and texts during the composing process? Students came to the lab at every historical moment of composing, bringing with them the representations—iconic and linguistic—that captured momentarily their evolving thought. I wanted an understanding of discourse structure, of discourse itself, that could account for the interactions between composers and the teachers–readers–critics–co-authors–conversational partners who leave traces in our texts as they are fixed—precipitated—from the energy of ongoing discourse, even before we let go of those texts to the larger world. (I switch pronouns here because I am a writer at this moment.)

DAVID: Her essay is in response to a problem, the disintegration of familiar understandings of what "structure" is in a text. (She starts with the fundamental question of why we understand structure to be "in" a text, even. Structure is of particular interest to composition teachers, of course, especially because much of their occupation has been understood as the search for some form of structure, expressed in "outlining, . . . rules . . . , and the 'correcting' of texts by teachers" [see above, p. 34].)

LOUISE: To put "Dance" in the context of my own writing, I reread parts of my dissertation on discourse mapping. There discourse structure is a teaching question about finding objective correlatives for structure in process. Composing is seen as "forming," structuring; and "text" is increasingly characterized by discursive features. There, and in "Dance," I am exploring what it means to think of composing as the progressive textualizing of language/thought. It would be interesting now to take this further, with a richer sense of the way conversational, conventional, rhetorical, even political structuring is going on, as well as the linguistic or language-like features of text.

"Dance" is open to misappropriation as a variation of literary theories which begin with the finished text and examine its vicarious life through the activities—uptake, response, criticism, deconstruction, amplification, citation—of readers. While the concept of "dance" here applies to all transactions over and through text, the ones that interested me when I wrote it—and still—are those that take place during composing. It's inspired by the experience of pedagogical reading, with its complex overlays and parallels between written discourse "events" triggered by text, and the talk and writing that surround them as they come into being, with virtual and actual writers and readers inextricably entangled until the co-authorship of all reading, the role of writer as reader, of reader as writer, become visible. For me, the dynamic patterns of pedagogical writing-reading transactions are the living model for understanding the event nature of all written discourse, the virtual life of all texts. Here's another irony: in order to "set all points in the communication triangle in motion," as Jim Kinneavy once urged me, I made the text, the dynamic, historical text—not the reader—the hero of my dance.

TAKE 3

DAVID: I tried first to understand the forces which structure the essay (forces which, as a newcomer to composition, are often invisible to me).

There's a sense in which through its very structure, its divisions and movement of thought, "Dance" presents a meta-account (and argument for) how composition might define and approach a problem: how practical experiences generate theoretical problems, and how one can appeal to concepts and images from outside the field of a problem to provide a tool for solving it.

DAVID: LWP's use of physics—a science that has a lot in common with poetry or phenomenology (gone so far Western that it becomes Eastern, so far male that it becomes feminized)—is in terms of a metaphor, of course. She is not a physicist. . . . The essay is a search for a way to understand practical actions as mediated by guiding metaphors . . . but retaining a vision of the metaphors as originating from some concrete source (in this case, science). In this way the essay maintains a grip on an empirical reality even as it commits itself to the metaphorical, balancing truth and method.

TAKE 4

CHARLIE: I think some people would characterize Louise's discussion of discourse apolitical . . . and would object to Louise's de-emphasis on power relations.

EVA: Does the language one uses to talk about process vs. product resemble the language used to talk about female vs. male experience? Is the compartmentalization of process and product akin to the way traditional academic discourse has compartmentalized body and mind, female and male? Have compositionists unconsciously been characterizing the finished text as male—and explaining the process in terms that are associated with female experience?

Some choices we call in retrospect "political": to locate myself squarely in composition and seek to influence its development; to challenge the governing discourse of process; to appeal to physics instead of literary theory, deliberately rejecting the exclusive composition/literature pair to open composition to multiple, even incompatible discourses and influences; to balance as motives the needs of practitioners, which define initial problems, and the cultural pressures and shifts that synergistically shape change; to develop and practice (says Eva, quoting Carol Christ) as "ethos of eros and empathy" as a model for scholarship, for reading student texts.[5]

> LOUISE: This piece is taking shape as circles . . . in the structure of *this* text and in my own composing and teaching history over time. Reading and remembering has brought me back concretely to the practices that generated this piece. I'm playing them out, reinventing them in our course, now, not with individual texts but with portfolios and portraits of writers.

> PATTI: It's a waltz. Find a partner, do the dance, return to the party. . .

But changed.

> HENRY: I am reminded of Borges' discussing Heraclitus's dictum, "You can't step into the same river twice." He notes its double implication, only one of which is a function of running water.

NOTES

1. Excerpts from our class correspondences over this essay appear as indented extracts. David Franke, Eva Heisler, Charles Howell, Henry Jankiewicz, Donna Marsh, and Patricia Stock are the friends and co-authors who (re)read "Dance" with me so provocatively. I thank my colleague Patricia Stock for leading our discussion generously and generatively, and for further conversations on this retrospective during walks near the Erie Canal. I've given her the last word. Well, almost.

2. An alternate version of this retrospective might have been to read my piece in context and in dialogue with Carolyn Miller's wonderful review-article "Public Knowledge in Science and Society," in the same issue of *Pre/Text* (Spring 1982), 31–49.

3. For these readers the primary context for "Dance" was the collection of essays in which it was reprinted, although they knew its full composing and publishing history. See Louise Wetherbee Phelps, *Composition as a Human Science: Contributions to the Self-Understanding of a Field* (New York: Oxford Univ. Press, 1988).

4. Discourse structure and discourse mapping are most fully explored in my unpublished 1980 dissertation, "Acts, Texts, and the Teaching Context: Their Relations Within a Dramatistic Philosophy of Composition."

5. Carol P. Christ, "Toward a Paradigm Shift in the Academy and in Religious Studies," in *The Impact of Feminist Research in the Academy,* ed. Christie Farnham (Bloomington: Indiana Univ. Press, 1987), p. 58.

3 : Cognition, Convention, and Certainty: What We Need to Know About Writing

Patricia Bizzell
College of the Holy Cross

What do we need to know about writing? Only recently have we needed to ask this question, and the asking has created composition studies. We have needed to ask it because of changing circumstances in the classroom, and our answers will be put to the test there with a speed uncommon in other academic disciplines. The current theoretical debate over how to go about finding these answers, therefore, is not merely an empty exercise. Students' lives will be affected in profound ways.

This profound effect on students is the more to be expected because of the terms in which the "writing problem" has appeared to us — terms that suggest that students' thinking needs remediation as much as their writing. Seeing the problem this way makes it very clear that our teaching task is not only to convey information but also to transform students' whole world view. But if this indeed is our project, we must be aware that it has such scope. Otherwise, we risk burying ethical and political questions under supposedly neutral pedagogical technique. Some of our answers to the question of what we need to know about writing are riskier in this regard than others.

We now see the "writing problem" as a thinking problem primarily because we used to take our students' thinking for granted. We used to assume that students came to us with ideas and we helped them put those ideas into words. We taught style, explaining the formal properties of model essays and evaluating students' products in the light of these models. Some students came to us with better ideas than others, but these were simply the brighter or more mature students. All we could do for the duller, more immature students was to hope that exposure to good models might push them along the developmental path.[1]

Over the last twenty years, however, we have encountered in our classrooms more and more students whose ideas seem so ill-considered, by academic standards, that we can no longer see the problem as primarily one of expression. Rather, we feel, "Now I have to teach them to think, too!" And at the same time, students have so much trouble writing Standard English that we are driven away from stylistic considerations back to the basics of grammar and mechanics. Teaching style from model essays has not prepared us to explain or repair these students' deficiencies. The new demands on us as teachers can only be met, it seems, by a reconsideration of the relationship between thought and language. We are pretty much agreed, in other words, that what we need to know about writing has to do with the thinking processes involved in it.

Composition specialists generally agree about some fundamental elements in the development of language and thought. We agree that the normal human individual possesses innate mental capacities to learn a language and to assemble complex conceptual structures. As the individual develops, these capacities are realized in her learning a native tongue and forming thought patterns that organize and interpret experience. The mature exercise of these thought and language capacities takes place in society, in interaction with other individuals, and this interaction modifies the individual's reasoning, speaking, and writing within society. Groups of society members can become accustomed to modifying each other's reasoning and language use in certain ways. Eventually, these familiar ways achieve the status of conventions that bind the group in a discourse community, at work together on some project of interaction with the material world. An individual can belong to more than one discourse community, but her access to the various communities will be unequally conditioned by her social situation.

If composition specialists generally agree about this description, however, we disagree about what part of it is relevant to composition studies. One theoretical camp sees writing as primarily inner-directed, and so is more interested in the structure of language-learning and thinking processes in their earliest state, prior to social influence. The other main theoretical camp sees writing as primarily outer-directed, and so is more interested in the social processes whereby language-learning and thinking capacities are shaped and used in particular communities. In the current debate, each camp seeks to define what we *most* need to know about writing.

Inner-directed theorists seek to discover writing processes that are so fundamental as to be universal. Later elaborations of thinking and language-using should be understood as outgrowths of individual capacities (see Figure 1). Hence, inner-directed theorists are most interested in individual capacities and their earliest interactions with experience (locations 1 and 2, Figure 1). The inner-directed theorists tend to see the kinds of reasoning occurring at all four locations as isomorphic — all the same basic logical structures.[2] They also tend to see differences

> 4. Writing situation: instance of language use directed to a particular audience, for a particular purpose.

↑

> 3. Society: conditions language use and thinking according to historical, cultural circumstances.

↑

> 2. Experience: leads individual to learn a native tongue, begin to form conceptual structures.

↑

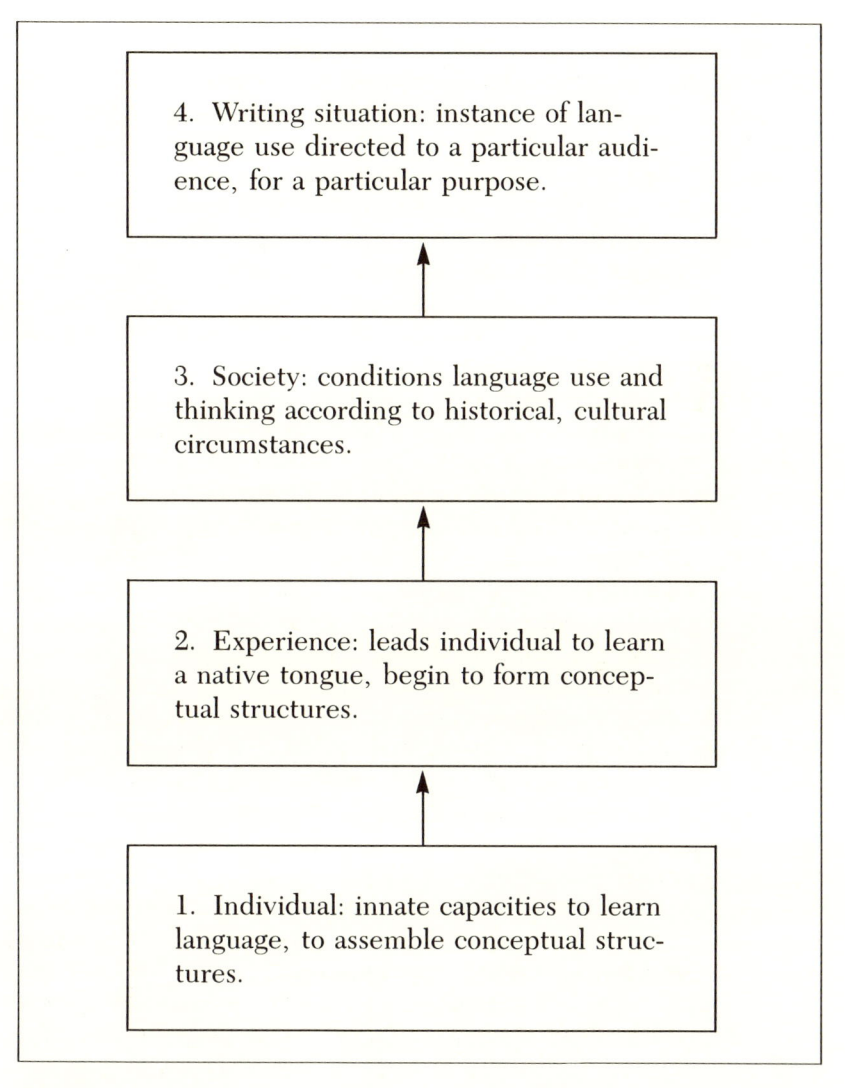

> 1. Individual: innate capacities to learn language, to assemble conceptual structures.

Figure 1. An inner-directed model of the development of language and thought writing. Arrows indicate direction of individual's development, beginning with innate capacities and issuing finally in particular instances of use.

in language use at different locations as superficial matters of lexical choice; the basic structure of the language cannot change from location to location because this structure is isomorphic with the innate mental structures that enabled one to learn a language, and hence presumably universal and independent of lexical choice. Nevertheless, looking for an argument to justify teaching one form of a language, some inner-directed theorists treat one set of lexical choices as better able than others to make language embody the innate structures. Insofar as these better choices fall into the patterns of, for example, a "standard" form of a native tongue, they make the standard intellectually superior to other forms.[3]

Inner-directed theorists further claim, in a similar paradox, that the universal, fundamental structures of thought and language can be taught. If our students are unable to have ideas, we should look around locations 1 and 2 for structural models of the mental processes that are not happening in these students' minds. Once we find these models, we can guide students through the processes until the students' own thought-forming mechanisms "kick on" and they can make concepts on their own. An heuristic procedure is often presented as such a process model.[4] Similarly, if our students are unable to write English, we should look in the same locations for patterns of correct syntax, which we can then ask the students to practice until they internalize the patterns. Sentence-combining exercises offer such pattern practice.[5]

Once students are capable of cognitively sophisticated thinking and writing, they are ready to tackle the problems of a particular writing situation. These problems are usually treated by inner-directed theory as problems of audience analysis. Audience analysis seeks to identify the personal idiosyncracies of readers so that the writer can communicate her message to them in the most persuasive form. The changes made to accommodate an audience, however, are not seen as substantially altering the meaning of the piece of writing because that is based in the underlying structure of thought and language.[6]

In contrast, outer-directed theorists believe that universal, fundamental structures can't be taught; thinking and language use can never occur free of a social context that conditions them (see Figure 2). The outer-directed theorists believe that teaching style from model essays failed not because we were doing the wrong thing but because we weren't aware of what we were doing. Teaching style from model essays, in this view, is teaching the discourse conventions of a particular community—in this case, a community of intellectuals including, but not limited to, academics. But because we were unaware that we were in a discourse community, we taught the conventions as formal structures, as if they were universal

2. Society: aggregate of discourse communities that all share certain patterns of language-using, thinking conditioned by historical, cultural circumstances.

d. another discourse community

e. another discourse community

b. work discourse community: some other conventions, some common with native community

f. another discourse community

a. native discourse community: conventions for preferred language-using, thinking directed toward a project of interaction with the world

c. school discourse community: some other conventions, some common with native community

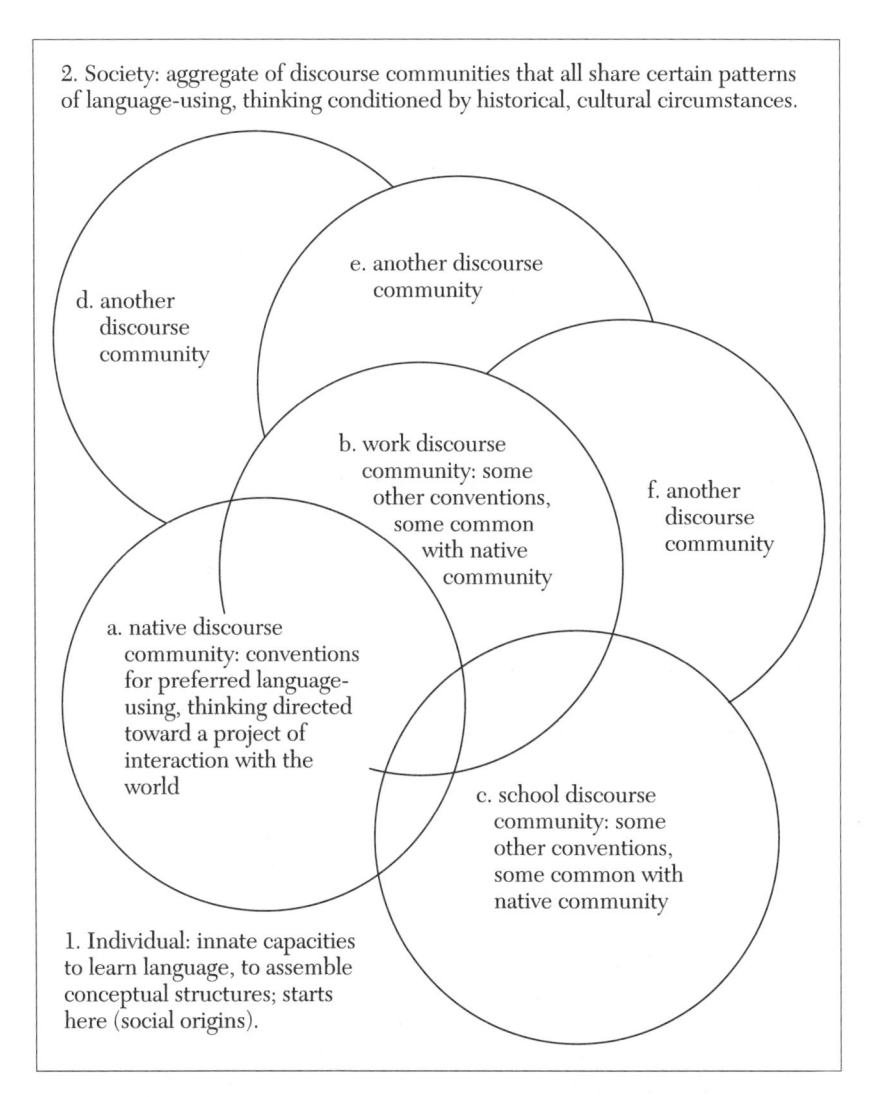

1. Individual: innate capacities to learn language, to assemble conceptual structures; starts here (social origins).

Figure 2. An outer-directed model of the development of language and thought. Note that innate capacities have no expression outside discourse communities and that society is made up entirely of discourse communities. Individual has unequal access to different communities. Direction of development is outward from native community.

patterns of thought and language. What we should do is to teach students that there are such things as discourse conventions.

The outer-directed theorists are sceptical about how we can obtain knowledge of what thinking and language-learning processes are innate. Moreover, they would argue that the individual is already inside a discourse community when she learns a native tongue, since the infant does not learn some generalized form of language but rather the habits of language use in the neighborhood, or the discourse community into which she is born.[7] Since this discourse community already possesses traditional, shared ways of understanding experience, the infant doesn't learn to conceptualize in a social vacuum, either, but is constantly being advised by more mature community members whether her inferences are correct, whether her groupings of experiential data into evidence are significant, and so on.[8] Some outer-directed theorists would go so far as to say that the lines of development of thought and language merge when the native tongue is learned, since one learns to think only by learning a language and one can't have an idea one doesn't have a word for.[9]

Outer-directed theorists would argue that we have no reason to believe, and no convincing way to determine, that our students can't think or use language in complex ways. It's just that they can't think or use language in the ways we want them to. To help them, then, we should be looking for ways to explain discourse conventions. We might find patterns of language use and reasoning that are common to all members of a society, patterns that are part of the set of conventions of every discourse community within the society. Conventions that are common in the society could be used as bridges between different discourse communities — for example, to ease the transition into the academic discourse community for students who come from discourse communities far removed from it.[10]

The staple activity of outer-directed writing instruction will be analysis of the conventions of particular discourse communities (see Figure 2). For example, a major focus of writing-across-the-curriculum programs is to demystify the conventions of the academic discourse community.[11] Discourse analysis goes beyond audience analysis because what is most significant about members of a discourse community is not their personal preferences, prejudices, and so on, but rather the expectations they share by virtue of belonging to that particular community. These expectations are embodied in the discourse conventions, which are in turn conditioned by the community's work. Audience analysis aims to persuade readers that you're right; it is to dress your argument in flattering apparel. Discourse analysis aims to enable you to make that argument, to do intellectual work of significance to the community, and hence, to persuade readers that you are a worthy co-worker.[12]

Answers to what we need to know about writing will have to come from both the inner-directed and the outer-directed theoretical schools if we wish to have a complete picture of the composing process. We need to explain the cognitive and the social factors in writing development, and even more important, the relationship between them. Therefore, we should think of the current debate between the two schools as the kind of fruitful exchange that enlarges knowledge, not as a process that will lead to its own termination, to a theory that silences debate. I would like to show here how one inner-directed theoretical model of writing can be enlarged by an outer-directed critique.

The inner-directed school has been distinguished by its fostering of research on writing that follows scientific methodology, and two of the most important researchers are Linda Flower, a professor of English at Carnegie-Mellon University, and John R. Hayes, a professor of psychology at the same school. They have been conducting research for about six years on what people do when they compose. The goal of this research is to formulate "A Cognitive Process Theory of Writing," according to the title of their recent *College Composition and Communication* essay, under review here.[13] Their work's roots in cognitive psychology can be seen in *Cognitive Processes in Writing,* also reviewed here, the proceedings of a 1978 symposium at Carnegie-Mellon.[14] Flower and Hayes see composing as a kind of problem-solving activity; what interests them are the "invariant" thought processes called into play whenever one is confronted with a writing task. In other words, they assume that although each writing task will have its own environment of purposes and constraints, the mental activity involved in juggling these constraints while moving to accomplish one's purposes does not change from task to task. This problem-solving thought process is the "cognitive process of writing."

In Figure 1, location 2 is approximately where Flower and Hayes would place what they are studying. The cognitive process is triggered by what goes on at location 4 (imposition of a particular writing task); the process may also be shaped by attitudes absorbed at location 3 and modified in the light of success or failure in problem-solving at location 4. Not everyone uses the same cognitive process in writing, some processes are more successful than others, and one's process can be consciously or unconsciously modified. Flower and Hayes seek to describe a model of the most complete and successful composing process they can find through their research.

Protocol analysis is their principal research tool. First, the researcher asks a person (the test subject) to say aloud whatever she is thinking while solving a problem posed by the researcher. For example, Flower and Hayes have asked English teachers to describe what goes through their minds while composing an article describing their jobs for the readers of *Seventeen* magazine. The transcription of what the subject says is the protocol. Next, the researcher scans the protocol looking in the subject's self-description for features predicted by the theory of cognitive activity guiding the research. Flower and Hayes have looked for descriptions of behavior common to current accounts of the writing process, such as "organizing" and "revising." In analyzing the protocol, the researcher must bridge gaps in the protocol caused by the subject's forgetting to mention some of her problem-solving steps. The theory is tested by its ability to bridge these gaps as well as by the appearance in the protocol of features it predicts (Flower and Hayes explain their procedure in "Identifying the Organization of Writing Processes," *Cognitive Processes,* pp. 3–30).

Through their research, Flower and Hayes have been gradually refining a process model of composing (see "Process Theory," p. 370). Its most current version divides the writing situation into three main parts: one, the "task environment," subdivided into "rhetorical problem" and "text produced so far"; two, the "writing process," subdivided into "reviewing" (further subdivided into "revising" and "evaluating"), "translating," and "planning" (further subdivided into "generating," "goal-setting," and "organizing"); and three, the "writer's long-term memory." The task environment is outside the writer, the writing process is inside the writer, and long-term memory can be both inside and outside — that is, in the writer's mind or in books. Task environment and memory are seen as information sources upon which the writer draws while performing the composing activities grouped under "writing process."

This model is hierarchical and recursive rather than sequential in structure; that is, Flower and Hayes do not see the writing process as an invariant order of steps. What is invariant, in their view, is the structural relation of the steps. A writer can "access" memory or task environment, and switch from one composing subprocess to another, at any time while the writing task is being completed; an entity in the model called "monitor" executes these switches. This model does not tell us how to proceed through the composing process, but only that in proceeding, there are certain subprocesses we must include if we want to compose successfully.

Flower and Hayes see this model as resolving current theoretical disagreements about what guides composing. Beginning their "Process Theory" essay with summaries of different but compatible views on composing, Flower and Hayes seem to suggest that while other theorists are like blind men describing an elephant, in the Flower-Hayes model we see the whole beast — or at least we can infer its shape when the porpoise occasionally breaks water, to switch to the animal metaphor Flower and

Hayes use (*Cognitive Processes,* pp. 9-10). It is the hierarchical and recursive structure of this model, in Flower and Hayes's view, that makes it superior to other theorists' work and able to control and reconcile other theorists' work.

The Flower-Hayes model may, however, strike many readers as a surprising mix of daunting complexity and disappointing familiarity. When we finally get the new terminology straight in our minds, we find in the model's elaborate cognitive processes just the same writing activities we have been debating about. Consider, for example, the Flower-Hayes model's "monitor," the entity that executes switches between composing subprocesses. On the one hand, the term, borrowed from computer programming, is rather intimidating, especially if we imagine that it names something we didn't know was there before. On the other hand, we find out eventually that "monitor" means simply "the writer's mind making decisions." Borrowing a term from programming masks the question of *why* the writer makes certain decisions. The Flower-Hayes model consistently presents a description of *how* the writing process goes on as if it were capable of answering questions about *why* the writer makes certain choices in certain situations. While it is useful for us to have an overview of the "how," such as the Flower-Hayes model offers, we should not suppose that this will enable us to advise students on difficult questions of practice. To put it another way, if we are going to see students as problem-solvers, we must also see them as problem-solvers situated in discourse communities that guide problem definition and the range of alternative solutions. Outer-directed theory can thus shore up the Flower-Hayes model in two critical areas, planning and translating.

"Translating," according to Flower and Hayes, is "the process of putting ideas into visible language" ("Process Theory," p. 373). They treat written English as a set of containers into which we pour meaning, regardless of how meaning exists before the pouring. The containers may not seem to be in convenient sizes at first — we have to struggle with their "constraints" or "special demands" — but once we internalize these, written language as a factor in the composing process essentially disappears. Writing does not so much contribute to thinking as provide an occasion for thinking — or, more precisely, a substrate upon which thinking can grow. Beyond minor matters of spelling, diction, and so on, we do not have to worry about how students are going to find out about the features of written language because these are already innate.

"Translating," then, remains the emptiest box in the Flower-Hayes model, while "planning" becomes the fullest. During planning, the writer generates and organizes ideas before struggling to put them into words. Language itself is not seen as having a generative force in the planning process, except insofar as it stands as a record of the current progress of the writer's thinking in "text produced so far." Planning processes, therefore, have to be elaborated because they are all the writer has to guide her toward a solution to the particular writing problem. What's missing here is the connection to social context afforded by recognition of the dialectical relationship between thought and language. We can have thoughts for which we have no words, I think, but learning language, though it doesn't exactly teach us to think, teaches us what thoughts matter. To put it another way, we can *know* nothing but what we have words for, if knowledge is what language makes of experience.

Vygotsky has characterized this dialectical relationship of thought and language as the development of "verbal thought." At first, language use and thinking develop separately in the child. But eventually the child comes to understand that language not only names ideas but develops and evaluates them, and then, "*The nature of the [child's] development itself changes,* from biological to historical."[15] The child's linguistic and cognitive development culminates in "verbal thought," which "is not a natural, innate form of behavior but is determined by a historical-cultural process and has specific properties and laws that cannot be found in the natural forms of thought and speech" (Vygotsky, p. 51). To illustrate the mature relationship between thought and language, Vygotsky uses situations that are strongly context-bound, such as conversations between lovers or among actors in a play.

Vygotsky's analysis suggests that a model that separates planning and translating will not be fruitful for describing adult language-using because these activities are never separate in adult language-using. There is, to be sure, a basis in the human organism for language-using behavior; Vygotsky calls it "biological," Flower and Hayes call it "cognitive." But while this basis is a legitimate object of study in its own right, even the most complete anatomy of it will not explain adult language-using because, as Vygotsky emphasizes, with the advent of verbal thought the very nature of language-using processes changes. The writing process can only take place after this change occurred. Vygotsky's analysis would suggest, then, not only that we should not separate planning and translating but also that we should understand them as conditioned by social context.

If we accept Vygotsky's analysis as indicating the need to fill in Flower and Hayes's empty "translating" box, then to look for knowledge to fill it, we can turn to sociolinguistics. This discipline seeks to analyze the ways thinking and language-using are conditioned by social context. In studying writing, sociolinguists look for the verbal ties with context. They argue that certain genres, implying certain relations between people, are typical of certain situations. Furthermore, readers do not perceive a text as hanging together logically unless its connections with the social con-

Cognition, Convention, and Certainty 75

text are as clear as the markers of internal coherence.[16] Therefore, for example, students who struggle to write Standard English need knowledge beyond the rules of grammar, spelling, and so on. They need to know: the habitual attitudes of Standard English users toward this preferred form; the linguistic features that most strongly mark group identity; the conventions that can sometimes be ignored; and so on. Students who do know the rules of Standard English may still seem to academics to be writing "incorrectly" if the students are insensitive to all these other features of language use in the community—then the students are using academic language in unacademic ways.[17]

Composition specialists can learn from sociolinguists to avoid what George Dillon has called the "bottom-to-top" fallacy: the notion that a writer first finds meaning, then puts it into words, then organizes the words into sentences, sentences into paragraphs, etc.[18] Dillon argues, rather, that it is the sense of her whole project that most stimulates a writer's thinking and guides her language use. The discourse gives meaning to the words and not vice versa. For example, such phrases as "it seems to me" and "these results suggest . . ." do not themselves tell us how to interpret such a pattern of qualifying statements. When we encounter these words in a student paper, we are likely to chide the writer for covering up poor research or for being unduly humble. When we encounter the very same words in a scholarly paper, we simply take them to mean that the writer is establishing a properly inquiring persona (see Dillon, p. 91).

Even something as cognitively fundamental as sentence structure takes on meaning from the discourse in which it is deployed. For this reason, for example, revising rules are notoriously unhelpful: they always require further knowledge in order to be applied. We can't "omit needless words" unless we have some additional criteria for "needlessness." We can't even "avoid passive voice" all the time. Passive voice might be preferred by a writer who wants to head her sentence with words that tie it closely to the previous sentence, especially if the kind of discourse she is producing places a high value on markers of internal coherence.[19]

"Putting meaning into words," then, cannot be seen as a mechanical process of finding the right size containers. Instead, with a form of discourse we take on a whole range of possibilities for making meaning. Language-using in social contexts is connected not only to the immediate situation but to the larger society, too, in the form of conventions for construing reality. This relationship between language and world view has prompted M. A. K. Halliday to argue that "the problem of educational failure is not a linguistic problem, if by linguistic we mean a problem of different urban dialects"; at bottom, "it is a semiotic problem, concerned with the different ways in which we have constructed our social reality, and the styles of meaning we have learned to associate with the various aspects of it."[20] In short, educational problems associated with language use should be understood as difficulties with joining an unfamiliar discourse community.

To look at writing as situated in a discourse community is to blur over the lines between translating and planning in the Flower-Hayes model. Finding words is not a separate process from setting goals. It *is* setting goals, because finding words is always a matter of aligning oneself with a particular discourse community. The community's conventions will include instructions on a preferred form of the native tongue, a specialized vocabulary, a polite technique for establishing persona, and so on. To some extent, the community's conventions can be inferred from analyzing the community's texts. But because the conventions also shape world view, the texts can never be an adequate index of community practice.

Therefore, we should not think of what I am calling a discourse community simply as a group who have decided to abide by certain language-using rules. Rather, we should see the group as an "interpretive community," to use Stanley Fish's term, whose language-using habits are part of a larger pattern of regular interaction with the material world.[21] Because this interaction is always an historical process, changing over time, the community's conventions also change over time. This is not to say that the community's interpretive conventions are arbitrary or that they totally determine individual behavior. They are not arbitrary because they are always conditioned by the ongoing work in the community and sanctioned by consensus. At any given time, community members should have no trouble specifying that some kinds of thinking and language-using are obviously appropriate to the community and some are not. Changes in conventions can only define themselves in terms of what is already acceptable (even if such definition means negation of the currently acceptable).

At the same time, some kinds of thinking and language-using are not obviously either appropriate or inappropriate; they are open to debate. An individual who abides by the community's conventions, therefore, can still find areas for initiative—adherence is slavish adherence only for the least productive community members. These "open" areas may be the unsolved problems of the community, experiences that remain anomalous in the community's interpretive scheme, or they may be areas the community has never even considered dealing with. An individual may, however, bring one of these open areas into the range of the community's discourse if her argument for an interpretation of it is sufficiently persuasive in terms the community already understands. As an example of this activity, Mina Shaughnessy has cited Freud's introductory lectures on psychoanalysis.[22]

Producing text within a discourse community, then, cannot take place unless the writer can define her goals in terms of the community's interpretive conventions. Writing is always already writing for some purpose that can only be understood in its community context. Fish has argued not only that the community of literary critics proceeds in this way but furthermore, that the main business of English studies should be to investigate the nature of discourse communities (see Fish, pp. 338-55). It is exactly this sort of analysis that the Flower-Hayes model lacks when trying to explain planning. For Flower and Hayes, "generating" (a subdivision of planning) means finding ideas by using heuristics, not by responding with individual initiative to the community's needs. "Organizing" (another subdivision) means fitting ideas into the range of logical structures available from human thought processes, not finding out what's reasonable in terms of a community's interpretive conventions. In other words, all that's needed for generating and organizing is access to the invariant, universal structures of human cognition (for a critique of this assumption, see Dillon, pp. 50-82).

The weakness of this approach is most apparent in Flower and Hayes's treatment of "goal-setting." They correctly identify goal-setting as the motor of the composing process, its most important element, but in their model they close it off in the most subordinate position (a subdivision of a subdivision of the writing process). In the "Process Theory" essay, Flower and Hayes elaborate their description into "process goals" (directions for the writing process) and "content goals" (directions for affecting the audience), and they also classify goals in terms of levels of abstraction (see "Process Theory," p. 377). Their model's structure cannot order this multifarious account.

Flower and Hayes end the "Process Theory" essay with analysis of a "good" writer's protocol, aimed to explicate the process of goal-setting. The writer is having trouble deciding how to tell *Seventeen* readers about his job as a college English teacher until he decides that many girls think of English as a "tidy" and "prim" subject and that "By God I can change that notion for them." He goes on to frame an introduction that recounts a "crazy skit" his 101 class liked on the first day of school ("Process Theory," pp. 383, 385). Of his "By God" moment of decision, Flower and Hayes say that "he has regenerated and elaborated his top-level goals," and "this consolidation leaves the writer with a new, relatively complex, rhetorically sophisticated working goal, one which encompasses plans for a topic, a persona, and an audience" (p. 383).

Notice the verbs in this explanation: "regenerating" and "elaborating" goals "leave" the writer with regenerated ("new") and elaborated ("complex") goals—which "encompass" what he needs to know to go on writing. The action described here has no force as an explanation not only because it is circular (regeneration causes regeneration), but also because we still don't know where the new goals come from. Flower and Hayes suggest that going through a process simply "leaves" one with the goals, as if the process itself brought them into being. Upon arrival, the goals are found to contain ("encompass") the necessary knowledge— but we still don't know how that knowledge got there.

The *Seventeen* article writer's process of goal-setting, I think, can be better understood if we see it in terms of writing for a discourse community. His initial problem (which seems to be typical of most subjects confronted with this writing task) is to find a way to include these readers in a discourse community for which he is comfortable writing. He places them in the academic discourse community by imagining the girls as students ("they will all have had English," p. 383). Once he has included them in a familiar discourse community, he can find a way to address them that is common in the community: he will argue with them, putting a new interpretation on information they possess in order to correct misconceptions (his "By God" decision). In arguing, he can draw on all the familiar habits of persuasion he has built up in his experience as a teacher (his "crazy skit" decision). He could not have found a way to write this article if he did not have knowledge of a discourse community to draw on.

The Flower-Hayes model does, of course, include a "long-term memory" where such knowledge could be stored, and Flower and Hayes even acknowledge its importance:

> Sometimes a single cue in an assignment, such as "write a persuasive . . . ," can let a writer tap a stored representation of a problem and bring a whole raft of writing plans into play. (p. 371)

A "stored representation of a problem" must be a set of directions for producing a certain kind of text—what I have been calling discourse conventions. I would argue that the writer doesn't just tap this representation sometimes but every time a writing task is successfully accomplished. Flower and Hayes give this crucial determinant of text production very off-hand treatment, however. They seem to see writing in response to discourse conventions as response to "semiautomatic plans and goals" that contrast with "goals writers create for a particular paper" (p. 381). Evidently they are seeing discourse conventions simply as rules to be internalized, similar to their treatment of the "constraints" of written English. This reduction of conventions to sets of rules is also

Cognition, Convention, and Certainty   79

suggested by their choice of the limerick as a good example of a "genre" (p. 379).

Hence, although Flower and Hayes acknowledge the existence of discourse conventions, they fail to see conventions' generative power, which is to say that their notion of conventions does not include the interpretive function for which I have been arguing. This neglect of the role of knowledge in composing makes the Flower-Hayes theory particularly insensitive to the problems of poor writers.

> Poor writers will frequently depend on very abstract, undeveloped top-level goals, such as "appeal to a broad range of intellect," even though such goals are much harder to work with than a more operational goal such as "give a brief history of my job." Sondra Perl has seen this phenomenon in the basic writers who kept returning to reread the assignment, searching, it would seem, for ready-made goals, instead of forming their own. Alternatively, poor writers will depend on only very low-level goals, such as finishing a sentence or correctly spelling a word. They will be, as Nancy Sommers's student revisers were, locked in by the myopia in their own goals and criteria. (p. 379)

The implication here seems to be that cognitive deficiency keeps poor writers from forming their own goals, keeps them locked in the myopia of goals appropriate to a much earlier stage of cognitive development. The physical image of poor eyesight is revealing of Flower and Hayes's assumptions about the innate sources of writing problems.

I think these students' difficulties with goal-setting are better understood in terms of their unfamiliarity with the academic discourse community, combined, perhaps, with such limited experience outside their native discourse communities that they are unaware that there is such a thing as a discourse community with conventions to be mastered. What is underdeveloped is their knowledge of the ways experience is constituted and interpreted in the academic discourse community and of the fact that all discourse communities constitute and interpret experience. Basil Bernstein has shown that British working-class students are not cognitively deficient but that, first, their native discourse community's conventions are very different from school conventions, and, second, their lack of a variety of speech partners makes it hard for them to see their problems in school as problems of learning to relate to new speech partners (or an unfamiliar discourse community).[23]

Such students may be unable to set a more operational goal because they do not know the conventions of language-using that define such goals as, for example, a "history." Without such knowledge, they may fall back on goals that worked in the past—perhaps in grammar school where close attention to spelling and grammar was rewarded. Or they may sensibly try to enlarge their knowledge by rereading the assignment, seeking clues to the conventions of this new discourse community or those "ready-made goals" without which no writing gets accomplished. Of course, their search of the assignment may be fruitless if the teacher has not been sufficiently explicit about her expectations. Academics are, perhaps, too ready to assume that such operations as "describe" or "analyze" are self-evident, when in fact they have meanings specific to the academic discourse community and specific to disciplines within that community.

To help poor writers, then, we need to explain that their writing takes place within a community, and to explain what the community's conventions are. Another way of putting this would be to borrow Thomas Kuhn's terminology and explain that "puzzle-solving" writing can go on only under the direction of an established "paradigm" for community activity.[24] As Charles Bazerman's work has shown, the writer within the academic community knows how to relate her text to "the object under study, the literature of the field, the anticipated audience, and the author's own self" via discipline-specific conventions governing "lexicon," "explicit citation and implicit knowledge," "knowledge and attitudes the text assumes that the readers will have," and the "features" of a "public face" (Bazerman, pp. 362–63).

The Flower-Hayes model of writing, then, cannot alone give us a complete picture of the process. We might say that if this model describes the *form* of the composing process, the process cannot go on without the *content* which is knowledge of the conventions of discourse communities. In practice, however, form and content cannot be separated in this way, since discourse conventions shape the goals that drive the writing process. To let the model stand alone as an account of composing is to mask the necessity for the socially situated knowledge without which no writing project gets under way. The problems of letting this model stand alone can be seen in the pedagogy emerging from Flower and Hayes's work. They are inclined to treat the model itself as an heuristic:

> Our model is a model of competent writers. Some writers, though, perhaps to their disadvantage, may fail to use some of the processes. (*Cognitive Processes,* p. 29)

Flower has recently published a textbook that aims to guide students through a complete repertoire of composing strategies.[25]

The difficulty with the textbook's view of writing as problem-solving is that it treats problem-solving as an unfiltered encounter with the underlying structure of reality—"the act of discovering key issues in a problem that often lie hidden under the noisy details of the situation" (p. 21). Having defined a problem, one should: first, "fit it into a category of similar problems"; next, decide on a possible course of action against the problem ("make the problem definition more operational"); "tree" the problem or analyze its parts into a hierarchical structure; "generate alternative solutions"; present a conclusion, which weighs alternatives and acknowledges assumptions and implications of the conclusion (see pp. 21-26). But *first,* how does one define a problem? Although Flower says that "problems are only problems for someone," she doesn't talk about this necessary link between problem definition and interpretive communities (p. 21). Rather, it seems that we will *find* (not make) the problem if we strip away the "noisy details of the situation." I would argue, in contrast, that only the noisy details of the situation can define a problem. To "define" a problem is to interact with the material world according to the conventions of a particular discourse community; these conventions are the only source for categories of similar problems, operational definitions, and alternative solutions, and a conclusion can only be evaluated as "well supported" in terms of a particular community's standards.

I certainly do not mean to suggest that students should not be encouraged to look at reality when they compose—far from it, since I have emphasized the function of writing in doing (intellectual) work in the world. But I do mean to point out that we cannot look at reality in an unfiltered way—"reality" only makes sense when organized by the interpretive conventions of a discourse community. Students often complain that they have nothing to say, whereas "real-world" writers almost never do, precisely because real-world writers are writing for discouse communities in which they know their work can matter, whereas students can see little purpose for their own attempts ("essais") other than to get a grade. For example, Erwin Steinberg has suggested that the superior organization of an electrical engineer's report, as compared to a freshman composition, stems from the engineer's superior knowledge of and experience in a field; what looks like a cognitive difference turns out to have a large social component (see "A Garden of Opportunities and a Thicket of Dangers," *Cognitive Processes,* pp. 163-165). Hence, although Steinberg is sympathetic to the project of finding writing models and heuristics, he cautions, "We must always be careful not to think in terms of a single model, because if we do we'll find one and force everyone to use it—the way English teachers used to require students to make formal outlines before they wrote" (p. 163).

The cognitive psychology approach cuts off writing-as-problem-solving from the context of a discourse community precisely because one model is sought (Steinberg's caveat notwithstanding). Discourse communities are tied to historical and cultural circumstances, and hence can only be seen as unenlightening instances of the general theory the cognitive approach seeks: the one model is the universal one. All of the theoretical essays in *Cognitive Processes in Writing* seek to find this model. Carl Bereiter offers an account of the stages of development in children's writing processes. Like the Flower-Hayes model, his is recursive—that is, he suggests that children's development includes a certain set of stages but that the order of these stages can be changed. There is, however, a "preferred or 'natural' order of writing development," an order in which the constraints on composing imposed by the necessity of putting thoughts into words are gradually reduced by being "automatized." Bereiter suggests that this order should be adopted in the schools (see "Development in Writing," p. 89).

Collins and Gentner seek to go even further in schematizing their theory as a rule-governed model because they hope to end with a program enabling a computer to compose (see "A Framework for a Cognitive Theory of Writing," pp. 51-52). This would permit the creation of "Writing Land," where computers would guide students through the patterns of the writing process and enhance the students' cognitive activities (see "Framework," pp. 67-70). Computer-assisted composition will help students reduce the constraints imposed by the struggle to put thoughts into words by separating "idea production" and "text production" ("Framework," p. 53). Once the ideas are under control, "the next stage is to impose text structure on the ideas" ("Framework," p. 59).

During text production, Collins and Gentner confidently state, the writer can call on "structural devices, stylistic devices, and content devices"—the term "devices" suggesting rule-governed mechanisms. Yet "unfortunately for the writer, there is no one-to-one correspondence between means and end here"—in other words, no consistency in situation that would permit reliance on rule-governed mechanisms ("Framework," p. 60). Collins and Gentner's analysis frequently bumps up against language's opacity, the contribution to thinking of densely situation-bound meanings embodied in habits of language-using. Because they cannot account for this situational aspect of writing, Collins and Gentner can only define "good writing" as writing that conforms to a set of rules set by some authority (see "Framework," pp. 52-53). This approach leaves them no way to justify the authority's decisions as other than arbitrary, and hence their "rules" turn out to be situation-bound: "Delete extraneous material," "Shorten long paragraphs," and so on ("Framework," p. 65). Such advice is unhelpful to students without other knowledge that enables them to identify the extraneous and over-lengthy, as I noted earlier in my discussion on revising rules.

The fundamental problem with this approach is that it assumes that the rules we can formulate to describe behavior are the same rules that produce the behavior. As attempts to program language-using computers have shown, such structures reveal their lack of explanatory power when applied to an actual situation in which discourse conventions come into play. Programming a computer to use language comes up against a problem of infinite regress of context—or, how do we tell the computer how to tell what's important when things are important only in terms of purposive activity? How can we define, for example, what is "extraneous material," when the quality of being extraneous resides not in the material itself but in its relation to discourse? Or, to use a simpler example, how can we tell the computer when a paragraph is too long except by specifying a range of lines that constitute acceptable lengths? Is there any form of discourse in which 20-line paragraphs are acceptable and 21-line paragraphs are not? As the competence/performance debate in linguistics has suggested, it may be that we cannot have a completely descriptive theory of behavior in widely varying specific situations—that is, we cannot formulate universal rules for context-bound activities. If language-using isn't rule-governed in this sense, however, it still may be regular—that is, we may be able to group situations as likely to share a number of language-using features. But to do this is to describe the conventions of discourse communities.[26]

As I have been arguing, then, both the inner-directed and the outer-directed theoretical schools will have to contribute to a synthesis capable of providing a comprehensive new agenda for composition studies. My critique of Flower and Hayes's work is intended to contribute to such a synthesis, not to delegitimate what they are doing. I do want to raise a serious question, however, about another feature of the inner-directed school, a feature that works against fruitful discussion and synthesis: the quest for certainty. In seeking one universal model of the composing process, inner-directed theorists seek a new set of principles for our discipline that will raise their arguments, as one has put it, "above mere ideology" (Hirsch, p. 4). They seek a kind of certainty they believe is accessible only to science, and their talk of paradigm-shifting invokes Kuhn to announce that our discipline will soon have a scientific basis.[27]

This kind of certainty is presumably analogous to the commonplace elevation of fact over opinion, since it is supposed to end all debate. The inner-directed school therefore has redefined composition research to mean a search for the facts in the real world that prove a theory beyond debate. The Flower-Hayes model claims much prestige from being derived from such supposedly unimpeachable evidence. But its reliance on empirical evidence can be questioned on several grounds. For one thing, protocol analysis is a controversial method even within cognitive psychology because it tends to affect what is being observed (see Gould's remarks, *Cognitive Processes,* p. 125). Flower and Hayes's work is particularly vulnerable because most of their adult subjects have been English teachers who are familiar with the specialized vocabulary of the theory of Flower and Hayes have used to analyze the protocols. Under any circumstances, protocol analysis can lead to "self-fulfilling" prophecy because its assumption that the subject's words mirror her thinking allows the researcher to claim that certain thought processes have occured if certain words appear in the protocol. Self-fulfilling prophecy is even more likely when test subjects share expert knowledge of these words with the researchers.

The larger point to be made here, however, is that no scientific research, no matter how rigorously it is conducted, possesses the kind of authoritative certainty inner-directed theorists are seeking.[28] It is always desirable, of course, to know more about composing, but it is also necessary to treat this knowledge as provisional, the way scientists treat their findings, if inquiry is not to end. We may wonder, then, why inner-directed theorists are so ready to invest their results with final authority and rush to pedagogical applications. I think it is that certainty appeals to composition specialists these days for various reasons. For one, until recently composition studies was a low-status enclave it was hard to escape; a powerful theory would help us retaliate against the literary critics who dominate English studies. Moreover, such a theory might help us survive what appears to be the long slide of all humanistic disciplines into a low-status enclave. A scientific-sounding theory promises an "accountability" hedge against hard times.

The strongest appeal of certainty, however, is its offer of a solution to our new students' problems that will enable us to undertake their socialization into the academic discourse community without having to consider the ethical and political dimensions of this act. We are reluctant to take up ethical and political questions about what we do because writing teachers have been under a terrific strain. Pressured with increasing asperity by our colleges to prepare students for their other courses, we have also felt anxious in the classroom both when our teaching worked—because we sensed that we were wiping out the students' own culture—and when it didn't—because we were cheating them of a chance to better their situations. Inner-directed pedagogy meets teachers' emotional needs because it can be defended on grounds that are likely to satisfy complaining faculty and administrators, and because its claim to a basis in universals assures us that when we inculcate it, we aren't touching the students' own culture but merely giving them a way around it and up the ladder of success. The corollary is that students for whom the pedagogy doesn't work need no longer be seen as victims of our incompetence but simply as innately inferior.

Invocation of certainty, then, performs the rhetorical function of invocation of the Deity. It guarantees the transcendent authority of values for which we do not need to argue but which we can now apply with the confidence of a "good cause." I would argue, however, that we must understand such a move as the assigning of superhuman authority to a human construction. All knowledge, that is, is of human origin, even scientific knowledge. Indeed, modern philosophy has centered around a critique of scientific knowledge precisely because such knowledge is most likely now to be treated as certain. As Richard Rorty has recently shown, the history of Western philosophy since the Renaissance can be seen as a series of unsuccessful attempts to fight off the admission that such claims for certainty are no longer tenable.[29] There is no way out of confrontation, except among fellow believers, with the necessity of arguing for one's ethical choices.

This confrontation is especially necessary in a pluralistic society such as the United States, in which a heterogeneous school population ensures that pedagogical choices will affect students unequally. Under such circumstances, as Rorty cautions, claims to certainty often express simply a desire for agreement which masks the question of whose interests are being served (see Rorty, p. 335). Teachers' individual ethical choices add up to political consequences, responsibility for which we cannot avoid. We are better off, then, with a disciplinary theory that encourages examination of consequences. For example, inner-directed research might come up with an heuristic that is useful in Basic Writing classes. But if we use it there, we should not imagine that the heuristic allows us to forget who the students are in Basic Writing classes, where they come from, what their prospects are — in short, why these particular students are having educational difficulties.

Ultimately, I am calling for the inspection of what some curriculum theorists have called the "hidden curriculum": the project of initiating students into a particular world view that gives rise to the daily classroom tasks without being consciously examined by teacher or students.[30] If we call what we are teaching "universal" structures or processes, we bury the hidden curriculum even deeper by claiming that our choice of material owes nothing to historical circumstances. To do this is to deny the school's function as an agent of cultural hegemony, or the selective valuation and transmission of world views. The result for students who don't share the school's preferred world views is either failure or deracination. I think we must acknowledge cultural differences in the classroom, even though this means increasing our emotional strain as members of one group trying to mediate contacts among various others.

The kind of pedagogy that would foster responsible inspection of the politically loaded hidden curriculum in composition class is discourse analysis. The exercise of cultural hegemony can be seen as the treatment of one community's discourse conventions as if they simply mirrored reality. To point out that discourse conventions exist would be to politicize the classroom — or rather, to make everyone aware that it is already politicized. World views would become more clearly a matter of conscious commitment, instead of unconscious conformity, if the ways in which they are constituted in discourse communities were analyzed.

This is not to say that we can make the school an ideologically neutral place. The whole force of my argument is that there is no way to *escape* all discourse communities, stand outside them and pronounce judgment. Furthermore, I assent to most of the conventions of the academic discourse community and believe that students from other communities can benefit from learning about them, and learning them. But perhaps we can break up the failure/deracination dilemma for students from communities at a distance from academe. Through discourse analysis we might offer them an understanding of their school difficulties as the problems of a traveler to an unfamiliar country — yet a country in which it is possible to learn the language and the manners and even "go native" while still remembering the land from which one has come.

In his discussion of literary criticism and interpretive communities, Stanley Fish has offered us one set of suggestions for how such ethically and politically conscious education might proceed. Richard Rorty offers another in his vision of philosophy becoming not the arbiter of disciplines but the mediator among them. This "edifying" philosophy will have as its task making us realize that agreement that looks like certainty can occur only "because when a practice has continued long enough the conventions which make it possible — and which permit a consensus on how to divide it into parts — are relatively easy to isolate" (p. 321). Rorty's is not a positivist notion of arbitrary conventions; he sees conventions as the product of communities, situation-bound but also subject to change. Rorty generalizes Kuhn's notions of "normal" and "revolutionary" science to argue that the edifying philosopher's task is to keep reminding us that "normal" discourse is evidently clear and above debate only because we agree about its conventions. Education must begin with normal discourse but should not be limited to it, with its unhelpful distinction between facts and values (see p. 363). For the goal of discovering Truth, Rorty substitutes the goal of continuing conversation, but this will not be a dangerously relativistic goal because always conditioned by and having to answer to an historical framework. Rorty's philosophical community thus resembles Fish's interpretive community.

Finally, then, we should see our answers to the question of what we need to know about writing in the light of a new humanistic synthesis. Philosophy has moved to the position that discourse communities are all we have to rely upon in our quest for certainty. Literary criticism is analyzing how discourse communities function as historically situated interpretive communities. Composition studies should focus upon practice within interpretive communities — exactly how conventions work in the world and how they are transmitted. If the work of these disciplines continues to converge, a new synthesis will emerge that revivifies rhetoric as the central discipline of human intellectual endeavor. In view of such a synthesis, the project to make composition studies merely scientific looks obsolete.

I hope that his rhetorical synthesis, because it turns our attention to questions of value and persuasion, will also reawaken us to the collective nature of the whole educational endeavor. There should be no disgrace in discovering that one's work and the understanding that guides it cannot be achieved autonomously. Then the main casualty of our theoretical debate can be the debilitating individualism that adds so much to classroom strain. In other words, let us emphasize not only discourse but also community. I do not mean that we should seek to eliminate the conflicts that arise from our coming from different historical and cultural situations. We should recognize that being so situated is the most important thing we have in common.[31]

Notes

1. The attitude I'm describing here has been called current-traditionalism, and it still dominates textbooks in the field; see Donald C. Stewart, "Composition Textbooks and the Assault on Tradition," *College Composition and Communication,* 29 (May 1978), pp. 171-76.

2. I am taking this sense of "isomorphic" from Frank D'Angelo, *A Conceptual Theory of Rhetoric* (Cambridge, Mass.: Winthrop, 1975), pp. 16, 26-36.

3. I have in mind here the justification for teaching Standard English advanced in E. D. Hirsch, Jr., *The Philosophy of Composition* (Chicago: Univ. of Chicago Press, 1977).

4. For example, Richard Young has recently characterized his particle-wave-field heuristic as based on "universal invariants that underlie all human experience as characteristic of rationality itself"; in "Arts, Crafts, Gifts, and Knacks: Some Disharmonies in the New Rhetoric," *Visible Language,* 14, no. 4 (1980), 347.

5. For an overview of research on sentence-combining and the arguments for teaching it, see Frank O'Hare, *Sentence Combining: Improving Student*

Writing without Formal Grammar Instruction (Urbana, Illinois: NCTE, 1973).

6. A new textbook that operates from these principles of audience analysis (and other inner-directed pedagogy) is Janice M. Lauer, Gene Montague, Andrea Lunsford, and Janet Emig, *Four Worlds of Writing* (New York: Harper and Row, 1981).

7. Typically, a discourse community prefers one form of the native tongue, which may be characterized simply by level of formality and specialized vocabulary, or which may be a dialect, or a fully constituted language (in the native tongue's family) with its own grammar rules. The outer-directed theorists thus emphasize "parole" over "langue," to use de Saussure's terms, "performance" over "competence," to use Chomsky's terms. For a good account of such language differences in an American setting, see William Labov, *The Study of Nonstandard English* (1969; revised and enlarged, Urbana, Illinois: NCTE, 1975).

8. See, for example, M. A. K. Halliday, "Language as Social Semiotic," *Language as Social Semiotic* (Baltimore: University Park Press, 1978), pp. 108–26.

9. This attitude has been called the Sapir-Whorf hypothesis, because arguments are advanced for it by linguists Edward Sapir and his pupil, Benjamin Lee Whorf; for a good summary and critique of the Sapir-Whorf hypothesis, see Adam Schaff, *Language and Cognition* (1964; trans. Olgierd Wojtasiewicz, ed. Robert S. Cohen; New York: McGraw-Hill, 1973).

10. This, I think, is the gist of the analysis offered by Mina Shaughnessy, "Beyond the Sentence," *Errors and Expectations* (New York: Oxford Univ. Press, 1977), pp. 226–72.

11. A new textbook that operates from some principles of outer-directed pedagogy is Elaine Maimon, Gerald L. Belcher, Gail W. Hearn, Barbara F. Nodine, and Finbarr W. O'Connor, *Writing in the Arts and Sciences* (Cambridge, Massachusetts: Winthrop, 1981).

12. For an exemplary analysis of academic discourse conventions and how they lead to the accomplishment of the community's work, see Charles Bazerman, "What Written Knowledge Does: Three Examples of Academic Discourse," *Philosophy of the Social Sciences,* 11 (September 1981), pp. 361–87; further references in text.

13. Linda Flower and John R. Hayes, "A Cognitive Process Theory of Writing," *College Composition and Communication,* 32 (December 1981), pp. 365–87; further references in text.

14. Lee W. Gregg and Erwin R. Steinberg, editors, *Cognitive Processes in Writing* (Hillsdale, New Jersey: Lawrence Erlbaum, 1980); further references in text.

15. Lev Vygotsky, *Thought and Language* (1934; rpt. ed. & trans. Eugenia Hanfmann and Gertrude Vakar; Cambridge, Mass.: MIT Press, 1962), p. 51, author's emphasis; further references in text. Vygotsky's pupil A. R. Luria did research among Uzbek peasants which suggests that thought and language interpenetrate to such a degree that perception of optical illusions, for example, changes with cultural experience and level of education; see A. R. Luria, *Cognitive Development,* trans. Martin Lopez-Morillas and Lynn Solotaroff, ed. Michael Cole (1974; reprint, Cambridge, Mass.: Harvard Univ. Press, 1976).

16. See M. A. K. Halliday and Ruqaiya Hasan, *Cohesion in English* (London: Longman, 1976), pp. 19-26.

17. My line of argument here is based on Dell Hymes, "Bilingual Education: Linguistic vs. Sociolinguistic Bases," *Foundations in Sociolinguistics* (Philadelphia: Univ. of Pennsylvania Press, 1974), pp. 119-24; in the same volume, Hymes argues that to uncover the extra-linguistic attitudes lending significance to language use, linguists need more contributions from folklorists.

18. George L. Dillon, *Constructing Texts* (Bloomington, Indiana: Indiana Univ. Press, 1981), pp. 1-20; further references in text.

19. A critique of the notion of simplicity-as-clarity has been offered by Richard Lanham, *Style: An Anti-Textbook* (New Haven, Conn.: Yale Univ. Press, 1974). Lanham's later work in composition pedagogy suggests, however, that he is cynical about the position taken in *Style* and not really ready to defend "ornate" language choices outside of special literary circumstances; see Richard Lanham, *Revising Prose* (New York: Scribner, 1979). Dillon, pp. 21-49, is more helpful on understanding the problems with revising rules.

20. Halliday, "Language in Urban Society," p. 163; Halliday suggests that our current difficulties in the composition class may be at least in part a function of the increasing number of students who come from urban areas.

21. See Stanley Fish, *Is There a Text in this Class?* (Cambridge, Mass.: Harvard Univ. Press, 1980), further references in text; the following argument is heavily indebted to Fish's work.

22. Mina Shaughnessy, "Some Needed Research on Writing," *College Composition and Communication,* 27 (December 1977), p. 319.

23. See Basil Bernstein, *Class, Codes and Control* (1971; rpt. New York: Schocken, 1975); and to correct the vulgar error that Bernstein is diagnosing a cognitive deficiency in working-class language, see "The Significance of Bernstein's Work for Sociolinguistic Theory" in Halliday, pp. 101-107. Many dangerous misinterpretations of Bernstein could perhaps have been avoided if he had not chosen to call working-class language-using habits a "restricted code" and middle-class (school-oriented) habits an "elaborated code."

24. The seminal text here is Thomas Kuhn, *The Structure of Scientific Revolutions,* 2d. edition, enlarged (Chicago: Univ. of Chicago Press, 1970). Kuhn is now going so far as to say that "proponents of different theories (or different paradigms, in the broader sense of the term) speak different languages—languages expressing different cognitive commitments, suitable for different worlds"; he announces the study of language's function in theory-making as his current project. See Thomas Kuhn, *The Essential Tension* (Chicago: Univ. of Chicago Press, 1977), pp. 22-23.

25. Linda Flower, *Problem-Solving Strategies for Writing* (New York: Harcourt Brace Jovanovich, 1981); further references in text.

26. In my discussion of Collins and Gentner, I am following the line of argument offered by Hubert L. Dreyfus, *What Computers Can't Do* (New York: Harper and Row, 1972; rpt. 2d. edition, San Francisco: Freeman, 1979). Flower and Hayes's sympathy with the Collins-Gentner approach is suggested not only by the large amount of agreement between the two accounts of composing, but

also by the numerous borrowings in the Flower-Hayes model from computer terminology and by Flower and Hayes's suggestions that their model will contribute toward "building a Writer" ("Process Theory" p. 368).

27. For an example of this use of Kuhn, see Maxine Hairston, "The Winds of Change: Thomas Kuhn and the Revolution in the Teaching of Writing," *College Composition and Communication,* 33 (February 1982); pp. 76–88.

28. This argument follows the account of rhetoric's function in the scientific discourse community given by Kuhn in *Structure* and (in a more radical version) by Paul Feyerabend, *Against Method* (1975; rpt. London: Verso, 1978).

29. Richard Rorty, *Philosophy and the Mirror of Nature* (Princeton, NJ: Princeton Univ. Press, 1979); further references in text.

30. On the hidden curriculum and its reproduction of oppressive social power relations, see Michael Apple, *Ideology and Curriculum* (London: Routledge and Kegan Paul, 1979).

31. I would like to thank Bruce Herzberg for the many ideas and the editorial guidance that he has, as usual, contributed to my work.

Afterthought: Cognition, Convention, and Certainty

As it now seems to me, my main motives in writing this essay were to undermine the authority of universalistic composition research and to make space for a different, more culturally or rhetorically oriented kind of research. I still think that my strictures on early cognitivist work and my recommendations for the study of writing in context are sound positions. What seems to have become the most influential aspect of "Cognition, Convention, and Certainty," however, is the concept of discourse community articulated there. I do have some concerns about how this concept has been read in the essay over time.

My principal objection here to the early work of Linda Flower and John R. Hayes was that they sought a kind of "authoritative certainty" that, I argued, drawing on Thomas Kuhn, no scientific research can provide. I did not want to allow them certainty because I feared that any model claiming to be above debate would be imposed Procrustean-fashion on all students, with relatively greater harm being done to students at greater social removes from the culture-bound assumptions about thinking and writing that, in my view, informed the model.

Rather than attack empirical work directly, however, my tactic here was to argue that it presents an incomplete view of composing. In part this tactic was motivated by respect for the many scholars who were eagerly taking up cognitive research as a way to "do" composition studies,

Cognition, Convention, and Certainty 91

a modus operandi the then-fledgling field badly needed. But I also wanted to create space for research that would focus upon the elements of the social context that influence writing, such as the textual conventions of discourse communities, which I suggested might be studied by more humanities-oriented research techniques. The concept of "discourse community" thus was initially used to define an alternate research site for scholars in composition studies. Indeed, in this essay I pretended that research was already going on at that site; as far as I knew it really wasn't, but I hoped to invoke it with my essay.

In recent years, I have been alarmed to learn that this concept of discourse community is being read as if it were intended to be a totally unified entity with impermeable boundaries, a reading that suggests that teaching the discourse of the academic community would mean imposing it on all students Procrustean-fashion with total disregard for whatever knowledge they might bring to school from other discourse communities. I reject this view.

It is true that in "Cognition, Convention, and Certainty" I was at pains to establish the currency of the concept of discourse community, using it to name an alternate research site so as to get the research going and break the momentum of cognitive work. Also, I emphasized the forces that make a discourse community cohere, that make it resistant to the entry of outsiders, in order to offer an alternate model for the difficulties of basic writers rather than seeing them as cognitively deficient. Thus I may have made the concept seem more reified that I would actually like to regard it.

I think, however, that I did also emphasize the multiplicity of personal, social, cultural, and political factors that condition discourse in a community, thus calling attention to factors that make for potential change. If the concept of discourse community is to remain useful for composition studies, we must now focus not on what makes it cohere, but what makes it unstable—in other words, we must focus on how discourse communities change, so that we can learn better how to make them change the way we might want them to.

This focus on change should also lead to serious reconsiderations of the task of teaching academic discourse. I think that at the time I wrote "Cognition, Convention, and Certainty," I was still hoping that learning academic discourse could foster in college students what Paulo Freire calls critical consciousness. Thus I could defend the project of teaching academic discourse as not inimical to radically democratic political goals. Although the argument was not developed fully in this essay, its lurking in the background may have encouraged the reading I deplore above, that I wanted academic discourse to be imposed forcibly on all. I don't think I ever wanted that. But I think I did have more confidence in the possible benefits of learning traditional academic discourse than I now have.

I now would say that "teaching academic discourse" must mean collaborating with students to both introduce them to the traditional discourse and work to change the traditional discourse along lines that seem good to them in terms of the discursive practices they bring to college from other communities. My current position does also involve a revisionist view of Freire, which is addressed in an essay in *Contending with Words,* eds. Patricia Harkin and John Schilb (MLA, 1991).

I have no strong feeling, though, that I must fight for the concept of discourse community, either in the sense of fighting for my own conception of this speculative instrument, or in the sense of fighting to keep the term current in debate in the field. I can't even remember now whether the concept of discourse community was "my own idea." I don't really believe that people have their "own" ideas or "own" them. The formulation of the concept in this essay was not taken from anywhere else in its present form. But it was certainly profoundly influenced by reading in Kuhn, Stanley Fish, Richard Rorty, and the sociolinguists, and by discussions with Bruce Herzberg. Indeed, given the concept's provenance in a review-essay — which Dominic LaCapra calls the characteristic genre of our intellectual era — I think it would be fair to say that Flower and Hayes also influenced its development. I am perfectly willing to await developments in the field of composition studies, even as I contribute to them, of course, to see what future the ideas in this essay may have.

4 : Rhetoric in the American College Curriculum: The Decline of Public Discourse

S. Michael Halloran
Rensselaer Polytechnic Institute

Richard Young has popularized the term "current-traditional rhetoric" for the theory and pedagogy that until recently dominated the wasteland of freshman composition.[1] The term "current-traditional rhetoric" seems to me an odd one. First, it's an oxymoron of sorts: what's current is almost by definition not traditional. More importantly, current-traditional rhetoric bears very little resemblance to the rhetorical tradition. The question I'd like to address in this essay is, How did we get from the rhetorical tradition to current-traditional rhetoric? This is an enormous question to which I don't pretend to have a complete answer. What I'm going to develop here is in effect a brief for an argument that I hope eventually to develop more fully.

First I'll offer some definitions and then spend some time trying to say what the teaching of rhetoric was like in the 17th and 18th century American colleges. Then I'll try to identify some important aspects of a change that took place during the 19th century, the change that produced current-traditional rhetoric. Finally, I want to suggest an important deficiency of current-traditional rhetoric which the recent revival of rhetoric in English departments has so far failed to address. As my title suggests, this deficiency has to do with something I call public discourse.

By rhetoric, I mean the art of effective communication.[2] As an art, rhetoric stands somewhere between a purely intuitive knack and an exact science; it provides techniques together with principles to govern their use, but it cannot say with total confidence that a given technique will achieve a desired effect. As an art of communication, rhetoric deals with the symbols — chiefly words — through which humans make and exchange meaning. As an art of effective communication, rhetoric focuses upon the adaptation of symbols to the demands of particular audiences, purposes, and situations.

By the rhetorical tradition, I mean a tradition of teaching and practice in the art of effective communication that flourished in classical Greece and Rome, survived in attenuated form through the middle ages, and revived in the Renaissance.[3] its fullest expression was in the works of Cicero and Quintilian. Aristotle was its principal theorist, but the tradition was defined most importantly not by its theory, but rather by its cultural ideal—the orator.[4] The rhetorical tradition portrayed the orator as a person who embodies all that is best in a culture and brings it to bear on public problems through eloquent discourse. Quintilian wrote of the good man skilled in speaking; Cicero of the *doctus orator,* the learned speaker. Both of them referred to a civic leader who understood all the values of his culture and used artful speech to make those values effective in the arena of public affairs. The purpose of education in the rhetorical tradition was to prepare such leaders.

As an art of effective communication, then, the tradition of classical rhetoric gives primary emphasis to communication on public problems, problems that arise from our life in political communities. The many other sorts of problems that might be addressed through an art of communication—problems of business and commerce, of self-understanding and personal relationships, of scientific and philosophical investigation, of aesthetic experience, for example—are in the tradition of classical rhetoric subordinate. This point of emphasis is central to the argument of this essay. My thesis is that rhetoric in the sense of an art of public discourse flourished in American colleges of the 18th century and died out during the 19th. I argue further that the revival of rhetoric in the field of English composition has thus far failed to address the need for a revival of public discourse. I call attention to the history of rhetoric in American colleges because I believe we have lost something that is worth trying to recover.

The rhetoric that was imported to the first American college (Harvard, founded in 1636) was in effect a much truncated version of classical rhetoric. One historian of rhetoric has characterized it as decadent.[5] Samuel Eliot Morison, looking not just at rhetoric but at the whole of Puritan culture, suggests that its thinness was not decadence or even anemia, but leanness appropriate to the conditions of frontier life.[6] In his view the Puritans brought to the new world as much of European Humanism as was likely to survive in an environment that directed one's attention relentlessly to the most basic material things—food and shelter. And it is true that while the rhetorical doctrine of 17th century Harvard was a pale shadow of classical rhetoric, it would later become a full revival of the tradition of Cicero and Quintilian.

There are two important respects in which 17th century American rhetoric was anti-classical. The first is that it made a sharp distinction between substance and form in discourse. What was called "rhetoric" dealt exclusively with what we might call the surface features of discourse. It had to do with variations of word order and with metaphors of various kinds, or as they were known in the rhetorical theory of the time, figures and tropes. The purpose of this rhetoric was simply to provide a pleasing surface for argumentative structures derived from other fields of study, such as theology, philosophy, and natural science. The more-or-less standard definition for rhetoric at this time was the art of ornamenting discourse.[7] Its parts were style and delivery, and it placed heaviest emphasis on style. The classical tradition, by contrast, had seen rhetoric as an art of persuasion, of moving an audience to act or think or feel in a particular way. The stylistic ornaments were simply means to this end, and they were understood as much more closely wedded to the substance and purpose of discourse.

The rhetoric I have characterized was of course not invented by the Puritan founders of Harvard College. What they imported was the rhetoric of Peter Ramus, or more properly of Omer Talon, Ramus's disciple in the program of curricular reform he undertook at the University of Paris during the 16th century.[8] A question one might reasonably ask is whether this art of ornamenting discourse can rightly be considered a rhetoric in the sense I have given to that term. In what sense is this an art of effective communication? Where is the notion of adaptation to the demands of audience, purpose, and situation? The answer, I believe, is that Ramistic rhetoric must be grounded in a highly stereotyped understanding of rhetorical situations. Standards of propriety are relatively simple and rigid, so they need not be considered explicitly. Ramistic rhetoric is thus suitable for a homogeneous and stable society, or at least for a society that wants to be homogeneous and stable. It adopts what might be called the verbal technology of traditional rhetoric, but rejects its sense of culture as complex and evolving. Later, this fragment of classical rhetoric would grow into the full tradition, and it would support the growth of a more complex and dynamic body politic.

The second anti-classical aspect of the rhetoric taught in the early years at Harvard was its relative indifference to communication in the vernacular. Both texts and classroom exercises were in Latin. Speaking English was prohibited, even in informal conversation, though scholars doubt that students observed the rule meticulously.[9] But in the curriculum, the language of social and political affairs had no place. The practical end of higher education in early colonial times seems to have been to produce mastery in the classical languages — first Latin, then Greek, finally Hebrew, which was at the time thought to be the original of all languages. The three classical tongues were understood as the key to all learning, both human and divine. A student was supposed to be more or less fluent in Latin and in command of the rudiments of Greek before being admitted to Harvard. The actual standard of performance was somewhat below this ideal, and one explanation of the simplified rhetorical doctrine in use is that it served as a sort of advanced grammar to shore up instruction in Latin.[10] The schemes and tropes of rhetoric according to this view simply elaborated the principles behind the grammatical paradigms.

In any event, no formal attention was paid to the students' ability to communicate effectively in their native language. This "classical" emphasis was in reality alien to the classical tradition. Quintilian's program for the formation of the ideal orator had placed considerable emphasis on Greek, a language that was to the students he had in mind foreign (though by no means dead), but his educational goal was to produce mastery in the artful use of Latin, the language of everyday political and social affairs.[11] Much of his theory and pedagogy focused minutely on style and strategy in Latin. An equivalent program for students at 17th century Harvard would have subordinated the study of classical languages to the study of English. An equivalent rhetoric would have said much about style and strategy in English, would have concentrated on making students artful in the language of everyday political and social affairs. There was, of course, a great deal of "spillover" from the study of rhetoric in Latin to the practice of discourse in English. It would be difficult to make sense of a Puritan sermon except as a deliberate application of Ramistic rhetoric. But the notion that one achieves eloquence in the vernacular not by studying and working in the vernacular, but as a by-product of work in foreign languages—this curious notion which on its face seems to respect the classics is in fact a clear violation of classical educational and rhetorical thinking.[12]

During the 18th century, the rhetoric taught at Harvard and at the newer colleges such as William and Mary (1693) and Yale (1700) gradually took on a more fully classical flavor. Classical texts that had been unavailable on this side of the Atlantic during the 17th century were imported. During the second decade of the 18th century, the works of Cicero and Quintilian began to appear in college libraries, and by mid-century *De Oratore* was widely known. It was, for example, required reading for students at what is now the University of Pennsylvania.[13] From Cicero and Quintilian, students would learn to understand rhetoric as an art of moving an audience through eloquent speech, not merely of ornamenting discourse according to tacit and stereotypic notions of propriety.

This broadening view of rhetoric can be seen in the theses listed for disputation at Harvard commencements. Throughout the 17th and into the 18th century, thesis lists regularly included definitions of rhetoric as the art of ornamenting discourse, and dividing it into the standard

Ramistic parts: style and delivery. But a 1748 thesis states that rhetoric has four parts: invention, arrangement, style, and delivery.[14] This approximates the full classical understanding of rhetoric, omitting only the canon of memory. This four part division of rhetoric means that by 1748 the art is understood to include deciding what to say and what order to put it in, as well as the specific verbal flourishes to use and matters of voice and gesture. Rhetoric had in effect been redefined as an art of adapting knowledge to specific occasions and audiences, which was essentially what Cicero and Quintilian had understood it to be.

The emergence of the full classical idea of rhetoric is also reflected in the increasing emphasis given in the curriculum to the English language. At least one English language treatise on rhetoric had been available in the Harvard College library by 1683 — John Smith's *The Mysterie of Rhetorique Unveiled.*[15] This was simply a conventional Ramistic rhetoric of tropes and figures with illustrations taken mainly from the Bible. An English translation of the Port Royal *Art of Speaking,* which presented something much closer to the full classical doctrine, was available at Harvard by 1716 and at Yale by 1722.[16] When John Ward's *A System of Oratory* appeared in 1759, it was very quickly taken up by colleges in America and remained the dominant text until 1780. Ward's *System* relied heavily on Quintilian and Cicero, and is regarded by some scholars as the fullest expression of classical rhetoric ever to appear in the English language. It is worth noting that this work enjoyed far greater popularity in American colleges than in its native England.[17]

The new emphasis on English was reflected in faculty appointments and college exercises as well as in the books in use. Pennsylvania appointed a professor of "English and oratory" in 1753, and by 1768 he needed an assistant. Timothy Dwight, who would later become president of Yale, was appointed in 1776 to teach "rhetoric, history, and the belles lettres" in English. Harvard adopted a tutorial plan that included "composition in English, Rhetoric, and other Belles Lettres" in 1766. Both Harvard and Yale instituted public speaking exercises in English during the 1750s. Prior to that time these very important exercises, in which all students were supposed to perform in order to achieve a degree, had been done exclusively in the classical languages. The new emphasis on English was also expressed in the student literary and debate societies that sprang up in great numbers during the 18th century.[18] From the beginning, English was the standard language of these groups, in contrast to the long-standing tradition that serious intellectual discourse was to be conducted in Latin. Some of the societies had explicit rules against speaking Latin.

The shift to English meant that learning could more readily be brought to bear on problems in the world of practical affairs, the world defined by the English language. And the growing interest of students in public affairs can be read in this list of questions disputed publicly at Harvard commencements:

> In 1729, Is unlimited obedience to rulers taught by Christ and his apostles?
> In 1733, Is the voice of the people the voice of God?
> In 1743, Is it lawful to resist the Supreme Magistrate, if the Commonwealth cannot otherwise be preserved? (Samuel Adams argued the affirmative.)
> In 1743, 1747, 1761, and 1762, Does Civil Government originate from compact?
> In 1758, Is civil government absolutely necessary for men? (John Adams argued the affirmative.)
> In 1759, Is an absolute and arbitrary monarchy contrary to right reason?
> In 1765, Can the new prohibitary duties, which make it useless for the people to engage in commerce, be evaded by them as faithful subjects? (Here is a headlong leap from the abstract world of philosophy and political theory, to the concrete world of affairs.)
> In 1769, Is a just government the only stable foundation of public peace?
> Again in 1769, Are the people the sole judges of their rights and liberties?
> In 1770, Is a government tyrannical in which the rulers consult their own interest more than that of their subjects?
> Again in 1770, Is a government despotic in which the people have no check on the legislative power?[19]

Other colleges exhibited a similar interest in the application of learning to public issues. At the 1770 commencement of the College of New Jersey, James Witherspoon defended in Latin the thesis that the law of nature obliged subjects to resist tyrannical kinds; Witherspoon was the son of the college president. Two years later, president John Witherspoon would defend the students' inclination to speak on political subjects, declaring himself proud of "the spirit of liberty [which breaths] high and strong" among students and faculty.[20] He would himself serve as a member of the New Jersey Constitutional ratifying convention and hold other public offices, all the while carrying on his duties as the head of the faculty at what is now Princeton University.

Up to this point I've tried to show that rhetoric in the college curriculum evolved toward a full expression of the classical tradition, starting with a sharply truncated version of it in the 17th century. But there are two major respects in which the whole college curriculum in America was directly in line with the tradition of classical rhetoric from the very beginning.

In the first place, rhetoric was treated as the most important subject in the curriculum. Typically, it was taught throughout all four years, and in many cases lecturing on rhetoric was a stated responsibility of the college president. The original statutes at Harvard, for example, required the president to lecture on rhetoric each Friday morning. The first theory of rhetoric developed by an American was contained in the lectures on eloquence delivered by John Witherspoon during the time he was president of Princeton.[21] When Timothy Dwight became president of Yale, he continued to lecture on rhetoric and belles lettres, and one of his first official acts as president was to engage in a formal debate with the senior students; the topic was whether the Old and New Testaments are the Word of God.[22] Rhetoric was emphasized so heavily because it was understood as the art through which all other arts could become effective. The more specialized studies in philosophy and natural science and the classical languages and literatures would be brought to a focus by the art of rhetoric and made to shed light on problems in the world of social and political affairs. The purpose of education was to prepare men for positions of leadership in the community, as it had been for Cicero and Quintilian.

The second respect in which the American college curriculum was from the beginning rhetorical is that it made oral communication primary. The most common classroom procedure was oral disputation. A student would be appointed to defend a thesis taken from assigned reading material against counterarguments made by the instructor and other students. Originally the form of the disputation was strictly syllogistic, in line with late medieval practice. During the 18th century the forensic form, which demanded more fully elaborated discourse ranging beyond the limits of strictly logical appeal, became more and more common.[23] The evolution of the forensic disputation was an important aspect of the increasingly Ciceronian emphasis of the colleges during this period. While the older syllogistic disputation had been rhetorical in the prominence it gave to orality, it had been anti-rhetorical in the formal limits it had placed on discourse. In addition to these classroom exercises, students periodically gave declamations and orations publicly — that is, in forums open to the entire college and to people in the surrounding community.

Written examinations did not come into use until well into the 19th century. Instead, a three week period of "visitation" was held each June, during which students seeking a degree or promotion had to make themselves available for oral examination by "all Commers [sic]" in all the subjects for which they were responsible. The exams were essentially disputations similar in form to the classroom exercises: the student was expected to defend assigned theses against whatever counter-argument a visitor chose to make. A student could be held back for a year by the judgment of "any three of the visitors being overseers of the Colledge [sic]."[24] (The specific system described here, known as "sitting solstices," was prescribed at Harvard. I cannot say how closely examination systems at other colleges approximated the details of this one, but as late as 1842, Francis Wayland, President of Brown, speaks of oral examinations as standard in all American colleges. He advocates the adoption of written examinations, and the only example he can offer of a place where such a system is in use is Cambridge University in England.[25])

Students were expected to hand in written copies of their formal oral performances, and we can assume that their tutors paid some attention to the quality of this written work. The growth in the 18th century of a concern for the students' work in English seems to have included a growing focus on written as well as oral composition. But what the students composed were speeches, not term papers or essays. They wrote primarily as a means of preparing and documenting an oral performance. This can be a tricky issue, since the term "composition" has in our own time come to apply almost exclusively to written work. In elementary and high-school, we speak of students "doing a composition," and the term most commonly refers to the thing he or she hands in to the teacher, the sheet of paper with words inscribed on it. In more enlightened circles, "composition" is now understood as referring to a process rather than a sheet of paper, but it is still a process of producing written material. From this persepctive, then, a debate held in 1794 at Princeton might look like evidence that writing was in competition with orality for primacy in the curriculum; the question was, "Whether debating or composition be more improving."[26] I believe, however, that the real issue was not writing vs. speech, but formally composed oratory vs. the new form of extemporaneous debate, which had been introduced in the Phi Beta Kappa chapters at William and Mary in 1778, and Harvard in 1785. Orality was still the primary medium and the first concern of the curriculum.

The only primarily written exercise that I am aware of was the requirement at Harvard that candidates for the MA degree write a "Synopsis, or Compendium" of one of the arts. Samuel Eliot Morison believes that this was not so much a demonstration of the candidate's scholarly accomplishment as a convenient means by which the college acquired elementary texts for use by undergraduates.[27]

This is not to say that students didn't write much in the course of their studies. My guess is that they wrote considerably more than many undergraduates of today, but the nature of their writing tasks was rather different. Much of it was sheer copying for purposes that today are served by the Xerox machine and printing press. For example, a student's first

Rhetoric in the American College Curriculum 101

task upon being admitted to Harvard was to write out his own copy of the college laws, which he and the President would then sign as a kind of contract.[28] During the course of his studies, he would keep a series of "paper books" into which he would copy remarkable passages from his reading. He would write copious summaries and analyses of reading material—the cost of books would have made our modern ways of textual notation quite extravagant. He may have done less than the modern student does of what we would consider original composition, and the great bulk of that was intended for oral delivery.

What were the effects of all this emphasis on oral communication? First and perhaps most obviously, a certain readiness of mind and speech, and a zest for rhetorical encounters. Here is what one scholar has to say about the practice of disputation. (The quotation refers to disputation as a medieval practice, but in context it is a comment on 17th century English colleges, which were the original from which Harvard and Yale took the practice of syllogistic disputation.)

> The method became very successful under favorable circumstances, and was not the dry-as-dust, tedious, and stifling affair that pleaders for the perfections of the so-called Renaissance have pictured it. Public disputing, by the twelfth century (Aquinas and others), had become the highly developed art of quickly and logically defining one's thoughts as well as the thoughts of an opponent while face to face with him that taught a student to defend any topic or proposition against attack. The method brought into play all the excitement of a contest, the triumphant ecstasy of winning, or the disgrace of defeat, [here perhaps is the source of Jim McKay's famous opener for the ABC Wide World of Sports] that emphasized the value of what had been learned and the importance of an alert wit together with constant readiness to use it. The method was possible only within the limits of a closed system of knowledge as deduced from the same set of principles, thoroughly agreed upon as principles, and rarely scrutinized for their own sake.[29]

I think it's worth dwelling for a moment on the apparent absence among students of the 18th century of that much studied modern phenomenon called "communication anxiety."[30] We all suffer from it to some degree, and I recall seeing somewhere a report of a study allegedly demonstrating that the most common of all neurotic fears is the fear of speaking before an audience. A fair amount of energy in modern speech pedagogy seems to go into the simple task of getting students to the point where they can stand before a group of people and utter sentences. Yet American students of the eighteenth century so relished the opportunity to speak that every college had one or more literary and debate societies, all of them entirely student originated and governed, most of them highly active and successful. My own guess is that these students were no less subject to "communication anxiety" than students today, but that speaking mattered to them in a way it does not on most 20th century campuses. And this was simply a natural result of the overwhelming emphasis given to rhetoric in their curriculum.

The speaking emphasized was public in two senses. First, it dealt importantly with public problems. I've already quoted some of the more overtly political questions that were disputed at Harvard commencements during the 18th century. Similar issues were debated in classroom and public exercises at other colleges. The point was that learning in philosophy and literature and the other subjects was understood as bearing directly upon the nature of the commonwealth. A primary emphasis of the curriculum was, in the phrase of the Harvard college charter of 1650, "all good literature," writings worth preserving for their moral significance, the light they could shed on the life of the body politic.[31] Morison makes a point about his own alma mater that holds equally of the other colleges of the late 18th century: "it was the classics that made Harvard men of that day effective in politics and statesmanship. In Plutarch's lives, the orations of Cicero and Demosthenes, and ancient history, young men saw a mirror of their own times; in Plato's Dialogues and Aristotle's Politics they learned the wisdom to deal with men and events. The classical pseudonyms with which our Harvard signers of the great Declaration signed their early communications to the press were not mere pen-names chosen by chance, but represented a very definite point of view that every educated man recognized."[32] Simply stated, their point of view was that public life is the great topic of both learning and discourse. It informed the works of Cicero and Quintilian and John Ward, and thereby the lectures of John Witherspoon and Timothy Dwight and the other men who transmitted the rhetorical tradition to American students.

The second sense in which the speaking emphasized in 18th century colleges was public had to do with audience. As a student advanced through the four years of the curriculum, more and more of his speaking was done in forums open to anyone who chose to attend. On regular ceremonial occasions, the more advanced students were required to speak and dispute before audiences that included at least some dignitaries of the local community. (I say they were "required" to do this, but I have seen no evidence that the students regarded the duty as onerous.) The ordeal of "sitting solstices," remember, was open to "all Commers," and the students' performance was judged not by the tutors with whom they lived and studied, but by those of the visitors "being overseers of the Colledge"—a position equivalent to trustee in a modern college. On commencement day, every student who was to receive a degree would deliver at least one oration or dispute a question — by the latter half of the 18th century, the old style syllogistic disputations were commonly assigned to the duller students, while the forensic disputations and orations were given to the bright ones.[33] Every student had to be prepared to speak in a fully public forum. The common ground upon which he stood with his audience was simply membership in the commonwealth.

At the end of the 18th century, then, rhetoric at American colleges was the classical art of oral public discourse. It stood very near if not precisely at the center of pedagogical concern. It provided students with an art, and more importantly with copious experience and with a tacit set of values bearing directly on the use of language in managing public affairs.

Within a century the picture had changed drastically. While the classical idea of rhetoric had not disappeared altogether, it had gone into a severe eclipse from which it has not yet emerged, if indeed it ever will. The most obvious changes were the move to a primary focus on written rather than oral communication, the demotion of rhetoric to a minor place in the curriculum, and the detachment of classical learning from the general concerns of rhetoric. Insofar as the rhetoric then emerging as dominant had a theory, it was the theory that Young and others characterize as current-traditional rhetoric — i.e., emphasis on the written product rather than the process of composition or of communication; classification of discourse into the four so-called modes (description, narration, exposition, argumentation); concentration on correctness of usage and certain stylistic qualities, without much reference to the invention of substance for discourse.[34]

How can we explain this radical departure from the tradition of classical rhetoric? The only serious attempt I am aware of points to the emergence at the beginning of the 19th century of certain vitalistic assumptions about the human mind and the creative act, assumptions commonly associated with romanticism.[35] In my own view this explanation is at best only partly satisfactory. It may account for the emphasis of current-traditional rhetoric on products rather than processes and the consequent absence of any treatment of invention. But I don't think it explains the new theory's tendency toward downright obsession with correctness of usage and purity of style, or the demotion of rhetoric to its new, low estate. Further, this explanation treats rhetoric more-or-less in isolation; a full explanation must portray it in the larger contexts of curriculum and culture. While I don't pretend to offer a full explanation of the rise of current-traditional rhetoric in this essay, I want to sketch three points that will have to figure prominently in such an account. The first is a development within the tradition of rhetorical studies itself;

the other two have to do with the context within which rhetoric was studied.

First is the emergence of the concept of belles lettres. The term "belles lettres" was adopted into the English language during the first third of the 18th century by way of three French men of letters whose works were translated into English and achieved some currency. They are Rene Rapin, Dominique Bonheurs, and Charles Rollin.[36] All three authors used the term belles lettres to name a broad category subsuming at a minimum history, poetry, and rhetoric (meaning the theory and practice of persuasive oral discourse). Rapin included philosophy as well, and Rollin included the study of languages as well as the other four parts. The English version of Rollin's works added physics to the list, perhaps because physical science was still understood as having a loose connection with philosophy. Thus, by 1740, "belles lettres" had come into English as a generalized term for learning in philosophy, history, languages, poetry, rhetoric, and—perhaps—natural science. Common synonyms were "fine learning" and "polite literature."[37] But as it very shortly came to be used in English, belles lettres was somewhat less generalized and more vague than the original French term had been. Both Adam Smith and Hugh Blair gave lectures on rhetoric *and* belles lettres; the two terms were made coordinate, whereas in French belles lettres had subsumed rhetoric. Neither Smith nor Blair drew any clear distinction between the two notions, but in Blair's *Lectures,* which were to become the most widely used rhetoric text in America during the early 19th century, the addition of belles lettres to rhetoric seemed to consist in a new concern with poetry and the aesthetic experience as well as with oratory and persuasion.[38] In America the term likewise made coordinate with terms it had originally subsumed. Timothy Dwight was appointed at Yale to teach "rhetoric, history, and the belles lettres." The 1766 Harvard tutorial plan uses the term in what looks like its original sense—"Composition in English, Rhetoric, and other Belles Lettres"—but by 1819 George Ticknor is named professor of "French and Spanish Languages and Belles lettres." This chair would one day pass to Bliss Perry, under whom it would become a professorship of English literature.[39]

The emergence of this notion of belles lettres as something connected in an at best vaguely specified way with rhetoric had two crucial effects: first, it destabilized the boundaries of rhetoric—or, perhaps better, it distracted the gaze of rhetoricians from their central concern with public discourse; second, it encouraged a new interest in the purely aesthetic qualities of discourse. The old notion of "good literature," upon which the Harvard curriculum had been founded, valued texts for their moral and political significance. Samuel Eliot Morison claims that the term "good literature" as used in the Harvard charter of 1650 is simply a literal translation of the Ciceronian concept of "bonae litterae."[40] I have not been able to find where in the works of Cicero or any other Roman author a concept of "bonae litterae" is developed at length, but the idea squares perfectly with the thinking of Quintilian, Cicero's most ardent and theoretically significant admirer. In the tenth book of the *Institutio Oratoria* he develops a literary canon, and the criteria for selection make it more a canon of bonae litterae than of belles lettres. It was their contribution to social morality that made poetic and oratorical and philosophical texts worth preserving. The 18th century notion of belles lettres called attention to the purely aesthetic qualities of texts, thus laying the groundwork for development of the modern notion of literary studies, in which the primary qualification for inclusion in the canon is a work's aesthetic merit.[41]

There was perhaps a precedent for belles lettres in the 17th century curriculum of Cambridge University, the model from which Harvard drew its original plan of studies. This was the so-called "studia leviora," light pursuits deemed suitable for men who came to college not to be serious scholars, but rather to "gett such learning as may serve for delight and ornament and such as the want wherof would speake a defect in breeding rather then Scholarship."[42] Under this heading we find some English poetry, English translations of classical works, and more recent works in Latin that students might read strictly for pleasure. Harvard made no formal allowance for the pursuit of studia leviora, and in fact tried to enforce a more strict scholarly standard than Cambridge on the use of Latin among students and faculty. The growth of the literary and debate societies during the 18th century was motivated partly by the students' own desire to read and discuss critically works that would have been included in the studia leviora. Thus, "polite literature" was tolerated as a minor pursuit at English universities of the 17th century, and flourished as what we would call an extracurricular activity at American colleges of the 18th century. During the 19th century it achieved full status in the curriculum, eventually displacing rhetoric as the primary concern of what became the Department of English.

The second point to be taken into account in tracing the development of current-traditional rhetoric is specialization of the curriculum during the 19th century. The original system of instruction at Harvard and the other early Colleges was tutorial—a single tutor would take responsibility for an entering class, which throughout the 17th and into the 18th century might number no more than ten or a dozen boys.[43] Under the close supervision of the president, the tutor was responsible for directing the entire course of studies, and for overseeing the students' moral and spiritual development, during the next four years. Under such a system the boundaries between subjects in the curriculum wouldn't count for very much, since every teacher dealt with the whole curriculum. He told the students what books to read and at what time, how to read them, what sorts of notes to take and analyses to write.

During the second half of the 18th century, professorships associated with particular subjects began to be established, and by the 1840s the typical college faculty consisted of a few professors, each one responsible for a certain "department" of the curriculum, each one assisted by a few tutors.[44] In part, this institutionalizing of boundaries between subjects was simply a bow to the necessity created by expanding enrollments; more students needed more teachers, and a larger faculty called for some division of labor. But the process was fed by the influence of the German universities where American teachers were going to study, then returning and bringing with them new ideals of specialized scholarship and learning for its own sake rather than for the public use to which the rhetorical tradition would direct it. The inclination toward specialization became an avalanche with the institution of the elective system during the last half of the 19th century. By the turn of the 20th century, virtually every major college in America had given up the fully prescribed curriculum, and undergraduate students were being encouraged to emulate their professors by specializing in some particular discipline. More importantly, the students' readiness for advancement or for a degree was no longer judged by the broad and public standard of "sitting solstices." Instead, professors in specialized disciplines gave marks for narrowly circumscribed things called "courses." A student read Horace or Dante or Shakespeare for a fixed period of time, and then demonstrated his mastery of that body of reading to an expert in the field. The task of relating specialized knowledge to more general and public concerns dropped out of sight.

While many of the early professorships established at American colleges were in rhetoric, the rhetorical tradition was a natural casualty of the specializing tendency.[45] As Aristotle pointed out centuries ago, rhetoric is by its very nature an inexact and unspecialized faculty (Rhetoric I, 4). The rhetorical tradition was not so much a body of specialized knowledge as a way of trying together and focussing the specialized knowledge provided by other fields of study. To the degree that specialized knowledge pursued for its own sake became an ideal in American colleges, rhetoric would necessarily fall from the elevated position it had once held.

The third point I want to focus on is a subtle but profound shift in the way colleges perceived their social function. Harvard was founded because the Puritans "dread[ed] to leave an illiterate ministry to the churches when our present ministers shall lie in the dust."[46] Their eyes were fixed on the needs of the community. Students were to be educated for positions of leadership not so much for their own personal advantage, but because the community had need of them. During the 19th century, this emphasis shifted. A college education came to be understood as a means by which students could pursue their own advancement in society.[47] This was particularly true of the newer institutions specializing in science and engineering; applied scientific knowledge was frequently connected with the interests of farmers and merchants and mechanics.[48] But even in the older institutions that remained committed to the notion of classical or liberal education, the value of that education tended to shift. As early as 1819, Edward Tyrrell Channing gave expression to this shift in his inaugural lecture as the third Boylston Professor of Rhetoric at Harvard: "We look back to the best ages of those commonwealths, when society, letters, and all the liberal arts were advanced the farthest, and we find eloquence the favorite and necessary accomplishment of all who were ambitious of rising in the world."[49] His eyes were fixed upon the individual. Rather than providing leaders for the community, education was becoming an opportunity provided by the community for the individual.

A consequence of this shift was an increased emphasis on evaluation of the student's achievements. So long as the college served to provide leaders for the community, the issue of rigorous evaluation was not terribly crucial. If a man who was not particularly well qualified somehow got admitted to the baccalaureate degree, no real harm or injustice had been done, since the community—the church or the body politic—had its own means of judging the quality of men. But when higher education came to be understood as an opportunity for individual advancement, the degree became something more like a certificate of qualification, and the institution had to concern itself with "quality control." Together with the steady growth in numbers of students, the new emphasis on rigorous evaluation produced the shift to writing as the primary medium in which students exercised their mastery of subject matter. A paper took up far less classroom time than a disputation or an oration, and it could be subjected to the most meticulous scrutiny.[50]

My claim, then, is that the shift from the 18th century revival of Ciceronian rhetoric to current-traditional rhetoric was shaped by three factors in addition to the rise of romantic vitalism: 1. the evolution of the concept of belles lettres as a concern of rhetorical theory and pedagogy; 2. the steady specialization of knowledge and the curriculum; 3. a shift in the social function of colleges toward emphasis on providing opportunities for individual advancement. There are no doubt other aspects of this change, and they deserve serious attention because the demise of the rhetorical tradition was a significant event in our educational and cultural history.

I hope I'm not just being nostalgic in believing that, while many of the changes that took place in American colleges during the 19th century were laudable, something of real value was lost in the eclipse of the rhetorical tradition by current-traditional rhetoric. Part of it is being regained and even improved upon by the developments that are finally robbing the current-traditional paradigm of its currency. I'm thinking primarily of research into the composing process, which has recovered the ancient idea of rhetoric as an art, an imprecise but still enormously helpful methodizing of a task we must otherwise accomplish by trial and error.

But there is one aspect of the rhetorical tradition that so far as I can tell remains quite dead—its focus on public discourse. I suggested toward the beginning of this paper that a rhetoric is defined not just by its theory, but by the sorts of rhetorical problems it gives most emphasis to. The rhetorical tradition gave primary emphasis to public discourse, and subordinated the many other sorts of rhetorical problems people must deal with to the public arena; it was in essence a rhetoric of citizenship. In its mature form, current-traditional rhetoric gave primary emphasis to expository essays of the sort students would have to write in their other courses; at its worst, it was a series of unhelpful lessons in how to get through college. The new rhetoric that has been developing over the past two decades or so retains some of this emphasis on the discourse of academic disciplines, and it has added a concern for rhetorical problems of self-understanding and personal relationships, and of business, commerce, and industry. It addresses students under three aspects of their identity: personal, intellectual-academic, and professional. It does not address students as political beings, as members of a body politic in which they have a responsibility to form judgments and influence the judgments of others on public issues. In the college as in the pre-college curriculum, English remains separate from social studies, the arts of discourse from the arts of citizenship.

In fall of 1981, when the U.S. Senate was considering President Reagan's proposal to sell the Awacs air defense system to Saudi Arabia, James Reston of the New York Times wrote half wistfully, half cynically of "The Forgotten Debate." What we had a right to expect of the President and Congress, in Reston's view, was a serious debate on the issues of Middle East foreign and defense policy, a debate that would convince us that "these devilish questions are being decided in the national interest by serious people in a serious way . . . and not fiddled by backdoor deals and personal tradeoffs."[51] Such a debate might even have enabled some ordinary citizens to form their own intelligent views on these matters, though this was more than Reston would hope for.

There was a time when politicians engaged in serious debate on such matters, debate that helped to shape reasonable and sound opinion on matters of public policy. When Daniel Webster debated the nature of the Constitution with Hayne and later with Calhoun, his arguments and those of his opponents were printed and the copies read and discussed in general stores and barber shops around the country. Webster had learned the art of rhetoric at Dartmouth. I believe that the vitality of the classical rhetorical tradition in the colleges of the 18th and early 19th centuries helped to maintain a standard of public discourse far superior to what we have in politics today. I think further that as rhetorical studies begin to regain some of their antique vitality and prominence, we might well turn some of our attention to the discourse of public life.

NOTES

Earlier versions of this paper were read at Carnegie-Mellon University and Mercyhurst College. Among the many people who offered helpful comments, I would like especially to thank Profs. Richard Leo Enos and David Kaufer of Carnegie-Mellon, and Prof. George Garrelts of Mercyhurst.

1. Richard E. Young, "Paradigms and Problems: Needed Research in Rhetorical Invention," in Charles R. Cooper and Lee Odell, *Research on Composing: Points of Departure* (Urbana, Ill.: NCTE, 1978), pp. 29-47.

2. I have extrapolated this definition from the discussion of classical and contemporary rhetoric in Richard E. Young, Alton L. Becker, and Kenneth L. Pike, *Rhetoric: Discovery and Change* (New York: Harcourt, 1970), pp. 1-9. I believe it is sufficiently general to avoid commitment to any particular system of rhetoric, yet sufficiently precise to avoid making the term mean everything, and thus nothing.

3. For a compact historical survey, see Edward P. J. Corbett, "Survey of Rhetoric," in *Classical Rhetoric for the Modern Student* (New York: Oxford Univ. Press, 1965), pp. 535-68; for a more complete yet still compact overview, see George A. Kennedy, *Classical Rhetoric and its Christian and Secular Tradition from Ancient to Modern Times* (Chapel Hill: Univ. of North Carolina Press, 1980).

4. See S. M. Halloran, "On the End of Rhetoric, Classical and Modern," *College English,* 36 (Feb. 1975), 621-31, and "Tradition and Theory in Rhetoric," *Quarterly Journal of Speech,* 62 (Oct. 1976), 234-41.

5. Warren Guthrie, "The Development of Rhetorical Theory in America I," *Speech Monographs,* 13 (1946), 14-22.

6. Samuel Eliot Morison, *The Intellectual of Colonial New England* (New York: New York Univ. Press, 1956).

7. This definition appears in William Dugard, *Rhetorices Elementa,* a standard text at Harvard throughout the 17th and into the 18th century. This same definition appears in lists of commencement theses at both Harvard and Yale. See Guthrie, op. cit.; Guthrie, "Rhetorical Theory in Colonial America," in Karl R. Wallace, ed., *History of Speech Education in America: Background*

Studies (New York: Appleton, 1954), pp. 48-59; Porter Gale Perrin, *The Teaching of Rhetoric in the American Colleges before 1750,* (Diss., Univ. of Chicago, 1936).

8. Guthrie, "The Development of Rhetorical Theory in America I," pp. 16-18. See also Perry Miller, *The New England Mind: the Seventeenth Century* (Boston: Beacon, 1939; rpt. 1961), pp. 300-62.

9. Samuel Eliot Morison, *Harvard College in the Seventeenth Century* (Cambridge: Harvard, 1936), p. 85.

10. Guthrie, "The Development of Rhetorical Theory in America I," p. 21.

11. See Quintilian, *On the Early Education of the Citizen-Orator* (*Institutio Oratoria* Book I, and Book II, chs. 1-10) trans. John Selby Watson, ed. James J. Murphy (Indianapolis: The Bobbs-Merrill, 1965). Morison notes that the *Institutio Oratoria* was unavailable at Harvard during the 17th century (*Harvard College in the Seventeenth Century,* p. 172).

12. The idea nonetheless flourished well into the 20th century. Bliss Perry, Harvard's first formally designated professor of English literature wrote in 1935 that the best way to form students in English composition is to require them to learn Latin and Greek and to drill them in translation. *And Gladly Teach: Reminiscences* (Boston: Houghton Mifflin, 1935), pp. 254-55.

13. Guthrie, "The Development of Rhetorical Theory in America, 1635-1850 II," *Speech Monographs,* 14 (1947), 38-54; Guthrie, "Rhetorical Theory in Colonial America," p. 54.

14. Perrin, p. 53.

15. Guthrie, "The Development of Rhetorical Theory in America, 1635-1850 I," p. 19.

16. Guthrie, "The Development of Rhetorical Theory in America, 1635-1850 II," p. 38.

17. For an analysis of Ward's work and its influence, see Douglas Ehninger, "John Ward and His Rhetoric," *Speech Monographs,* 18 (151), 1-16.

18. David Potter, "The Literary Society," in Wallace, ed., *History of Speech Education in America: Background Studies,* pp. 238-58.

19. Samuel Eliot Morison, *Three Centuries of Harvard 1636-1936* [Cambridge: Harvard Univ. Press 1936), pp. 90-91.

20. Ralph Ketcham, *James Madison: A Biography* (New York: Macmillan, 1971), pp. 37-38.

21. John Witherspoon, *Lectures on Moral Philosophy and Eloquence* (Philadelphia: Woodward, 1810). Guthrie identifies Witherspoon's Lectures as the "first complete American rhetoric" in his "Rhetorical Theory in Colonial America." See also: Wilson B. Paul, "John Witherspoon's Theory and Practice of Public Speaking," *Speech Monographs,* 16 (1949), 272-89; Wilbur Samuel Howell, *Eighteenth-Century British Logic and Rhetoric* (Princeton: Princeton Univ. Press, 1971), pp. 671-91.

22. Barbara Miller Solomon, Introduction to Timothy Dwight, *Travels in New England and New York,* ed. Barbara Miller Solomon (Cambridge: Harvard Univ. Press, 1969), xvii-xviii.

23. George V. Bohman, "Rhetorical Practice in Colonial America," in

Wallace, ed., *History of Speech Education in America: Background Studies,* pp. 60-79.

24. Morison, *Harvard College in the Seventeenth Century,* pp. 67-68.

25. Francis Wayland, *Thoughts on the Present Collegiate System in the United States* (New York: Arno Press and The New York Times, 1842; rpt. 1969), pp. 93-99.

26. Potter, "The Literary Society," in Wallace, ed., *History of Speech Education in America: Background Readings,* p. 250.

27. Morison, *Harvard College in the Seventeenth Century,* p. 148-50.

28. Morison, p. 81.

29. Harris Francis Fletcher, *The Intellectual Development of John Milton* II (Urbana: Univ. of Illinois Press, 1961), pp. 231-32.

30. For a recent example of the research, see Malcolm R. Parks, "A Test of the Cross-Situational Consistency of Communication Apprehension," *Communication Monographs,* 47 (Aug. 1980), 220-32.

31. Morison, *Harvard College in the Seventeenth Century,* p. 5.

32. Morison, *Three Centuries of Harvard 1636-1936,* p. 136.

33. Bohman, "Rhetorical Practice in Colonial America," pp. 70-71.

34. Young, "Paradigms and Problems: Needed Research in Rhetorical Invention," pp. 30-33.

35. Hal Rivers Weidner, *Three Models of Rhetoric: Traditional, Mechanical and Vital,* (Diss., Univ. of Michigan, 1975).

36. The English language versions of their works are: Rene Rapin, *The Whole Critical Works of Monsieur Rapin, in Two Volumes . . . Newly Translated into English by Several Hands* (London, 1706); Dominique Bonheurs, *The Art of Criticism: or, The Method Of Making a Right Judgment Upon Subjects of Wit and Learning* (London, 1705); Charles Rollin, *The Method of Teaching and Studying the Belles Lettres, or An Introduction to Languages, Poetry, Rhetoric, History, Moral Philosophy, Physicks, &c.* (London, 1734). The significance of these works for the history of rhetoric in English is discussed in Howell, *Eighteenth-Century British Logic and Rhetoric,* pp. 519-35.

37. See, for example, Alexander Jamieson, *Grammar of Rhetoric and Polite Literature,* which was used as a text at Amherst, Bowdoin, Wesleyan and Yale during the early part of the 19th century. Samuel Eliot Morison uses the term "polite literature" as a synonym for bonae litterae and associates the notion with the interests of well-to-do young men who came to college not for serious scholarly pursuits but to acquire the outward marks of gentility. (*The Founding of Harvard College,* [Cambridge: Harvard Univ. Press, 1936], p. 56; *The Intellectual Life of Colonial New England,* p. 32.) In my own view, conflating "good literature" and "polite literature" misses a subtle but important distinction.

38. Note, for example, the emphasis given to the development of taste in Hugh Blair, *Lectures on Rhetoric and Belles Lettres,* ed. David Potter (Carbondale: Southern Illinois Univ. Press, 1783; rpt. 1965). This emphasis is even more pronounced in some of the later rhetorics that were influenced by Blair. Samuel P. Newman, *A Practical System of Rhetoric* (Portland: Shirleyand Hyde,

1827) devotes two of its five chapters to the notion of taste; Newman's *System* is probably the first rhetoric of written composition, and perhaps also the first textbook in the modern sense of that curiously redundant term, written by an American.

39. Perry's intellectual memoire, *And Gladly Teach,* offers a case study in the displacement of the rhetorical tradition by modern literary studies. He started his career as teacher of rhetoric and oratory at Williams College during the 1880s, then moved to Princeton where he taught courses in both literature and rhetoric and eventually was appointed Holmes Professor of English Literature and Belles Lettres. Of this chair, he writes that it "freed me, after many years, from the claims of Oratory" (p. 160), though as a younger man he seems to have felt a real affection for the study of rhetoric and oratory. After a time as editor of *The Atlantic Monthly,* he joined the faculty at Harvard, becoming in 1906 its first formally designated Professor of English Literature.

40. Morison, *The Founding of Harvard College,* p. 248.

41. My account of the relationship between rhetoric and belles lettres conflicts with the view developed in Howell, pp. 441 ff. Howell portrays the matter in fairly neat, categorical terms: classical rhetoric "limit[ed] itself to persuasive popular discourse as exemplified by political, forensic and ceremonial speeches;" the new rhetoric of the late eighteenth century "expand[ed] its interests to include learned and didactic discourses and perhaps even the forms of poetry." I believe that this view misrepresents both classical and "new" rhetoric. With the exception of Aristotle, classical rhetoricians were not much inclined to limit the compass of rhetoric, though they did tend to subordinate other forms of discourse to "persuasive popular discourse." In the long term the issue raised by eighteenth century rhetoricians was not simply whether rhetoric should expand its purview, but what kind(s) of discourse should dominate its field of interest. The relevant question about a rhetorical tradition is not whether it does or does not profess to account for a given form of discourse, but what importance it attaches to that form relative to others.

42. Richard Holdsworth, "Directions for a Student in the Universitie," in Fletcher, *The Intellectual Development of John Milton* II, 623-64. The significance of Holdsworth's "Directions" for understanding the original Harvard plan of study is discussed in Morison, *The Founding of Harvard College,* pp. 62-74.

43. Morison, *Harvard College in the Seventeenth Century,* pp. 50-53; *Three Centuries of Harvard 1636-1936,* p. 90.

44. Wayland, *Thoughts on the Present Collegiate System in the United States,* pp. 25-26.

45. The transformation of one of the early professorships is told in Ronald F. Reid, "The Boylston Professorship of Rhetoric and Oratory, 1806: 1904: A Case Study of Changing Concepts of Rhetoric and Pedagogy," *Quarterly Journal of Speech,* 45 (Oct. 1959), 239-57.

46. Morison, "New England's First Fruits," *The Founding of Harvard College,* p. 432.

47. This view is apparent throughout Wayland's *Thoughts on the Present Collegiate System in the United States.*

48. Stephen Van Rensselaer announced the founding of one of the earliest American schools of engineering thus: "I have established a school . . . for the purpose of instructing persons, who may choose to apply themselves, in the application of science to the common purposes of life. My principal object is, to qualify teachers for instructing the sons and daughters of farmers and mechanics . . . in the application of experimental chemistry, philosophy and natural history, to agriculture, domestic economy, the arts and manufactures." Samuel Rezneck, *Education for a Technological Society: A Sesquicentennial History of Rensselaer Polytechnic Institute* (Troy, N.Y.: Rensselaer Polytechnic Institute, 1968), p. 3. The specific reference to daughters as well as sons is worth noting. At that time (1824), the liberal arts colleges were exclusively and emphatically male.

49. Edward T. Channing, *Lectures Read to the Seniors in Harvard College,* ed. Dorothy I. Anderson and Waldo W. Braden (Carbondale: Southern Illinois Univ. Press, 1856; rpt. 1968), p. 2.

50. This is the rationale of Wayland's brief for written examinations in *Thoughts on the Present Collegiate System in the United States.*

51. James Reston, "The Forgotten Debate," *New York Times,* Oct. 18, 1981, sect. 4, p. 21.

Afterthoughts on Rhetoric and Public Discourse

Last night the City Council of Troy, New York, was visited by a group of angry and frustrated residents of the section known as "South Troy." They were trying to prevent construction of an asphalt plant in their neighborhood. South Troy is a working-class area situated on the flood plain of the Hudson River; parts of it could be a set for filming Joyce's *Dubliners.* When I was very young it often stank of methane and sulfur from the giant ovens where coal was baked into coke for steel production and home heating. My father, who had kept his job at the coke plant throughout the Great Depression, used to call that odor: "the smell of prosperity." No rhetoricians from Rensselaer Polytechnic Institute, a school located "on the hill" in Troy, participated in or observed last night's confrontation. None of us lives in South Troy proper, though a few live in more elegant row houses that were built far enough north to be beyond the stink.

I offer this incident as a synecdoche of both something I had in mind and something I failed to recognize when I wrote "Rhetoric in the American College Curriculum." Prior to its nineteenth-century transformation into freshman composition, the academic study of rhetoric in America focussed heavily on participation in civic affairs. The efforts of citizens like the residents of South Troy to shape the fate of their community would surely have been of interest to American neoclassical rhetoricians of the late eighteenth and early nineteenth centuries. I was concerned in 1982 about the apparent lack of interest in such "public discourse" among the new rhetoricians of late twentieth-century English departments.

But I failed then to acknowledge the relevance of social and economic class to the study and practice of public discourse. The geographical situation of South Troy and Rensselaer Polytechnic Institute, the one quite literally looking down on the other, is symbolic of a gulf that has long separated academic rhetorical studies from the strivings of working-class people. American neoclassical rhetoric was among other things an instrument of patrician domination in the Federal period, and the economic interest of the academic rhetoricians of that time would have motivated them to align with those trying to build the asphalt plant, against those whose neighborhood will be degraded by it. The forms and conventions of this rhetoric are in fact copiously illustrated in speeches by men who defended slavery in the South and an industrial system in the North that was almost as exploitative. Those forms and conventions are much less often illustrated in works by women, blacks, and working-class people, since such people were denied access to the public forum. When I used the Senate debate on selling weapons systems to Saudi Arabia as an example in concluding my 1982 essay, I was evading this issue of class (and the related issues of gender and race), since foreign affairs is a domain sufficiently remote from the day-to-day economic realities of most people's lives to mask many conflicting interests. I could maintain the illusion that we are all just citizens, motivated by a common interest in peace and prosperity.

Rensselaer Polytechnic Institute was not always on the hill, literally or figuratively. It was founded as the Rensselaer School in 1824 for the avowed purpose of training itinerant teachers who would lecture to "the sons and daughters of farmers and mechanics," enabling them to apply scientific knowledge in their own pursuits. The first director, Amos Eaton, envisioned his school at the center of a lecture circuit, similar to what flourished for a while as the lyceum movement, through which scientific learning would be spread for the purpose of elevating the competency of ordinary people. His vision of a kind of populist science never got very far, and Rensselaer instead became a place for training professional engineers. The knowledge of applied science, which Eaton had wanted to disseminate as common property for the benefit of all, became instead a marketable commodity possessed by specialists whose knowledge set them apart from ordinary people. His school had started in a building situated on the flood plain, where working people lived, and it had an educational philosophy to match. Before long it moved up the hill, both literally and figuratively.

The change was part of a broader transformation of American society from a traditional hierarchy based on property and hereditary privilege, to one in which merit and achievement figured more strongly, while the boundaries were drawn ever more sharply. The egalitarian visions of Amos Eaton and others became part of a middle-class ethos that celebrated social mobility, but at the same time hid the reality of increasing stratification by wealth and class. In school rhetoric, the new emphasis on correctness served a parallel and likewise paradoxical function. By codifying explicitly the dialect of the privileged class, textbooks by A. S. Hill and others gave outsiders a means of learning it and gaining access. But by portraying that dialect in hyper-correct terms, they accentuated its distinctness from the speech of ordinary people and thus reinforced the linguistic barriers to mobility. The line between the stink of South Troy and the clean air on the hill was thus inscribed in the rhetoric texts used by American college students, including those at the growing number of non-traditional schools (such as Rensselaer Polytechnic Institute) that were relatively effective as vehicles of upward mobility.

Today the smell of the coke ovens is a dim memory in South Troy, and the houses are festooned with yellow ribbons. Big industry has long since fled south, west, and overseas, and young men and women are fighting in the Persian Gulf. We do after all share a common interest in peace and prosperity, even as we are divided by these and many equally "common" interests. Had I thought about South Troy and all it represents while writing "Rhetoric in the American College Curriculum," I might have taken a more complex and ambivalent view of the tradition of neoclassical rhetoric. I would have placed its history more firmly in the context of the nineteenth-century transformations of American society, economy, and culture, and I would have recognized its complicity in the exploitation of people. But I would nonetheless have insisted on its largely unrealized potential as an instrument of participation in the discourse that continues to shape American society.

5 : THE RHETOR AS *Eiron:* Plato's Defense of Dialogue

C. Jan Swearingen
University of Arizona

Plato's critique of sophistic rhetoric is a recurrent theme in the dialogues, and a primary subject in two, the *Phaedrus* and the *Gorgias*.[1] In his critique, Plato recurrently links the flaws in sophistic rhetoric with writing and literacy, which were rapidly gaining popularity in his time, and with intentional dissembling, which was being advocated by the sophists as a constituent of suasive oratory.[2] In one of the later dialogues, the *Sophist*, Plato extends the critique of sophistic rhetoric to include the sophistic philosopher, and concludes the dialogue with the observation that there are two kinds of sophists, each a dissembling imitator (*eironikon mimeten*) of truth:

> One who can dissemble in long speeches in public before a multitude, and the other who does it in private in short speeches and forces the person who converses with him to contradict himself.[3]

The first type of sophist is the more familiar target of Plato's critique: the sophistic rhetor who cleverly twists his words and dissembles knowledge he does not possess in order to sway public opinion. The second type of sophist bears a suspicious resemblance to Socrates, whose short speeches and questions in private dialogue often force an interlocutor to contradict himself.

Plato's persistent association of the flaws in sophistic rhetoric with writing, textuality, and intentional dissembling, along with his extension of the critique of rhetoric to include the philosopher, can be approached as a consistent and precocious analysis of linguistic models and assumptions which were being disseminated by the sophists. Rhetoric *per se,* which is often regarded as the primary target of Plato's critique, was, I will argue, only part of a larger whole. My discussion of Plato's defense of dialogue as an antidote to sophistic rhetoric will propose that

Plato's critique of sophistic rhetoric comprises interdependent analyses of literacy, rhetoric, and irony as dangerous concomitants of the formulaic language models which the sophists employed in their teaching: formal rules of grammar and style; tabular summaries of argumentative, expository, and narrative structures; and lists of the effects of specific styles and arrangements on specific kinds of audiences.

The objectives of my discussion are several. First, I want to suggest that Plato's critique of sophistic rhetoric remains a viable critique of rhetoric, and that it was in no way superceded by Aristotle's carefully elaborate partitioning of rhetoric, poetics, logic, and ethics — "subjects" which were integrated in the sophistic teachings that Plato denounces. Aristotle's work was designed to dispel the abuses which Plato attacks, but, I will suggest, it had the effect of institutionalizing the linguistic, aesthetic, and ethical instrumentalism which, Plato argued, generated the abuses in the first place.[4] An instrumentalist view of language and linguistic interactions is one which posits that language is used to do something, to effect a change in thinking or in other human beings. Primacy is given to the efficaciousness of a given utterance, over and above its ultimate truth or meaning. The sophistic emphasis on *techne*, a craft or technique, was one of the sources of their instrumentalist conception of language, and the one which Plato singles out more than any other for scrutiny. Thus, Aristotle's place of technique at the center of both the rhetorical and logical treatises, far from reversing the abuses Plato worried most about, had the effect of systematizing them. Among the assumptions which Aristotle borrowed from the sophists and institutionalized are three which Plato places at the center of his analysis:

1. that a diversity of intentionally formulaic discourse structures are an improvement over the traditional, less self-conscious, formulas which structured Attic epic-oral discourse;

2. that writing records, represents, and communicates thought efficiently, and that it is an ideal medium for instruction because of its mnemonic power and its capacity to "fix" thought and language, thereby making them more accessible objects of scrutiny; and

3. that intentional dissembling, understood as both a rhetorical technique and as a literary style, is an inevitable, even welcome, concomitant of linguistic sophistication.

Aristotle's role as a perpetuator of these assumptions is noteworthy primarily because he and his interpreters have often regarded his work as a successful improvement over the sophistic teachings which Plato objected to. I will note the points at which sophistic teachings parallel time-honored elements in Aristotle's work only in passing, and primarily to mark the channels through which sophistic assumptions have been transmitted to subsequent linguistic and literary theories.

A second purpose of my discussion will be to establish that there are many important parallels among Plato's critiques of rhetoric, writing, literacy, and dissembling which are more than incidental. The structure of the dialogues is both the source and an example of the "confusing" and seemingly incidental parallels which Plato draws. As I draw together the threads of his interdependent analyses of rhetoric, writing, literacy, and dissembling, I will be violating both the form and the substance of the only kind of written discourse Plato produced. I am not writing a dialogue, and I am arranging my discussion in a linear, hierarchical fashion which, in Plato's recurrent phrase, "gives the appearance of truth." No one, he remarks in *Letter VII,* will commit his (or her) most serious thoughts to writing because once written they will circulate uncontrollably among those who do and those who do not understand the subject and the terms being used.[5] The form of the dialogues, as I will demonstrate, replicates the interlocution of *viva-voce* dialogue with two kinds of circumlocution: the literal give and take of a multi-speaker discourse, and the developmental structure of dialectical question and answer, both of which are indigenous to conversation but discouraged by the conventions of linear, written and spoken, monologue discourse. While Plato has rightly been chastized for writing while opposing writing, it is essential to note that the form and content of his dialogues forces the reader to do what I will be doing — to become an interlocutor in an extremely long-winded, frustratingly wandering discussion of many topics at once, out of which slowly emerges an improved but never final understanding of several topics. Since one of my objectives is to show the consistency and coherence of Plato's critique of sophistic rhetoric, I will be assembling the pieces of that critique in what I hope will be an organized and coherent fashion. As I assemble these pieces, however, I will also be demonstrating how and why Plato objected to linear, hierarchical, monologue discourse both in writing and in speaking.

The third objective of this discussion will be to define parallels among Plato's interdependent analyses of rhetoric, writing, and dissembling and contemporary critical debates which are anticipated quite strikingly in Plato's critique. The work of Eric Havelock and Walter Ong has revived an interest in the relationship between literacy and orality, or literate cultures and oral cultures. The work of the Russian linguist A. R. Luria, sociologist Erving Goffman, and sociolinguist John Gumperz hs extended the interest in literacy and orality, provoking numerous questions about the influence of literacy on thought structure, concept formation, and discourse patterns in literate versus oral cultures and, within literate cultures, on spoken discourse. Plato's promotion of the dialogue form as an antidote to the various "sophistries" indigenous to monologue rhetoric and textuality anticipate many of these questions, albeit in a highly polemical fashion, and are particularly valuable, because they were produced by a participant-observer in a culture which was just on the brink of literacy.

Recent debates in interpretation theory have revived a question which is articulated throughout the dialogues. Plato refuses to separate intention from meaning, a refusal which is central to his rejection of rhetorical monologue, rhetorical dissembling, and textuality. For Plato, the intention of the speaker is an intrinsic part of the meaning of what he says; thus, the context in which something is said must be accessible to anyone who seeks understanding. This view rules out full understanding of written texts and of rhetorical speeches, a parallel which is central to Plato's objection to both.

Modern critical theory has revived the question of intentionality as a criterion of interpretation. Some, like Jacques Derrida, simultaneously reject the notion that "the speaking subject" is present in a "text," written or spoken, and reject the notion that the text itself "contains" meaning. Even though Derrida blames Plato for fathering the belief in the primacy of the spoken word, he agrees with Plato, in that he defends the inseparability of linguistic form and "content," and regards the individual as inevitably unsuccessful at "producing" meaning. Like other critics who place deconstruction at the center of the interpretive act, Derrida suggests that interpretation consists of understanding what was not said, an examination of linguistic absences and failed attempts at communication and meaning. To a certain extent, but for very different reasons, Plato concurs with this conception of understanding.

A second group of interpretation theorists, represented by Hans Georg Gadamer and Paul Ricoeur, are attempting to repair the historicity and intersubjectivity which has, in their view, plagued continental hermeneutic methods since Schliermacher, Dilthey, and, most recently, Heidegger. Heidegger's hermeneutic circle, which posits that the historical context of the text and the individuality of the interpreter alter the meaning of a given text, so that each text means something different to each age and ultimately to each interpreter, is criticized by Gadamer and Ricoeur because it has introduced a hopeless relativism and solipsism into interpretation theory and methods. Gadamer and Ricoeur posit different ways out of the hermeneutic circle. Gadamer argues for the weight of incremental interpretations, "the tradition," as a means by which the original text, along with the layers of acquired meaning it has accumulated, serve as an antidote to an infinite solipsism of individual interpretations. Ricoeur emphasizes that the intention of the author, which is necessarily rendered inaccessible by textuality, should be a part but not the whole authority in the act of interpretation, and that those elements of the text which are autonomous and fixed in meaning, should lie at the center of the interpretive act. Ricoeur's defense of the semantic autonomy of the text is based on an extensive analysis of the nature of textuality, an analysis which he utilizes to celebrate the autonomy and freedom of the written text as a release from intersubjectivity. Ricoeur's analysis of textuality is an interesting foil for Plato's, for up to a certain point it is identical—the speaker is absent from the text. Beyond that point the two differ, and Ricoeur differs from Gadamer, who, like Plato, encourages the concept of interpretation as dialogue.

The nature of textuality, and its relationship to both meaning and understanding, is one question which links Plato's critique with developments in modern critical theory. Insofar as authorial intention is an important component in contemporary discussions of textuality and interpretation, it will be approached in part with reference to the studies of literacy and orality, and to the studies of hermeneutic methods I have described above. A second aspect of authorial intention, represented by critical theories which focus on the rhetoric of fiction and of irony, links modern critical theory to a second area of concern to Plato—the problem of intentional dissembling in rhetoric and, more broadly, in discourse structures which have the effect of misrepresenting truth. Critical debates about the role which should be played by the author's intention as a constituent of meaning focus on the act of interpretation and understanding. Critical theories which provide means for determining the extent to which an author was being calculating, or ironic, focus on ferreting out deliberately crafted discrepancies between what is said and what is meant, or between different accounts of the "same" reality articulated, for example, by different characters.

Rhetorical criticism and point-of-view criticism represent interpretive methods which focus on inconsistencies and incongruities which are assumed to be carefully crafted by an author in an attempt at creating an ironic effect, or an effect more neutrally labelled "cognitive dissonance." The celebration of literary irony, which reached epidemic proportions during the hegemony of the new critics, is a critical stance which takes the construction of discrepancies between intent and meaning, or between what is and what is reported, to be an admirable and sophisticated activity on the art of the author. Such dissembling, or deliberate constructing of contradictory points of view, has also been valued because the successful recognition and appreciation of these duplicities is regarded as a mark of intelligence and sophistication on the part of the reader.

Wayne Booth's defense of irony is, I think, a representative articulation of the degree to which we have come to accept and appreciate the intentional dissembling which is part and parcel of literary irony. *A Rhetoric of Irony* classifies irony in terms of overt/covert, and stable/

unstable. Booth accepts and applauds overt stable irony, such as that found in 18th century fiction, as a clever, sophisticated, and instructive species of literary art. He is less comfortable with covert unstable irony, such as that found in Melville's *The Confidence Man,* Nietzsche, and Beckett because, he notes, it has the effect of inculcating a profound distrust of both authorial voice and of texts themselves, leading, ultimately to nihilistic fragmentation, alienation and, finally, despair. Booth's taxomony is useful, but does not fully address the problem of how "stable" irony lays the groundwork for its more "unstable," destructive successors, a sequence which we can observe in the literature of the 19th and 20th centuries.[6]

Booth's description of how and why we appreciate irony is an accurate profile of assumptions about irony in literature and in life which we have slowly come to take as axiomatic. In my discussion of Plato's critique of rhetorical and philosophical dissembling, I will argue that he anticipated the evolution of our modern assumptions by predicting that they would be an inevitable result of the terms and discourse models which were being disseminated by the sophists. He was a part of that dissemination insofar as he encouraged the development of abstract terms and of discourse structures which would best house their use as propaedeutics to a conceptual understanding of reality.

The Platonic *eidon,* ideas, and the Platonic *episteme,* means of knowing, were, however, distinctly different from the instrumentalist rhetoric of the sophists. The fact that Plato links the philosopher with the sophist in the *Sophist* indicates that he foresaw the difficulty of avoiding intentional and inadvertent dissembling with the new linguistic tools which he and the sophists alike had evolved. While he clearly suspects that dissembling will become more likely with the increasing consciousness of the forms of thought and language, he persists in denouncing dissembling, and particularly intentional dissembling, on the grounds that both *logos* and *ethos* — meaningful discourse and character — will be irremediably damaged by intentional dissembling. His defense of dialogue, then, can and should be examined as a proposal that if dialogue is sustained as the normative discourse structure, many if not all of the abuses he defines under the heading of dissembling can be reduced to a minimum.

Plato's proposed dialogue norm was unsuccessful, and was supplanted by the Aristotelian divisions of discourse types and purposes which influenced most subsequent rhetoric, logic, and poetics. It is useful to note that Plato's recurrent characterization of the nature of speech is that its primary function is "to influence the soul."[7] Aristotle's recurrent characterizations of rhetoric, that it is the art of persuasion, and that it is the study of those things which "move men's minds to decision," mark the shift from an emphasis on language as a means of knowing and language as a means of effecting changes in other people.[8] It is no accident that Aristotle's taxonomy is the first place in which *eironeia* is first praised as a literary-rhetorical device, and as a manner of speaking which is suitable for the gentleman to use when speaking to "the vulgar."[9] With the divorce of rhetoric from ethics, the Platonic concern with the ethical aspects of rhetorical dissembling was put to rest, just as Aristotle's divorce of poetry and rhetoric from logic rendered them outside the domain of "meaning-bearing statements," the *logos* which Plato had helped bring into being and which he had hoped would remain an integrated whole.[10]

In the sections that follow, I will describe the context and substance of the sophistic assumptions regarding writing and literacy, rhetoric, and dissembling, at which Plato directed his critique. Then, I will examine his defense of dialogue as an attempt to reverse the abuses which he feared would become institutionalized in the Attic *paideia* if the sophistic teachings came to dominate the curriculum.

A methodological problem in this discussion is the fact that Plato's dialogues are one of the most extensive surviving records of sophistic beliefs and teachings. Unfortunately, this places us in the position of having to use Plato's characterizations of the sophists as the primary source of information. Two pieces of external evidence, however, help correct the distortion likely in using the accuser as the primary source of information about the accused.

First, up to the time of Plato *sophistes* had not had negative connotations. A term traditionally used to refer to intellectuals and poets, it had, by the fifth century, been extended to the teachers of practical knowledge and verbal skill who were gradually supplanting the poets at the center of the Attic *paideia*.[11] The distinction which Plato draws between "true" *philosophistes* and "false" *sophistes* is his own. Thus, when Plato, Aristophanes, and Xenophon speak of the "sophists" with full pejorative connotations they are referring to all of the proponents of what Aristophanes terms the "new education."[12] The objections to the sophists and to their teachings should be understood as generally held objections, and as objections which had just emerged in the last third of the fifth century B.C.[13]

Second, Plato's improvements on sophistic teaching should be understood as improvements from within, that is, as improvements generated in and through dialogues with other "sophists." When he emphasizes distinctions between himself, or "philosophy," and "sophistry," Plato is introducing internal distinctions for the first time, even though his initial objections are often corroborated by external sources. One of the most important of these distinctions, between the sophist and the poet on the one hand, and the philosopher, on the other hand, is uniquely Platonic, for all other opponents of the sophists objected to them as upstart rivals to the traditional *paideia* rightly dominated by the poets and dramatists.

Even though we must use the dialogues as the major source of information about the specific elements in sophistic rhetoric and linguistic assumptions, these qualifications should allay any facile, *a priori* assumptions that the sophists were clearly bad, and set the scene for an examination of Plato's critique of the sophists in its own terms.

THE SOPHISTIC TEACHINGS

Writing and Literacy The vehemence of the Aristophanic and Platonic denunciations of writing suggests, as Eric Havelock argues in *Preface to Plato,* that writing had become firmly entrenched in the curriculum by the fifth century B.C. and that traditionalists were unhappy about it. Socrates' retelling of the Egyptian myth of the invention of writing in the *Phaedrus,* Plato's *Letter VII,* and sections of the *Protagoras* and the *Laws* provide extensive descriptions of how writing was utilized in the schools, and of what kinds of texts were available to students and to the culture at large. The evidence suggests that although writing was a new but firmly entrenched part of the elementary curriculum, where it was used primarily as a mnemonic, texts were virtually non-existent during the period when Plato wrote the dialogues. Thus, writing and literacy, both of which are targets of Plato's critique, must be taken separately even though it is curious to do so.[14]

Havelock's reconstruction of Attic literacy in the fifth century provides documentation for the provocative, and controversial, theses that (a) although the poets had been composing in writing beginning in the seventh century, writing skill was not widespread in Greece until the fifth century, and (b) there was no "corresponding increase in fluent reading." It was not until the middle of the fourth century that the transition to full literacy had been accomplished. The fifth century, then, constitutes what Havelock terms a period of "craft literacy," or "semi-literacy," in which writing skill (*grammatike*) was taught at the elementary level, but reading skill was taught rarely and, if at all, in adolescence.[15] The evidence for these rather startling propositions is incomplete but nonetheless suggestive. During the Periclean decades, there is little evidence of books or journals circulating and widely known; all evidence from the fifth century points to the conclusion that the term *biblion* (book) denoted single sheets, "notes," texts of speeches which were to be delivered orally, and tabular manuals; most literary and rhetorical works, on the evidence of fifth century orators and, later, Plutarch, were published orally; public inscriptions were virtually the only form of readily available, readable, text; the spelling and orthography of the inscriptions is erratic; and all available records of the classrooms describe writing as a child's exercise used in memorization and composition exercises.[16] Both the *Phaedrus* and the *Frogs* record instances of composition texts used solely as preparation for oral delivery, and ridicule performers caught using their notes. At the same time, references to "manuals" for rhetorical composition in the *Phaedrus,* and to "compendia" of selections from the poets in the *Laws VII* suggest that during this inordinately long transition period from semi to full literacy, in Havelock's words, "the new reading habits were already impairing the traditional ability to memorize 'whole poets'."[17] The traditional facility for repeating poets in their entirety had been imparted by aural drills, listening and repeating the performance of oral poets. Thus the traditionalist objections to writing taught by the sophists were objections not only to a new technology but to a discernible difference in the form and substance of the things memorized. With the development of Attic democracy during the Periclean decades it had become important for the public speakers to be able to compose speeches, as distinct from performances of traditional epic poetry, and to insert appropriate excerpts into their speeches. That writing was the means by which composition and invention were taught to public speakers marked it as a tool not only of the new education but of the new political order as well.

When we examine Plato's critique of writing in these contexts it appears much less polemical and much less bizarre than it seems at first reading. Plato's descriptions of writing and how it was taught seem polemical at first, because they seem to overemphasize the mnemonic and composition-drill capacities of writing over and above what to us are its many more important functions. However, Plato's descriptions are contextually accurate, for all the evidence suggests that writing in the fifth century was exclusively a *techne* (skill) used only at the elementary level, and only for the purposes he describes. Thus, writing was a child's skill, shed with maturity and with the "internalization" of the material and composition techniques it had imparted. Phaedrus's curious remark to Socrates, in the *Phaedrus,* that the great public speakers are afraid to leave written speeches behind them in fear they will be called sophists, denotes among other things the association of writing with mere elementary skill.[18]

The myth of the invention of writing told by Socrates in the *Phaedrus* emphasizes a more complex phenomenon—the psychological effects of using writing as a mnemonic which in turn was utilized as a composition drill. Socrates says that students who learn to write receive "a quantity of information without proper instruction," and that writing makes them "forgetful."[19] He charges that by depending on "external signs" rather than on their own "internal resources" students become intellectually lazy, confuse recollection with memory, and fail to learn the difference between information and knowledge. Havelock notes that these confusions had always been present in the oral *paideia* through which students learned to perform epic poetry, but the fixed form and content of epic poetry were neither "information" nor "knowledge" in the Socratic sense. Thus, Socrates' objections to the sophists' use of writing parallel his objections to the unthinking nature of the epic encyclopedia. The parallel is only partial, however, for the content of Attic rhetoric in the fifth century was distinctly different from the content of the fixed epic canon. The sophists taught speakers to memorize compositions which stated their own views, using excerpts from the poets and from other speeches as exempla. Plato's lengthy analyses of sayings (*rhema*) versus statements (*lege*) and meaning-bearing statements (*logon*) are more than grammatical or even semantic inquiries, for their purpose is to sort out the proliferation of kinds of discourse which were being generated helter skelter once the hegemony of epic poetry and epic poets began to fade. To these classifications I will return in subsequent sections, but here, in my analysis of the sophists' and Plato's views of writing, the distinction must be touched on in order to explain what Socrates is referring to when he distinguishes among memory, recollection, information, and knowledge. Not only writing, but the compositions which writing was used to teach, were, in Plato's analysis, fostering confusions among discourse distinctions which Plato and other *philosophistes* had only recently achieved.

The *Phaedrus* and *Letter VII* record not only what and how the sophists taught when they taught writing but also the attitudes which were developing concerning writers and writings. Those who can write, Socrates says in the *Phaedrus,* have the reputation for wisdom.[20] At the same time, the writings themselves are ridiculed, and those who circulate them are suspected of ambition.[21] "Leaving a writing behind," as Phaedrus notes, is avoided by the great speakers. Knowing how to write, that is, perhaps, "having gone to school," was clearly prestigious but distributing writings, or speaking from a written text, were regarded as bad form.

Havelock notes that long-standing Greek tradition evidenced in passages stretching from Aeschylus' *Suppliants* through Plato's *Letter VII,* mistrusted the written word, and particularly the document detached from the writer. Attic Greece was alone among the ancient Near Eastern cultures in never evolving a scribe culture which split the mechanisms of power between "the men of physical brawn or crude cunning and the men of skill, trained to use the clumsy elaborate script system."[22] When writing came to be used in Greek culture it was assimilated very gradually and over a three century period, by the entire ruling class. During Plato's century writing was a part of the sophistic curriculum but not yet a medium for mass communication. Plato objected to the uses of writing in the sophists' classrooms in part because those uses perpetuated the mechanical memorization techniques which had for so long structured the oral *paideia*. A second part of his objection focused on the probability that if writings came to be used as means of disseminating knowledge (*episteme*) and discourse (*logoi*) the nature of both would be permanently altered.

Havelock notes that Plato's preference for spoken discourse is illogical, "since the Platonic episteme which was to supplant *doxa* was being nursed to birth by the literate revolution."[23] However, I propose that if we look at Plato's analysis of the technology and psychology of writing alongside his critique of rhetorical discourse and rhetorical dissembling, we can observe the parallels which he perceived among these three contemporaneous developments. Each of these formulaic discourse types was objectionable to Plato precisely because it could be and was being formulized. Writing, rhetoric, and types of dissembling were being presented to students in memorizable, tabular, manual forms destined for use in situations where the ability to appear knowledgeable had priority over the hard-won "true" knowledge of philosophical inquiry.

Writing, in Plato's analysis, lends itself to the giving of an appearance (*phainetein*), in two ways. First, its physical reality, the fact that it is an observable phenomenon, makes it an outstanding but dangerous mnemonic whose use fosters confusions among memory, recollection, information, and knowledge. Second, since writing can appear to "say" things on its own it lends itself to deliberate misrepresentations. It can, and will, transmit quantities of information without proper instruction, thus without the possibility of full understanding. Since writing is a representation of what is already a representation — spoken language — it is twice as likely to function misrepresentationally. Because of this double jeopardy intrinsic to writing, Plato argues, writing cannot contain record or represent "thought" and "knowledge." It is the potential for deliberate misrepresentation which concerns Plato most and it is this characteristic which links writing to rhetoric in his critique.

Rhetoric   The earliest rhetors were "natural leaders," as we would call them today, whose character and powers of persuasion placed them in positions of power when tribal elder governance was gradually replaced by the public assembly in Attica. As previously noted, Attic Greece was unique in the primacy it had always given the spoken word, the poet, and, finally, the speaker (*rhetor*). Thus, to speak of the development of rhetoric in Greece is simply to note that Greek culture had for centuries encouraged and rewarded oral performative skill. The Greek dramatists record the preoccupation with verbal power, which marked the cultural changes of the sixth and fifth centuries B.C. Plato borrowed the dialogue form traditionally utilized by the dramatists when he sought an acceptable form for recording the process used by Socrates and other *philosophistes*.[24] Like drama, dialogue represents exchange, interaction, response, and process in ways which cannot be fully realized in narrative or expository monologue discourse. And, the dramatists' depictions of the relationship between people and ruler, those who are ruled and those who rule, increasingly focused on the pathological excesses of the powerful. Rhetoric, and rhetoricians, then, emerged during a period when the traditional seats of power—the hereditary rulers, their priest-counselors, and the *aiodoi* (poet-singers)—were being challenged by new ideas of governance which had emerged in the wake of abused power. The tyrant was the villain; the people were represented in the increasingly prominent choric voice of the dramas, functioning simultaneously as the hero and forum in which debate took place. In Plato's dramatic dialogues, the sophist-rhetor functions as the tyrant-villain.

The necessity for training in debate placed successful rhetors, who were often retired public figures, in great demand. Thus, retired rhetors were the first teachers of rhetoric, but as their *techne* came to be studied rhetoric came to be regarded as a set of learnable techniques independent of an individual's character, position, or individual performances. One of the concepts which was central to rhetoric once it began to be regarded as a learnable technique was that of "giving the appearance of." *Phainetai*, from which we derive "phenomenon," with its emphasis on semblance, the perceived and experienced. Aristotle extended the emphasis on semblance and appearance even further by equating the effective rhetor with the actor (*hypocritike*).[25] Just as Plato objected to the sophistic emphasis on giving the appearance of knowledge through the written medium, he objected to the explicit emphasis on appearance as distinct from substance in the sophists' rhetorical teachings. In the *Gorgias*, Socrates notes that the rhetorician who knows nothing of medicine can outstrip a knowledgeable doctor in a public assembly meeting because the audience will give priority to the one who appears most knowledgeable.[26]

Persuasion without reference to knowledge, "without instruction," in Socrates' recurrent phrase, was supplanting hereditary tribal authority in the assembly meetings. This substitution was not only a dubious replacement of one kind of *aristos* with another; it was also for Plato a dangerous, because deliberate, driving apart of the distinction between opinion/belief (*doxa*) and knowledge. A parodic rendering of this sophistic teaching appears in the *Phaedrus,* where Socrates describes an all too familiar technique:

> There are even some occasions when both prosecution and defense should positively suppress the facts in favor of probability if the facts are improbable. Never mind the truth—pursue probability through thick and thin in every kind of speech; the whole secret of the art of speaking lies in consistent adherence to this principle.[27]

The distinctions parodied here—between probabilities and facts, and between truth and probability—were further reinforced by Aristotle's adoption of the enthymeme as the line of demarcation between logic, in which syllogistic premises state "general truths" and rhetoric, in which enthymenic premises state "probabilities," "signs" and "commonplaces."[28] The "incompleteness" of the rhetorical enthymeme, in Aristotle, is one of substance rather than form.

Because the sophists taught the rhetor to deal in persuasion based exclusively on opinion, and to effect this persuasion through giving the appearance of knowledge, Plato terms the sophistic rhetor a "dissembling imitator" of truth.[29] Just as writing is, physically, the representation of a representation, and thereby an "image" (*eidolon*) thrice removed from what it represents rhetorical semblances are termed semblances, appearances (*phainetai*). Rhetoric's double jeopardy is not that it is thrice removed, but that it is deliberately incomplete, a partial representation which will appear correct and thereby persuasive.

Eric Havelock substantiates the associations Plato draws between rhetoric and poetry by describing the sense in which both rhetoric and poetry, in their Attic context, were based on opinion:

> *Doxa* is therefore well chosen as a label not only of the poet's image of reality but of that general image of reality which constituted the content of the Greek mind before Plato. Its general significance prevailed in the end over its poetic one. If it originally united the two, this is precisely because in the long centuries of oral culture and oral communication it was the poet and his narrative that bore the responsibility for creating the general vision and preserving it and fastening it upon the minds of succeeding generations of the Hellenes.[30]

Rhetoric simply replaced one kind of opinion with another, and in a context of new discourse structures and new modes of authority where there was no weight of tradition to ground or check the substance and suasiveness of the neologisms. Havelock's focus on the centrality of *doxa* to Plato's critique of the poets is particularly noteworthy in a second connection. *Doxa* denoted not only "opinion," or "belief," but also, and orginally, the decision reached in the assembly meeting — a commonly held belief. Manipulating opinion, then, was potentially much more powerful in Plato's context than in our contemporary lexicon where "opinion" does not carry the weight of a ruling paradigm. For Plato, rhetoric replaced one order of *doxa* with another, and reduplicated the "error" of poetic "semblance" with the rhetorical "commonplaces" and "topoi" disseminated in the rhetoricians' manuals.

If we examine Plato's version of one of these manuals we find a list of structures and strategies which looks quite familiar. It is clear from the discussion of rhetorical manuals, devices, and strategies which stretches from *Phaedrus* 257-274 that rhetoric as taught and practiced by the "sophists" was neither homogeneous nor fully distinguished from the various philosophical schools which were developing the prototypes for what would become technical formulae for definition and logical proof. The most tabular representation for organizing an effective speech occurs at 266d and following, where "the technical treatises on the subject" are summarized. The summary given contains these elements:

- an introduction
- a statement of the facts supported by the evidence of witnesses
- indirect evidence
- arguments from probability
- proof and supplementary proof
- insinuation
- indirect compliments and indirect blame.

Throughout his composition, the rhetor is advised to rate probability higher than truth, to make trivial matters appear great and great matters appear trivial, to clothe old ideas in new language and new ideas in old language, and to end with a recapitulation or summary.

To this methodology Socrates juxtaposes two countersuggestions, which have been illustrated in his own speech, earlier in the *Phaedrus*. First, he recommends a synoptic view in which many scattered particulars are gathered under a single generic term, "so as to form a definition," and to then proceed to "divide the genus into species again" in order to test the definition and present it for fuller understanding.[31] Second, he proposes an ongoing process of dialectic, comprised of the moving back and forth between definitions of *gene* and testings of that definition against particulars. He poses the question, "Is there anything worth having that can be systematically acquired if it is divorced from dialectic?"[32]

Plato's position is that terms cannot be manipulated, and cannot be used to manipulate others, if they are persistently submitted to the scrutiny of dialectic. Most of the rhetorical arts, as defined in the manuals, depend on creating discourse structures and techniques which deliberately avoid defining terms and which are presented in situations where the testing of dialectic does not and cannot take place. His argument suggests that the techniques of logic and those of suasive rhetoic had not yet been divorced from one another, as they were to be by Aristotle's taxonomy. His description of the "technical manuals" of rhetoric suggests how that divorce was beginning: for practical and strategic reasons the suasive orator should not define his terms too exhaustively. The testing of terms and propositions in dialectical dialogue, the second suggestion which Socrates offers as a replacement for monologue rhetoric, was practiced by many rhetoricians in assembly debate. The Megarians, in particular, were famed for their use of *dialegesthai:* dialectical debate structured as question and answer. Zeno and Euclides, among others, developed a more radical strategy: monologue dialectics in which an argument was posed in interrogative form. Among the most representative examples are the Cretan Liar paradox attributed to Zeno, the Megarian *reductio ad absurdum,* and the elenchic rebuttal of inferences which could be derived from premises rather than of the premises themselves.[33]

It is clear from Socrates' comments on extant rhetoric manuals, and from his own suggestions, that the rhetorical structures and strategies which he objects to were simultaneously rhetorical and logical. He notes recurrently that the use to which a given structure is put, that is, its rhetorical purpose, is as much a determinant of its meaning and efficacy as its content or logical validity. His defense of dialogue, then, is not only a defense of the logical and epistemological virtues of a question-answer structure, but also of the interpersonal good will which distinguishes dialogue from public assembly debate. Socrates' comments to Gorgias', a sceptic, exemplify the emphasis which he placed on interpersonal context. Gorgias persistently maintains that rhetoric is designed to be used "in a crowd," and refuses to define it outside that context.[34] Socrates emphasizes that the rhetor's wisdom is always specious, since "in a crowd" means "among the ignorant." Gorgias concedes the point.[35]

Gorgias' sceptic background is an important element in his position on rhetoric, for it places him in the tradition of Heraclitus, and Parmenides, who promoted the study of *phainomena,* or appearance, on the grounds that it alone is directly accessible to observation. Parmenides and Protagoras were credited with developing a version of dialectic to which Plato objects: the ability to argue *pro* and *con* the same issue, or thesis.[36] Gorgias' teaching of rhetoric was neutral in the same sense. It is precisely this neutrality, the lack of reference to "what is really so," that Socrates objects to in the *Gorgias,* and that Plato objects to throughout the dialogues. The grounds for the objection are, first, that the lack of any ultimate resolution, or reference to the "truth" is philosophically inadequate, because a discussion without that reference becomes an infinite regress. Second, in speaking before crowds, or "among the ignorant," the rhetor using the "neutral" dialectical technique is deliberately misleading the audience in that the audience, by definition, will not make the philosophical distinction between what appears to be the case and what is "really" the case. Thus, Plato objects to any public rhetoric, and to the teaching of rhetoric as a means of persuading "crowds."

The sophists taught the rhetor to deal in persuasion with no reference to truth, and in situations where that omission would go unnoticed by the audience. Thus, Plato's objections to rhetoric should be appreciated as one of the first critiques of rhetoric as a culturally sanctioned species of dissembling. In the hands of the philosophers, the *dissoi logoi* — proofs of opposite propositions — were a useful propadeutic for inquiry and an agonistic sport which Plato himself utilizes. Among "the ignorant," however, the same argumentative and logical structures become ethically and philosophically questionable. It is the dual — ethical and philosophical — problem of dissembling and imitating truth which leads Plato to equate rhetor, philosopher, and *eiron* in the *Sophist*.[37]

Irony   *Eironeia,* in the literature and usage of Plato's time, was a term of rebuke, meaning "you dissembling scoundrel." G. G. Sedgewick and D. C. Muecke document the fact that it was not until Aristotle that irony denoted anything other than low class, mocking, pretence.[38] Sedgewick notes that Thrasymachus hurls *"eiron"* at Socrates during a heated argument in the *Republic,* and that there it is clearly meant abusively.[39] I have already noted a second instance of *eiron,* in the *Sophist* where, albeit not in fully nominalized form, it clearly means "dissembler," with full negative connotations. That Socratic Irony later came to denote a philosophically subtle and aesthetically sophisticated manner of articulation should not be confused with the fact that for Socrates and Plato alike it denoted deceit pure and simple.[40]

The multiple meanings and connotations which "irony" has for us today make it difficult to talk about Plato's equations among sophistic rhetor, philosopher, and *eiron;* however, the prominence of Plato's emphasis on rhetoric as dissembling and manipulating "the ignorant," particularly when it is placed alongside our subsequent acceptance of both rhetoric and irony as tolerable, even attractive, species of guile, justify the difficulty. Irony did not mean to Plato what it means to us, but then, neither did rhetoric.

My discussion of Plato's critiques of writing and rhetoric has emphasized that in both of these cases, one of the targets of Plato's critique was the presence or absence of the speaker/thinker to his audience. Oral discourse is preferable to written discourse, in Plato's analysis, because the statements of interlocutors can be tested against the interlocutors' perceptions and understanding of the subject at issue. Dialogue discourse is preferable to textual or rhetorical monologue discourse in Plato's analysis for the same reason: there is less likelihood of misunderstanding and, concomitantly, more likelihood of a productive and instructive process of inquiry, leading ideally to a fuller understanding of the subject at hand. It is instructive to compare Plato's definition of speech, "the function of speech is to influence the mind/soul (*psyche*)," with Aristotle's, "rhetoric is the art of persuasion" and "rhetoric is the study of those things which move men's minds to decision."[41] Aristotle replicates Gorgias' defense of rhetoric as a technique which already exists in the public forum of the assembly by arguing that after all, "men's minds" are already being moved by rhetoric; and we might as well improve on the extant excesses used to move them; and that the virtue or vice of the rhetor is not the fault of rhetoric; it is a characteristic of the individual. Gorgias argues that "those who misuse the art I hold to be responsible"; Aristotle, that "What makes a man a 'sophist' is not his faculty but his moral purpose."[42]

Both of these defenses beg the question in the sense that they do not deal with the more difficult, systemic question which Plato poses. If people are taught that speech (*rhetorike*), in both the everyday and technical sense, deals with constructing apparent truths and with influencing opinion, won't they be more likely to use speech to construct only apparent, hopefully persuasive utterances whose final "acceptability" is determined by the extent to which the utterance "sells" rather than by the extent to which the utterance is true?[43] These larger questions, perhaps because they are more difficult to answer, were not tackled by the sceptic Gorgias or by the pragmatist Aristotle. However, the fact that both Gorgias and Aristotle bothered to respond to the moral implications of Plato's question suggests at the very least that they regarded it as a viable, if difficult to answer, question.

The Aristotelian defense of rhetoric, and subsequent descriptions of textuality, have maintained that what a discourse, text, or utterance "means," once it is uttered, is to some extent independent of the act of understanding and of the intention of the speaker or writer. Plato's position is, I propose, almost unique in its refusal to admit this neutrality to "semantic" meaning, and the refusal of neutrality is based on two very different propositions. An utterance or text is not only incapable of being fully "detached" from the speaker's context and intention; it is also either true or false. Thus, for Plato, "intent" is not only a determinant of semantic meaning, but also a criterion for epistemological and ethical evalutation. Aristotle divorces "rhetoric, poetry, and prayer" from "meaning-bearing discourse" on the grounds that they are "neither true nor false."[44] In contrast, Plato posits that the speaker's semantic intention must be used to determine the meaning of terms and propositions. If a speaker "meant" other than what he "said," the meaning must be defined before the discussion can continue lest all subsequent discussion be marred by a misunderstanding. The truth or falsehood of a term or proposition is a part of "understanding" what it means, and going through the process of inquiry which determines truth or falsehood is part of what makes dialogue so ideal to Plato.[45] Not only the truth of the utterance, but the collaborative efforts which generate a shared understanding of its truth, are for Plato ideally situated in the dialogue form.[46]

The ethical sense of "truth" and "falsehood" is, for Plato, a constitutive component of meaning. If, for example, a speaker says something which is factually "true" in order to deceive, the "meaning," understood as "understandability" of the utterance, is forfeited. This crime is more objectionable to Plato than a similar instance of misrepresentation: inadvertently saying something which is not true. "For some of these imitators are simple-minded and think they know about that which they have only opinion. . . . we call one the simple imitator (*haploun mimeten*) and the other the dissembling imitator (*eironikon mimeten*)."[47] Only the latter receives full moral censure, but the truthfulness of the former's utterance is as important as Plato as its inadvertentness. Both cases of misrepresentation would be greatly reduced, in Plato's analysis, if dialogue were the primary medium of discourse, for in dialogue the ethical and epistemological flaws of natural language find an equally natural corrective.

Discourse, for Plato, is a "class of being." It exists, and through it, we exist. "If we were deprived of discourse," he argues, "we should be deprived of philosophy . . . ; we must come to an agreement about the nature of discourse, and if we were robbed of it by its absolute nonexistence, we could no longer discourse."[48] The *Sophist*, at 258b and following, entails a lengthy discussion of "not-being" and "being," which establishes that "not-being" exists as one of the "classes of being permeating all being" but only insofar as understanding consists of knowing what something is not. This premise is extended to discourse, so that the question becomes, does not-being mingle with opinion (*doxa*), speech (*lege*), and discourse (*logon*)? If not-being does not mingle with them, then both false opinion and false discourse come into being: ". . . to think or say what is not—that is, I suppose, falsehood arising in mind or in words."[49] The discussion goes on to determine that "if falsehood exists, then deceit exists," a conclusion that jars the modern reader in part because we tend to distinguish "reference mistakes" from "deceit" quite habitually.

Instead of arguing that Plato was right, I propose that we examine the implicit assumptions behind these questions, and the instructive value of discourse, but also allow for a scrutiny of the semantic and interpersonal components of irony in its limited Platonic sense of dissembling. The terminology of the *Sophist* 258 and following persistently links "saying something which is not" with "falsehood." "Falsehood," in turn, is linked with deceit, in the sense that "dissembling" (*eironeia*) in the Greek lexicon of that time meant deceit and nothing else. Thus, false discourse is any discourse which states nonentities in any context other than the dialectical discovery of what "is" as opposed to what "is not." The statement of such nonentities outside the context of dialectical heuristics understood as such by all participants constitutes "falsehood." Finally, the deliberate statement of such falsehoods is said to constitute dissembling, to be morally reprehensible, and to undermine the "existence" of discourse itself:

> To take pleasure in thus always bringing forward opposites in the argument—all that is no true refutation, but is plainly the offspring of some brain that has just begun to lay hold upon the problem of realities. For certainly, my friend, the attempt to separate everything from everything else is not only not in good taste but also shows that a man is utterly uncultivated and unphilosophical. . . . The complete separation of each thing from all is the utterly final obliteration of all discourse. For our power of discourse is derived from the interweaving of the classes or ideas with one another.[50]

The logical, analytical procedures of dialectic, understood in its technical sense—the *dissoi logoi* proofs *pro* and *con* the same thesis, the elenchic questions challenging the premises of an opponent, and the breaking down of a genus or term into its specific parts—are linked not only with an unproductive epistemological procedure, but also with immature competitiveness, destructiveness, and, finally, dishonorable behavior. If analysis is not accompanied by synthesis it is not only incomplete but meaningless. If separating everything from everything else, and bringing forward opposites in argument is not directed at subsequent integrations and articulations of truth, then the agent of separations and oppositions is guilty of a moral crime.

The Elean Stranger provides two characterizations of the bad motives which convict the sophist of wrongdoing. ". . . because of their experience in the rough and tumble of arguments, (they) strongly suspect and fear that they are ignorant of the things which they pretend before the public to know."[51] The aggressiveness, then, of the sophist in argument is motivated by the fear of being discovered. A second motive, that of appearing knowledgeable to those who are not capable of discerning ignorance from true knowledge, appearance from reality, characterizes the public orator as, in Plato's assessment, despicable. The link between the two types of wrong motive, one indigenous to exchanges among those trained in dialectic, the other to the setting of public oratory, is that of knowingly stating that which is not true. The motive of the speaker, as well as the nature of what is said, brand orator and dialectician alike as sophists.

Wayne Booth's characterization of the test which irony presents to its beholder illustrates the curious inversion of Plato's depiction of dialectical sophistry in the irony embraced by the modern literary and interpretive tradition.

> Our pride is more engaged in being right about irony than about many matters that might seem important — being logical or consistent, for example. If I am wrong about irony, I am wrong at deeper levels than I like to have exposed. When I am 'taken in,' my profoundest beliefs and my most deeply rooted intellectual habits are under judgment. But is it not also true that I am equally under judgment if not by my fellow men then by the mocking spirit of irony, when I see ironies that are not there?[52]

The pride implicit in the fear of discovery, targeted by Plato as a defining sin in dialectical sophistry, has become, in Booth's analysis at least, one of the sources of the modern appreciation of irony. When and if we detect that we have been duped we "are wrong," in Booth's phrase, at deeper and more troubling levels than normally define mistakes. To suspect an irony that is not present is equally troubling, Booth maintains, for it marks us as capable of suspecting an interlocutor or author of deliberate deception. Booth's characterization of modern irony and the perceiver's relationship to that irony parallels Plato's description of rhetorical dissembling in that it focuses on interpersonal intention. It was the intent to dupe an "ignorant" audience that led to Plato's objection to rhetorical dissembling. Booth depicts the same process from the point of view of the recipient in order to define what it is that makes irony troubling, but also enjoyable as a test of judgment.

The second type of dissembling condemned by Plato — the deliberate misrepresentation and undermining of truth which can take place among dialecticians — focuses on the bad faith and wrong intent of the would-be philosopher among other philosophers. The Elean Stranger argues that dialectic should not be granted to "any but the man who pursues philosophy in purity and righteousness."[53] The sophistical dialectician, in contrast, "runs to earth in the darkness of Not-being, where long practice has taught him to feel his way about; and the very darkness of that place makes it hard to discern him."[54] The argumentative and logical divisiveness of the wrongly motivated dialectician marks him as a dissembler in the sense that he imitates the form—dialectic—but not the true or right purpose—seeking truth through the interweaving of terms and propositions—of philosophy. This second kind of dissembling has its parallel in a second category of modern depictions of irony: those which posit that language itself, or knowledge itself, are fragmentary, incomplete, and fraught with absences. Hayden White has depicted this set of beliefs in an articulation which parallels Plato's emphasis on the linguistic and epistemological consequences of abused dialectic:

> The linguistic mode of the Ironic consciousness reflects a doubt in the capacity of language itself to render adequately what perception gives and thought constructs about the nature of reality. It develops in the context of an awareness of a fatal asymmetry between the processes of reality and any verbal characterization of those processes.[55]

Modern deconstructivist and semiological characterizations of language represent this view and are, like Plato's sophist, proponents of negation in the sense of being exponents and analytical methodologies whose purpose is to break down the elements of discourse with no subsequent reassemblage. "The complete separation of each thing from all is the utterly final obliteration of all discourse," warns the Elean Stranger.[56] Modern poetics, however, has constituted critical approaches which yield discourses of anti-discourse, "writing zero degree," in Roland Barthes' phrase; "the poetics of absence," in Jacques Derrida's.

Julia Kristeva has described modern critical discourse as a process through which "The *death drive* of the writer becomes *irony* in the critic, because there is irony each time an ephemeral meaning crystallizes for such a reader."[57] The Elean Stranger concedes the ephemerality of knowledge when he asserts that "the nature of the other is all cut up into little bits, like knowledge."[58] In Plato's "true discourse" this fragmentation "interweaves" and reassembles. If it does not, it cannot exist. In the modern view, however, two kinds of irony can and do emerge out of division, incompleteness, and negation: the irony of crystallizing an ephemeral meaning which wasn't "really" there, and the irony of pure negation in which fragmentation is the avowed intention of the author or critic. "Experiencing the trajectory of this negativity, writing is contestation, rupture, flight, and irony. . . . Acting with the subject, it breaks its individual, contengent, and superficial representations and makes of them an *inorganic nature,* a pulverization of fragmented elements."[59]

Kristeva depicts the linguistic and representational chaos which is deliberately constructed by the modern critic and author in their flight from conventional form and substance. Unlike the modern critic's and author's "playing against" convention, Plato's dialogue and dialectic are novel yet anti-ironic modes of seeking truth, promoted, as I have argued, in an explicit attempt to reverse the sophistic tendency toward linguistic games and counters, precisely those aesthetic structures which Kristeva describes and which we have come to associate with literary and critical sophistication. In describing sophistic gamesmanship, and in defining the abuses of dialectic practiced by the sophists, however, Plato comes very close to depicting the linguistic and intersubjective contingencies which are central to the modern concept of irony. Plato's arguments against textuality, rhetorical dissembling as a moral crime, and eristic dialectic depend on a firm distinction between these abuses and proper enactment of discourse in dialectical dialogue. The following sections will demonstrate that even though Plato's arguments against the sophist depend in large part on a distinction between false sophist and true philosopher, the *Sophist* undermines that distinction in a scrupulously honest concession of the difficulty of drawing that line, paving the way for later, particularly German Romantic, adoptions of the dialogues as an exemplary instance of irony as a function of the intersubjective contingencies of dialogue.

DIALOGUE: ANTIDOTE FOR SOPHISTIC RHETORIC

Euclid: Here is the roll, Terpison; I may observe that I have introduced Socrates, not as narrating to me, but as actually conversing with the persons whom he mentioned—these were Theodorus the geometrician (of Cyrene), and Theaetetus. I have omitted, for the sake of convenience, the interlocutory words "I said," "I remarked," which he used when he spoke of himself, and again, "he agreed," or "disagreed," in the answer, lest the repetition of them should be troublesome. — *Theaetetus* 143 b-c

The introduction of the *Theaetetus* is unusual in that Plato explicitly states a convention which has been used throughout the dialogues. Conversations which were, in fact, remembered by Socrates or witnessed by Plato are rendered in the form used for written drama: Title, Listing of Characters, Dialogue. Before the *Theaetetus* proper begins there is this short dialogue between Euclid and Terpison recounting how Euclid brought the transcription from Megara and why he chose to write it in dialogue form. Unlike Plato in the other dialogues, Euclid explains at the start that he has adapted his notes "for convenience" into dialogue form. He omitted some of what Socrates actually said because, he claims, the dialogue form gives a more *direct* account of what was said.[60]

We might suspect Plato of a subtle joke in writing this introduction. He does not, after all, include the frame outside the frame of the *Theaetetus:* a dialogue explaining how Plato acquired the text. Or we might dismiss all this as a simple problem of narrative economy and dramatic craft. However, Plato rigorously condemns drama and poetry throughout the dialogues, a fact which should make us beware of assuming that Plato is exercising poetic license. The aim of the dialogues is not to encourage a willing suspension of disbelief, or, conversely, a belief in the illusion that this dialogue is really taking place. Moreover, the later dialogues, to which the *Theaetetus* belongs, focus relentlessly on the formal conventions of written and spoken language, calling constant attention to the fact that the forms of language should not be confused with the realities to which they refer.[61]

It is by no means farfetched for us to read this passage from the *Theaetetus* as an instance of Plato's playing with the frame of the dialogues. But to do so, I think, tells us more about ourselves, our assumptions, and modern interpretive proprieties than it tells us about Plato. Play with formal conventions is an aesthetic activity which we both enjoy and admire. Plato, while he carefully analyzes the forms of discourse, does not *play* with formal conventions in our sense of the word. To do so would, in his terms, constitute false rhetoric: deliberate misrepresentation, guile, and the manipulation of forms as art-for-art's sake.

Plato understands conventions, and describes a good number of them as he comments on rhetoric and rhetorical situations. In the *Phaedrus,* Socrates defines ". . . two kinds of madness, one arising from human disease, the other when heaven sets us free from established convention."[62] Freedom from established convention is termed "madness" because its intense pleasure is akin in degree, but not kind, to that madness which is a "human disease." Freedom from convention is said to be "heaven sent" because it consists of the apprehension of concepts in and of themselves, without mediation by physical or linguistic embodiments. When the *eideon* are apprehended as realities in and of themselves, they inaugurate a revolutionary epistemology in the beholder because they supplant both the old gods and tradition (custom) as explanations of causality, human purpose, correct behavior, understanding itself. "The mass of men," as Socrates puts it in the *Apology,* "cannot accept the idea that there is a beauty itself rather than many beautiful things."[63]

Havelock asserts that "Platonism at bottom is an appeal to substitute a conceptual discourse for an imagistic one. As it becomes conceptual, the syntax changes, to connect abstractions in timeless relationships instead of counting up events in a time series; such discourse yields the abstracted objects of intellection."[64] Until the sophists, and then Socrates, began to disseminate the new lexicon and syntax of abstractions — the *topoi* stating abstracted premises such as "The wise are good"; the class terms such as "justice" presented for definition — there had been no propositional, abstract discourse. Thus, the fight between Plato and the "sophists" is, in part, a fight over the conventions which will govern this new discourse and its uses. In a double paradox, Socrates defined the concept of convention only to denounce many conventions as a prisonhouse, and Plato employed a dramatic convention, the dialogue form, as the best medium for recording Socratic philosophy.[65]

When Euclid announces that he has replaced Socrates' narrative with a dialogue form in order to be more "direct," he enacts a paradox. The aim of the transcription is to recount, as faithfully as possible, the exchange that took place between Socrates and Theaetetus. The most faithful, and direct, rendering of that exchange, he asserts, is the dialogue form because it best represents the subject and structure of the dialogue: syntax and epistemology, examined in a question and answer process. Plato, an opponent of writing, epic drama, and conventional forms, builds into the *Theaetetus* an explanation of why he has utilized all three of these targets of his critique.

The Platonic dialogue, I propose, is more than a straightforward borrowing of an extant literary convention. Instead, it is a novel invention, a new set of discourse conventions developed by Plato. How best to record dialectical, as opposed to linear, propositional discourse? How, moreover, to recapture the evolution of a vocabulary of thought–about–thought which occurred not in the mind of one man but in a lifetime of careful conversations?[66] Plato evolved the dialogue form as the answer to these questions, I propose, because other versions of abstract, formulaic discourse were already being circulated in the practice of sophistic rhetoricians and in the writings of Socrates' and his own students, such as Dionysus. The dialogues themselves function as both exempla and defense of the dialogue form as preferable to both sophistic rhetoric and eristic dialectic. The embodiment of dialectic in the dialogue form quickly came to be misconstrued, by Diogenes Laertius and Aristotle among others, as an unhappy hybrid of two distinct logical formulae: the dialogue as "a discourse consisting of question and answer," and dialectic as "the art of discourse (*techne logon*) by which we either refute or establish some position, by means of question and answer on the part of the interlocutors."[67]

It was Aristotle's divorce of rhetoric from logic, and his development of propositional and dialectical logic as rule-governed heuristic and proof procedures which, in effect, silenced the Platonic dialogue as a mode of philosophical reasoning and discourse. Platonic dialogue persisted as a lilterary genre throughout classical times, but not as exemplary and most productive mode of philosophical inquiry which Plato had hoped it would become. The onset of widespread literacy facilitated the atrophy of Platonic dialogue, as Walter Ong has demonstrated.[68] Modern critics have revived the analysis of literacy and textuality and have singled out two aspects of spoken discourse which parallel Plato's defense of the dialogue form: the tendency of written discourse to be monologue discourse, and the absence of writer from reader in the "exchange" which takes place through written discourse. The primacy of spoken discourse is central but not constitutive of Plato's concept of the dialogue, a point which is missed by modern critics such as Derrida who argue that Plato prefers spoken to written discourse because it is "more natural."[69] I have tried to demonstrate that Plato's defense of spoken discourse is thoroughly embedded in his defense of the dialogue form, and that thus understood Plato is the originator of a new conception of philosophical discourse and not simply a traditionalist resisting textuality. Both dialogue and dialectic as conceived by Plato were novelties in their original context. However, two important confusions have persisted regarding Plato's views on the relationship between dialogue and dialectic and the relationship between dialogue and rhetoric. From Aristotle forward, syllogistic dialectic has often been regarded as an improvement over Plato's dialogue dialectic, missing the point that dialogue is a non-monologue form, and that the interrelationship among interlocutors in dialogue was, for Plato, as definitive or dialectical philosophizing as the divergence between logically contradictory propositions. Similarly, Plato's distinction between the "true rhetoric" of dialogical philosophizing and the "false rhetoric" of speaking before a public audience has seemed vague because both dialogue and public speaking are oral discourse modes, an analogy which misses Plato's ethical point: dissembling is less likely among interlocutors in private dialogue. However, Plato himself caused some of the confusion, as I will argue in the next section, when he analyzed the probability and kinds of dissembling which can take place even in dialogue. Indeed, when Plato collapsed the distinctions between sophists and philosopher and rhetoric and philosophical dialogue in the *Sophist* he anticipated, perhaps even encouraged, others to do the same. The conflations, I propose, are one source of our modern, extended, concept of irony.

Irony is often typified as a rhetorical phenomenon. The semantic, epistemological, and ethical contingencies central to irony and elaborated by Plato in the *Sophist* are readily available in the rhetorical situation which is the object of his attack in the earlier dialogues. Paradoxically, it is within the integrated language model which Plato invented as an antidote to sophistry—the dialogue—that we find a reduction in "rhetorical" distance only to be that much closer to the clever *eiron* who must purchase our trust if the irony is to succeed. A dissembling orator is less disturbing than a dissembling friend. But Plato's point then, well worth reviving now, is "why?" The contingencies which operate, in Plato's analysis, in public rhetoric and in private dialogue constitute an integrated field of potential misrepresentations and deceptions at which, I propose, he directs both his critique of rhetoric in the earlier dialogues, and his critique of abused dialectic in the *Sophist*.

Plato's promotion of dialogue as an antidote to sophistic rhetoric is developed slowly but powerfully in the *Phaedrus, Gorgias, Theaetetus,* and *Sophist,* through the recurrent utilization of three metaphorical structures which depict dialogue as true rhetoric.[70] The metaphor of parents and offspring is introduced in the *Phaedrus* to depict the relationship which should exist between the individual and his thoughts and utterances. The metaphor of *maieutics*—midwifery—is central to the depiction of philosophical inquiry which is a central topic of the *Theaetetus*. The metaphor of weaving-blending appears in all four dialogues but is oddly prominent in the *Sophist,* the most sceptical of the depictions of dialogue. We might welcome the substitution of an "if-then," "since," and "therefore" lexicon which occurs in place of "weaving together," "blending," "mixing" in parts of the *Sophist* and persistently in the *Parmenides*. The former, more familiar, terms are clearer, in a sense. And, as Gilbert Ryle has asserted, "philosophy progresses from the opaque to the clear."[71] But there is an important sense in which the "weaving together," "blending," "mixing" metaphors are clearer: Plato was not up to devising a logical lexicon which would stand on its own, independent of the "weaver," the "blender," and the "mixer." It is significant, in this regard, that in *Letter VII,* where all three sets of metaphors recur in a summary and recapitulation of Plato's views, the "weaving together" terminology is back in force.

Plato uses the metaphor of parents and offspring to characterize the semantic and semiotic aspects of discourse. Whether a statement has meaning (semantics) and what a statement refers to (semiotics) depend in part on the relationship between individuals and on the attitude they adopt toward what they say. By equating what an individual says with offspring, Plato emphasizes the connection between intent and meaning. There are many discourse types in which we no longer insist on congruence between intent and meaning, or on any necessary link between intention and semantic content.[72] For Plato, however, the meaning of a statement is contingent on its speaker's avowal of what is said and on that speaker's "good will" and "care" for his audience. These connections among attitude, intent, and meaning are embodied in the metaphor of parents (speakers) and offspring (their statements and writings).

Understanding and knowledge, Plato argues, can only be achieved through a long process of dialectical dialogues among colleagues conducted in a spirit of "knowledge, good will, and candor."[73] Moreover, the understanding and knowledge thus attained cannot be stated in a treatise:

> even the best of such compositions can do no more than help the memory of those who already know; whereas lucidity and finality and serious importance are to be found only in words spoken by way of instruction, or, to use a truer phrase, written on the soul of the hearer to enable him to learn about the right, the beautiful, and the good;
>
> Such spoken truths are to be reckoned a man's legitimate sons, primarily if they originate within himself, but to a secondary degree if what we may call their children and kindred come to birth, as they should, in the minds of others.[74]

What a given discourse means is, for Plato, irrevocably linked to what the speaker meant and depends on the immediate presence of both the speaker and the hearer so that they can be sure they have understood each other, and, thereby, the discourse as a whole. Both the intrinsic meaning and the referential efficacy of statements are, for Plato, grounded in the dialogue process rather than in the discourse *per se*. The analogy between "treatises" and abandoned children is more complex than it appears to be. Through the analogy, Plato suggests that misinterpretation is a subspecies of misunderstanding, and, moreover, that it is an abuse rather than an inevitability because interpretation itself is incomplete understanding.[75] The interpretive situation occurs when individuals misuse language by placing it outside of a dialogical situation. When he hears that Dionysus of Sicily, a former student, has written a manual on the techniques he learned from him, he responds by saying, "He put it together as if it were a treatise of his own, quite different from what I taught him."[76] What Plato objects to in this portion of *Letter VII* is not simply plagiarism, but Dionysus' failure to understand that neither the technique nor the content of the dialogue can be stated discursively because the content is, in part, the dialectical process by which one individual understood what another individual was saying. To formulate a discursive summary of "what was said" is "different from what (Plato) taught him," because part of what Plato taught was that to summarize statements is to leave out the experience of sudden insight and mutual understanding which cannot be recorded:

> It is not something that can be put into words like other branches of learning; only after long partnership in a common life devoted to this very thing does truth flash upon the soul, like a flame kindled by a leaping spark. . . .
>
> If I thought that any adequate spoken or written account could be given to the world at large, what more glorious life work could I have undertaken than to put into writing what would be of great benefit to mankind and to bring the nature of reality to light for all to see.[77]

Dionysus evidently attempted to produce a manual on dialectic and dialogue in which he sought to define their matter and processes in a treatise which Plato terms "a dishonor" to himself and his techniques.[78]

Like the "abandoned" children which figure prominently in the *Phaedrus,* Dionysus' treatise is emblematic, for Plato, of the misuses and abuses of discourse. The detaching of discourse from its true home: dialogue, will inaugurate, in Plato's mind, a succession of semblances, misunderstandings, and abuses occasioned by the detachment of discourse from its speaker and from its original context. Detachment and abandonment are used metaphorically to emphasize that method alone cannot produce or contain truth, that individuals over a lifetime of conversation with one another experience the process of understanding through which, occasionally, insight is attained.

A second metaphor, that of midwifery, is utilized by Plato to characterize the relationship among the individuals engaged in dialogue, and the sense in which even ordinary conversation can be an act of knowing. Where the metaphor of abandonment and detachment emphasized the relationship between an individual and the discourse produced, the metaphor of maieutics emphasizes the relationship which should exist among participants in dialogue, the situational and interactional aspects of discourse. In the *Theaetetus,* Socrates likens himself to a midwife in an extended analogy which begins with the announcement that his mother was a "brave and burly" midwife.[79] The midwife, he asserts, "is also the true and only matchmaker"—a facility which he parallels with the philosopher's ability to put classes of things together in order to produce the best offspring: truth.[80] "I tell you this long story, friend Theaetetus," he continues, "because I suspect, as indeed you seem to think yourself, that you are in labor—great with some conception. Come then to me, who am a midwife's son and myself a midwife, and do your best to answer the questions which I will ask you."[81]

Maieutics defines the kind of relationship that exists, ideally among the participants in a dialogue. Their good intentions and trust of one another are as esential as their candor in saying, to the best of their abilities, what is true. Thus, the dialogue is, like any conversation among friends, an exchange in which each participant helps the others to say what they are trying to say by candidly responding when they find error, lack of clarity, or wrong intent. Even though neither the dialogues of Plato nor conversations among friends always attain this ideal, the metaphor of maieutics reminds us, I think, of an aspect of conversation which we frequently forget. Conversation, like Plato's concept of maieutic dialogue, is more than an exchange of random opinions; it is an epistemological activity grounded in trust and good will. Conversation, and dialogue, generate a mutually constructed reality, and mutually defined terms. When we have that sense of you and I finding words to talk about a subject we want to know more about we are, quite literally, helping one another give birth to new ideas, perhaps even to truth. Maieutics, then, characterizes the attitudes which the participants in philosophical dialogue should have towards one another, and extends the metaphor of parents and offspring to include a characterization of the relationship among "parents," or, among those who are in the process of trying to give birth to meaningful, productive, discourse.

The third metaphor which Plato utilizes to characterize dialogue as the ideal medium for philosophy and discourse is that of weaving, blending, and mixing. These related metaphors characterize the relationship among terms, statements, and ideas which the participant in dialogue should keep uppermost in mind as the process of discussion proceeds. In the *Phaedrus,* at 266 and following, where Socrates criticizes the extant rhetoric manuals and formulae, he utilizes the distinction between drawing likenesses and establishing differences among classes of things to distinguish between the "true rhetoric" of seeking genuine truth from the false rhetoric of using techniques like definition, analysis, and proof to produce suasive rhetoric which has no relationship to truth or reality. Drawing likenesses, or, as he puts it in the *Sophist,* mixing and blending, is a process of knowing, not a technique of rhetoric. Yet, as he notes, those who learn the processes of definition, analysis, and proof in the context of dialogue can and do utilize those processes as techniques:

> Simply to demonstrate that in some undetermined way the same is different or vice versa, the tall short, the like unlike, and to delight in continually brandishing such contradictions in argument, is not legitimate criticism; it is the new-born babe of a mind that has only recently made contact with reality.[82]

Plato's point is that the objective of discourse ought not to be the rather empty exercise of providing obligatory comparisons or contrived distinctions, as the sophists do in their public speeches to give the appearance of logic. Instead, the purpose of both discourse and philosophical inquiry should be to move through the process of definition, analysis, proof, and synthesis in order to arrive at and communicate truth.

It is synthesis, more than any other process, which Plato represents with weaving, blending, and mixing. Analysis, definition, and proof are, in his portrayal, preliminary steps in a process which should always culminate in understanding, which he portrays as the weaving together of words, sentences, and the dialectical testing by question and answer which takes place in dialogue. "A statement does more than just name something. It gets us somewhere by interweaving verbs and nouns."[83] This portrayal is simultaneously grammatical and moral, for it defines not only the logic of statement-making but also the spirit in which statements should be made. "Those [names] which are spoken in order and mean something do unite, but those that mean nothing in their sequence do not unite."[84] While apparently tautological, this depiction of the interdependence of grammatical entities—nouns—and a sense-making utilizer of nouns is important, particularly to the modern mind schooled in precisely the divisions which Plato was worried about. We normally think of nouns as minimal units of referential meaning, but Plato emphasizes that nouns alone do not have meaning, that even strings of nouns do not necessarily have meaning, and that those which are spoken in order and mean something do not simply mean, but unite. "All discourse originates in the weaving together of Forms."[85] That is, discourse as an exchange of ideas originates not with the atoms of verbs and nouns but with the act of weaving, uniting, bringing together. Not only are the parts of speech brought together in the meaningful unities of sentences, but sentences are brought together in the processes of definition, analysis, testing, and reformulation. Finally, the weavers themselves, the agents of the sentences and of the dialogue, are brought together in their shared apprehension of a subject.

Plato chastizes the practitioners of pure analysis and eristic debate not only for being sophistic rhetors interested in little more than display, but also for being destroyers of dialogue and discourse. "The endeavor to separate everything from everything else is not only out of place, but is also the mark of a man who has no link whatever with the Muse of Philosophy."[86] These *anti logoi* are the human counterparts of the *dissoi logoi*—proofs of opposite propositions—in the sense that they destroy discourse by taking it apart without reassembling it or worrying about its truth. They violate the Parmenidian dictum quoted by the Elean Stranger in the *Sophist:* "Never shall this be proved, that things which are not, are;/And do thou, in thy inquiry, deter thy thought from this way."[87] The two negations, speaking of that which is not, and using logic to prove that which is not, generating an *anti logoi* of negation, are at the center of Plato's critique of abused dialectic. To say or speak that which is not is "falsehood"; to separate without reuniting is destructive. Much of the *Sophist* is taken up with trying to draw the very fine line which divides the evil negator from the good philosopher who uses analysis to refine and reformulate thinking. In the concluding section which follows I will argue that if we examine Plato's distinction between the abusive dialectician, the dissembling imitator of philosophical truth, and the true philosopher, we will arrive at the point where modern irony begins. Plato's growing recognition of the ultimate inseparability of the true philosopher and the sophistical dialectician manifests itself, I think, in the conclusion to the *Sophist,* in which the philosopher and the sophist merge in the figure of the dissembling imitator. It was the German Romantic retrieval and celebration of Plato's *Socrates* which inaugurated the modern concept of irony.

Dialogue and Dialectic: The Dissembler and His Double

> Logos and logic, crystal hypothesis,
> Incipit and a form to speak the word
> And every latent double in the word.
>
> — Wallace Stevens[88]

"Every latent double in the word," in Plato's all too exhaustive analysis, is matched and magnified by the duplicity of the speaker and by the audiences's willingness to be teased, pleased, and even duped. Plato's depiction of dialectic as the Socratic method of discovering truth by asking questions has been supplanted in the *Sophist,* by the notion of dialectic as the logical technique of arguing opposing propositions. Thus, Plato's attempt to forge an inseparable integration between dialogue and dialectic failed. Even within the dialogues, I propose, we find evidence that Plato himself recognized the contingencies and relativisms which result from even a properly dialogical exercise of dialectic. The analysis of nouns and verbs and propositions leads to an awareness that definitions can be arbitrary, and can be used arbitrarily. The more we know, the more the materials and processes of knowing seem to be contingent. Technically speaking, the rhetoricians seem to be right. I have suggested that Plato sought to temper some of this contingency by inventing and promoting the dialogue as the proper setting for discourse. However, the conclusion to the *Sophist* indicates Plato's recognition that existentially and epistemologically the distinction between sophist and philosopher is inaccessible to the outside observer. The examination of dialectic which takes up much of the *Sophist* suggests, I propose, that the origins of modern irony are to be found, quite appropriately, in the debate about the institutionalization of rhetoric which culminated in Plato's attempt to distinguish not just rhetoric from dialectic but right from wrong dialectic itself.

The sophists, in Plato's judgment, exploited the fact that audiences often prefer to be delighted and flattered in their unexamined opinions rather than being challenged with the truth. Thus, the rhetorician encourages a kind of ignorance in the audience. Plato's emphasis on the implicit relationship between the speaker and audience which is tacitly contracted in a rhetorical situation constitutes one of the earliest systematic accounts of the verbal and situational duplicities which are necessary to irony. Paradoxically, the relationship between Socrates and his interlocutors in the dialogues has struck many as paradigmatically ironic. He seems to be pretending ignorance only to outstrip his opponents in a display of seemingly eristic debate. He seems to state positions which he doesn't really hold for the purposes of argument, only to show how flawed those positions are once his listeners have agreed to them. He asks his interlocutors in seeming good faith to define "justice" or "truth" only to proceed by a series of questions to refute their definitions. Socrates seems to be the master of irony. He was the model taken by the German Romantics when they evolved the modern concept of irony; thus, to speak now of Socrates as not ironic involves us in a paradox. However, if we look closely at what Socrates does and why he does it, we will see that he doesn't really fit the role of arch-*eiron* even though he served as its *exemplum*.

Socrates' motive is not what it seems. It appears to be aggresively interrogative, but it is maieutic and didactic as well. The truth of his statements is questionable, in the sense that he seems to say things he doesn't mean, or the opposite of what he means, or to state answers which he rapidly converts into questions. He seems, in short, to use all the tricks he and Plato condemn the sophists for. But if we scrutinize Socrates' apparent logic-chopping and seemingly manipulative dissembling we find, I propose, that Plato's portrait of Socrates in dialogue conveys a subtle lesson, just as he says dialogue should. Socrates pretends ignorance, not knowledge, a distinction which immediately separates him from the sophists. His conclusions, rather than his questions, are fictions, embodied in dialogues which, as more than one philosophy student can attest to, never conclude. Still, Socrates' motive does seem to be to frustrate and tease his audience as much as to engage in helpful, benign maieutics. Kierkegaard characterized this quality in Socrates as an ironic attitude which goes far deeper than mere (!) dissembling:

> He brought the individual under the force of his dialectical vacuum pump, deprived him of the atmospheric air in which he was accustomed

to breathe, and abandoned him. The expression "know thyself" means: separate yourself from the "other."[89]

"The nature of the 'other,'" says the Socratic voice of the Elean Stranger in the *Sophist*, "is cut up into little bits, like knowledge."[90] Socrates' questions and testing of his interlocutors' thoughts do "deprive" them, in Kierkegaard's term, of the received opinion and common knowledge which were imparted to them by their culture. Thus, it is fair to say that Socratic inquiry "creates" the alienated individual who is no longer capable of immediate experience or unexamined thought. It is the modern voice of Kierkegaard, however, who links these capabilities with "abandonment" and with irony. His accusation reverses Socrates' metaphor of maieutic parenting and replaces it with that of "abandonment," precisely the activity which Plato condemns. The missing portion of the portrait Kierkegaard gives us is the theme of a maieutic and life-long common life with others engaged in dialogue. In Kierkegaard and subsequent denouncers of philosophical abstraction, Socratic thought has been conceived in the modern setting of an isolated individual thinking alone. The setting, and not the way of thinking itself, constitutes alienation and abandonment. If we recall the recurrent criticism of eristic debate, negation, and monologue discourse which runs throughout the dialogues, we can see, I think, the very interesting borrowing of part but not all of Plato's Socrates in the proponents and opponents of modern irony.

Socrates explains how knowledge and understanding depend on the ability to see distinctions, opposites, and negations. The nature of truth becomes clearer when we examine the false. Even at the level of syntax and grammar, he shows, we make statements only be separating — knowing the difference between — one part of speech and another. His point, however, is that "weaving together" of forms into meaning relies on our ability to make distinctions. We make what we "know" an "other" at the moment that we begin to make propositions about it. We separate and divide in order to know, and in order to know we must recombine parts into discourse which means with and through others. For all his implicit superiority in asking hard questions, then, the Socrates of the dialogues does not play on his superiority. His refusal of his interlocutor's yearning for conclusions seems cruel, but it is crucially different from the *eiron's* pretended omniscience. The Socrates given us by Plato doesn't teach conclusions. Nor does he ultimately give the impression that he really knows. Instead, he teaches the methods of dialectical inquiry through dialogues which should be directed toward the discovery of truth while sustaining the belief that truth cannot be stated discursively.

Plato emphasizes the human context of dialectic when he calls it the art of true opinion. Knowledge is not simply a matter of logical consistency, or of testing propositions as an end in itself. Without an emphasis on knowledge as a process in which one person understands another person, dialectic can and did become an empty analytical method generating endless antinomies. Aristotle's creation of the syllogism out of the raw materials of dialogue dialectic which he shared with Plato guaranteed that logical analysis rather than dialogue would be the primary function of philosophical inquiry. For Plato, however, dialogue and dialectical testing were improved versions of rhetoric, and Socrates the "true philosopher" an improved version of the eristic dialectician. But in a parodic emulation of sophistic definition, Plato concludes the *Sophist* with a statement of the identity between sophist and philosopher:

> The imitative kind of the dissembling part of the art of opinion which is part of the art of contradiction and belongs to the fantasy class of the image-making art, and is not divine, but human, and has been defined in arguments as the juggling part of productive acticity — he who says that the sophist is of this descent and blood will, in my opinion, speak the exact truth.[91]

This parody of sophistic definition enacts the intensity of Plato's aversion to definition and logic chopping as ends in themselves. It is voiced by the Elean Stranger who has, throughout the *Sophist,* replaced Socrates, a hint perhaps that his is not an orthodox Socratic position. The Elean Stranger and Thaetetus have concluded their attempt to define the sophist, and here is the definition, more conclusive than most of the conclusions to the dialogues.

Both the parodic quality and the conclusive form of this passage hint at a subtle irony. The phrase "in my opinion," spoken by the Elean Stranger, evokes a parallelism with the opinion-mongering sophists, and at the same time conveys the Socratic message that philosophizing is the art of true opinion. Yet if this is "true" opinion, the Elean Stranger has committed the Socratic crime of dissembling by claiming to speak, as he says here, the "exact" truth. Anyone trying to say what is true will necessarily utter unexamined opinion in the attempt to get at the truth. But to state, "this is the exact truth" borders on dissembling because in the Socratic scheme of things no one can speak the exact truth. "The dissembling part of the art of opinion" and the "juggling part of productive activity" here define the false philosopher, the dissembling imitator of truth. The true philosopher, too, however, must be able to make distinctions, and to juggle seeming contradictions in order to generate productive discourse. A subtle pun, if we get it, demonstrates the identity of the sophist with the true philosopher in all but motive. "This, in my opinion, is the exact truth." Knowledge is always stated through an individual's incompletely verified opinion. The true philosopher here says "in my opinion" to communicate that what he says may or may not be "the exact truth." The sophist, on the other hand, would never say "in my opinion," for to do so would undermine his apparent authority.

Those of us who are proper Socratic dialecticians should be suspicious of these combinations. If we regard this subtle punning as a confidence game perpetrated by an arch-*eiron* we can very easily judge this true philosopher a sophist because he is saying what he doesn't mean: "I speak the exact truth." If we judge him a sophist in this articulation of his definition of the sophist, we have learned something which is based on our experience with the dialogues which have preceded this utterance: truth is always incompletely apprehended; knowledge is a slow, ongoing process which doesn't ever conclude. And if we detect that this passage violates the letter and the spirit of the dialogues which have preceded it, then a paradoxically maieutic relationship emerges among ourselves, the Elean Stranger, and the Platonic voice behind this dialogue. The motive behind the seeming motive of concluding has been to instruct, test, and ultimately further our understanding. In all of this double and triple *entendre* there is much teasing and much irony, as those terms are now understood. We now have the critical and interpretive equipment to appreciate that teasing and that irony in ways which, paradoxically, Plato would probably have disapproved of. We will never know what his true intention was because, as he says so recurrently, writings are like abandoned children who without their parent to come to their rescue, may be misunderstood.

Today, we do not, as Plato did, conflate interpretation and misunderstanding, because we understand interpretation as a benign necessity coextensive with textuality and monologue discourse, all those separations of the speaker from the hearer to which Plato objected. Because we live and interpret in contexts unknown by Plato, it is useful, I think, to observe what he warned against, and to test our assumptions against his provocative guesses about what would happen should rhetoric and textuality become pervasive discourse norms. While he was not successful in replacing rhetoric with a merger of dialogue and dialectic, Plato, I propose, successfully articulated the importance of the interdependent relationship between our understanding of a speaker's motives and our understanding of what is said. Moreover, I have argued, Plato was among the first to describe the way in which irony, understood as a rhetorical sensibility shared by speaker and listener allowing for the possibility of dissembling, undercuts meaning. Irony is an assumption about language and about human nature which functions as a perceptual context, a stance by which we "read" utterances and texts with an awareness of the possibility of duplicity. "Every latent double in the word" becomes dialectic—two words, two sides to an argument—and finally, the deliberate exploitation of duplicity. Plato leaves us with the opposing proposition, that every latent double in the word can be embodied in benign, maieutic dialogue.

NOTES

1. Throughout my discussion I will refer to "Plato" rather than "Socrates," because my focus is more on the systematic critical pattern which Plato evolves throughout the dialogues, a part of which is his characterization of Socrates. Thus, unless I am directly referring to something Socrates says I will speak of "Plato's argument," "Plato's thesis," etc. In addition, I wish to emphasize that the dialogues, including the portrait of Socrates they contain, are Plato's construction rather than an accurate transcript of Socrates.

2. Neither writing nor dissembling has been central to most of the scholarship on Plato and the sophists. The "logical fallacies" of the sophists, and their willingness to argue something they don't believe in, are close to dissembling, but these more familiar renderings of what it was that Plato objected to neglect, I would argue, the interesting parallels between Plato's depiction of sophistic dissembling and irony, understood as a sophisticated linguistic art and skill.

I am greatly indebted to Eric Havelock's *Preface to Plato* (New York: Grossett and Dunlap, 1963) for the suggestion that the sophists were, among other things, the first teachers of writing to the Greeks (pp. 292 and ff., p. 306, n.8.).

3. Plato, *Sophist,* trans. H. N. Fowler (Cambridge: Harvard University Press, 1977), 268b; alternate translations from John Warrington, trans., *Sophist,* in *Parmenides and Other Dialogues* (New York: Dutton/Everyman, 1969). The "later dialogues"—the *Philebus, Theaetetus, Sophist, Parmenides, Statesman, Timaeus,* and *Laws*—have traditionally been assumed to have been composed after Plato's second voyage to Syracuse, in 361. His dismay at Dion of Syracuse's banishment by Dionysus II, Plato's student, led him to avoid politics entirely in his later years, and is thought by many to be the source of the "cynicism" of the later dialogues. For an interesting alternative dating of the sequence and topics of the dialogues, see Gilbert Ryle, *Plato's Progress* (Cambridge: Harvard University Press, 1966), pp. 216-300.

4. Aristotle, *Rhetoric,* trans. J. R. Freese (Cambridge: Harvard Univ. Press, 1975), 1355b establishes that rhetoric, like dialectic, is of general application to a variety of subjects; that it is *useful;* that it is not so much "the art of persuasion" (the traditional sophistic definition) as it is a means of finding out in each case the available means of persuasion; that it is distinct from dialectic in that it discovers the real versus apparent means of persuasion whereas dialectic discovers the real versus apparent syllogism. Finally, he adds, what makes the sophist is "the moral purpose" rather than the ability to use rhetoric. While each of these definitions and divisions is intended to "answer" charges which Plato brought against rhetoric, each further extends the neutrality, utility, and manipulability of the "faculty" of rhetoric.

The Rhetor as *Eiron* 153

I have adapted the term "instrumentalist" from Hans Georg Gadamer, *Truth and Method* (New York: Seabury, 1975), who uses it to define an incorrect, because incomplete, model of language and its use: "an instrumentalist theory of signs that sees words and concepts as *handy tools* has missed the point of the hermeneutic phenomenon" (p. 364); "There is a development from the complete unconsciousness of language that we find in classical Greece to the instrumentalist devaluation of language that we find in modern times" (p. 365); and "It can be stated as a fundamental principle that wherever words assume a mere sign function, the original connection between speaking and thinking, with which we are concerned is changed into an instrumental relationship" (p. 392).

5. Plato, *Letter VII*, in *Phaedrus and Letters VII and VIII*, trans. Walter Hamilton (Harmondsworth, England: Penguin, 1973) 344a-d.

6. Wayne Booth, *A Rhetoric of Irony* (Chicago: Univ. of Chicago Press, 1974).

7. Plato, *Phaedrus*, 271b, 278a.

8. Aristotle, *Rhetoric*, 1355b and 1377b, at the beginnings of Book I and Book II, respectively. The introduction to Book III places yet another construction on the nature and purpose of rhetoric: "Since the whole business of Rhetoric is to influence opinion, we must pay attention to delivery, not as being right, but necessary" (1404a).

9. *Ibid.*, 1419b and 1420a, and *Nichomachean Ethics* 1124b, where Aristotle recommends freedom and candor in speaking to the virtuous man who ". . . is given to telling the truth except when he speaks in irony to the vulgar."

10. Aristotle, *On Interpretation*, trans. H. P. Cooke, H. Tredennick (Cambridge: Harvard Univ. Press, 1973), 17a.

11. Havelock, p. 163 n. 28, p. 306 n. 8.

12. For a useful analysis of the battle between the new and old education which takes up much of the *Clouds*, see William Arrowsmith, trans., *The Clouds* (New York: Mentor, 1962), pp. 135-58.

13. Havelock, pp. 50-52 n. 4.

14. *Ibid.*, pp. 40-41.

15. *Ibid.*, p. 40, p. 52 n. 6.

16. *Ibid.*, p. 39, p. 54 n. 10.

17. *Ibid.*, p. 55 n. 16.

18. It is noteworthy that Jacques Derrida, *Of Grammatology*, trans. Gayatri Chakrovorty Spivak (Baltimore: John Hopkins Univ. Press, 1974), mentions the association between writing and childishness which Plato draws even though Derrida's purpose is to demonstrate that Plato himself romanticizes the spoken word in a somewhat simplistic, if not childlike, manner. See pp. 50-52.

19. Plato, *Phaedrus*, 275a.

20. *Ibid.*

21. Plato, *Letter VII*, 344d.

22. Havelock, p. 127.

23. *Ibid.*, p. 56 n. 17.

24. To give only two examples, the priest Calchas figures prominently in the *Iliad*, the *Agamemnon*, and *Iphigenia at Aulis*, where his interpretations

of oracular and sacrificial auguries is roundly questioned, and directly associated with suspect verbal skill. Likewise, Oedipus' problematic status as a stranger and rescuer, but also a man who places his own wits ahead of traditional authorities, provides a classic case of the tension which is created in any culture when "intelligence" supplants "tradition" at the center of political power.

25. Aristotle, *Rhetoric,* 1404a, and 1404b: "We can now see that a writer must disguise his art and give the impression of speaking naturally and not artificially" (W. Rhys Roberts translation).

26. Plato, *Gorgias,* trans. W. C. Helmbold (New York: Library of Liberal Arts, 1952), 459a, and in the discussion which runs through 455a-456d.

27. Plato, *Phaedrus,* 272d.

28. Aristotle, *Rhetoric,* 1356b-1357a, 1401d-1403b.

29. Plato, *Sophist,* 268a.

30. Havelock, p. 251.

31. Plato, *Phaedrus,* 265d.

32. *Ibid.,* 266a.

33. Ryle, *Plato's Progress,* pp. 110-17.

34. Plato, *Gorgias,* 459a.

35. *Ibid.,* 459b, paralleled in Aristotle, *Rhetoric,* 1357a, where the audience of Rhetoric is defined as "... such hearers as are unable to take a general view of many stages, or to follow a lengthy chain of argument"—an audience characteristic which, Plato would argue, means that no intelligible discourse can take place. And, at *Rhetoric,* 1408b, as throughout Book III, Aristotle gives a number of suggestions for semblance, such as "... one ought not to make use of all kinds of correspondence together; for in this manner the hearer is deceived." Not surprisingly, Aristotle recommends "an ironic manner" like Gorgias' to the orator in the same passage.

36. Ryle, pp. 124-26, describes the replacement of debate by dialogue.

37. *Sophist,* 268a and ff. emphasizes moral censure with "dissembling."

38. G. G. Sedgewick, *Of Irony, Especially in Drama* (Toronto: Univ. of Toronto Press, 1948), pp. 11-18. D. C. Muecke, *Irony* (London: Methuen, 1970), p. 50.

39. Sedgewick, p. 50.

40. Deceit, and, implicitly, the contempt which deceit entails. Successful deceit, like the more subtle, or "unstable" forms of modern irony, depends on the speaker or writer correctly gauging the ability of the listener or reader. A failed deception reflects badly on its perpetrator, a successful one on its victim. For an analysis of literary irony which emphasizes the victimizing of the audience and the oral problems often ignored in that victimization, see John B. McKee, *Literary Irony and the Literary Audience* (Amsterdam: Rodopi, 1974).

41. Aristotle, *Rhetoric,* 1355a-b, 1377b.

42. Plato, *Gorgias,* 457a; *Phaedrus,* 271d; Aristotle, *Rhetoric* 1355b.

43. Cf. the root *rhema:* a speech or saying, that which is spoken; and Aristotle's influential divorce of rhetoric, as continuous, uninterrupted speech, from dialectic, a process of question and answer.

44. Aristotle, *On Interpretation,* 16b-17a.

45. Plato, *Letter VII,* 342-345. In this summary of the hierarchies of knowl-

edge, articulation, and understanding, Plato gives equal primacy to the objects of knowledge, the tools — both mental and linguistic — by which they are articulated, and the individual acts of understanding "in good faith and without malice" which comprise discourse.

46. *Ibid.,* 344b.
47. Plato, *Sophist,* 268a. This distinction between unintentional and intentional misrepresentation is paralleled in Augustine, *Enchiridion,* trans. Albert C. Outler (Philadelphia: Westminster Press, 1940) VI, 18: ". . . he is the better man who unknowingly speaks falsely, because he judges his statement to be true, than the one who unknowingly speaks the truth while in his heart he is attempting to deceive."
48. Plato, *Sophist,* 260b.
49. *Ibid.,* 260c.
50. *Ibid.,* 259 d–e.
51. *Ibid.,* 253e.
52. Booth, *A Rhetoric of Irony,* p. 44.
53. Plato, *Sophist,* 253e.
54. *Ibid.,* 254a (John Warrington, trans.).
55. Hayden White, *Metahistory* (Baltimore: Johns Hopkins University Press, 1973), p. 232.
56. Plato, *Sophist,* 259d.
57. Julia Kristeva, *Desire in Language* (New York: Columbia University Press, 1980), p. 109.
58. Plato, *Sophist,* 257c.
59. Kristeva, pp. 107–108.
60. Compare the two translations of the *Theaetetus'* introduction on which I base my remarks. Plato, *Theaitetos,* trans. John Warrington (New York: Dutton, 1969), 142b:

"Euclid: Here now is the book, Terpison. Notice the shape in which I have cast the dialogue. Instead of the narrative form used by Socrates when he told me about it, I have preferred *direct speech* as between him and his two interlocutors — Theodorus the geometer, and Theaitetos. I was anxious that my written account should not be cluttered up with *bits of narrative breaking in on the conversation.* You know, things like 'and I said,' or 'and I remarked' whenever Socrates referred to his own words, and 'he agreed,' or 'he would not agree' when it came to the reply. I therefore left out all such matter and *represented Socrates as talking with them in person*" (my italics).

And, Plato, *Theaetetus,* trans. Benjamin Jowett with introduction by Irving M. Copi (New York: Bobbs-Merrill, 1949), 143b:

"Euclid: Here is the roll, Terpison; I may observe that I have introduced Socrates not as narrating to me but *as actually conversing* with the persons whom he mentioned — these were Theodorus the geometrician (of Cyrene), and Theaetetus. I have omitted, *for the sake of convenience,* the interlocutory words 'I said,' 'I remarked,' which he used when he spoke of himself, and again, 'he agreed,' or 'disagreed,' in the answer, *lest the repetition of them* be troublesome" (my italics).

61. The issue of the relationship between words and their referents, as well

as the relationship between propositions and truth, is one of the more important issues which divides Plato's from Aristotle's analysis of discourse meaning. Where Plato said, in effect, "the sophistic models are wrong: we must change them before they gain more momentum;" Aristotle said, "the system is already well established; let us improve upon it." Unlike Plato, who resisted systematizing, and who repeatedly emphasized the incompleteness of the semiotic model of linguistic meaning, Aristotle built an entire system on the referential aspect of discourse. Where Plato utilizes *semenoi* (signs), *onomai* (names), and *eikonoi* (representations, images), to denote "words," Aristotle uses *onomai* almost exclusively, with full emphasis on the root *o nomos* (the custom, the law). Thus, Aristotle's emphasis, like the modern, is on conventional usage as the primary determinant of meaning.

62. Plato, *Phaedrus,* 265b.
63. Plato, *Apology,* 493e-494a.
64. Havelock, p. 261. See also pp. 270 and 304.
65. The sequence from observing conventions at work to describing them as having certain generic features to generalizing about "convention," was, I propose, slower and more painstaking than we might initially think. The gradual evolution of such a critique and subsequent concept is paralleled in the modern development of literary critical terms. For example, the novel came of age in the 19th century, but it was not until the 20th that an entire range of phenomena embodied in the novel were elaborated by literary critics. All of the nuances of reader-audience relationships, several different degrees of omniscience, the notion of an "implied" author emanating from the text itself, the epistemological dependence of the reader on the narrator — all of these very interesting incipient events-of-the-text emerged, like "convention" for the Greeks, only after a period of semi-consciousness of the phenomena involved, and after a series of unrelated individual attempts at articulating the experience of those phenomena.

66. Plato, *Letter VII,* 341.
67. Ryle, *Plato's Progress,* 125-26.
68. See Walter Ong, *Ramus: Method, and the Decay of Dialogue* (Cambridge: Harvard Univ. Press, 1958), and "From Mimesis to Irony: the Distancing of Voice" *Midwestern MLA Bulletin* IX:2 (1976) 1-24.
69. See Derrida, *Of Grammatology.* Derrida notes that Plato, like Levi Strauss, Rousseau and a host of others, posits the superiority of spoken discourse to text discourse on the grounds that it is more natural. That many have defended the premise that the letter kills is true; and Derrida gives an excellent account of the genealogy of this belief going back to Plato. However, I propose that it is incorrect to say that Plato prefers dialogue because it is spoken and thus more natural. As I have tried to suggest, dialogue as defined and practiced by Socrates was anything but natural; it was a difficult discipline which occasioned notable rebellions on the part of Socrates' interlocutors and Plato's students.

70. Few treatments of Plato treat his theory of language as anything other than primitive or obscurely metaphysical and polemical. Ong and Havelock,

despite their different purposes, come to remarkably similar conclusions regarding Plato's importance as a mediator between the poetic oral culture of pre-literate Greece and the logico-rhetorical culture initiated by Aristotle. Hans Georg Gadamer's *Truth and Method* demonstrates the importance of the *Cratylus, Parmenides, Theaetetus* and *Sophist* to subsequent semantic theory, and their role as precursors to modern semiotic explorations of the nature of the sign. While I am focusing on Plato's analysis of rhetoric and dialetic in the *Phaedrus, Gorgias, Theaetetus* and *Sophist,* I should note that the additional dialogues mentioned above are important and underrated explorations of many linguistic and logical problems which have been revived in recent critical theory.

71. Ryle, *Plato's Progress,* p. 293.

72. The debate about the importance of intent to meaning has been revived in two recent critical debates, one concerning Heideggerean hermeneutics and its limitations in historicity and intersubjectivity, the other in the emergence of speech-act theory, which proposes that the meaning of an utterance must be determined in part by the intent of the speaker and the tacit assumptions which that intent activates in the hearer. Hans Georg Gadamer and Paul Ricoeur provide useful retrospectives on Plato as they engage in slightly different proposals for finding a way out of the Heideggerean hermeneutic circle. While both these recent debates are interesting revivals of some of Plato's questions about intention, it is worth noting that they do not focus on the explicitly interpersonal, ethical aspects of intention used and abused which Plato's regards as central to the problem of discourse meaning and production.

73. Plato, *Gorgias,* 487a.

74. Plato, *Phaedrus,* 278.

75. Paul Ricoeur, *Interpretation Theory: Discourse, and the Surplus of Meaning* (Ft. Worth: TCU Press, 1976), p. 32, makes the *a propos* observation that "Hermeneutics begins where dialogue ends." He argues that the need for interpretation emerges only when the immediate presence of speaker and hearer is broken by the conventions of formalized discourse types such as rhetoric and poetry. Unlike Plato, however, Ricoeur sees the need for interpretation as a liberation from the restrictions imposed by face-to-face dialogue.

76. Plato, *Letter VII,* 341.

77. *Ibid.*

78. *Ibid.,* 345b.

79. Plato, *Theaetetus,* 149.

80. *Ibid.,* 150.

81. *Ibid.,* 150 and ff.

82. Plato, *Sophist,* 259d.

83. *Ibid.,* 262d.

84. *Ibid.,* 261d.

85. *Ibid.,* 259e.

86. *Ibid.,* 259e.

87. *Ibid.,* 237a.

88. Wallace Stevens, "Notes Toward a Supreme Fiction," *Collected Poems of Wallace Stevens* (New York: Knopf, 1972), pp. 380–408, p. 387.

89. Soren Kierkegaard, *The Concept of Irony* (New York: Harper and Row, 1966), pp. 202-03.
90. Plato, *Sophist,* 257c.
91. *Ibid.,* 268d.

Afterplay: A Fore Letter Word

The years spanning the completion of "The Rhetor as *Eiron*" and the present volume have been the first ten years of my son's life, a context that has encouraged in many ways the interest in paideia, nurture, and discourse training that occupied some of my attention in dealing with Plato's delineations of dialogue. We learn by doing to have conversations, to use dialogue in different ways, to fight for keeps and *per bellum purificandum,* to use agon dialogically and dialogue agonistically. These have also been years spent at two different universities, taken up with the completion, revision, and polishing of the inevitably rushed tenure books. I remain eternally grateful to the two editors involved, not just for their patience, but for encouraging the time taken in revision and polishing because they, like the rest of us, dislike a system that encourages mass-produced, redundant tangled messes, a kind of fast food approach to thought and publication. This has been a decade of manifold changes in the media, languages, and objectives of scholarship; and an era of particularly rapid growth and diversification in the field of rhetorical criticism and theory. *PRE/TEXT* has fostered that growth, spawned wars as well as debates, and performed the always thankless role of court gadfly—in several different courts. Victor Vitanza should be credited with sheer endurance as well as for his more obvious perspicuities—and perversities—of thought. My reflections on "The Rhetor as *Eiron,*" ten years later, will be set in all of these contexts and will enact some of the meanings of the title as well. Like Heraclitus' always-turning universe in which the road up and the road down are eternally the same road, the *palintropos harmonia* of rhetor and *eiron* eternally suggests that she who would speak must speak (*eiro*) irenically at times, eristically at others, elenchically with some opponents, maieutically with the young and tender hearted, and inescapably with the irony of those who believe in the incompleteness and incommunicability of thought that relentlessly necessitates dialogue. The concluding sentence of "The Rhetor as *Eiron,*" complete with the inevitable illumination of an uncaught typo ("maietic"), defends as Plato's effort the attempt to represent and defend rhetoric as a truth-seeking enterprise, as benign, maieutic dialogue.

I continue to defend a reading of Plato shaped by the contemporary revival of dialogical hermeneutics, a body of work in which Bakhtin, Gadamer, and Ricoeur have been special touchstones and guides. To read Plato's works on rhetoric, the rhetor, and the sophist through these lenses is even more important to me now than it was ten years ago because of the various caricatures and cartoons of Plato that have been advanced within deconstructologos and among related postmodern critiques of idealism. In 1986, I was delighted to catch on tape and incorporate into the *PRE/TEXT* Literacy/Orality issue Eric Havelock's observation that many modern views of Plato's "idealism" are in fact rooted in nineteenth-century neo-Kantian German idealism, the kind of highly abstracted conceptualism that informs Liddell and Scott's Greek-English lexicon. Many modern critiques of Plato and of his idealism should be re-viewed, and perhaps re-cast, as attacks on German idealism and Cambridge Platonism around the turn of the century. I find among recent neo-Nietzscheisms a tacit and perhaps unconscious awareness of the very recent origin of this "Plato" who is the object of ritual rebuke.

The fin-de-siècle era and its fascination—both pro and con— universals and idealisms—is of renewed interest just now for other reasons as well. In it can be found some of the roots of those "essentialist" ideas as well as of the attentions they now receive from various quarters. The memory has faded all too quickly of the idealisms and essentialisms of race, class, and color that in the teens and twenties provoked race riots when Southern African-Americans moved into Northern cities; when Eastern Europeans emigrated in large numbers; when quotas limiting the numbers of Jews admitted to colleges and universities were introduced without apology or disguise. Even feminists like Charlotte Perkins Gilman, and other "liberal" thinkers, could in that era be found espousing views that today would be seen as despicably anti-semitic.

Only slightly later, Bakhtin and other soviet "formalists" inaugurated the Eastern European version of what would, later and further west, come to be termed structuralism. Formalism's initial effort was to free literary aesthetics from race and class biases—from the classicism that frustrated dialogue because it would not listen or talk to things spoken in a different voice. This understanding of dialogical polyvocality and hermeneutics bears repeating at the end of a decade in which Plato has been so routinely associated with fascist idealism and his concept of dialogue convicted of guilt by association. Along with Gadamer and Ricoeur, Bakhtin has provided a trifocal approach to reading Plato's dialogics, a polyvocality of hermeneutic screens, as it were, that has facilitated a synthesis of that reading with a similarly polyherm history of rhetoric. Plato's dialogics is central to Bakhtin's and Gadamer's thinking, but in different ways. Each reads Plato's concept and practice of dialogue in different ratios to his uses of dialectic, on the one hand, and to his critiques of writing and of rhetoric on the other. Within Bakhtin's early work, represented best in my view by *Dostoevsky's Poetics,* there is a focus on defining a phenomenology of meaning that can be linked to the development of soul, self, and spirit. Prompted perhaps by a discomfort with the developmental, edifying, hierarchical, and aristocratic aesthetics, poetics, and epistemology implicit in the *bildungsroman* paradigm, this emphasis is gradually supplanted by an attention to contemporary language as already spoken that we find in *Speech Genres.* Like contemporary critiques of the expressive self as reactionary, as retrograde romanticism, or as advancing Cartesianism, Bakhtin's later work adopts the spare lines of aphoristic conjecture, a mode that resembles the late Wittgenstein and the early Heidegger. Though polyvocal, this is not a particularly dialogical mode. Instead, it resembles the mantic pronouncement of oracles who seek to stimulate thought in silent — or empty — mental spaces.

Dialogue and dialectic continue to receive extended and renewed attention, appraisal, redefinition, and realignment. The retrieval of Plato's concept of dialogue has been rebuked on several grounds: that it assumes or promotes conceptions of self, knowledge, and truth that are "Cartesian," masculinist, idealist, or all three. The characterization of Plato's dialogue that I advanced in "The Rhetor as *Eiron*" emphasized a dual — simultaneously ethical and epistemological — goal of dialogue as knowledge-seeking and meaning-making among equals, as an ongoing process rather than as the attainment or capturing of truth. This characterization is no more an appropriative imposition of modern views than the Rambo notion of Plato as a fascist idealist. Both are possible readings; each can be done well, or poorly, prompting the dialogical question of where we get our criteria of "well" or "poorly." Richard Rorty, Stanley Rosen, and Martha Nussbaum have encouraged reappraisals of the dialogues as dialogues, a seemingly obvious undertaking but one that has not been fostered by analytic philosophy. In a different quarter, the burgeoning revival of social-constructionist notions of identity, meaning, and discourse has redirected attention to collective and collaborative processes of knowing that have during the past decade-plus also been promoted within composition pedagogy and theory. Among the many nostalgias for the sixties that shape contemporary academia this one is particularly appealing for me for it hearkens back to undergraduate phenomenology classes where Berger and Luckmann's *The Social Construction of Reality,* and journals, not essays, about same, were all the rage.

Is the knowing subject, the self implicit in Plato's representation of dialogical exchange, drawing on and referring to a collective set of meanings, understandings, and truths? Are these truths outside of the individuals who "seek" them or are they, as in Descartes' radical mentalism, the entities that Kant would call "noumena?" Since these questions are themselves subjects of discussions in several dialogues, the process of asking where "Plato" stands on any one issue necessarily involves us as interlocutors in the dialogues by way of observing his construction of the dialogue. It was this stance that, in his later work, Bakhtin came to call "thirdness." The observation of dialogue is not participation in a dialogue, necessarily. However, I will persist in insisting that the structure and ambiguities of meaning in Plato's dialogues do an awfully good job, as does post-romantic literary irony, of forcing the involvement of the reader in making, or completing—depending on your textual politics—the meaning of a text. In this sense, end-stop deconstruction and some versions of reading theory resemble conservative paradigms of validity in interpretation, for both narrowly prescribe what can and can't and should and shouldn't be done. Radical reader-centered reading theory produces little more than tales of how I couldn't read this text, narratives of the impossibility of reading. This, too, is nondialogical.

The affinities of dialogical hermeneutics with recent developments in composition theory and pedagogy remain central to my interests, encouraged by the need to sustain ties among composition theory and teaching, rhetorical theory and criticism, and literary studies. We all deal with texts. We all produce as well as interpret texts. We all convey to students understandings of what a text is, what their writing is, and thereby of who they are, understandings and practices that they will take with them into their futures. Our theories of reading, as Edward White has put it, inevitably affect our theories of writing. The way we teach writing influences how students come to conceptualize themselves and is the first time many students have encountered the process of conceptualizing themselves. The meaning of meaning and how to read a page were of interest in the newly democratized university classrooms of the twenties and thirties. The forms and objectives of basic writing similarly received painful but productive scrutiny in the wake of open admissions in the sixties. Culture, class, ethnicity, and gender are today's battlefields, as witnessed by the recent debates over cultural diversity and curriculum at Stanford and the University of Texas at Austin. All of these events and issues suggest to me an urgent need to keep talking about how theories of reading affect theories of writing, and about how the hermeneutics of text and of self are mutually defining and irreducibly dialogical.

Per oratio, I'll divest myself of a few gripes and conclude with a few words of thanks. *Oremus.* Lead us not into sticking labels all over one another lest we fall into the grave error of taxonomania. In the past decade I have been taxonomized and classified a bit more than is comfortable, particularly for someone who is trying to lose weight. It is peculiar to have people at conferences and students in classes remark, as if this were in the *Encyclopedia Britannica,* "well, since you're a neo-Platonist you think . . ." Or, "you're going to disagree with this, since you're a positivist historian." However, having just delivered myself of the categories neo-Nietzschean and deconstructologos, I will appeal to the dialogical concept that categories, if used and understood heuristically and not literally, can help us when crossing the street. This I believe is what Plato meant when he said that discourse can't just name things; it has to get us somewhere by naming.

Lead us not into the temptation of self-righteousness, a temptation, it will surprise no one to learn, to which I am particularly prone. Righteousness is fine in small measure, but it is far too easy to confuse one's temper with moral justice. Or, as Joan Baez sings, self-parodically:

> May you grow up to be righteous [but not too]
> May you grow up to be true
> May you always do for others
> What you'd have them do for you.

But then there's the abandonment of all value, too, on the grounds that any value is politically and ideologically incorrect. Somewhere between overqualified scepticism to the point of silence and barbaric self-importance perhaps we can create a few new spaces for talk, as opposed to lines drawn in the sand, standoffs, shoot-outs, and the other martial metaphors that in this era of desert storms and canon blasting we can hardly encourage.

Coda. Thanks to Victor for running the show, keeping it up, and getting the ball rolling. Thanks to Sharon Crowley for eloquence, good spirits, and new rhetorical tropes; I especially like *refusio,* and "in your face." Thanks to the Poulakoi for introducing new discourses and new issues. Thanks to Louise Wetherbee Phelps for recurring Ricoeur. Thanks to all the beloved adversaries and beloved infidels who keep this curious crossroads puzzling along.

6 : THOMAS DE QUINCEY IN A REVISIONIST HISTORY OF RHETORIC

William Covino
San Diego State University

The rhetorician's art in its glory and power has silently faded away before the stern tendencies of the age; and, if, by any peculiarity of taste or strong determination of the intellect, a rhetorician *en grande costume* were again to appear amongst us, it is certain that he would have no better welcome than a stare of surprise as a posturemaker or balancer, not more elevated in the general estimate, but far less amusing, than the acrobat, or funambulist, or equestrian gymnast. No; the age of Rhetoric, like that of Chivalry, has passed among forgotten things.

—Thomas De Quincey, "Rhetoric," 1828[1]

For De Quincey, rhetoric is the art of wondering: "to hang upon one's own thoughts as an object of conscious interest, to play with them, to watch and pursue them through a maze of inversions, evolutions, and harlequin changes" (p. 97). Such wondering finds an audience among those willing to share the freeplay of the mind that the rhetor exploits. But De Quincey holds little hope that the promise of excursive, speculative discourse will lure anyone away from the instant pleasure of "daily novelties" and the urgency of "public business": "So multiplied are the modes of intellectual enjoyment in modern times that the choice is absolutely distracted; and in a boundless theatre of pleasure, to be had at little or no cost of intellectual activity, it would be marvellous indeed if any considerable audience could be found for an exhibition which presupposes a state of tense exertion on the part of both auditor and performer" (p. 97).

De Quincey's appreciation for "a state of tense exertion" in reading and writing resonates against the most popular contemporary advice, from Hugh Blair's *Lectures on Rhetoric and Belles Lettres:*

We are pleased with an author, we consider him as deserving praise, who frees us from all fatigue of searching for his meaning; who carries us through his subject without embarassment or confusion; whose style flows always like a limpid stream, where we see to the very bottom.[2]

For De Quincey, the "elegant but desultory" Blair represents the "mechanic system," rhetoric reduced to perspicuity and ornament, rhetoric which panders to a society that aggrandizes communicative efficiency, that dismisses the language of patient exploration and speculation as wasteful, "as pure foppery and trifling with time" (pp. 100, 192-93).

De Quincey's rhetorical theory deserves close attention because it addresses the differences between thoughtless, instant communication and speculative imagination, and warns us about the social and cultural mediocrity that results when the preferred style represents efficiency more than strength of mind. Furthermore, he represents a conception of rhetoric largely ignored in the rhetorical tradition, but pertinent to modern rhetoric and its intensified questioning of those norms, conventions, and pragmatics which restrict the play of discourse. Traditional rhetoric consistently stresses the importance of moving an audience toward resolution or conviction, and associates rhetorical effectiveness with the establishment of some "truth": the spiritual truth of Platonic and Augustinian rhetoric, the probable truth of Aristotelian and Ciceronian rhetoric, the empirical truth idolized by London's Royal Society and holding sway from the seventeenth century onward. Over the last fifteen years, a new "New Rhetoric" (counterpart to the new "New Criticism") has seemed to emerge, with its emphasis on the invention of multiple perspectives, the illusiveness of truth, and resistance to certainty and closure; Jacques Derrida, Hayden White, Clifford Geertz, Paul Feyerabend, Richard Rorty, and others of the academic *avant-garde* insist that although language offers the resources for inventory, it is always a "strategy without finality,"[3] and they reinforce Kenneth Burke's longstanding position that the main ideal of rhetoric is "to use all that is there to use."[4]

New appreciation of the human capacity for intellectual freeplay calls the received tradition into question. As an art which promotes wondering rather than conviction, modern rhetoric must write a new history for itself; this history enters into dialogue with the classical canon, speaking with another voice about the aims of discourse. De Quincey numbers among the heroes in such a history, and I will briefly nominate some others at the conclusion of this essay. An early estimate of De Quincey's contribution to rhetoric was voiced by David Masson in his 1890 comment on De Quincey's 1828 essay, "Rhetoric": "Indeed, from the point of view of previous tradition respecting the business of Rhetoric, the title of the paper is to a considerable extent a misnomer."[5] Scarcely a handful of essays over the last sixty years oppose Masson's assessment by trying to legitimize De Quincey's work as a rhetorical theory.[6] Only Paul Talley's 1965 piece and Marie Secor's more recent summary of De Quincey's theory of style acknowledge his special affinity with modern conceptions of rhetoric. The lack of critical appreciation for De Quincey's rhetorical theory attests to the power of traditional definitions to delimit importance, and sustains Masson's remark as the prevailing view. Rene Wellek offers a strong and influential voice against the practice of redefining established terms when he declares that De Quincey's "Rhetoric" has merely "wrenched an acceptable term into a new meaning."[7]

Along with an adherence to tradition goes the suspicion of intellectual play whose end seems to be personal pleasure and novelty only, a suspicion lurking behind the remarks of Masson and Wellek. De Quincey invites this suspicion with his characterization of rhetoric as play with one's own thoughts, and especially when he writes elsewhere that "to think reasonably upon any question has never been allowed by me as a sufficient ground for writing upon it, unless I believed myself able to offer some considerable novelty" (*Collected Writings* IV, 2). Stressing the word "offer" in this remark, I think we have the key to De Quincey's importance. Whatever novelty he achieves stands as an offer that reaches outside the rhetor's fanciful mind and aims at social consequences, the activity of novelty within a community of rhetors who are also citizens and friends. Creating such a community means eschewing definitions and concepts which compartmentalize thought and isolate individuals one from another.

De Quincey's rhetorical theory emerges from four essays on language: "Rhetoric" (1828), "Style" (1840-41), "Language" (date unknown), and "Conversation" (1847).[8] He begins "Rhetoric" by rejecting popular definitions:

> Here then we have in popular use two separate ideas of rhetoric: one of which is occupied with the general end of the fine arts—that is to say, intellectual pleasure; the other applies itself more specifically to a definite purpose of utility, viz. fraud. (p. 82)

In one view, rhetoric is the art of ornament; in the other, the art of persuasion. Rhetoric as ornament stresses the *manner* of presentation; rhetoric as persuasion stresses the *matter,* the content of arguments devised "to dash maturest counsels and to make the worse appear the better reason." Setting aside for a time De Quincey's emphasis on the dishonesty attendant to persuasion, we might summarize his distinction in classical terms by labelling the rhetoric of ornament as style and the rhetoric of persuasion as invention.

De Quincey rejects these two views of rhetoric and offers a third "which excludes both." However, he does not really exclude both views; rather, he rejects their designation as *separate* processes, arguing throughout his essays on language that manner and matter, style and invention, become one in the act of a "moving intellect." One of his most explicit arguments against the division of style from invention comes in the essay on "Language":

> Now, these offices of style are really not essentially below the level of those offices attached to the original *discovery* of truth . . . Light to *see* the road, power to *advance along* it — such being amongst the promises and proper functions of style, it is a capital error, under the idea of ministeriality, to undervalue this great organ of the advancing intellect . . . The vice of that appreciation which we English apply to style lies in representing it as a mere ornamental accident of written composition — a trivial embellishment, like the mouldings of furniture, the cornices of ceilings, or the arabesques of tea urns. (p. 261)

Agreeing with Wordsworth that style is the *incarnation* rather than the "dress" of thoughts, De Quincey criticizes the British tendency to "set the matter above the manner"; this "gross mechanical separation" sterilizes both matter and manner, and severely limits one's ability to voice more than "external facts, tangible realities, and circumstantial details" (p. 227), predetermined data extraneous to the resources of the intellect. Without the inclination or ability to at once invent and compose thought, "an orator cannot think on his feet, and a writer cannot move beyond the facile and commonplace; he cannot modulate out of one key into the other" (p. 229). One who recognizes that the manner of composition *creates* matter is more able to keep thinking, talking, speculating; and that recognition coincides with tapping one's subjective sensibilities; calling forth the "internal and individual." Only to the degree that one allows subjectivity its exercise, "does the style or the embodying of the thoughts cease to be a mere separable ornament" and take on the quality of the moving intellect (p. 229). Rhetoric consists of style which exhibits the confluence of manner and matter as it plays through the possibilities for exploring a subject; De Quincey recognizes that *conviction* is anathema to restless, shifting queries: "Where conviction begins, the field of Rhetoric ends" (p. 82).

Rhetoric's energy is "elliptical," illustrating the rhetor's own labyrinthine movement of mind, and significantly, the polymorphous shape of reflective and fanciful discourse corresponds to the act of reasoning: "All reasoning is carried on discursively; that is, *discurrendo* — by running about to the right and the left, laying the separate notices together, and thence mediately deriving some third apprehension" (p. 103). The dialectical pattern of the rhetor does not conform to the neat lines of a thesis–antithesis–synthesis, much less the linear march through a causal chain, but instead derives new conclusions from the activity of "running about." This mode suits not only the variegated play of subjectivity informing the manner of rhetoric, but also the indeterminate questions which comprise the matter: "Whatsoever is certain, or matter of fixed science, can be no subject of the rhetorician: where it is possible for the understanding to be convinced, no field is open for rhetorical persuasion" (pp. 90–91). Leaving aside the question whether "certainty" or "fixed science" can hold any stability at all against the energy of the intellect, we can still say that matters are *un*fixed, and "with the chance of right and wrong, true and false, distributed in varying proportions between them" supply the rhetor with a range of possibilities so necessary to his art.

De Quincey mentions his affinity with Aristotle as he acknowledges the power of rhetoric for developing a probable truth, and admits that rhetorical expression can involve stressing only one side of an issue, and "withdrawing the mind so steadily from all thoughts or images which support the other as to leave it practically under the possession of a one-sided estimate" (p. 91). With intellectual dexterity, the rhetor may so fully exploit his bias that a "mob" of auditors is razzle-dazzled into his camp: "Like boys who are throwing the sun's rays into the eyes of a mob by means of a mirror, you must shift your lights and vibrate your reflections at every possible angle, if you would agitate the popular mind extensively" (p. 139). This statement both acknowledges the stubborn fixity of the popular mind, and suggests the licentious potential of rhetorical skill; in view of this potential De Quincey offers the curious remark that a licentious technique should be viewed as the "just style in respect of those licentious circumstances," suggesting that the dull-witted authors deserve what they get (p. 140).

However, the invention of a richly supported bias is only a portion of the rhetorical process, whose most full expression demonstrates a habit of analogical thinking which does not limit the scope of the understanding. Edmund Burke stands as De Quincey's hero in this regard:

> All hail to Edmund Burke, the supreme writer of his century, the man of the largest and finest understanding . . . His great and peculiar distinction was that he viewed all objects of the understanding under more relations than other men, and under more complex relations. According to the multiplicity of these relations, a man is said to have a *large* understanding; according to their subtlety, a *fine* one; and in an angelic understanding all things would appear to be related to all. (p. 115)

The supreme composition spirals outward with "progress and motion, everlasting motion," generated by the rhetor "morbidly impatient of tautology" (p. 129). And rhetoric fully exercised does not encourage blind adherence, but rather, full participation in the art of wondering, that "state of tense exertion on the part of both auditor and performer."

De Quincey distinguishes oratory from writing enough to suggest the ways in which the prevalent style of the former taints that of the latter, and lessens popular appreciation for the complexity of prose rhetoric: *"The modes of style appropriate to popular eloquence being essentially different from those of written composition,* any possible experience on the hustings, or in the senate, would *pro tanto* tend rather to disqualify the mind for appreciating the more chaste and more elaborate qualities of style fitted for books" (p. 141). The practice of setting the "matter above the manner," using style to merely ornament content, prevails in oratory partly because of the "licentious" designs of some orators, but also because the auditors cannot take advantage of "re-reading" an oration:

> It is the advantage of a book that you can return to the last page if anything in the present depends on it. But, return being impossible in the case of a spoken harangue, where each sentence perishes as it is born, both the speaker and the hearer become aware of a mutual interest in a much looser style, and a personal dispensation from the severities of abstract discussion. (p. 140)

That looser style is repetitious rather than generative; the orator re-presents the same proposition through "running variations," in order "to mask, by slight differences in the manner, a virtual identity in the substance" (p. 140). And so audiences become conditioned to extract a simple "message," reinforced through repetition, rather than to share a more wide-ranging, less contrived exploration. Thus conditioned, readers approach books as they do speeches, satisfied to apprehend a single thesis echoed through various stylistic devices.

Along with the influence of popular eloquence, the "necessities of public business" contribute to the foreclosure of contemplation, and the surrender to facts and maxims. De Quincey laments the contemporary reduction in philosophical scope that results while each individual struggles with the "agitations of eternal change" which intensify as society becomes more complex. In modern life, the consideration of indeterminate questions disappears, and the urgency of "determinate questions of everyday life" takes over:

> Suppose yourself an Ancient Athenian at some customary display of Athenian oratory, what will be the topic? Peace or war, vengeance for

public wrongs, or mercy to prostrate submission, national honour and national gratitude, glory and shame, and every aspect of open appeal to the primal sensibilities of man. On the other hand, enter an English Parliament, having the most of a popular character in its constitution and practice that is anywhere to be found in the Christendom of this day, and the subject of debate will probably be a road bill, a bill for enabling a coal-gas company to assume certain privileges against a competitor in oil-gas, a bill for disfranchising a corrupt borough, or perhaps some technical point of form in the Exchequer Bills bill. So much is the face of public business vulgarized by details. (p. 98)

As science, business, and politics enlarge and aggrandize the objective and concrete, one's interest is considering and questioning more abstract, basic issues and assumptions weakens, "because the rights and wrongs of the case are almost inevitably absorbed to an unlearned eye by the technicalities of the law, or by the intricacy of the fact" (p. 99). The intellect required to engage in rhetoric *en grande costume* languishes on a diet of facts and maxims:

"Rhetoric prospered most at a time when science was unborn as a popular interest, and the commercial activities of aftertimes were not sleeping in their rudiments." (p. 100)

In an age obsessed with data extraneous to the "subjective exercises of the mind," rhetorical freeplay is not an exigency, and neither is the "conscious valuation of style" characteristic of a rhetor focussed upon the manner in which his prose gives "evanescent, external projection to what is internal, outline to what is fluxionary, and body to what is vague"; lack of concern for the personal import and creative life of language leaves style aside, and demonstrates the writer's belief that "the matter tells without any manner at all" (pp. 226–7). And so the popular prose of the age, written by and for the shareholders of public business, reveals scant attention to craft:

Whatever words tumble out under the blindest accidents of the moment, these are the words retained; whatever sweep is impressed by chance upon the motion of a period, that is the arrangement ratified. (p. 142)

Faced with the bulky periodic *surplusage* of careless writers, "every man who puts a business value on his time slips naturally into a trick of shorthand reading." And so a nation of turgid writers has its readers skimming; "an evil of modern growth is met by a modern remedy" (p. 162).

Prose aspiring to the finest abilities of human discourse bodies forth not a stuffing of thoughtless facts, but the human energy of engagement with an open question, energy seeking a community of intellectual exchange. The model for this searching language, this rhetoric, is conversation. De Quincey's interest in conversation extends throughout the essays on language, and the properties of the best conversation are identical to the properties of the best rhetoric. Citing the British tendency, in speaking and writing, to remain self-absorbed, "tumid and tumultuary," in- flexible, De Quincey, proposes that the more lively prose to France results "from the intense adaptation of the national mind of real colloquial intercourse." The French prize the rapid exchange of views, so that each statement in a conversation remains "brief, terse, simple," always open to reciprocation:

> It passes by necessity to and from, backwards and forwards . . . the momentary subject of interest never *can* settle or linger for any length of time in any one individual without violating the rules of the sport, or suspending its movement. Inevitably, therefore, the structure of sentence must for ever be adapted to this primary function of the French national intellect, the function of communicativeness, and to the necessities . . . of interminable garrulity. (pp. 150-57)

The individual sentences of colloquial intercourse stay short and simple, but interplay among sentences forms the conversation at large, and we might characterize this larger discourse as a continual sentence of growing, changing theses, couched in the rhythm of the communal mind. The interminable garrulity of "flux and reflux, swell and cadence" models the intellectual play of a discourse resisting closure. So conversation and prose rhetoric share common virtues, as we must conclude when De Quincey exalts Edmund Burke's conversational ability for the same reason that he names Burke a representative master of rhetoric:

> One remarkable evidence of a *specific* power lying hid in conversation may be seen in such writings as have moved by impulses most nearly resembling those of conversation—for instance, in those of Edmund Burke—such was the prodigious elasticity of his thinking, equally in his conversation and in his writings, the mere act of movement became the principle or cause of movement. Motion propagated motion, and life threw off life. (pp. 269-70)

Associational fluency powers conversation, a fluency uncommon to the "bookish" idiom infecting De Quincey's Britain, but not to rhetoric *en grande costume*.

Discourse that embodies intensity and play arises from a positive liking for human diversity, and faith in the essentially constructive nature of novel possibilities. De Quincey calls Samuel Johnson a defentive conversationalist and rhetor, who shuns wondering and speculation for one reason:

> Because he had little interest in man. Having no sympathy with human nature in its struggles, or faith in the progress of man, he could not be supposed to regard with much interest any forerunning symptoms of changes that to him were themselves indifferent. (p. 273)

In De Quincey's view, the "desponding taint" in Johnson's blood renders him incapable of "the positive and creative," and limits him to inflexible, monotonous pronouncements. Apart from the question whether Johnson deserves such criticisms, and Burke such praise, the idea remains that creative power requires a positive interest in the human condition: "From the heart, from an interest of love or hatred, of hope or care, springs all permanent eloquence" (p. 273).

Insulation from a diversity of language and thought blinds a culture to its own disclosure, and informs the kind of selfabsorption that feeds indifference. De Quincey recognizes that modern rhetoricians might call entrapment in one's own "observation language": "The eye cannot see itself; we cannot project from ourselves, and contemplate as an object, our own contemplating faculty, or appreciate our own appreciating power" (p. 153). And in the face of this problem, changes in the popular conception and practice of rhetoric are not likely. A people immersed in language which dulls rather than refreshes thought, cannot see the limitation of their style, because the usual way of seeing is itself that style, with its attendant deficiencies and manipulative power: "Easily, therefore, it may have happened that, under the constant action and practical effects of a style, a nation may have failed to notice the cause (style itself) as the cause" (p. 139). Style creates and restricts content, and so does *expertise,* because it enfranchises privileged and exclusive viewpoints; De Quincey develops this idea in "A Brief Appraisal of Greek Literature in Its Foremost Pretentions," where he attacks the Greek Scholar who puts "a preposterous value upon the knowledge":

> So it will always be. Those who ... possess no accomplishment *but* Greek will, of necessity, set a superhuman value upon that literature in all its parts to which their own narrow skill becomes an available key ... It is the habit (well known to psychologists) of transferring of anything created by our own skill, or which reflects our own skill, as if it lay causatively and objectively in the reflecting thing itself, that

pleasurable power which in very truth belongs subjectively to the mind of him who surveys it, from conscious success in the exercise of his own energies. (pp. 292-93)

Coincident with the proposal that rhetoric consists of a subjective play that challenges established priorities and received modes of expression, De Quincey reiterates the necessity for exploding the conventions of manner and matter while he admits our inescapable dependence upon them.

Rhetoric maintains a tension between convention and invention, mechanic and organic, closure and wonder, and one becomes a rhetorical animal through involvement in the process of intellectual play. Following De Quincey through the "evolutions, inversions, and harlequin changes" of his own prose, we engage in the very rhetoric he conceives. In the essay on "Style," De Quincey continually reminds us that he is exploiting both the desire of readers for perspicuous prose, and the capacity of both writers and readers for sustaining the exploration of a subject:

> Reader, you are beginning to suspect us. "How long do we purpose to detain people?" . . . "And *whither* are we going? towards what object?"—which is as urgent a query as *how far* . . . You feel symptoms of doubt and restiveness . . . unless we explain what it is that we are in quest of.
>
> We shall endeavor to bring up our reader to the fence, and persuade him, if possible, to take the leap. . . . But as we have reason to believe that he will "refuse" it, we shall wheel him round and bring him up to it from another quarter. (pp. 190-191)

This essay and others move through contemporary anecdotes, historical surveys, stylistic analyses and critiques, and addresses to the reader largely through apparent digression, through a wandering away from the subject which might be termed more properly a *wandering into* the subject, given the idea of rhetoric that motivates the prose.

And in the individual sentences, this same presentation of a subjective mind in process contributes to our amazed sense of the number and complexity of perspectives the rhetor may compose. Consider, for example, this description of Herodotus about to speak to the Greeks of his extensive foreign travels and of the war with Persia; for De Quincey, Herodotus epitomizes two characters, a great explorer and a "patriotic historian":

> Now, if we consider how rare was either character in ancient times, how difficult it was to travel where no passport made it safe, where no preparations in roads, inns, carriages made it convenient; that even five centuries in advance of this era, little knowledge was generally circulated

of any region unless so far it had been traversed by the Roman legions; considering the vast credulity of the audience assembled, a gulf capable of swallowing mountains, and, on the other hand, that here was a man fresh from the Pyramids and the Nile, from Tyre, from Babylon and the temple of Belus, a traveller who had gone in with his sickle to a harvest yet untouched; that this same man, considered as a historian, spoke of a struggle with which the earth still agitated; that the people who had triumphed so memorably in this war happened to be the same people who were then listening; that the leaders in this glorious war, whose names had already passed into spiritual powers, were the fathers of the present audience; combining into one picture all these circumstances, one must admit that no such meeting between giddy expectation and the very excess of power to meet its most clamorous calls is likely to have occurred before or since upon this earth. (p. 180)

Here we experience the cumulative effect of associative thinking, that "flux and reflux, swell and cadence" which results when the views illuminating an issue, like voices in an intense conversation, chime one upon another, until the very point of the sentence—that Herodotus' speech betokened the scope of human history—becomes inextricable from the threads of time and place that weave through the fabric.[9] Reading means participation in De Quincey's movement of mind; understanding emerges only *through* that movement, and the reader bent on extracting plain information efficiently will find himself rebuked.

De Quincey gives alternatives, in theory and in practice, to the traditional affirmation of perspicuity, certainty, and closure as the virtues of rhetoric, and looks toward the modern advocacies of a liberated discourse, advocacies set in these times even more dedicated to communicative efficiency and the necessities of public business, and less tolerant of play, intellectual or physical. As Christopher Lasch has argued recently, "When the play element disappears from law, statecraft, and other cultural forms then men turn to play not to witness the dramatic reenactment of their common life but to find diversion and sensation."[10] And so arcades of video games replace the play of human discourse with instant mechanical gratification, and allow us to remove ourselves so completely from participation in a community of ideas and people.

Like De Quincey, others in other ages have regarded discourse as a medley of perspectives without absolute terms. Such thinkers inform a revisionist history of rhetoric which illuminates the problem of community and critical thinking in our accelerated, post-modern world. They too would trade the primacy of certainty, closure, and communicative efficiency for "the art of intellectual and fantastic play with any subject to its utmost capabilities." Three such figures are Montaigne, Vico, and

Hume; a glimpse of their largely undervalued counterstatements to establishment rhetoric suggests their kinship with De Quincey and their present value, and also suggests a reconsideration of rhetoric in Antiquity, especially Aristotle's contribution.

Montaigne rebukes the Ciceronian emphasis on style at the expense of invention, and his *Essays* exploit the generative power of the imagination. The *Essays* appear in England at about the same time that Francis Bacon's *Advancement of Learning* (1605) issues an influential warning against the "lawless" activity of free imagination in rhetoric.[11] As faith in scientific truth increases, and the plain style begins to prevail in England, Montaigne's work stresses the inherent ambiguity of language, ambiguity which allows the essayist never-ending paths of inquiry. For Montaigne, generosity of spirit coincides with endless reformulations; the writer's pursuits are *"termelesse and formlesse. His nourishment is admiration, questing, and ambiguity. . . . It is an irregular uncertain motion, perpetual, paternlesse and without end. His inventions enflame, follow and interproduce one another."*[12]

By 1708, when Giambattista Vico delivers his address *On the Study Methods of Our Time* at the University of Naples, Descartes' mechanistic view of language and learning has swept Europe. Mindful that "human events are dominated by Chance and Choice," Vico dismisses the "clear and distinct perception" valorized by Descartes for a more complex and unsettled vision that invites metaphorical invention; locating oneself within a variegated reality requires the "capacity to perceive the analogies existing between matters lying far apart and, apparently, most dissimilar."[13] Vico's later, larger work, *The New Science,* demonstrates most extensively his involvement in the tangle of associational thinking that is the root of community.

Later in the eighteenth century, in England, David Hume recalls the spirit of both Vico and Montaigne as he explains the intellectual power to associate impressions and ideas. Hume repeatedly insists that this power frees us to question and revise matters taken for granted, to create new perspectives. One of the central statements of Hume's skepticism, "Whatever *is,* may not be," is tied to his belief in the primacy of intellectual freeplay:

> Nothing is more free than the imagination of man . . . it has unlimited power of mixing, compounding, separating, and dividing (matters of fact) in all the varieties of fiction and vision.

Once we consider Hume's philosophy as a rhetorical theory, what emerges is his increasing admiration for unconventional ideas embodied in imaginative juxtapositions.[14]

The views of Montaigne, Vico, Hume, and De Quincey maintain the equivalence of rhetoric and intellectual freeplay through the three centuries in which rhetoric became a mechanized ornament of thought and critical thinking became schematized. The rationalist, schematic, post-Renaissance view of rhetoric may not only have muffled these renegade voices, but also straitened the value of our rhetorical "heroes" from Antiquity. Consider, for instance, that the positions of Montaigne, Vico, Hume and De Quincey are not at all inimical to the spirit of Aristotle's *Rhetoric*. Pursuing this revisionist history of rhetoric, we may finally arrive at a reconsideration of Aristotle, and by ignoring all the deadly charts that reduce the *Rhetoric* to divisions and subdivisions of types of argument and proof, we may investigate instead the ways in which Aristotle resists closure as he enacts the process of rhetorical invention, and demonstrates a mind ranging through possibilities and analogies with greater uncertainty and less "system" than most analyses presume. Understood in this way the prototypical *Rhetoric* assures those whose theories of discourse set them apart from the mainstream that they have been right all along.

Notes

1. Quotations from De Quincey throughout this essay are from his *Selected Essays on Rhetoric,* ed. Frederick Burwick (Carbondale: Southern Illinois Univ. Press, 1967), p. 97.

2. Ed. Harold F. Harding (Carbondale: Southern Illinois Univ. Press, 1956), p. 186. For discussions of Blair's popularity, see especially two articles by Douglas Ehninger and James Golden, "The Intrinsic Sources of Blair's Popularity," *The Southern Speech Journal* 21 (1956), 12-30; and "The Extrinsic Sources of Blair's Popularity," *The Southern Speech Journal* (1956), 16-32.

3. Derrida discusses writing as a "strategy without finality" in "Differance," *Speech and Phenomena* (Evanston, Illinois: Northwestern Univ. Press, 1973), p. 135.

4. I have transposed this conclusion from Burke's *Philosophy of Literary Form* (1941; 3rd ed. rev. Berkeley: Univ. of California Press, 1973). Burke regards a literary text as an act affected by changing contexts, exhibiting multiple identities. The study of literature, then, involves the many factors influencing a text, and Burke concludes that "The main ideal of criticism . . . is to use all that is there to use" (p. 23).

5. *The Collected Writing of Thomas De Quincey,* ed. David Masson (1890); rpt. New York: AMS Press, 1968), X,2.

6. See Hoyt Hudson's 1925 essay, "De Quincey on Rhetoric and Public Speaking," reprinted in *Historical Studies of Rhetoric and Rhetoricians*, ed. Raymond F. Howes (Ithaca: Cornell Univ. Press, 1961), pp. 198-214; Frederick Haberman, "De Quincey's Theory of Rhetoric," *Eastern Public Speaking Conference, 1940, Papers and Addresses* (New York: H. W. Wilson, 1940), pp. 191-203; Sig-

mund Proctor, *Thomas De Quincey's Theory of Literature* (Ann Arbor: Univ. of Michigan Pub. in Language and Literature, 1943); Paul Talley, "De Quincey on Persuasion, Invention, and Style," *Central States Speech Journal* 16 (1965), 243-54; Frederick Burwick, "Introduction" to De Quincey's *Selected Essays on Rhetoric,* pp. xi-xlviii; Weldon Durham, "The Elements of Thomas De Quincey's Rhetoric," *Speech Monographs* 37 (1970), 240-48; Andrew King, "Thomas De Quincey on Rhetoric and the National Character," *Central States Speech Journal* 24 (1974), 128-134; Marie Secor, "The Legacy of Nineteenth-Century Style Theory," *Rhetoric Society Quarterly* 22, No. 2 (1982), 76-84.

7. Wellek, "De Quincey's Status in the History of Ideas," *Philological Quarterly* 23 (1944), 269. Wellek repeats this criticism as *A History of Modern Criticism: 1750-1950* (New Haven: Yale Univ. Press, 1965), pp. 110-120. Another devaluation of De Quincey from an equally influential critic comes in Wilbur Samuel Howell's "De Quincey on Science, Rhetoric, and Poetry," *Speech Monographs* 13 (1946), 1-13.

8. Because De Quincey's full rhetorical theory emerges from an understanding of these essays *in concert,* my discussion will range freely among all four. To avoid numerous distractions, I will usually restrict citations to page numbers, instead of repeatedly naming the essay of reference. The essays occupy the following pages in the Burwick edition: "Rhetoric," pp. 81-133; "Style," pp. 134-245; "Language," pp. 246-263; and "Conversation," pp. 264-88.

9. Soon after the sentence about Herodotus, De Quincey seems to comment on his own process when he says, "The labour of composition begins when you have to put your several threads of thought into a loom; to weave them into a continuous whole; to connect, to introduce them; to blow them out or expand them; to carry them to a close" (p. 181).

10. Christopher Lasch, *The Culture of Narcissism* (New York: Warner Books, 1979), pp. 217-18. Lasch sets this statement within a discussion of "The Degradation of Sport" in American life, but he shares with Johan Huizinga a general advocacy of play in all cultural activities, and a fear that "the spirit of arbitrary invention" has been obliterated by behaviors "which seek precisely to predict and control the future and to eliminate risk" (p. 185).

11. Of course, Montaigne and Bacon are both critics of Cicero, but Bacon's treatment of invention and imagination is ever so restrained, rationalistic, and cautious. See *The Advancement of Learning,* ed. G. W. Kitchin (Totowa, New Jersey: Rowman and Littlefield, 1973), especially pp. 120-121.

12. Montaigne's *Essays,* tr. John Florio (1630; rpt. New York: AMS Press, 1967), III, 332.

13. Giambattista Vico, *On the Study Methods of Our Time,* tr. Elio Gianturco (Indianapolis: Bobbs-Merril, 1965), pp. 25, 34.

14. The quotations are from Hume's *Enquiry Concerning Human Understanding,* in his *Philosophical Works,* ed. T. H. Green and T. H. Grose (Germany: Scientia Verlag Aallen, 1964), IV, 134, 40. David Hume's belief in the freeplay of the mind and his skepticism about conventional forms increased through his career, so that by the time he published the authoritative version of *Human Understanding* just before his death in 1777, he had removed the

pages that stressed the value of unity and coherence in literature, and was writing to friends that *Tristram Shandy* was his favorite book.

This essay is reproduced with permission from William A. Covino. An expanded version appears in *The Art of Wondering: A Revisionist Return to the History of Rhetoric* (Portsmouth, N.H.: Boynton/Cook, 1988).

AFTERTHOUGHTS

Aiming to re-contextualize "Thomas De Quincey in a Revisionist History of Rhetoric," I might first note the history of recent revisionism. My call for a revisionist history appeared at the leading edge of a movement that was itself responding to the newly established importance of the history of rhetoric. Scholars such as Edward Corbett, James Murphy, and James Kinneavy called repeatedly through the 1960s and 1970s for new respect for the teaching of writing, as a continuation of a rhetorical tradition that had been for so long the centerpiece of the humanities. Articles and books and courses in the history of rhetoric began to multiply, and as the 1980s began, students in composition studies were learning an already canonical history, which presented an idealistic Plato, a systematic Aristotle, and a formulaic Cicero, all aped and amplified through the Middle Ages and the Renaissance, and then replaced by a new triumvirate—Blair, Campbell, Whately—in the eighteenth century.

Schooled in both this history of rhetoric and post-modern critical theory, a younger generation of scholars (Berlin, Brannon, Clifford, Jarratt, Knoblauch, S. Miller, Schilb, Swearingen, Vitanza, Welch) began to complicate the canonical version of history, questioning in ideological terms the methods, aims, and effects of the history of rhetoric. It became clear at the 1989 conference on "Writing Histories of Rhetoric" that self-scrutinizing historicism—written by a self-conscious historian who confesses a political agenda and a propensity for intellectual license—had arrived in force.

"Thomas De Quincey in a Revisionist History of Rhetoric" was, in many ways, *not* a call for the revisionist historicism that has now arrived. Methodologically and stylistically, it is more a piece of New Criticism than anything else: a close reading of a literary essay which explicates—in conventional scholarly form—De Quincey's "theme." The article does not demonstrate the rhetoric that it admires. Instead, there is a good deal of certainty and disciplined propositionalizing about the value of uncertainty and intellectual play. There is none of the renegade De Quincey in Covino's well-behaved prose. A disappointing performance.

This said, I welcome the opportunity to do better, to be a full-bodied revisionist historian. First, let me confess my biases and limitations. I have not written or thought much about De Quincey for nearly ten years and find myself unable to rewrite my interest in him, except in terms of my present concerns. Doing so will mean *distorting* my 1983 De Quincey to fit the Covino of the 1990s. Of course, the 1983 De Quincey was already a distortion: wrenching an opium-soaked hallucinogenic hack into a model rhetor is — few would deny — a bald act of critical transformation.

My current interest — in the will to distort as the motive force of historical rhetoric, indeed as the motive force of all discourse — stems from both scholarly *ennui* and radical politics. The ongoing post-modern debate in all arenas of English studies, between the advocates of "presence" and the advocates of "absence," between the canonicals and the pluralists, is now commonplace, and no longer very interesting. At the same time, the necessity for generating new categories of thought that shake up the bureaucratized intellect is — in view of events in Grenada, Panama, and the Persian Gulf — no less urgent. Boredom and urgency have led me away from my own pluralist dirge, a version of revisionist history that establishes a pantheon of run-amoks like Montaigne, Vico, De Quincey, and Byron (see Covino, *The Art of Wondering* [Portsmouth, N.H.: Heinemann-Boynton/Cook, 1988]), to a more explicitly political and post-postmodern explication of coercive discourse.

Here is my present position: Coercive discourse (that is, *all* discourse), is *magic*. It transforms the *phenomenal* world through *noumenal* enchantment. De Quincey writes within a Romantic poetics that accords language magical power. It is a power at once reactionary, visionary, and erotic.

Now, briefly, let me explain: Brian Vickers, Ioan Couliano, and others have explained that the Enlightenment model of a mechanistic universe displaces a Renaissance magic cosmology. For Couliano (*Eros and Magic in the Renaissance* [Chicago: University of Chicago Press, 1987]) this epistemic shift *changes the nature of the imagination.* For Morris Berman (*The End of Enchantment* [Ithaca, N.Y.: Cornell Univ. Press, 1981]), the end of magic corresponds with the transformation of rhetoric, from the art of intellectual exploration — which partakes of the magic plasticity of language — to the strict observation of scientific clarity and precision within the confines of a rule-laden positivistic logic. As Anya Taylor points out in *Magic and English Romanticism* (Athens: Univ. of Georgia Press, 1979), magic (from Antiquity through the Renaissance) is that study of "the strange and mysterious potencies of words" which is recalled by Romantic poets who employ language to create "the infinity of worlds."

The Romantic movement is an attempt to reaffirm the magical properties of language, and to define writing as a liberatory force that constructs realities. Erotic power—that is, the power to draw the elemental forces of the universe into communion—is the activity of the Romantic magical imagination, "coercing all things into sympathy" (Wordsworth, *Prelude* 2.390). What I call the "art of wondering," that restlessly associative habit of mind so evident in the manner and matter of De Quincey's prose, is essentially erotic. Plainly sexual fantasies in his *Suspiria de Profundis* exhibit the Romantic fascination with intercourse between the spiritual and physical, dream and reality, a fascination also evident in Blake, Shelley, and Keats.

Romantic writers call themselves magi, and their major critical theses—Wordsworth's *Preface to Lyrical Ballads,* Coleridge's *Biographia Literaria,* Shelley's *Defense of Poetry*—claim that the time has come to react against scientific reductionism with visionary scope; like alchemists forging new realities, they call up a sympathetic universe. As the poet/magus charts elemental and celestial forces whose movement and transformation affect the human condition, he enters into the soul of the world, the *anima mundi,* to participate in the mobility and connectedness of all things.

De Quincey's rhetoric is a recollection of the mystical powers of contemplative discourse that he associates with the monastic writers of Middle Ages, the last rhetoricians. As a new meditative visionary, he issues a political indictment of the mechanistic, reductive discourses that he would replace with dialectical play within a universe of free signifiers, and the "flux and reflux, swell and cadence" of an incantatory style. Thus he joins the Romantic magi who consistently appeal to the "witchery" of language to re-order the imagination and reform the public mind.

7 : THE WRITING OF SCIENTIFIC NON-FICTION: CONTEXTS, CHOICES, CONSTRAINTS

Charles Bazerman
Baruch College, N.Y.

In the sociology of science recent studies of scientific texts and writing practices consistently indicate two themes: (1) scientific writing arises within and is responsive to specific social situations, and (2) the author controls (or constructs) what appears in the scientific text and thus can use the text to advance the author's interests.[1] These studies, together examining a wide disciplinary and historical range of texts, convincingly refute the traditional view that scientific texts simply and unproblematically report on nature as revealed through empirical investigation.

But recognizing that scientists indeed write their papers and that they write within a set of historical-social exigencies seems to make problematic science's claim to make valid, successful, or successively better formulations about nature, unless validity, success, and goodness are defined purely in terms of social and personal interest. In short, indexicality and interest seem to cut the ground of reference to nature out from underneath scientific non-fiction. If scientific non-fiction, moreover, finds itself with little to distinguish itself from fiction, then all other forms of non-fiction would seem to lose whatever claim they have to the representation of reality.

From a relativist perspective, such problematization of nonfiction is not troublesome; it is indeed the point. But for any more agnostic investigation, the question of the status of non-fiction cannot be set aside, if for no other reason than scientists themselves operate on the assumption that they are formulating statements of at least provisional validity about nature. In order to understand scientists' practices on their own terms and to evaluate the substance of their operative existential belief, we need to take seriously the claim that scientists write a kind of non-fiction. Furthermore, if scientific papers do succeed in encapsulating some knowledge of nature beyond the social operations of participation in the scientific community, we must spell out the mechanisms by which this is accomplished.

This paper investigates how scientific texts are made accountable to nature even though a text arises within a scientific community, employs communal language and concepts, pursues the concerns of that community, and furthers the individual's interests within that community. The investigation here, however, turns to the process by which a text is created to find out how meanings are created and embodied in the text. This study goes beyond a reconstruction of the implied relations embodied in the text to examine the material relations between the emerging text and the author/scientist, the relevant community, the prior knowledge, and observed nature. These relations will be examined by the positioning of the emerging text against the contexts and interests within which it arises and by notes, drafts, and revisions that reveal the text's coming into being.

The case to be studied is the emergence of a paper "Measurements of β-Rays Associated with Scattered X-Rays" by Arthur H. Compton and Alfred W. Simon, originally appearing in *Physical Review,* 25 (March 1925), pages 306–313. This case material was chosen because of the completeness and availability of the relevant notes, drafts, and revisions in Compton's notebooks. I worked from the photocopy of Compton's notebooks at The Center for the History of Physics at the American Institute of Physics in New York; the originals are deposited in St. Louis at the library of George Washington University. Such draft materials for writing in physics are rare in the public archives. Unlike writers of fiction and poetry, who recognize that a text emerges only gradually and who therefore save the record of the literary workshop for posterity, physicists seem to save very little of their intermediate paper.

Although both Compton and Simon are credited as joint authors of the "Measurements" article, all notes, drafts, and revisions appear in Compton's third notebook in Compton's handwriting. The assumption that Compton was the actual writer and the shaping intelligence is further supported by the fact that Simon was still a graduate student when the article was written; moreover, the paper fits closely to the theme and issues of Compton's research program while Simon never pursued similar work except in collaboration with Compton.[2] Finally in the draft of the article, Compton unthinkingly starts to refer to himself as the author. Thus it appears safe to assume that Simon's role was to assist in the laboratory, and all the shaping and formulating was Compton's.[3]

The materials from Compton's notebook consist of about a dozen pages of notes on works by other authors, twenty-two pages of calculations and design sketches for a polyphase transformer, fourteen pages of analysis of photographic data, and seventeen pages of draft and revisions. Material related to other work Compton was engaged in is interspersed, such as a draft of exam questions from a course Compton was teaching.

CONTEXT AND RESPONSE

The article in question is one of a series of follow-up articles to Compton's major discovery paper, "A Quantum Theory of the Scattering of X-Rays by Light Elements," in which he announced what is now called the Compton Effect.[4] In retrospect the Compton Effect is considered the first empirical verification of the quantum theory, but verification of quantum theory was not Compton's purpose in pursuing his experimental program or publishing his findings.[5] He was instead concerned with explaining X-ray scattering effects which he had been investigating in classical electrodynamic terms.[6] He found that the only way to account for the wavelength shift of X-rays occurring during scattering was to assume that the incident radiation imparted a quantum of energy to the target electron, which then recoiled in a definite direction; in order to conserve momentum and energy a new quantum of scattered radiation (of longer wavelength and thus less energy than the incident radiation) had to be emitted in an appropriate direction.

Almost immediately upon publication, Compton's discovery underwent a series of challenges, which Compton answered by carrying out further experiments and publishing the results, disconfirming the challenges and refining the theory.[7] It was in this context of challenge and response, of elaboration and bolstering, that Compton pursued the work that would lead to the "Measurements" paper. The more evidence of the most varied kind he could find, the more likely he would be to gain acceptance of his original discovery claims.

At about the same time as Compton had published "A Quantum Theory of the Scattering of X-Rays by Light Elements" in May 1923, C. T. R. Wilson (and slightly later W. Bothe) identified in cloud chamber experiments on X-ray scattering secondary β-ray tracks substantially shorter than photo-electron tracks.[8] Compton immediately saw that these shorter tracks could represent the recoil electrons he hypothesized in the quantum theory article. He wrote a letter dated August 4, 1923, to that effect to *Nature,* which published the letter in the issue of September 22, 1923.[9] Although at that time Compton continued to be mostly concerned with data revealing wave-length shifts, which data he kept gathering during the following year, he clearly understood how the cloud chamber findings filled out his work. He assimilated the cloud chamber findings into his consequent papers, often in lengthy discussions indicating how they supported his theory.[10]

Wilson's and Bothe's data, however, only offered a rough correspondence to Compton's theory, as Compton later noted: "They have shown that the direction of these rays is right, and that their range is of the proper order of magnitude."[11] The roughness Compton ascribes to the use of insufficiently hard and too heterogeneous X-rays. The "Measurements" article can thus be seen as Compton's attempt to tie down the connection between his theory and the cloud chamber tracks more firmly and precisely by redoing other people's experiments in a way more appropriate to his programmatic purposes. He would then obtain support for his theory from a kind of data not at all available when the theory was first framed; such data, confirming the predictive power of the theory, is rather persuasive.

In this way we can see the "Measurements" paper motivated and shaped in specific ways by Compton's theoretical program, discoveries by other scientists as reported in the literature, the desire for closer measurement of the phenomenon, and Compton's persuasive intentions. Contextual factors provide pressures and offer opportunities to gather fuller, more precise, and more focused data about the observed radiation—confirming and adding detail to the representation of nature embodied in Compton's theory. His social interest in establishing the proposed phenomenon leads Compton to search actively for passive constraints of new and more precise kinds; criticisms in the literature actively push him again to seek passive constraints that make his formulation more likely; finally, new techniques, actively created (although embodying passive constraints in what they can accomplish and in the results they produce), provide opportunities for closer looks at the purported phenomenon, adding new passive constraints to the formulation.

Specifically, this set of forces and opportunities led Compton to design experiments and write a paper reporting those experiments:

1. adopting Wilson's cloud expansion apparatus;
2. referring to and discussing his own quantum theory of scattering;
3. employing higher energy (shorter wave-length) incident radiation than Wilson and Bothe;
4. designing and employing a method of obtaining more homogeneous incident radiation than Wilson and Bothe (consequently reporting data for higher energy, more homogeneous data);
5. developing theoretical predictions about aspects of the recoil electrons measurable through the Wilson apparatus;
6. and discussing the correspondence between the theoretical predictions and the experimental data.

These effects of the rhetorical situation correspond to the major structural features of the resulting paper. Compton, indeed, alludes to these effects when he describes the paper at the end of the opening paragraph:

> The present paper describes stereoscopic photographs of these new rays which we have recently made by Wilson's cloud expansion method. In taking the pictures, sufficiently hard X-rays were used to make possible a more quantitative study of the properties of these rays.[12]

Within the stylized terms of the field, the paper describes constraints imposed by the results of more precise measurements. By showing that Compton's theory is in conformity with ever-increasing passive constraints, the article seeks to establish fact-like status for Compton's claims.[13]

Another aspect of the rhetorical context consisted of one particular challenge to Compton's quantum theory of scattering. Bohr, Kramers, and Slater claimed that at the particle level the laws of conservation applied only statistically.[14] Compton's theory required event by event application of the conservation laws; up to that point, however, Compton had established the recoil phenomenon only on an aggregate basis through measurement of radiation wavelengths. Wilson's cloud photographs provided a way of capturing and measuring single incidents and were, therefore, the ideal means of refuting Bohr, Kramers, and Slater. The full and explicit refutation of the statistical argument was to be made by Compton and Simon in a subsequent article—"Directed Quanta of Scattered X-Rays"[15] which appeared in *Physical Review* six months after the "Measurements" article—but the desire to refute the challenge remains an implicit shaping force on the earlier article. The effect can be seen in the emphasis given in both the abstract and the full paper on conclusions and evidence that the scattering occurs on an event by event basis, with each event maintaining conservation of momentum and energy. This emphasis is in fact increased in revision. Again, attack on the formulation provides pressure to seek and reveal passive constraints, consonant with the original formulation.

Laboratory Decisions, Events, and Results

The effects of the rhetorical situation are first realized in Compton's laboratory decisions before their full implications in the text are realized. The laboratory decisions, such as the use of the Wilson cloud apparatus, designing a more precise control over the incident radiation, the design of the scattering experiment, the choice of which plates to use as data, and the particular measurements taken from those plates, all have an effect on the final article, both in terms of the procedures described and the data reported. The first three decisions are design decisions based on the characteristics of the phenomenon investigated and the properties of the equipment, as both have been revealed through previous investigations. The Wilson apparatus, for example, is used only because it had earlier revealed tracks that Compton can identify with recoil electrons. Compton goes to great lengths to make design decisions that will permit observation with the desired precision; twenty-two pages of his notebooks are devoted to designs for a polyphase transformer that will provide him with stable enough voltage to provide homogeneous incident radiation of calculable energies.[16] The experimenter can choose from among available technologies, but those technologies suffer many passive constraints. The experimenter cannot use impossible machines, nor can he make machines do what they cannot do.[17] The latter two decisions—the choice of plates and the choice of measurements to take from the plates—depend on what happens in the laboratory, on what turns up on the plates. Once the experimenter sets up the conditions of the experiment, what turns up is beyond his control. Only after can the experimenter reassert control through selection and manipulation.

In the final article Compton reports that he is using data from "the best 14 of a series of 30 plates taken," but the notebooks show him making calculations for 14 numbered plates running from number 15 to number 47.[18] Assuming that plates 1 through 14 served as practice runs, that still leaves three plates unaccounted for, presumably so bad that they do not even count as plates. Although Compton gives no overt definition of what makes the selected plates 'best,' the sixteen deleted plates worst, and the three not plates at all, his notebooks offer two clues about his criteria of selection. First, he tends to select the higher number plates; in fact he records measurements for plates 38, 39, 40, 43, 45, 46, and 47. This suggests that Compton and Simon were still gaining the technical skill to produce plates that clearly revealed the tracks they were interested in. Second, at the bottom of the column of measurements for plate 38—which in fact was deleted from the article partway through the writing of the draft—the notation "uncertain because too crowded" appears. This notation reinforces the impression that selection was based on how clearly the plates represented and allowed distinctive counts of the data associated with the scattering phenomenon. That is, Compton and Simon were simply looking for clear and distinct tracks.

The tracks on the photographic plates are Compton and Simon's closest glimpse at the scattering phenomenon, and reproductions of some photographic plates are included in the final document to give the readers qualitative visual evidence. How those tracks are interpreted quantitatively, however, depends on a number of manipulations of measurement and calculation. The data tables in Compton's notebook, even in parts of the rough draft of the article, are filled with corrections. These corrections seem all to derive from two incorrect assumptions about the equipment which led to mistaken values for the potential of the X-ray tube and consequently for the energy of the incident radiation. The two causes for error — a warping in a frame and the effect of a condenser — are both carefully noted in the notebook and in the final article. Although on first glance all the corrections appear to be manipulation of the numerical data after the fact, they really only serve to adjust the secondary numerical data to the actual event as occurring in the equipment and recorded on the plates. In addition, although Compton for the most part adheres to Knorr's observation that scientists tend not to report their wrong turnings and errors in the final report[19] (Compton, for example, does not discuss what went wrong in the first fourteen parts nor in the later deleted ones), Compton is very careful to cover this error in both notes and text. His great care, and indeed the great detail with which he reveals this error in the article, suggests that this error is of a different order in that it comes after the laboratory event but seems to change the reality of what happened. To retain the integrity of the data, to make clear that he is constrained by the data and not fiddling with it, he must expose the error of calculation and measurement which leaves the reality of machinery and photographic plates untouched. Thus the representation of a certain class of error is necessary in the article to keep the relation between laboratory happenings and the report of those happenings as clean as possible. The purpose of exposing the error is not, as Medawar would like,[20] to reveal the psychology of discovery.

THE WRITING-UP

The previous sections have examined some of the constraints and decisions that determined what the measurements article would look like, but still we do not have a text. Compton must sit down with blank paper in his notebook and create a string of words, equations, numbers, and graphics to fulfill the possibilities of the constraints. As part of that fulfillment he must represent nature at various levels of mediation: nature as perceived through the literature, as formulated in a problem and hypothesized answer, as inherent in the experimental design and the actual experimental happenings, as represented by the experimental data and the secondary calculations, as interpreted through discussions and conclusions. Thus the article, even while describing the forces that shaped it, is reconstructing views of nature at a number of levels of intellectual and physical mediation. By the convention and logic of the scientific report, however, all these representations must be weighed against the least mediated representation, the data—the photographs and numbers one carries away from the laboratory.

At this point of writing-up the task of the scientist then becomes using language to create these various representations at a level of precision and completeness that adds no further confusion or lack of clarity at any of the levels and that allows an intelligible comparison between the data and the other more mediated representations. When we look at Compton's draft and revisions of the article "Measurements of β-rays Associated with Scattered X-rays," we see indications of just this concern for creating an adequately full and precise representation of nature at several levels of mediation. The larger part of the many changes and corrections he makes as he writes and revises manage the representation of the X-ray-electron interaction, the theory of that interaction, the experimental design and happenings, and the kinds of interpretations and conclusions that can be drawn on the basis of the data.

The following discussion of the drafts and revisions will first present the three major tactics of revision that Compton uses—postponing, extending, and fine tuning—and then will examine epistemological, phenomenological, and social issues raised by the draft and revisions.

Postponing Postponing is a structural decision made in the course of writing the draft. Four times Compton starts to raise major subjects, then decides he must first reveal some preliminary information. At the end of the opening paragraph in the draft, after only mentioning the photographs, he is about to present a set of reproductions with the phrase, "A typical series of these photographs is shown in figures . . ." Before completing the sentence, however, he strikes it out in order to insert a paragraph spelling out the cloud chamber, X-ray, and photographic equipment. Then in the third paragraph (line 28)[21] he returns to presenting the reproductions of the plates. In the second case, after qualitatively discussing the photographs, Compton begins to raise a major theoretical issue with a new paragraph beginning, "One of the most important questions is whether . . ." He backs away from his direct assault, however, by striking the incomplete sentence and beginning a different paragraph introducing quantitative theory to be matched against empirical data (39). The quantitative material then continues as the main body of the paper. Although it is unclear what important question Compton has in mind, the discussion of all the major questions follows the quantitative presentation. The third case involves the presentation of the first data table. Some time after copying the first two columns of data Compton realized the errors in the potential and energy figures discussed earlier. He apparently then went back to check his equipment and recalculate his figures. He then corrected the figures in the first two columns and copied in the correct figures for column seven, which is calculated from the first two columns. Then in the draft immediately following the table he added a paragraph explaining the error (47–59). In the final paper, however, the table is postponed until after the explanation of the error. In the last case, Compton splits his first draft of the second table, which included data on both maximum range of R-tracks and the distribution of the ranges of the full set of tracks. The latter part of the original table appears later in the article in a slightly different array as Table III. The effect is to allow complete discussion of the issue of maximum range before raising the issue of relative distributions.

In all four cases the postponement is to allow the presentation of additional detailed information prior to the postponed material. In the first and third cases the additional material explains the equipment that produced the postponed data; in the second and fourth cases the inserted material is data logically prior to the postponed material.

Extending Extensions, giving more information about some item already under discussion, serve to clarify or make precise the item being discussed. For example, "primary beam" is changed to "primary X-ray beam" (5); "photographs" becomes "stereoscopic photographs" (11); "the X-ray tube, enclosed in a lead box" becomes "the Coolidge X-ray tube, enclosed in a heavy lead box" (19–20); and "$\tau + \sigma$" becomes "$\mu = \tau + \sigma$" (80). In a more extensive example, "To calculate the relative number to be expected, we have arranged this expression over the range of wavelengths used in our experiments," grows in several steps into "To calculate the relative number of tracks for different relative wave-lengths to be expected, we have arranged this expression by a rough graphical method over the range of wave-lengths used in our experiments." (138–141).

In one case the addition serves to justify a statement. The phrase "in view of the fact that the photographs were stereoscopic" adds a reason to the original phrase which now follows, "it was possible to estimate . . ." (161).

In all the above cases the addition gives detail to the originally mentioned object or event, but in at least three cases the additions redefine the object of concern more precisely. "Track" becomes "length of a given track" (135); "40 tracks" becomes "the directions of 40 tracks" (159); and "short tracks . . . and long tracks" becomes "short tracks (type R) . . . long tracks (type P)" (41). The last example involves a change in epistemic level, to be discussed below.

Fine-tuning Word substitutions fine tune the language through more specific, correct, or appropriate phasing. Compton achieves greater specificity by such changes as "an" to "the" (110), "the" to "its" (103), and "those" to "the quantity S" (125). More substantive specifications are made in such changes as "acquires" becoming "moves forward with" (109).

In some cases Compton is correcting an outright error, as when he miscopies an equation from a previous article (112), or he incorrectly calls an "expression" an "equation" (147). Elsewhere he must correct an inverted ratio (85), report that there was more than one "condenser" by making the word plural (52), and relabel a "scattering quantum" as a "scattered quantum" (151). More frequently the corrections are more subtle, as when measured values are described as "summarized" rather than "Shown on the following table" (117) or when "C. T. R. Wilson's datum" is changed to "C. T. R. Wilson's result" (119). A repeated subtle error needing frequent correction is referring directly to an object instead of the appropriate quality. Compton in the draft consistently refers to R and P and R/P when discussing the number of electrons but in the final version the notation is consistently changed to N_r, N_p, and N_r/N_p (42, Table 1, 75, 83, 88, 96). Related are the wavering from "apparatus" to "chamber" back to "apparatus" (15), the change from "photoelectric absorption coefficient" to "true absorption coefficient" (43), and the revision of "amplitude" to "magnitude" (185).

The last category of fine tuning revisions corrects tactical errors of exposition and thereby modifies slightly the impression of what is being discussed. Compton first begins to describe the maximum frequency "required to" and then switches to "excited by the voltage" (122); a bit later Compton cites a finding "for the number" but then changes that to a finding "that the probability" (134); and a few lines later Compton starts a sentence, "This expression assumes that the electrons all . . ." then recasts the thought changing the subject of the assumption, "This expression assumes that the exciting primary beam . . ." (137). A more clearly consequential example occurs when Compton begins to discuss "the origin of the short" tracks but then changes the focus to "the origin of the two classes of β-rays" (40). Here he changes the topic from one phenomenon to two phenomena in order to prepare for an equation for the ratio of the two later in the sentence. The original singular focus, although not a factual or technical error, was a tactical error in not providing for the continuity of the exposition; the writer must keep in mind what he will discuss in what order, and he must focus the discussion accordingly.

All three types of revision—postponing, extending, and fine-tuning— indicate that the writer is moving through the imprecision and incompleteness of formulations to come to a more focused, accurate representation of what he did, saw, measured, and thought. The language of the original draft is in parts skimpy, fuzzy, misleading, and even wrong, but by struggling with the language the scientist writer can achieve a bit better fit between symbolization and experienced world.

The Writing of Scientific Non-Fiction 191

Criteria of adequacy The symbolic representation of nature is inevitably an approximation in an alien mode; absolute precision and completeness of formulation would be an endless task. Criteria are necessary for a writer to decide whether a linguistic representation is adequate. Compton's draft and revisions offer clues as to his criteria in the instances where he deletes detail or foregoes specificity. Compton seems to follow two criteria: what one can say and what one needs to say — that is, assessments of how finely one knows what one is discussing and of what level of distinction is necessary to carry the particular argument forward.

The rounding off Compton does in Table II shows how these criteria are applied. In the original data tables in the notebook the observed maximum ranges are all measured to the first decimal, but in the transfer of the table to the draft and the consequent revision three observed ranges are rounded off to the nearest integer, in accordance with a prior admission that the observed track lengths "could be estimated probably within 10 or 20 percent" (115-116). That is, the decimals give an appearance of greater accuracy than was probable. Two calculated values, as well, are rounded off to the nearest integer. On these calculated values no error range restrictions apply, but since the degree of statistical correspondence being demonstrated is quite broad (as large as ±3 mm. or 33 percent of the measured value) the decimals are unnecessary for the demonstration. Compton gives no greater statistical precision than he legitimately can or needs to.

Unneeded specificity is deleted in a number of cases, trivial and substantive. In trivial cases the specification has already been achieved elsewhere in the text as in the deletion of "X-ray" in "primary X-ray beam" (18). In more substantive examples the deleted material raises extraneous theory or inappropriately narrows the discussion. The expression V_c/h is eliminated after the phrase "maximum frequency" because the expression is not used in any of the ensuing calculations (121). The phrases "but radiates uniformly in all directions" (110) and "depending on the direction" (116) are similarly deleted for raising unnecessary qualifications. Another deletion, "mean of the experimentally" from the larger phrase comparing "calculated values with the mean of the experimentally observed relative ranges" (143), emphasizes that the data fit is independent of the voltage and therefore is valid for each of the cases individually rather than only in the mean. Thus the force of an entire set of data is strengthened by the removal of an unnecessarily narrowing qualifier.

The most interesting example of deletion occurs in the description of the photographic equipment (25-27). Compton twice tries to include phrases noting that the full aperture of the lens was employed, but he twice deletes this as unnecessary. Then he twice tries to give positive judgments about the quality of the lenses and plates—"which gave excellent defin . . ." and "very satisfactory." He deleted the first completely and removed the "very" from the second so that the text is left with only the comment that the plates "were found satisfactory." This judgment is all that is needed for the exposition of the experiment. Without a scale of excellence, the more effusive judgments, moreover, do not appear legitimately knowable or supportable to Compton; only the word *satisfactory* carries a criterion of adequacy to the task at hand. Compton's obvious technological pride in the laboratory accomplishment of capturing the scattering phenomenon on photographic plates seems to motivate all four deleted phrases, but he recognizes that such feelings are extraneous to the argument.

Control of Theory, Persona, and Audience

In addition to controlling the more obvious representations of nature, Compton is careful to control the definition of the epistemic level of the discussion, the projection of his persona, and the relationship to the audience. These factors are important to maintain under control, because if improperly treated they could not only obscure the description of nature being proposed, but undermine the purpose of the discourse. By carefully identifying the epistemic level of discussion, Compton is able to identify exactly what he is representing and at what level of mediation. By controlling persona he is able to assert his individual ownership interests, identify where his judgment enters, and limit his intellectual risks, while still keeping attention on what the data and theory suggest. By controlling the relationship to the audience, he serves the reader's convenience,[22] helps the reader follow the argument, and submits himself to the audience's criteria of judgment, again while keeping focus of the article on the formulation and data; his most important task with respect to the audience is to maintain credibility, which is done by remaining responsible to and for the data.

Epistemic Level As part of the process of adjusting language to necessary and possible levels of precision and completeness, Compton carefully assigns each statement to the appropriate epistemic level. That is, items can be represented at different levels of theoretical and empirical mediation. For example, near the beginning of the draft Compton shows uncertainty whether to discuss *rays* or *tracks*. *Rays* of course directly represents the purported object in nature, but *tracks* represents a manifestation of those rays as they pass through a cloud chamber to create vapor trails that are recorded on photographic plates. After a few equivocations and changes, Compton decides to discuss *rays* in the introduction and switch to *tracks* only after the photographic data are introduced. Thereafter the track terminology dominates the rest of the article. Thus Compton indicates that although rays are the object of interest, recorded tracks are all he has to observe and work with.

Even in the discussion of the purported object of nature there is recognition that the discussion is really about objects constructed in the literature. The opening sentence of the published article reads "In recently published papers, C. T. R. Wilson and W. Bothe have shown the existence of a new type of β-ray excited by hard X-rays." The word *new* is added in the draft, so its use is clearly a conscious choice. The word *new,* however, is only appropriate as meaning new in the literature, not new in nature.

Once the linguistic representation of an object is recognized as being a construction of the literature, then it is only appropriate that alternative terms should be used depending on the theoretical context invoked. Thus Compton changes "ray" to "quanta" (89) in accordance with the invocation of quantum theory a few lines earlier. Similarly, Compton begins to write "an [electron]" then corrects this to "a β-particle" (120) in accordance with an earlier switch in discussion from colliding objects to an analysis of ranges of particles. In both cases the changes are not compelled by technical accuracy, but they do help to maintain clear focus on the appropriate theoretical contexts.

Authorial Persona Despite the familiar conjecture that scientists remove themselves from their writing so as to make their work appear less particular and so as to evade epistemological responsibility, Compton maintains an authorial presence in the article. The revisions in some ways enhance this presence and in other ways diminish it. The pattern is that authorial presence is decreased for the prior work, which is merged into the literature of the field, but authorial presence is increased for the current work, for which Compton and his co-worker Simon take responsibility as the thinkers, doers, and owners.

The merging of the individual into the collective of the literature for the scientist's prior work appears in a number of revisions involving self-citations. In the first paragraph of the draft, for example, Compton refers to his previous work "the quantum theory of X-ray scattering proposed by the [author]." Then Compton remembers that Simon is nominally co-authoring the article; he strikes out "the" and substitutes "one of us," to which he appends a footnote to his monograph for the National Research Council. But in the final version the entire phrase "proposed by one of us" is deleted (8–9), suggesting no credit in the text, and a citation to Debye is added to the footnote, sharing credit in the literature and emphasizing that the self-citation is part of a wider literature that is communal. Similar demotions of textual self-reference to footnotes occur at lines 101–103 and 128. In another case the self-reference is removed from the head of the sentence and given a less definitive verb; "Compton and Hubbard give for the . . ." becomes, "If the maximum range of the recoil electrons is S_m, Compton and Hubbard find . . ." (133–134). The most extreme case occurs in the last sentence, when Compton is stressing how well the current work fits with the findings of the literature. The phrase "strong confirmation of the assumptions used by one of us to explain . . ." is shortened by the deletion of the self-reference (187–188); moreover, the self-citing footnote is also eliminated, but a final phrase—the closing phrase of the article—is added: "on the basis of quantum theory" (180). Compton's earlier work is subsumed into a theory which is a fact of the literature transcending individual ownership.

In the previous example, however, even while self-citation is vanishing into the literature, strong reference remains to the authors as conceivers, doers, and owners of the current work. In all versions the last sentence opens with "Our results . . ." (187). Other first person usages remain through all versions to indicate the doing of the work (e.g., "photographs . . . which we have recently made" (11–12), "apparatus used in our work" (15), and "we used a mercury spark" (22)), responsibility for reporting the work (e.g., "In Table 1 we have recorded the results" (47)), intellectual operations (e.g., "we have taken from his data" (78) and "the value of which we used" (81)), ownership of the data (e.g., "in our photographs (157)), the evaluation of the evidence (e.g., "In view, however, of the meager data as yet available on this point, we do not wish to emphasize this correspondence too strongly" (97–99)).

Three revisions, in addition, make the authors' role more explicit. The first two bring out the individual responsibility for the evidence. "Observed in the photographs" becomes "shown in our photographs" (115); "the experimental values" becomes "the observed lengths of the R tracks" (124). The third brings out the evaluative role; "can leave no reasonable doubt" becomes transformed to the more direct "we believe establishes" (83).

Authorial Judgments   Even where an author does not use first person to call attention to his evaluative role, he makes many evaluative judgments throughout the article through estimates of the reliability of various claims. Compton sharpens this evaluative role through revisions.

One set of judgments sharpened in revision assigns the way in which a relevant theory specifies a particular phenomenon. In the second sentence of the draft, radiation which has "been ascribed to photoelectrons"

The Writing of Scientific Non-Fiction 195

gets revised to radiation which has "been identified with photoelectrons," indicating a more specific association. A few lines later Compton flip-flops as to whether a particular interaction is "according to the predictions," "as predicted by," or "in accordance with the predictions of the quantum theory" (8); Compton winds up with the last, and weakest, assumption. As we shall see below, even the title of the article, characterizing the strength of the claim of the whole article, undergoes a similar weakening.

In the above examples the truth value of the claims was not questioned, but only the applicability to specific cases. But the larger set of revisions changes the certainty or character of a claim. "Fact" is weakened to "observation" (96); "suppose" is strengthened to "explained" (92); and a definite "are" wavers to "may be" then regroups to "are often" (68). "A satisfactory agreement" edges up to "a rather satisfactory agreement" (143–144); a "theory" is demoted to an "hypothesis" (154); and the direct identification of "are" weakens to the mediated explanation of "have tracks long enough to determine . . ." (157–158). Finally in the last paragraph an inserted "about" (183) admits that the conclusions rest on approximate evidence.

The most direct judgments are made in the concluding section, and here we see the most adjustment of the strength of claims. In the third from the last paragraph Compton begins to draw strong conclusions from the angles of ejection: "There can be no question but that the electrons ejected . . ." But he then reconsiders and replaces this strong statement with a sentence about the calculation (173–174). In the next sentence he tries again: "There is undoubtedly . . ." But he also crosses this out and starts anew with a qualification: "I spite of some discrepancy at the largest angles, the R electrons ejected at small angles undoubtedly have greater energy than those . . ." In the final version, however, even this certainty is excessive, and a weaker judgment is passed to the reader who inspects the data charts: "It will be seen that the observed ranges . . . are . . . in substantial agreement with the theory" (174–177).

Again in the next to the last paragraph, "thus constitutes a strong support of the . . ." becomes the weaker "is thus of special significance" (182). A judgment is again passed to the audience.

Despite these two weakenings the last sentence of the article is strengthened as much as it needs to be to assert the significance of the work. "Our results are thus in . . ." becomes "our results therefore afford a strong confirmation of . . ." (187). Compton thus urges no more than he has to, but does not evade responsibility for judgments. Elsewhere he calls attention to his judgments through italics in intermediate sets of conclusions (82–86 and 128–131).

Audience Concerns The revisions show almost no concern with trying to urge the audience. The only persuasion seems to be that built into the article by the early constraints and early choices that shape the article. If one wishes to study persuasive intent one should look to those early decisions that position the work against previous work, that frame the problem to be addressed, and that determine the kind of evidence to be generated by the experiment; such modes of persuasion are in support of a theoretical position rather than in support of a particular set of results. The only overt attempt to urge the audience in the revisions is the addition of the word "heavy" in front of "lead box" (20) in the apparatus description to dispel criticism of contamination through inadequate shielding. All other revisions in anticipation of audience reaction have to do with the conventions and felicity of language: spelling and word form corrections, removing redundancies and excess commas, and rearranging word order and equations for easier reading. Many of these corrections occur between the completion of the revised draft and the publication to the final version. At that time certain small features are also made consistent with the journal style. *Centimeter* is spelled out, but *equation* is abbreviated; the degree symbol is substituted for the word, and the angstrom symbol is simplified by removal of the superior cycle.

Thus, although the audience is accommodated, it is not pushed. The reasons why the audience might want to believe the article are imbedded in the article's structure. A representation of the literature establishing and positioning a problem, an accurate understanding of existing knowledge, the drawing of a question sharply, the appropriateness of the research design, the fit of the results—these are what convince, but these are determined before the writing-up by the early constraints and decisions. The only thing the scientist as writer can control at the writing up stage is the representation of these earlier constraints and choices. In the representation the scientist has some leeway, but the representations to be credible must still strike the audience as adequate accounts of actual situations. That audience has access to the same literature, has their own formulations of problems, knows what equipment is available and what the equipment can do, can inspect the author's equipment, and can replicate the author's experiment or run other experiments revealing the same phenomenon. In this light we can understand both Compton's throwing certain judgments to the reader under the assumption that the data is clear enough to speak for itself within the theoretical context established by the article, and Compton's efforts in his revisions to make his descriptions as accurate and precise as needed for the argument. His credibility and persuasiveness depend finally on how close a fit his readers find between what he says and what is.

In order to maintain credibility Compton takes great care not to misrepresent his data. Not only is the first person maintained in contexts indicating his responsibility, the author takes explicit responsibility for miscalculations and errors, both through the section added prior to Table I describing the sources of error and through another estimate of error (115–116). This latter discussion of error is difficult for Compton to formulate; he must make several revisions before he can make a reasonable and not misleading formulation of the probable errors. Finally, since the experimental error affecting the data was not discovered until Compton was part way through the draft, a number of corrections had to be made of figures in the text and in the first table.

TEXT AS OBJECT

Through all the constraints and choices we see the gradual emergence of a text—a literary object, separate from, although the consequence of, all that went before. Particularly as the text takes shape in drafting and revision, we can see it take on the quality of an object, open to all the limitations and manipulations of language. But still the text is a linguistic object that takes on the overriding task of the representation of nature.

The act of revision itself treats language as an object. Certain revisions in particular call attention to the text as linguistic construction: the sharpening of the recognition of the obscuring effect of reproduction on photographs (33); the retrospective addition of a phrase because certain terms are needed in an equation on the next line (41); deletions in recognition of later repetitions (90 and 116).

Large organizational shifts call attention both to the manipulable quality of a text and to the gradual construction or emergence of the textual object. The splitting of Table II indicates that Compton is developing an organizational sense of the article that he did not have as he started the draft. Similarly, he did not begin with the subtitles that mark the major divisions of the revised article in mind. The first subtitle in the draft, "*Number of Tracks*," is clearly an afterthought, squeezed in between lines. But when he reaches the second set of data, Compton realizes that the organization does have major divisions, so he rather emphatically begins the next section with the title "*Ranges of the R Tracks*" on a separate line and centered. By the time he reaches the third of the ultimate divisions, he seems to have gotten used to the organizational structure, and he presents the title "*Angles of Ejection of R. Tracks*" in a more subdued position, on the same line as the new paragraph. This is the position the subtitles take in the printed version.

If the subtitling indicates Compton's increasing awareness of the role of blocks of text, his titling of the whole article indicates his judgment of what the whole text does. The original title in the draft is "Measurements of β-rays Excited by Hard X-rays," but before publication the title was softened to "Measurements of β-rays Associated with Scattered X-rays." The changed title recognizes that the text is not so much concerned with the mechanisms of excitation so much as the association of the rays through measurement and photographs of individual incidents. The text is limited to just an aspect of the phenomenon and just an aspect of Compton's thoughts and convictions about the phenomenon. A text is a limited object.

The Abstract   The article's abstract serves as one further step in turning the article into an object, for the abstract considers the article as a whole and then makes a representation of it. In this regard the point at which Compton decides to write the abstract is a good indicator of when he gains a grasp of the whole text. The draft of the abstract appears about two-thirds the way through the draft of the main text, at a spot corresponding to line 142 of the published version. The earlier part of the abstract draft, in addition, contains the kinds of numerical errors that Compton was not aware of until he reached Table I (59). These facts indicate that Compton probably began the abstract when he was part way into the article; he apparently turned to a blank page where he thought the main draft would end. He did not have a grasp of the whole when he began the article and had to wait until he saw what he had written before he wrote the abstract; nonetheless, he felt he needed to write the abstract before completing the article, in order to articulate his sense of the whole and to keep the later parts logically and structurally consistent.

Even in the abstract itself he seems to need to recapitulate the entire argument before summarizing the conclusion. He reduces the summary of the data to a one-sentence statement recounting the main topics: "Measurements were made of the maximum range, the relative number of different ranges, the relative number ejected at different angles, and the relative ranges of the R tracks ejected at different angles." This sentence does not find its way into the published abstract, but rather seems more for Compton's own benefit.

Furthermore, the draft of the abstract is not complete on the notebook pages alloted it, suggesting that Compton returned to the main article before finishing the abstract and did not leave enough blank space for the completion of the abstract. The abstract draft breaks off in mid-sentence at the bottom of a page; the next page continues with the main text in mid-sentence. If the abstract did get written in stages coordinated with the writing of the main text, that correlation would further emphasize the interaction between the gradual creation of the text and the growing perception and command of the text as an object.

The specific content of the abstract and its revisions further reveal Compton's perception of what kind of object the text is. The substantial discussions in the main text of the background literature and the experimental apparatus become only sketchy mentions via secondary phrases in the first few sentences of the abstract. The sentences are more concerned with the data and findings; the grammatical subjects are reserved for "photographs," "kinds of tracks," and "ratio." Moreover, the problem addressed in the paper, "a more quantitative study of the properties of these rays" (14), does not receive explicit mention in the abstract.

The first eight of the nine sentences of the abstract are devoted to reporting the findings in some statistical detail. The organization of sentences three through eight follows exactly the structure of the body of the paper reporting the data and findings, with two sentences devoted to each of the topics announced in the subtitles of the paper. The conclusions are reported in the last sentence of the abstract; however, that sentence is very long, about eighty words, and manages to incorporate almost all the substance of the final two paragraphs of the full paper. The one sentence summary in fact incorporates verbatim many of the key phrases of the full version.

The abstract, therefore, focuses on the outcome of the experiment rather than on the background, formulation of the problem, or the experimental design. Nor does the abstract try to recapture a coherent argument, which would require more emphasis on theory and context. The emphasis is entirely on what can be formulated about the out-there physical phenomenon as a result of the experiment.

The revisions of the abstract draft emphasize this focus. Specifying phrases are added about the observed phenomenon, and excess theory and reference to calculations are eliminated. Finally, the original terse summary of conclusions is greatly expanded to incorporate almost all the substance of the full conclusions, as previously noted.

Conclusions

One must always be cautious about generalizing from a single case. The following conclusions, therefore, stay close to the particular case. These conclusions, nonetheless, are more generally suggestive for two reasons. First, although revealing a complex social, psychological, and intellectual dynamic of scientific formulation, this case gives some grounds for traditional empiricist simplifications. Second, this case suggests a mechanism whereby scientific discourse can become accountable to nature; even more, the mechanism subordinates other social and personal accountabilities to the accountability to nature. If such a mechanism appears in one case, it (or a similar mechanism) is likely to appear in others. This paper thus opens up a major area of analysis of scientific discourse — an area that is central to science's understanding of itself and its chosen tasks, yet an area which has been ignored in recent studies of scientific discourse. I will end, however, by suggesting some of the ways in which this particular case may be limited, as may be all detailed analyses of scientific discourse. The differences among such detailed studies open up several new questions for investigation.

A. H. Compton, as all authors do, chooses the words that go on the page and thereby creates a statement — a text, a linguistic object — that did not exist before. But Compton's choices are severely constrained by contextual forces, directed by procedures of scientific argumentation, and motivated by his personal commitment to record his claims and data as accurately as he is able. Some of the contextual constraints are active (in Fleck's terminology) in that they reflect the structure of the scientific community, the thought style and expressive habits of the period, the social position and interests of the investigator within the scientific community, the research program and theory commitments of the scientist, and the nature of the challenges to prior formulations of theory.

Within this context Compton has some freedom in choosing what claims to advance, in formulating or reformulating those claims, and in designing experiments or other means of advancing those claims. It is at this point that Compton seems to have the most leeway to frame his work strategically, positioning it against other claims and challenges. It is at this stage of basic positioning, I believe, that we should look for the locus of persuasive strategy rather than at the actual writing up stage with its narrower manipulation of language. At this stage Compton decided what the real issues in the problem area were and how he could address them in the way most persuasive to his colleagues.

These strategic choices, nonetheless, were subject to constraints, but the constraints were passive. Compton could not violate the bulk of previously gathered data (although he could actively reinterpret or offer alternate explanations for the data). He could not make equipment do what it could not do, and he could not control what data ultimately got recorded on the photographic plates. Moreover, given the canons of scientific argumentation which Compton observed, the center of the persuasive strategy was the active search for passive constraints. Compton bolstered his original discovery claim by developing a new source of data; he answered challenges by finding specific refuting data; and he advanced his own career by revealing more about the phenomenon and developing techniques for looking more intimately into nature.

Once the experiment has run its course, Compton could only choose to publish or not publish the results. Having chosen publication Compton is committed to presenting his theory and results as clearly, accurately, and precisely as the material and language allow. This precision, accuracy, and clarity in part serve the persuasive intention by identifying the tightness of fit among his claim, experimental procedures, and observed nature; in part they protect him from criticism of fuzziness or fraudulence (note particularly his careful revelations about the necessary recalculations to preserve the integrity of the data).

But the revisions are so careful on even such apparently inconsequential matters as his estimate of the quality of the photographic technique or the choice of "the" over "an" that they reveal a deeply internalized commitment to the best possible representation of the material within his theoretical, experimental, and linguistic scope.

Since there is no guarantee of an essential link between the objects of nature and the words and equations scientists formulate to describe those objects and their behavior, the non-fiction created by Compton, or any other scientist, cannot be taken as absolute, a transparent and congruent presentation of nature as it is. The formulating mechanisms suggested above, however, do provide a means by which Compton and other scientists may improve their formulations, holding those formulations more closely accountable to nature as it is perceived through the thought style of the scientist's thought collective.

It would, however, be premature to suggest how general the mechanisms described above actually are for several reasons beyond the normal cautions of the case study: (1) the fact that the Compton material was among the very few sets of rough drafts of writing in physics that I was able to locate may indicate that Compton was idiosyncratic among physicists in the seriousness with which he took writing; (2) the idiosyncratic care for language may be heightened by the high stakes involved with Compton's claims and reputation at this point; (3) in other scientific work of more directly practical consequence, other accountabilities may shape the discourse in different directions. (See, for example, Knorr-Cetina's analyses of writing in the area of protein resources, closely linked the pressing social needs of nutrition.[23]); and (4) the character of science, particularly the canons of scientific argumentation, appears to change through time, discipline, and situation. Yearley, analyzing a text in early nineteenth century geology, finds a very different mode of argumentation and a very different set of authorial commitments than found here[24]; further, Gilbert and Mulkay, working with a highly competitive field in contemporary biochemistry find strong evidence of interest laden distortion.[25]

Such cautions suggest the need for: (1) studies of general writing practices among contemporary scientists, including investigations of whether writing practices change with the anticipated importance, anticipated controversy, or the reputation of the author; (2) comparisons of scientific writing in different fields with different relations to wider social needs; and (3) studies of the changing nature of scientific discourse, with particular concern for the emergence of contemporary canons of scientific discourse.[26]

NOTES

I wish to thank E. Davenport, J. Dore, N. Mullins, C. Piltch, R. Stuewer, S. Weart, and H. Zuckerman and the referees for *Pre/Text* for their helpful comments, suggestions, and corrections as this paper passed through various forms. I especially wish to thank the librarians at the Center for the History of Physics, American Institute of Physics, New York, for their many kindnesses. An earlier version of this paper was delivered to the Society for the Social Studies of Science (Atlanta, 1981) and the New York Circle for the Theory of Literature and Criticism.

1. G. N. Gilbert, "The Transformation of Research Findings into Scientific Knowledge," *Social Studies of Science,* 6 (1976), 281-306; G. N. Gilbert, "Referencing as Persuasion," *Social Studies of Science,* 7 (1977), 113-122; G. N. Gilbert and N. Mulkay, "Contexts of Scientific Discourse: Social Accounting in Experimental Papers," *Sociology of the Sciences Yearbook,* (1980), 169-294; G. N. Gilbert and M. Mulkay, "Experiments are the Key" and "Warranting Scientific Belief," unpublished papers; M. Mulkay and G. N. Gilbert, "Joking Apart: Some Recommendations Concerning the Analysis of Scientific Culture," *Social Studies of Science,* 12 (1982), 585-614; J. Law and R. J. Williams, "Putting Facts Together: A Study of Scientific Persuasion," *Social Studies of Science,* 12 (1982), 535-558; K. Knorr-Cetina, *The Manufacture of Knowledge: An Essay on the Constructivist and Contextual Nature of Science* (Oxford: Pergamon, 1981); K. Knorr-Cetina, "Producing and Reproducing Knowledge: Descriptive or Constructive?" *Social Science Information* 16 (1977), 669-696; K. Knorr-Cetina, "Tinkering Toward Success: Prelude to a Theory of Scientific Practice," *Theory and Society,* 8 (1979), 347-376; K. Knorr-Cetina and D. Knorr, "From Scenes to Scripts: On the Relationship between Laboratory Research and Published Paper in Science," *Institute for Advanced Studies, Vienna, Research Memorandum* No. 132 (1978); B. Latour and S. Woolgar, *Laboratory Life* (Beverly Hills: Sage, 1979); S. Woolgar, "Discovery: Logic and Sequence in a Scientific Text," *Sociology of the Sciences Yearbook,* 1980, 239-268; S. Woolgar, "Writing an Intellectual History of Scientific Development: The Use of Discovery Accounts," *Social Studies of Science,* 6 (1976), 395-422; S. Yearley, "Textual Persuasion: The Social Accounting in the Construction of Scientific Arguments," *Philosophy of the Social Sciences,* 11 (1981), 409-435.

2. J. M. Cattell and J. Cattell, Eds., *American Men of Science,* 4th edition (New York: Science Press, 1927), p. 897.

3. Since a number of the revisions that appear in the published article are not marked in the revised draft, an editor may have suggested some of the

changes. Compton, however, would have had to approve any suggestions. I am therefore accepting the simplifying assumption that Compton is responsible for all revisions.

4. A. H. Compton, "A Quantum Theory of the Scattering of X-Rays by Light Elements," *Physical Review,* 21 (1923), 483–502.

5. The current view of Compton's work neglects his theoretical concern in developing an account of X-ray scattering consistent with electrodynamic theory in favor of an empirical result that was originally subordinate to theoretical issues. This interpretive shift began quite early. Compton's article appeared in volume 21 of *Physical Review.* Of the citations that appeared through volume 25 of that journal (a span of two years), excluding self-citations, nine appear in contexts that refer to his theory, and only one is concerned primarily with his empirical results. Of the citations in volumes 26 through 29, however, two are primarily theoretical, three are empirical, and one is mixed. Given the progress of quantum theory during that period and since and the consequent change of the importance of Compton's work, such a reinterpretation makes sense as part of the historically changing codification of the literature of a scientific field. But such reinterpretation based on current scientific belief in effect rewrites the original article.

I drew the citations from *A Citation Index for Physics: 1920–1929* (Philadelphia: Institute for Scientific Information, 1980); incidentally, Compton's Quantum Theory" article was the most cited article in physics during the decade.

Theory citations: 22, 283; 23, 122; 23, 135; 23, 316; 24, 179; 24, 591; 25, 314; 25, 444; 25, 723; 26, 435; 28, 875.

Experiment citations: 25, 193; 26, 299; 26, 657, 29, 758.

Mixed citation: 26, 691.

6. The importance of Compton's research program for the shape of his argument is made evident by a comparison to Debye's paper proposing a similar quantum theory of X-ray scattering, that might be taken as a case of simultaneous discovery. (P. Debye, "Zerstreuung von Rontgenstrahlen und Quantentheorie," *Physikalische Zeitschrift,* 24 (1923), 161–166.) Debye was not associated with the X-ray problem area, but rather was deeply committed to the quantum theory and its elaboration. Consequently, Debye's paper presents an extension of quantum theory that explains data anomalous to classical electrodynamic theory. Rather than presenting the progress and general types of difficulties run into by classical theory (as Compton does), Debye points to specific data anomalies. The derivation of the equations then follows, not as a proposed theory to be tested as in Compton's paper, but as a direct answer to difficulties. For Debye, quantum theory already stands, and this is only one more demonstration of its power; for Compton quantum theory is a last explanatory resource to be tested only after all classical explanations have been exhausted.

7. The full history of Compton's discovery, the challenges, and Compton's responses are recounted in R. Stuewer, *The Compton Effect* (New York: Science History, 1975). Compton's chief responses to challenges appear in the following articles: A. H. Compton, "Scattering of X-ray Quanta and the J Phenomena," *Nature,* 113 (1924), 160–61; A. H. Compton, "Absorption Measurements of the Change of Wave-length Accompanying the Scattering of X-Rays,"

Philosophical Magazine, 46 (1923), 897-911; A. H. Compton, "The Spectrum of Scattered X-rays," *Physical Review,* 22 (1923), 409-413; A. H. Compton and Y. H. Woo, "The Wave-Length of Molybdenum Kα Rays when Scattered by Light Elements," *Proceedings of the National Academy of Sciences,* 10 (1924), 271-273; A. H. Compton and J. A. Bearden, "The Effect of a Surrounding Box on the Spectrum of Scattered X-Rays," *Proceedings of the National Academy of Sciences,* 11 (1925), 117-119.

    8. C. T. R. Wilson, "Investigations on X-Rays and β-rays by the Cloud Method," Part I — X-Rays," *Proceedings of the Royal Society,* 104 (1923), 1-24; W. Bothe, "Über eine neu Sekundärstrahlung der Röntgenstrahlen," *Zeitschrift für Physik,* 16 (1923), 319-210, and 20 (1924), 237-255.

    9. A. H. Compton, "Recoil of Electrons from Scattered X-Rays," *Nature,* 112 (1923), 435.

    10. A. H. Compton and J. C. Hubbard, "The Recoil of Electrons from Scattered X-Rays," Physical Review, 23 (1924), 439-456; A. H. Compton, "The Scattering of X-rays," *Journal of the Franklin Institute,* 198 (1924), 57-72; A. H. Compton, "A General Quantum Theory of the Wave-length of Scattered X-rays," *Physical Review,* 24 (1924), 168-176.

    11. A. H. Compton and A. W. Simon, "Measurements of β-Rays Associated with Scattered X-Rays," *Physical Review,* 25 (1925), 306.

    12. *Ibid.,* p. 307.

    13. L. Fleck, *Genesis and Development of a Scientific Fact,* tr. F. Bradley and T. Trenn (Chicago: Univ. of Chicago Press, 1979) discusses how active and passive resistances give rise to formulations taken to be facts by a thought collective. These formulations are developed and expressed within the stylized terms of the thought collective.

    14. N. Bohr, H. A. Kramers, and J. C. Slater, "The Quantum Theory of Radiation," *Philosophical Magazine,* 47 (1924), 785-802.

    15. A. H. Compton and A. W. Simon, "Directed Quanta of Scattered X-Rays," *Physical Review,* 26 (1925), 289-299.

    16. Arthur H. Compton, *Notebook III,* pp. 20-41.

    17. Latour and Woolgar, *Laboratory Life, op. cit.* note 1, citing G. Bachelard, *Le matérialisme rationnel* (Paris: P.U.F., 1953), discuss laboratory equipment as a reification of theory. This idea is intriguing, but it must be kept in mind that no matter how fully suggested by theory, the equiment must accord with the functioning of nature to work; in this way the equipment is as much a test of theory as reification of theory.

    18. *Ibid.,* pp. 49-52. On the bottom right hand corner of page 51 there is a boxed off set of data that is unlabelled that may represent a fifteenth plate; if so this would compensate for the apparent discrepancy caused by the later deletion of plate 38.

    19. Knorr, "Tinkering Toward Success" and Knorr and Knorr, "From Scenes to Scripts," *op. cit.* note 1.

    20. P. B. Medawar, "Is the Scientific Paper Fraudulent?" *Saturday Review,* 1 August 1964, 42-43.

    21. The line references that continue to the end of the paper refer to the final published version of the 'Measurements' article, reproduced and given line

reference numbers in the appendix. Draft and revisions appear in Notebook III, pp. 59-75.

22. Such interest in the audience's convenience is the basis of the research reviewed in M. Ennis, "The Design and Presentation of Informational Material," *Journal of Research Communication Studies,* 2 (1980), 67-82.

23. "From Scenes to Scripts" and *The Manufacture of Knowledge, op. cit.* note 1.

24. *op. cit.* note 1.

25. "Contexts of Scientific Discourse," *op. cit.* note 1.

26. Recent contributions toward a history of the scientific paper are J. Paradis, "Historical Aspects of Language Reform in the Sciences: 1620-1840" and J. Stephens, "Styles as Therapy in Renaissance Science" both in *New Essays in Technical and Scientific Communication: Theory, Research, and Criticism,* ed. Anderson, Miller, Brockmann (Farmingdale, NY: Baywood, 1983); and C. Bazerman, "Modern Evolution of the Experimental Report in Physics: Spectroscopic Articles in *Physical Review,* 1893-1980," *Social Studies of Science,* 14 (1984), 163-196.

This essay appears, in somewhat altered form, in the author's book *Shaping Written Knowledge: The Genre and Activity of the Experimental Article in Science* (Madison: Univ. of Wisconsin Press, 1988).

APPENDIX

MEASUREMENTS OF β-RAYS ASSOCIATED WITH SCATTERED X-RAYS

By Arthur H. Compton and Alfred W. Simon

Abstract

Stereoscopic photographs of beta-ray tracks excited by strongly filtered x-rays in moist air have been taken by the Wilson cloud expansion method. In accord with earlier observations by Wilson and Bothe, two distinct types of tracks are found, a longer and a shorter type, which we call P and R tracks, respectively. Using x-rays varying in effective wave-length from about 0.7 to 0.13 A, the ratio of the observed number of R to that of P tracks varies with decreasing wave-length from 0.10 to 72, while the ratio of the x-ray energy dissipated by scattering to that absorbed (photo-electrically) varies from 0.27 to 32. This correspondence indicates that about 1 R track is produced for every quantum of scattered x-radiation, assuming one P track is produced by each quantum of absorbed x-radiation. The *ranges* of the observed R tracks increase roughly as the 4th power of the frequency, the maximum length for 0.13 A being 2.4 cm at atmospheric pressure. About half of the tracks, however, had less than 0.2 of the maximum range. As to *angular distribution*, of 40 R tracks produced by very hard x-rays (111 kv), 13 were ejected at between 0 and 30° with the incident beam, 16 at between 30° and 60°, 11 at between 60° and 90° and none at a greater angle than 90°. The R electrons ejected at small angles were on the average of much greater range than those ejected at larger angles. These results agree closely in every detail with the theoretical predictions made by Compton and Hubbard, and the fact that in comparing observed and calculated values, no arbitrary constant is assumed, makes this evidence particularly strong that the assumptions of the theory are correct, and that whenever a quantum of x-radiation is scattered, an R electron is ejected which possesses a momentum which is the vector difference between that of the incident and that of the scattered x-ray quantum.

IN recently published papers, C. T. R. Wilson[1] and W. Bothe[2] have shown the existence of a new type of β-ray excited by hard x-rays. The range of these new rays is much shorter than that of those which have been identified with photo-electrons. Moreover, they are found to move in the direction of the primary x-ray beam, whereas the photo-electrons move nearly at right angles to this beam.[3] Wilson, and later Bothe,[4] have both ascribed these new β-rays to electrons which recoil from scattered x-ray quanta in accordance with the predictions of the quantum theory

---

[1] C. T. R. Wilson, Proc. Roy. Soc. A **104**, 1 (1923).
[2] W. Bothe, Zeits. f. Phys. **16**, 319 (1923).
[3] See, e.g., F. W. Bubb, Phys. Rev. **23**, 137 (1924).
[4] W. Bothe, Zeits. f. Phys. **20**, 237 (1923).

of x-ray scattering.[5] In support of this view, they have shown that the direction of these rays is right, and that their range is of the proper order of magnitude. The present paper describes stereoscopic photographs of these new rays which we have recently made by Wilson's cloud expansion method. In taking the pictures, sufficiently hard x-rays were used to make possible a more quantitative study of the properties of these rays.

The cloud expansion apparatus used in our work was patterned closely after Wilson's well-known instrument except that all parts other than the glass cloud chamber itself were made of brass. The timing was done by a single pendulum, which carried a slit past the primary beam and actuated the various levers through electric contacts. The Coolidge x-ray tube, enclosed in a heavy lead box, was excited by a transformer and kenotron rectifiers capable of supplying 280 peak kilovolts. For illumination we used a mercury spark, similar to that of Wilson, through which discharged a 0.1 microfarad condenser charged by a separate transformer and kenotron to about 40 kv. The photographs were made by an "Ontoscope" stereoscopic camera, equipped with Zeiss Tessar $f/4.5$ lenses of 5.5 cm. focal length. Eastman "Speedway" plates (45×107 mm) were found satisfactory.

A typical series of the photographs[6] obtained are reproduced in Plate I, (a) to (f), which show the progressive change in appearance of the tracks as the potential across the x-ray tube is increased from about 21 to about 111 kv.

Especially in view of the fact that the original photographs are stereoscopic, the negatives of course show much more detail than do the reproductions. These suffice to show, however, the two types of tracks, the growth of the short tracks with potential, and the fact that while the long tracks are most numerous for the soft x-rays, the short tracks are most in evidence when hard rays are used. These results are in complete accord with Wilson's observations.

Number of tracks. It has been shown[7] that if the above interpretation of the origin of the two classes of β rays is correct, the ratio of the number of short tracks (type R) to that of long tracks (type P) should be

$$N_R/N_P = \sigma/\tau \qquad (1)$$

where σ is the scattering coefficient, and τ the true absorption coefficient of the x-rays in air; for σ is proportional to the number of scattered

---

[5] A. H. Compton, Bulletin Nat. Res. Council, No. 20, p. 19 (1922); and P. Debye, Phys. Zeits. (Apr. 15, 1923)

[6] These photographs were shown at the Toronto meeting of the British Association in August 1924.

[7] A. H. Compton and J. C. Hubbard, Phys. Rev. **23**, 448 (1924).

(a) 21 kv
No Filter
$\lambda_{eff.} = .71 A$

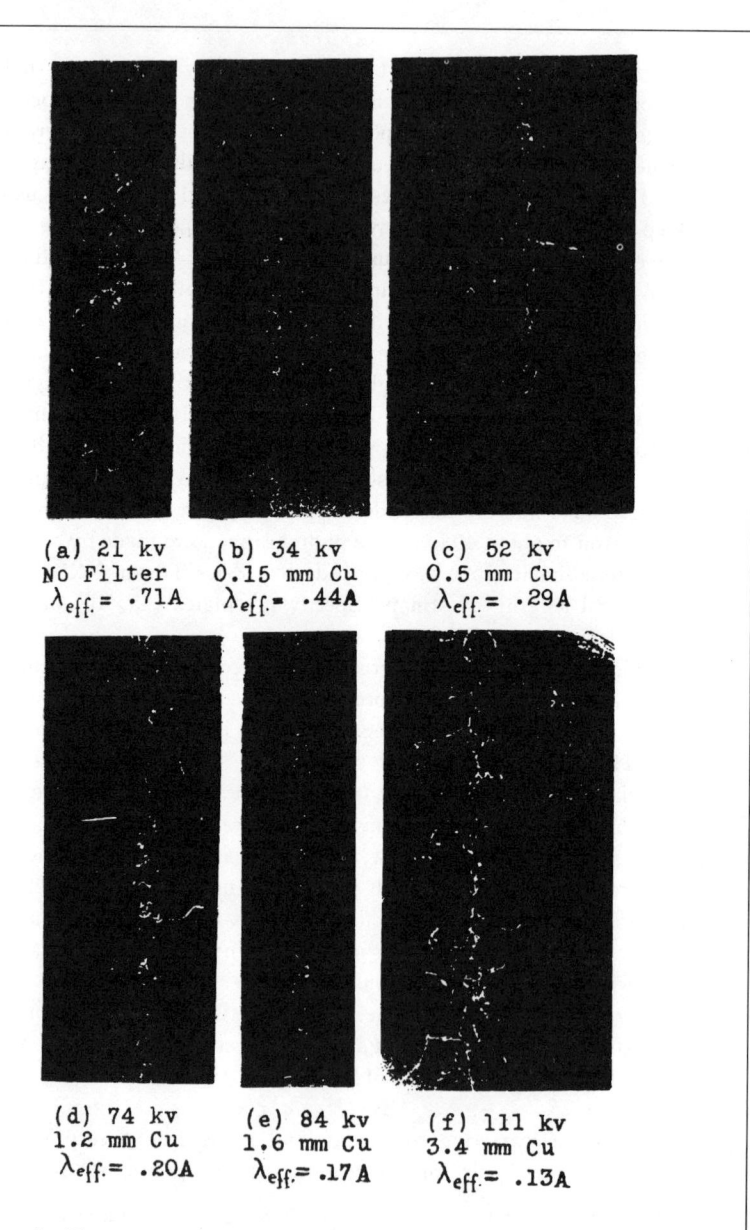

(b) 34 kv
0.15 mm Cu
$\lambda_{eff.} = .44 A$

(c) 52 kv
0.5 mm Cu
$\lambda_{eff.} = .29 A$

(d) 74 kv
1.2 mm Cu
$\lambda_{eff.} = .20 A$

(e) 84 kv
1.6 mm Cu
$\lambda_{eff.} = .17 A$

(f) 111 kv
3.4 mm Cu
$\lambda_{eff.} = .13 A$

Plate I. The x-rays pass from top to bottom. In addition to the copper filter, they traverse glass walls 4 mm thick. For the short waves the shorter (R) tracks increase rapidly in length and number. Thus while in (a) nearly all are P tracks, in (f) nearly all are R tracks.

quanta, and τ to the number of quanta spent in exciting photo-electrons, per centimeter path of the x-rays through the air.

In Table I we have recorded the results of the examination of the best 14 of a series of 30 plates taken at different potentials. The potentials given in column 1 of this table are based on measurements with a sphere gap. The potential measurements required corrections due to a slight warping of the frame holding the spheres, and to the lowering of the line voltage when the condenser was charged for the illuminating spark. The latter error was eliminated in the later photographs, at 34, 21, and 74 kv, and the former error was corrected by a subsequent measurement of the sphere gap distances, checked by a measurement of the lengths of the P tracks obtained at the lowest potential. The probable errors of potential measurements are thus unfortunately large, amounting to perhaps 10 percent in every case except that of 74 kv, which is probably accurate to within 5 per cent.

TABLE I
Number of tracks of types R and P.

Potential	Effective wave-length	Total tracks N	R tracks N_R	P tracks N_P	N_R/N_P	σ/τ
21kv	.71A	58	5	49	0.10	0.27
34	.44	24	10	11	0.9	1.2
52	.29	46	33	12	2.7	3.8
74	.20	84	74	8	9	10
84	.17	73	68	4	17	17
111	.13	79	72	1	72	32

The effective wave-lengths as given in column 2 are the centers of gravity of the spectral energy distribution curves after taking into account the effect of the filters employed. Because of the strong filtering, the band of wave-lengths present in each case is narrow, and the effective wave-length is known nearly as closely as the applied potential.

All the tracks originating in the path of the primary beam are recorded in column 3. Of these, the nature of some was uncertain. At the lower voltages it was difficult to distinguish the R tracks from the "sphere" tracks which Wilson has shown are often produced near the origin of a β-ray track by the fluorescent K rays from the oxygen or nitrogen atoms from which the ray is ejected. At the highest voltage the length of some of the R tracks is so great as to make it difficult to distinguish them from the P tracks. The numbers of R and P tracks shown in columns 4 and 5 are those of the tracks whose nature could be recognized with considerable certainty, the uncertain ones not being counted. This procedure probably makes the values of N_R/N_P in column 6 somewhat too small for the lower potentials and somewhat too great for the higher potentials.

The values of σ and τ given in column 7 are calculated from Hewlett's measurements[8] of the absorption of x-rays in oxygen and nitrogen. We have taken from his data the value of τ for 1 A to be 1.93 for air, and to vary as λ^3. The difference between the observed value of $\mu = \tau + \sigma$ and this value of τ gives the value of σ which we used.

The surprisingly close agreement between the observed values of N_P/N_R and the values of σ/τ we believe establishes the fact that the *R tracks are associated with the scattering of x-rays*. In view of the evidence that each truly absorbed quantum liberates a photo-electron or P track,[9] the equality of these ratios indicates that *for each quantum of scattered x-rays about one R track is produced.*

The fact that for the greater wave-lengths the ratio N_R/N_P seems to be smaller than σ/τ may mean that not all of the scattered quanta have R tracks associated with them. This would be in accord with the interpretation which has been given of the spectrum of scattered x-rays. The modified line has been explained by assuming the existence of a recoil electron, and the unmodified line as occurring when the scattering of a quantum results in no recoil electron. On this view the fact that the unmodified line is relatively stronger for the greater wave-lengths goes hand in hand with the observation that N_R/N_P is less than σ/τ for the greater wave-lengths. In view, however, of the meager data as yet available on this point, we do not wish to emphasize this correspondence too strongly.

Ranges of the R tracks. The range of the recoil electrons has been calculated on the basis of two alternative assumptions.[10] First, assuming that the electron recoils from a quantum scattered at a definite angle, its energy is found to be

$$E = h\nu \frac{2a \cos^2 \theta}{(1+a)^2 - a^2 \cos^2 \theta}, \tag{2}$$

where $a = h\nu/mc^2$, and θ is the angle between the primary x-ray beam and the direction of the electron's motion. This energy is a maximum when $\theta = 0$, and is then,

$$E_m = h\nu \frac{2a}{1+2a}. \tag{3}$$

[8] C. W. Hewlett, Phys. Rev. **17**, 284 (1921)
[9] See, e. g., A. H. Compton, Bull. Nat. Res. Council No. 20, p. 29, 1922
[10] See Compton and Hubbard, loc. cit.[7]

The second assumption is that the R electron moves forward with the momentum of the incident x-ray quantum. In this case the energy acquired is

$$E' = h\nu \cdot \tfrac{1}{2}\frac{a}{1+2a}(1-\tfrac{1}{4}a^2+ \cdots) . \qquad (4)$$

Eq. (3) was found to agree considerably better than Eq. (4) with Wilson's experimental results.

The lengths of the tracks shown on our photographs could be estimated probably within 10 or 20 per cent. These measured values, reduced to a final pressure of 1 atmosphere, are summarized in Table II. In column 2 are recorded the lengths of the longest tracks observed at each potential. S_m is the range calculated from Eq. 3, using C. T. R. Wilson's result[1] that the range of a β-particle in air is $V^2/44$ mm, where V is the potential in kilovolts required to give the particle its initial velocity, and the frequency ν employed is the maximum frequency excited by the voltage applied to the x-ray tube. S' is similarly calculated from Eq. (4).

TABLE II
Maximum lengths of R tracks.

Potential	Observed	Calc. (S_m)	Calc. (S')
21kv	0mm	0.06mm	0.004mm
34	0	0.3	0.02
52	2.5	1.8	0.1
74	6	6	0.4
88	9	12	0.7
111	24	25	1.5

It is evident that the observed lengths of the R tracks are not in accord with the quantity S' calculated from Eq. (4). They are, however, in very satisfactory agreement with the values of S_m given by Eq. (3). This result agrees with the conclusion drawn from Wilson's data,[11] but is now based upon more precise measurements. It follows that *the momentum acquired by an R particle* is not merely that of the incident quantum, but *is the vector difference between the momentum of the incident and that of the scattered quanta.*[12]

This conclusion is supported by a study of the relative number of tracks having different ranges. If the maximum range of the recoil electrons is S_m, Compton and Hubbard find[7] that the probability that the length of a given track will be S is proportional to

$$(2\sqrt{S/S_m}+\sqrt{S_m/S}-2) . \qquad (5)$$

[11] Compton and Hubbard, loc. cit.,[7] p. 449.
[12] That this is true for the β-rays excited by γ-rays has been shown in a similar manner by D. Skobeltzyn, Zeits. f. Phys. **28**, 278 (1924).

This expression assumes that the exciting primary beam has a definite wave-length. To calculate the relative number of tracks for different relative lengths to be expected, we have averaged this expression by a rough graphical method over the range of wave-lengths used in our experiments. These calculated values are given in the last column of Table III, for the relative ranges designated in column 1. A comparison of these

TABLE III
Relative lengths of R tracks.

Range of S/S_M	52kv	74kv	88kv	111kv	Mean	Calc.
0- .2	44	66	60	54	56	53
.2- .4	34	20	26	32	28	22
.4- .6	19	8	4	8	10	14
.6- .8	0	3	5	3	3	8
.8-1.0	3	3	5	3	3	3

(Per cent of R tracks within this range)

calculated values with the observed relative ranges shows a rather satisfactory agreement throughout. It will be noted further that the probabilities of tracks of different relative ranges is found to be about the same for x-rays excited at different potentials. This is in accord with the theoretical expression (5) for the probability, which is independent of the wave-length of the x-rays employed.

Angles of ejection of R tracks. On the view that the initial momentum of an R electron is the vector difference between the momenta of the incident and the scattered quantum, it is clear that these electrons should start at some angle between 0 and 90° with the primary beam. The probability that a given track will start between the angles θ_1 and θ_2 is on this hypothesis,[13]

$$\int_{\theta_1}^{\theta_2} P_\theta d\theta = 3ab \int_{\theta_1}^{\theta_2} \frac{a^2 \tan^4\theta + b^2}{(a \tan^2\theta + b)^4} \frac{\sin\theta}{\cos^3\theta} d\theta, \qquad (6)$$

where $a = (1 + h\nu/mc^2)^2$, and $b = (1 + 2h\nu/mc^2)$.

In our photographs only those taken at 111 kilovolts have tracks long enough to determine the initial direction with sufficient accuracy to make a reliable test of this expression. In all, the directions of 40 tracks were estimated, with the results tabulated in the second column of Table IV. In view of the fact that the photographs were stereoscopic, it was possible to estimate the angles in a vertical plane roughly, though not closer perhaps than within 10 or 15°. The values in the third column are calculated from Eq. (6). It is especially to be noted that, in accord with the

---

[13] See Compton and Hubbard, loc. cit.,[7] Eq. (14).

theory, no R tracks are found which start at an angle greater than 90° with the primary x-ray beam. In view of the small number of tracks observed and the approximate character of the angular estimates, the agreement between the two sets of values is as close as could be expected.

A more searching test of the assumption that the R tracks are electrons which have recoiled from scattered quanta is a study of the relative ranges of the tracks starting at different angles. (See columns 4 and 5 of Table IV.) The calculated ranges in column 5 are based on Eq. (2) for

TABLE IV
Number and range of R tracks at different angles, for 111 kv x-rays.

Angle of emission	Per cent of total number (obs.)	(calc.)	Average range (obs.)	(calc.)
0°-30°	34	28	9 mm	11 mm
30°-60°	39	50	4	4
60°-90°	27	22	0.9	0.3

the energy at different angles. In this calculation the effective wavelength, as estimated in connection with Table I, is employed. It will be seen that the observed ranges of the tracks ejected at small angles are much greater than that of those ejected at large angles, in substantial agreement with the theory.

It is worth calling particular attention to the fact that in comparing the theoretical and experimental values in these tables, no arbitrary constants have been employed. The complete accord between the predictions of the theory and the observed number, range, and angles of emission of the R tracks is thus of especial significance.

The evidence is thus very strong that there is about one R track or recoil electron associated with each quantum of scattered radiation, and that this electron possesses, both in direction and magnitude, the vector difference of momentum between the incident and the scattered x-ray quantum. Our results therefore afford a strong confirmation of the assumptions used to explain the change in wave-length of x-rays due to scattering, on the basis of the quantum theory.

RYERSON PHYSICAL LABORATORY,
UNIVERSITY OF CHICAGO.
November 15, 1924.

Reprinted by permission of the American Physical Society.

Afterthoughts:
Who Made Non-Fiction a Negation?

When I wrote "The Writing of Scientific Non-Fiction: Contexts, Choices, Constraints" in the early 1980s I was beginning to walk a line, a line I perceived then as so narrow and delicate I was afraid of falling — or being pushed — off. The line was between the marauding bands of radical relativists and what they claimed were the entrenched forces of positivist domination. Since then that line has become a broad and familiar path, passing through many locales, and intersecting with many other roads. At the same time, having walked with science studies so far through a changing landscape of representations, I no longer see simple battle lines formed between a well-disciplined band of radical relativists and hegemonic forces of scientific tradition. The relativists not only are divided among themselves, several (despite denials) are venturing into the intersection between material experience and processes of social interpretation and use. Moreover, as I have looked into the history of science, I have seen scientists and philosophers of science recurrently grappling with issues of individual perception and social representation. The legend of a fearsome positivist phalanx is a legend only, fostered by a small number of interested parties on both sides of a line they have mutually constructed.

Some of the interested parties in this construction of the positivist terror, curiously enough, have come from literary culture, which has categorized all texts which are not poetry, novels, or short stories as nonfiction. Non-fiction is a negative term, and therefore a term of marginality and exclusion.

Until the nineteenth century the term fiction — referring to made-up, deceptive, or lying discourse — was the marginal term. Following the romantic construction of the imagination as the privileged mode of knowing, the recognition of a body of texts which were admirable precisely for their fiction gave legitimacy to the term fiction in the nineteenth century, but still set against the more general body of texts assumed to be responsible for the quality of representation. Non-fiction as a term does not appear in general currency until the twentieth century. The term nonfiction appears neither in the original *Oxford English Dictionary* or the 1933 supplement. The 1976 supplement finally lists it with a first use as a noun in 1909 and as an adjective in 1903. Early uses of the term arise out of book distribution through libraries and publishers. The later adoption of non-fiction as a technical term of literary study, denoting a category of literary prose, excludes from study the wide body of texts that do not reflect literary values even while it readmits that small body of texts whose literary values designate them as subordinately part of literary culture and worthy of critical attention. This move seems to reflect the interests of an academic literary community needing to establish a privileged domain of discourse set against a perceived threat of scientific discourse delegitimating all other areas of culture and knowledge. Defining fiction as the privileged category carves out a protected socially important domain, even at the expense of demeaning the value and interest of all other forms of discourse.

The fiction/non-fiction divide reinforces the social definition of science as positivist and asserts that the shadow negative is in essence uninteresting from a literary perspective and therefore transparent as discourse. Non-fiction is simply a matter of fact, unless it is redeemed by looking a little bit like fiction. Thus the whole tradition of the complexity of representation is obscured to those people who study secular texts in the academy. The representational impulses of fictional texts are cast into the background, and texts which are predominantly representational vanish. In recent years when philosophically oriented literary theory reminded literary studies that representation was troublesome and could not be taken for granted, this cultural memory was immediately translated through the new cultural dichotomy of privileged literature and marginalized non-fiction with the result of an imperial assault of fiction upon non-fiction.

Because I now more clearly reject the whole fiction/non-fiction dichotomy, if I were rewriting this article today, I would no longer draw the rhetorical battle lines along that divide, not even to carve out a demilitarized zone of negotiation. When I revised material from this article to appear as a chapter in *Shaping Written Knowledge,* I replaced issues of non-fictionality with discussion of reference and accountability of representations to empirical experience. Indeed the substance of the article, even in the earlier form, concerns the ways in which the writer actively constructs reference through linguistic and material activity and uses this referential activity as a resource in persuasive scientific accounts. The referential activity, however, is persuasive only because it is constrained by resistances from empirical practices that pervade the entire process of the construction of representations—resistances that are reliably reconstitutable by other participants in the disciplinary practice. A. H. Compton, the scientist under study, through behavior in the writing process revealed in the notes and drafts, enacts this process of empirical accountability. In the surrounding chapters of *Shaping Written Knowledge,* accounts of experiments are placed within complex social matrices of institutions, relationships, and practices. Texts are not treated as fundamental accounts of truth in themselves but are seen as active parts of social processes of the production and reproduction of representations useful in the evolving discussion of the world we live in. Empiricism, which was the explicit project of modern science, is the issue which is to be understood in the texts and not non-fictionality (which is the discarded half of the post-Romantic literary project).

What was an issue in science studies a decade ago is no longer so poignantly an issue there, but has become increasingly an issue in literary studies and rhetoric. Some of the same impulses toward questioning the perceived hegemonic authority of modern science that led the strong program radical relativists in the sociology of knowledge to question the grounds on which texts claimed to stand, have led literary and rhetorical theorists to point toward the textuality of texts. Rhetoric of science and philosophy has again become an explicit issue as vigorously as it was in the eighteenth century, when Hume, Locke, Smith, Priestley, Vico, and many others wondered what it meant to create accounts of our experience. Our social position and the politics of knowledge are now different, but I hope we do not remain blinded by local battles so as to define these most serious issues too narrowly. As long as we desire to live in this world in ways that take account of the people, and life, and phenomena around us, we need to inquire how we can talk (and through our talk come to knowledge) about that which surrounds us.

8 : Neo-Romanticism and the History of Rhetoric

Sharon Crowley
Northern Arizona University

I can no longer resist the urge to take up my pen, having been incited to this act by reading the words of yet one more literary critic who is writing about rhetoric.

This time the critic is Jonathan Culler, an otherwise sensible interpreter of contemporary critical movements. In an essay on metaphor Culler allows that our "illustrious forebears" in rhetoric, while they would be delighted with a revival of interest in their discipline, would be puzzled by "the extraordinary privilege accorded to metaphor" in current literary criticism.[1] No doubt our forebears in rhetoric would be less surprised at Culler's limiting rhetoric to an aspect of *elocutio*—this very limitation having been imposed on rhetoric as several intervals in her history —than they would be astounded by his list of illustrious rhetoricians: Quintilian, Puttenham, DuMarsais, Fontanier. (At this point I took my copy of Kennedy's *Classical Rhetoric* off the shelf to confirm, as I suspected, that of the four names in Culler's list only Quintilian's appears in the index.)

We might attribute Culler's aberrant notions about rhetoric to the virtual absence of rhetorical training in graduate work in English in this country. Or we might place responsibility at the door of French criticism, from which much recent American critical thought takes its cue. In their introduction to *Rhetorique generale,* for example, the authors (known as Group *Mu* in homage to the Greek account of metaphor) puzzle themselves over Chaim Perelman's embarrassing habit of calling his work "rhetoric" when it deals with, of all things, a theory of reasoning.[2] While Group *Mu* heartily disavows Peter Ramus' influence on their work (except to hope that, like Ramus', their work will have a "revolutionary impact"), they are furthering the tendency begun by Ramus and continued by seventeenth-century French rhetoricians toward limiting rhetoric to a theory of communication, that is, to a theory of style (p.

viii). The French, it appears, are somewhat more familiar than are American critics with the history of rhetoric, although their version of it is peculiarly Francophile in overlooking parts of Aristotle in order to prefer Bernard de Lamy and Pierre Fontanier — the French *equivalents of* Hugh Blair.

A question arises. Should this make any difference to rhetoricians? That is, should students of rhetoric count the stance of contemporary literary criticism toward their discipline as simply another instance in a long series of misunderstandings about the scope of their work, or does the critics' appropriation of an emasculated rhetorical tradition have more serious ramifications? I think it does, obviously; and I will try to show why this is so by looking at some recent events in the history of the relation between rhetoric and literary criticism.

The definition of rhetoric as it is now understood in American literary criticism has its roots in the nineteenth century. While classical thought had tended to see literature as one of a collection of discursive arts which were alike in their being species of composition, Romantic literary theory repudiated classical notions about the mutual relation of kinds of discourse in order to elevate literature, specifically lyric poetry, to a dominant position among the discursive arts as "the breath and finer spirit of all knowledge" and "the very image of life expressed in its eternal truth."[3] The necessity to rationalize this concept of poetry prompted the appearance of a series of essays by influential Romantic critics who attempted to distinguish poetry from other kinds of discourse.

In 1833 John Stuart Mill contributed two essays on poetry to the *Monthly Repository,* the first of which, "What is Poetry?," states his famous dictum that "eloquence is *heard,* poetry is *over*heard" (Adams, p. 539). Mill argues that while poetry and eloquence are "both alike the expression or uttering forth of feeling," they differ in that "eloquence supposes an audience; the peculiarity of poetry appears to us to lie in the poet's utter unconsciousness of a listener." Mill's distinction, while it preserves the classical position that the aim of eloquence is to persuade an audience to the composer's point of view, adds the specifically Romantic notion that poetry is composed in a human vacuum. As Mill notes, when the composer's intent is the "desire of making an impression on another mind" the discourse "ceases to be poetry" (Adams, p. 540).

If Mill's distinction is accepted, discourse becomes less literary the further it moves away from lyric utterance toward frank acknowledgement of an audience. This notion no doubt has an affinity with Wordsworth's contention that poetry is "the spontaneous overflow of powerful feelings," where the poet aims solely to express a deeply-felt emotional experience. As Mill puts it, the poet bodies forth symbols "which are the nearest possible representations of the feeling in the exact shape in which it exists in the poet's mind." The important thing in Romantic theory is this mirroring of the poet's mind. Hence the priority accorded to lyric poetry, which is by convention "overheard" — the potential presence of an audience has nothing to do with the composition of the poem.

The romantic position regarding the poet's audience constitutes a more or less conscious attempt to remove poetry from contamination by everyday concerns, thus elevating it to a transcendental realm of permanence and beauty. Mill remarks, for example, that when a poet writes with the intention to publish, or for money, the chance that he will produce poetry "is far less probable" than were he to "succeed in excluding from his work every vestige of such lookings-forth into the outward and everyday world."

Romantic denial of the importance of the more mundane realities associated with writing poetry is a first step in the process of setting poetry apart from other sorts of discourse. A second, and related, step is to deny that poems are composed in any ordinary sense of that word. In an 1829 essay, Cardinal Newman bases his distinction between poetry and eloquence on just this criterion: for Newman, "dexterity in composition" is no essential part of poetry.[4] The poet "will be obscure, not only from the carelessness of genius, and from the originality of his conceptions, but it may be from natural deficiency in the power of clear and eloquent expression, which, we must repeat, is a talent distinct from poetry, though often mistaken for it." Thus "attention to language, for its own sake," that is, to eloquence, "evidences not the true poet, but the mere artist" (p. 25). Composition becomes an afterthought on the Romantic model, something attended to when inspiration, the real stuff of poetry, declines. "The mind in creation is as a fading coal," says Shelley (Adams, p. 511).

What Newman does not say is that the poetic audience must then consist of those who can tune in to the poet's inspiration in such a way as to obviate the need for clarity. Since the act of composing apparently comprises a hasty recording of the poet's insight readers must reconstruct the experience as best they can. It was left for Thomas De Quincey to provide a rationale for just such a conception of the poetic process.

De Quincey joined the discussion about the relation of literature to other sorts of discourse in 1848 in an essay reappraising the poetry of Pope, although he first published his famous distinction between "the literature of power" and "the literature of knowledge" in 1823.[5] De Quincey's distinction avowedly resorts to the relative effect on readers of each mode of discourse, a move which designates his criticism as rhetorical. And yet De Quincey, like Mill and Newman, writes as though poets are innocent of overt rhetorical intent, that it is instead the natural sympathy of human minds that permits the literature of power to affect readers. De Quincey's distinction proves on examination to be metaphysical rather than rhetorical, grounded as it is in a distinction between the kinds of truth revealed by the two kinds of discourse.

In the 1823 essay De Quincey waxes lyrical as he describes the required effect of the literature of power:

> I should be made to feel vividly, and with a vital consciousness, emotions which ordinary life rarely or never supplies occasion for exciting, and which had previously lain unwakened, and hardly within the dawn of consciousness — as myriads of modes of feeling are at this moment in every human mind for want of a poet to organize them. (Masson, X, 48)

For De Quincey power is the antithesis of knowledge, and "all that is literature seeks to communicate power; all that is not literature, to communicate knowledge." The antithesis implies an absolute opposition between discourse which organizes emotion and that which aims simply to communicate information.

In this early essay De Quincey explicitly rejects the classical notion that discourse either teaches or delights, arguing that *Paradise Lost* neither instructs nor amuses. In the 1848 essay, however, De Quincey opposes the effect of the literature of knowledge to that produced by the literature of power by utilizing the classical account: the functions of the kinds of discourse are to teach and to move, respectively (Masson, XI, 54). The distinction between teaching and moving has to do, he explains, with the relative newness of the material to its readers: "whenever we talk in ordinary language of seeking information or gaining knowledge, we understand the words as connected with something of absolute novelty." But De Quincey is really interested in establishing a hierarchy of value based on relative novelty: "it is the grandeur of all truth which can occupy a very high place in human interests that it is never absolutely novel to the meanest of minds: it exists eternally by way of germ or latent principle in the lowest as in the highest, needing to be developed, but never to be planted. To be capable of transplantation is the immediate criterion of a truth that ranges on a lower scale" (Masson, XI, 55). De Quincey illustrates his point by comparing the relative effort of reading a cookbook (where the reader learns "something new, something that you did not know before, in every paragraph") to that of reading *Paradise Lost,* which gives a reader "exercise and expansion to our own latent capacity of sympathy with the infinite."

There exist, then, two sorts of knowledge to which the two kinds of discourse appeal. The first is knowledge of the facts of the world, the discourse about which may be revised, expanded, or even "placed in a better order" and thus superceded (Masson, XI, 57). The second sort of knowledge appeals to some latent structure already in the reader's mind, reactivating it and bringing the reader's awareness of it to life. Perhaps De Quincey's point can be made clearer by juxtaposing it to a similar argument made by Mill in his essay "On Genius."[6] Mill argues that "to know an individual fact may be no exercise of the mind at all; merely an exercise of the senses." The discoverer of such a fact has only brought it "sufficiently close for the senses to judge of it" (Robson, p. 331). However the "knowledge of supersensual things, of man's eternal and moral nature, where the appeal is to internal consciousness and self-observation" is of a very different order. This second mode of knowing, the internal, is entitled to be called knowledge; all else is merely authority. Mill uses a similar argument in "What is Poetry?" to distinguish poetry from fiction; and for Mill as well as De Quincey, it is to the higher knowledge that poetry contributes, because readers of poetry can achieve complete identification with the poet (Adams, p. 538; Robson, p. 333).

If we accept De Quincey's contention that the literature of power appeals to all readers on some level of consciousness, it follows that such literature has universal appeal; and this provides De Quincey with a ground for giving higher rank to the literature of power than to its antithesis: "and hence the preeminency over all authors that merely teach of the meanest that moves." Literature of power, because of its appeal to innate structures of the mind, has permanence, too: "all the literature of knowledge builds only ground-nests, that are swept away by floods, or confounded by the plough; but the literature of power builds nests in aerial altitudes of temples sacred from violation, or of forests inaccessible to fraud" (Masson, XI, 59).

De Quincey thus introduces into Romantic theory the notion of the authoritative literary text which is different in kind, by virtue of its universal and timeless appeal, from those whose object is the communication of mere information. This appeal is based not only in its faithful *mimesis* of human thought but in its imitation of the mind's structures as well. As De Quincey writes, the texts of the literature of power "never can transmigrate into new incarnations. To reproduce these in new forms, or variations, even if in some things they should be improved, would be to plagiarize" (Masson, XI, 57). The forms taken by texts of the literature of power in some way resemble or recreate the universal structures of the human mind; that is the source of their power. The literature of knowledge, on the other hand, can derive its structural principles only by relying either on the organization of the facts themselves or by having form imposed on it by its author. The truth-value of the literature of knowledge, governed as it is by the necessity of adhering to empirical fact, is always available for revision, as is its shape. The latter is the case, De Quincey contends, with La Place's reworking of Newton's *Principia.*

Walter Pater begins his 1889 essay on style by putting De Quincey's distinction into suspension on the ground that it is difficult to draw a firm line between facts and someone's sense of what the facts are.[7] Pater's own distinction between modes of discourse, however, echoes De Quincey's in its reliance on the notion that discourse can reflect both exterior and interior truth. In non-literary and literary discourse respectively, one looks for "truth there as accuracy, truth here as expression, that finest and most intimate form of truth, the *vraie vérité*" (32). The artist deals in the finer, inner sort of truth: "for just in proportion as the writer's aim, consciously or unconsciously, comes to be the transcribing, not of the world, not of mere fact, but of the sense of it, he becomes an artist, his work fine art" (p. 6).

The distinction between interior and exterior truth seduces Pater into assuming a form/content dualism as the basis for his "eclectic principle of good style." Good style is the "absolute accordance of expression to idea." (p. 32). Artistry consists in the degree to which the composer is able to fit her expression to her inspiration; this is more likely to happen in poetry, of course. Pater is willing to allow the humbler sort of discourse pretensions to artistry, however, if its style permits it to convey inner truth: "all beauty is in the long run only fineness of truth, or what we call expression, the finer accommodation of speech to that vision within." In true works of art, then, inspiration and expression are perfectly matched to one another even if they happen to be written in prose.

The Romantic elevation of poetry seems to require that it be distinguished from imaginative prose as well as from more mundane sorts of discourse. For Shelley this distinction had revolved around the presumed universality of poetry: "stories," like history, are "detached facts," while poetry is "the creation of actions according to the unchangeable forms of human nature" (Adams, 502). Thus Pater wants to distinguish poetry from fiction on the grounds that the latter appeals to the exterior truth of fact rather than to higher, inner truth. Indeed, Pater goes so far as to apologize for the ubiquity of imaginative prose in his own era (p. 7). In fact, his uneasiness about the possibility that formal perfection may be achieved in prose provides the key to a hidden enterprise in his essay. According to Pater, "scientific writing," which includes all discourse except poetry and fiction, must never call on the writer's imaginative powers. Writers of scientific discourse — Pater's example is Gibbon — are to be confined by the facts of their subject, just as they are for De Quincey. Pater leaves the impression that he disapproves of the *Decline and Fall* precisely because Gibbon moulded his material "to a preconceived view" (p. 5). That Gibbon's more rhetorical age applauded his approach as that most suited to writers of history seems not to concern Pater. What is crucial in Romantic theory is that writers who are not poets be inextricably bound to the facts presented by their material. Such writers distort that material if they impose a predetermined order on it; in other words, Pater's principle of good style—the "absolute accordance of expression of idea"—is not available to writers who concern themselves with "exterior" truth.

Thus the Romantic program outlined a role for poetry which of necessity influenced conceptions about the scope of other modes of discourse. Poetry reflects valuable human truth through its being given to especially sensitive writers to transfer their insights to capable readers. Further, the linguistic surface of the poetic work is neatly fitted to the message it carries. The concept of the perfect fit between inspiration and expression fosters a disdain for composition as an art which serves only those readers who are unable to share the poetic insight without its assistance. Romantic theory leaves the more mundane work of appealing to audiences, dealing with facts, and addressing the niceties of composition to nonpoetic modes of discourse.

The impact of the Romantic model is still being felt in American literary criticism, as had been nicely demonstrated by Frank Lentricchia. The neo-Romantic tradition, according to Lentricchia, espouses "a theory that language in the aesthetic mode overcomes the arbitrariness of ordinary discourse by achieving ontological participation."[8] That literary criticism has bought into the Romantic enterprise is no surprise, since the privileging of literary discourse has created a comfortable professional niche for those so inclined.[9] What is remarkable is that rhetoricians have been so taken with Romantic notions about the status of literary discourse.

In an influential essay published in *PMLA* in 1904, Fred Newton Scott attempted to distinguish poetry from prose. That Scott undertook this dubious exercise at all is testimony to the influence on him of the Romantic assumption that in the universe of discourse there is poetry and there is everything else. Since he is a rhetorician, Scott wants to ground his distinction in the social nature of language. Consequently he draws on the anthropological knowledge of his day to formulate origins for prose and poetry: prose occurs in "the situation in which a member of society is moved to verbal utterance mainly by a desire to communicate himself to his fellow men," poetry when "one man, or a number of men acting in concert, are moved by a desire to express or give vent to the feelings and ideas which arise in them, the desire being the natural psychological necessity that thought and feeling in simple natures must have some motor outlet."[10] But as he explores his subject Scott realizes that to identify poetry with expression and prose with communication takes him into dangerous waters; to assume that one can define an author's intention by the form that the work takes is a shaky enterprise at best.

Scott's uneasiness about this distinction is betrayed by the fact that exceptions to the expression/communication rule appear in a series of footnotes to his essay. He does not know what to make of the fact that diaries, which ought to be wholly expressive, are written in prose, or of Gabriel Rossetti's comment that great artists identify themselves with the personalities of their readers, a feat which ought to be more in keeping with the aims of prose writers than of poets, if Scott's distinction between the two forms is the correct one. Consequently Scott continues to refine his initial distinction, arriving eventually at this formula: poetry is "expression for communication's sake," prose "communication for expression's sake" (257).

Yet even this blurring of the original dichotomy will not do. Scott creates a middle category, prose-poetry, which results, he tells us in a footnote:

> when a writer adhering to the traditional medium of communication — the forms invested by long use with communicative associations — becomes interested mainly in expression. Under the influence of the expressive impulse the words tend to fall into regular rhythms, but are prevented from doing so by the writer's sense of integrity — his sense of the artistic necessity of maintaining the structural form which he set out. (pp. 266-67)

Artists who lack a sense of structural integrity end up writing "bad blank verse." In other words, as the intention of the artist changes, so ought the form. If the artist's intention is muddled, we get bad (read "hybrid") writing, which is not sure whether it wants to emphasize inner, personal expression or outer, social, communicative truth.

Scott's confusion here stems from his unquestioning acceptance of the Romantic assumption that a text must somehow reflect its author's intention, or, to speak more broadly, that texts reflect the movement of their authors' minds. Objections to intentionality as a critical criterion are easy to raise of course: authors are not always conscious of an explicit intention when they compose, and even when they are, the completed discourse may be read in such a way as to defy its author's intention altogether. (If this were not the case there presumably would be no such thing as a negative review). A given text may be construed in nearly as many ways as it has readers, as even a cursory review of the pages of *PMLA* will demonstrate.[11]

Two influential rhetoricians published essays in the mid-twenties dealing with the relation of rhetoric to literature. In his "Rhetoric and Poetry" Hoyt Hudson initially adopts Scott's notion of intention as a criterion for distinguishing poetry from rhetoric.[12] According to Hudson, "poetry is for the sake of expression . . . rhetoric is for the sake of impression" (p. 146). Hudson does acknowledge, however, that poets do consider audiences while composing: "the poet thinks of a more general and more vaguely defined audience than the orator." Having said as much Hudson abruptly reverses himself and adopts De Quincey's criterion of universality to disqualify considerations of audience as part of the poetic performance: "we find that [the poet] is likely to think of himself as a fair representative of mankind and write to please himself, trusting thereby to please others—which is equivalent to taking no account of his audience at all" (p. 148).

Hudson next introduces the concept of display as a distinctive criterion of rhetoric. Display has to do with the surface trappings of language use: "order of words, with regard to emphasis and balance, clever paradox and specious reasoning, beauty and variety of figures and tropes, dignity and sonorousness of language" (p. 150). According to Hudson the rhetorician may more easily risk readers' recognition of such technical fireworks than may the poet; indeed, "the desire to make a display of skill should never enter the poet's impulse." Once again, poets are not to interest themselves in matters which are exterior to the essence of their discourse, nor are they to permit exteriority to reveal itself in obvious attention to the niceties of composition.

Herbert Wichelns' "The Literary Criticism of Oratory" has since been much reprinted in speech criticism circles.[13] While Wichelns' scholarly essay presents itself as an attempt to distinguish rhetorical from literary criticism, it can be read as a reaction to the dominance of Romantic assumptions in the criticism of both fields. The essay is, in fact, an *apologia* for the occasional nature of rhetorical discourse. Wichelns find an opportunity to distinguish poetical from rhetorical discourse when, late in the essay, he attempts to define "rhetoric." He quotes with approval Scott's definition of rhetoric as "the science and art of communication in language," while poetry is concerned with expression. But Wichelns is less sure that rhetorical discourse must always occur in prose (pp. 54–55). As he notes, the inclination of literary critics to muddle about a verse/prose distinction covers up a much more crucial one, the relation of the two kinds of discourse to their immediate cultural situations.

Wichelns is not afraid to defend rhetorical discourse and its criticism on the grounds of their concern with immediate effect. He deplores the negative attitude of the literary critic toward "the minor rhetoric, the suasive purpose" of discourse (p. 44). Rhetorical criticism would, in Wichelns' view, eschew the criteria of permanence and beauty with which literary critics evaluate discourse, preferring instead to engage in "analysis and appreciation of the orator's method of imparting his ideas to his hearers" (p. 54). Much criticism of oratory, Wichelns feels, distorts its nature by treating it as "a specimen of prose, or as an example of philosophic thought," thus ignoring its formal aspect (p. 36). Wichelns is especially disturbed by the literary critical habit of judging oratory in terms of its stylistic felicities, noting several times that such criticism overlooks the really salient property of rhetorical discourse, that is, "the larger pattern of ideas rather than the minute pattern of grammatical units," the "order and movement given to thought," its "strategy," and its "architectonic element." In other words, Wichelns approves of a formalist criticism for oratory; he just wants it to occur on a larger scale than does stylistic analysis. That is, Wichelns wants some oratory to be able to aspire to the Romantic criterion of formal perfection, a criterion which, where achieved, will elevate it to the realm of literature, which is always "free to fulfill its own law" (p. 56). The difficulty of employing formal perfection as a critical criterion for rhetorical discourse is of course that rhetoric is "perpetually in bondage to the audience and occasion," as Wichelns puts it in a revealing image.

Wichelns' advocacy of formal analysis as a suitable critical approach to both kinds of discourse anticipates a critical movement which peaked in popularity in the mid-twentieth century. "Rhetorical analysis of literature," as it was understood in the nineteen-sixties at least, assumed that readers' responses to a text are somehow enshrined in its surface rather than being shaped by a whole panoply of linguistic, cultural, and personal contexts brought to it by readers, as more recent reader response theory acknowledges.[14] Wilbur Samuel Howell places blame for the ubiquity of this critical school on Kenneth Burke, whom he accuses of having "gelded" rhetoric by conflating it with poetic.[15] In 1965 Howell argued in Burke's presence that the final chapter of *Counter-Statement* (1931) "makes the poetic utterance and the rhetorical utterance specifically alike" by assuming that "their common capacity to produce effects argues their identification in method and structure" (p. 238). Burke's literary theory is then constituted by the "study of mechanisms by which literary works produce effects on readers," a position which assumes that "literary theory and rhetorical theory are one in the same thing" (p. 37). According to Howell, Burke was led into his mistaken attempt to assert that the same critical principles governed both kinds of discourse by the "shaky rhetorical learning that was the rule rather than the exception in scholarly and critical circles of the early twentieth century."

Actually, Burke does not go so far in *Counter-Statement*. His strategy there is to borrow the long-established terminology of rhetoric in order to create a vocabulary for poetry, which had not yet developed its own set of critical terms in 1931. Burke did respond to Howell's charges, however, with a murky essay entitled "Rhetoric and Poetics" which appeared in 1968.[16] There Burke reaffirms the theory of formal effect he espoused in *Counter-statement* and puts its genesis down to his having begun "in the aesthete tradition, with the stress upon self-expression." Later, while writing *Counter-statement*, he "made the shift from 'self-expression' to 'communication'"; only later still did he add a third term to his critical vocabulary, "consummation" (p. 305). Burke's use of Scott's language is something other than coincidence, since Burke here betrays his continuing allegiance to neo-Romantic formalism when he writes that "questions to do with the arousing and fulfilling of expectations are, in the last analysis, but ways of asking pointed questions about a work's unity . . . they do serve well as goads, or arrows, prodding us to take a close look at the dynamics or musculature of either Poetical or Rhetorical performance" (p. 306). In other words, Howell's claim that Burke's method identifies poetry with rhetoric is a valid one. Thirty years after the publication of *Counter-statement* Burke continued to conflate the two kinds of discourse by insisting on formalist analysis as the critical approach appropriate to both, an analysis that borrows from rhetoric only the notion that readers' anticipated responses can be used for evaluating the worth of a work.

In 1964 the University of Iowa hosted a seminar aimed at clarifying the relation between rhetoric and poetry. Some of the best-known scholars of the sixties were invited to discuss what rhetorical critic Edwin Black called "the theoretical disshevelment" found at the boundary of the two fields.[17] Reading through a collection of essays that records the proceedings is a curious experience. The literary critics tend to talk about poems and plays in self-assured New Critical fashion, as though to do so is to illustrate the role of rhetoric in literature. For example, Murray Krieger discusses the literary use of persona at some length, apparently on the assumption that persona is a rhetorical concept. Krieger approves of its use in literature when it renders a work "more subtle," and hence more valuable. Nonetheless, Krieger inserts this discussion into a defense that he calls "contextualist criticism," which posits that poetry has to be kept free from contamination by reality (p. 47). Krieger's argument must have at least dismayed the rhetoricians who were present.

Chicago critic Bernard Weinberg used Romantic terminology to attempt a theoretical distinction between rhetoric and poetry. "In poetry," he writes in good Shelleyan fashion, we are led "inwards" rather than "outwards . . . to a form that is essentially self-contained." And in order that the self-reference of literature not be dismissed as an impossibility by those who worry about its impact on others, Weinberg asserts that the poet "writes his poem, and if he writes it well, the audience will respond to it as it should" (p. 38). Even though the poet may not have a specific audience in mind when he composes, Weinberg is sure that the formal effect built into every poem will trigger the appropriate effect in any audience who contemplates it.

The rhetoricians who spoke at the Iowa conference used the occasion to resurrect a sense of their field as a coherent domain, a move made necessary by the secondarization of rhetorical discourse in contemporary literary theory. Donald Bryant attributes the confusion about the relation between literature and rhetoric to literary critics' misapplication of the term "rhetoric." Bryant's list of critical definitions of rhetoric includes the sense of formal techniques codified in textbooks called "rhetorics"; the "full-blown sense" of "a coping with a public which is deliberately to be affected," a usage which is denigrated by literary critics because it has reference to an external world and thus cannot be art; and two uses in literary theory where rhetoric means either generic criticism (a la Northrop Frye) or is a catch-all term that refers to whatever linguistic element in a poem eludes its critics (pp. 2–12). Bryant efficiently demolishes one New Critical distinction between rhetoric and literature by demonstrating that overt attempts to persuade audiences are often made by literary artists. But he concludes what is an otherwise persuasive appeal to reconsider the current critical vocabulary by arguing, as Wichelns had done nearly forty years earlier, that some rhetorical discourse is of sufficient quality to be considered literary. Bryant defines quality as a genuine fusion of thought, feeling, and expression; we are left to conclude that where this fusion does not occur we have instead the "manipulation" of thought and feeling, that is, "mere" rhetoric.

Roger Hornsby closed the seminar by accusing modernism of taking a naive attitude toward literary form, an attitude which probably accounts "for the pejorative connotation rhetoric enjoys today" (p. 90). Noting that "the ancient writers never made the peculiar modern assumption that a work exists in some sort of vacuum, that it does not have an audience," Hornsby nonetheless betrays his own seduction by neo-Romantic notions about form when he quotes Allen Tate to the effect that "rhetoric is . . . the means of forming the work, or informing it." Like Kenneth Burke—but unlike Aristotle—Hornsby would consider plot as "a kind of rhetorical term" (p. 91).

Twentieth-century historians of rhetoric have generally appealed to the classical criterion of mimesis as a basis for distinguishing between rhetoric and literature, as do C. S. Baldwin, D. L. Clark, and Walter Ong.[18] As early as 1947, for example, Howell had argued the necessity for maintaining a clear distinction between the two arts, a distinction he would base on the classical assumption that poetry, being mimetic, refers only mediately to the experience for which it is a fictional deputy, while rhetoric refers directly to the world of things. Howell wants to reclaim rhetoric by arguing its claims to truth-telling, claims to which poetry has only secondary rights by virtue of its fictional nature. Unlike classical rhetoricians, who carefully hedged their bets about the truth value of rhetorical discourse, Howell states flatly that rhetoric, "the literature of statement," has truth as its end, while poetry, "the literature of symbol," is a purely aesthetic matter whose end is delight. Of course Howell's version of poetic *mimesis* borrows a card from the Romantic deck in assuming that discourse mirrors reality. He also retains the Romantic division of reality into interior and exterior realms to which poetry and rhetoric refer, respectively; as a rhetorician Howell finds that discourse which deals directly with the world of things more valuable than that which represents the postulated inner world of experience.

A very recent attempt to distinguish the province of rhetoric from that of literature does little to allay suspicion that pronouncements about the relative value of the two fields of study will cease to be made, even though new developments in literary critical theory and a revived respect for rhetoric have appeared in the last fifteen years or so. Almost in passing, George Kennedy gives a neat turn to the Romantic screw in order to demote literature by assigning to it the very qualities usually relegated to rhetoric in neo-Romantic literary theory. Kennedy privileges rhetoric as "primary" while literature is "secondary"; rhetoric is oral, public, grounded in civic matters, and persuasive, while literature is characterized by "commonplaces, figures of speech and thought, and tropes in elaborate writing."[19] Apparently, the relative value of exteriority in discourse depends on which blade of the discursive axe is being ground; overt concern with form, linguistic elaboration, or display can be positive or negative depending on whether these are perceived as central or extraneous to an artist's aim. And if these are negatively perceived they will be attributed to whichever kind of discourse a given critic is attempting to secondarize.

I have tried to demonstrate here that in twentieth-century criticism, at least, the Romantic habit of valorizing literary discourse has been met with a variety of defensive responses on the part of rhetoricians, responses which can be seen as culminating in Kennedy's reversal of the Romantic evaluative hierarchy. But the entire enterprise of hierarchizing the two kinds of discourse seems to me to have lost its reason for being. Literary study has succeeded in enthroning itself as a legitimate discipline; it need no longer attempt to secure its position by proclaiming itself to be the pinnacle of discursive art. It can continue to do so only because many of its practitioners remain ignorant of rhetorical history and theory.

Such ignorance still causes literary critics occasionally to broach rhetoric as though it were a branch of literature. Kennedy points out that this approach is a serious distortion of both rhetorical and literary history (p. 109). And as Howell notes in another context, "anyone who has conscientiously tried to take rhetoric seriously as a discipline knows how frustrating it is even yet to be associated with some of the degraded aspects of the rhetorician's procedures, and to be assumed in teaching those procedures to emphasize only what the pejorative senses of the term rhetoric would seem to allow" (*Poetics,* p. 237).

But confusion about what rhetoric is causes problems for literary criticism, too. It is amusing, if not sad, to watch good critics wrestle with insights that are prosaic in even those most prosaic of rhetorical circles, the speech-communication journals. For an example we can turn to *Is There a Text in This Class?*, where Stanley Fish acknowledges, after many pages (and presumably years) of searching, that "the mechanisms of persuasion . . . are context-specific," and that "shared assumptions" about values must exist in order for writers to be understood by readers.[20] And in the essay with which I began, Jonathan Culler makes an elaborate case for metaphor as a means of invention; a similar argument was made by rhetorician Alexander Bain well over a hundred years ago. It seems that James Murphy may have a valid complaint when he notes that the English profession's ignorance of its history tempts it into continual reinventions of the discursive wheel.[21]

What is to be done? At the risk of building a case for my own brand of chauvinism, I suggest a simple and relatively cheap remedy: give every graduate student in English a good course or two in the history of rhetoric. Such a course might go a long way toward helping students of literature to understand that the critical criteria championed by whatever school of literary thought is currently in fashion constitutes merely one of many revolutions in discursive theory, revolutions which have been occurring for over 2000 years. Such a historical context might bring scholars and teachers of literature to see, among other things, that no theory of discourse has ever been successful in maintaining metaphysical claims for language, that the priority of formalism waxes and wanes, that invention—the art of composing—used to hold an honored place in rhetoric, and that rhetoric itself was once a monolithic theory of discourse which included literary composition within its province. Failing the possibility that organized study in rhetorical history can be universally instituted, we can at least include the work of some of our illustrious rhetorical forebears on graduate reading lists: Gorgias, Aristotle, Cicero, Quintilian. Surely such readings are as central to Western culture as those of Spenser and Milton. Maybe even those of Wordsworth and Shelley.

NOTES

1. Jonathan Culler, *The Pursuit of Signs: Semiotics, Literature, Deconstruction* (Ithaca: Cornell Univ. Press, 1981), p. 188.

2. Group Mu, *A General Rhetoric,* trans. Paul B. Burrell and Edgar M. Slotkin (Baltimore: Johns Hopkins Univ. Press, 1981).

3. The first characterization is Wordsworth's, from the "Preface to the Second Edition of Lyrical Ballads," in Hazard Adams, ed., *Critical Theory Since Plato* (New York: Harcourt Brace Jovanovich, 1971), p. 439; the second is Shelley's, from "A Defense of Poetry," in Adams, p. 502. For the revolutionary nature of this definition of poetry the best source is still M. H. Abrams, *The Mirror and the Lamp* (New York: Oxford Univ. Press, 1953).

4. John Henry Newman, "Poetry with Reference to Aristotle's *Poetics,*" in *Essays Critical and Historical* (London: Longman's, 1919), I, 24.

5. Thomas De Quincey, "Letters to a Young Man Whose Education has been Neglected," in *The Collected Writings of Thomas De Quincey,* ed. David Masson (London: A. and C. Black, 1897), X, 46–48; and "The Poetry of Pope," in Masson, XI, 51–95.

6. John Stuart Mill, "On Genius," in *The Collected Works of John Stuart Mill,* ed. John M. Robson and Jack Stillinger (Toronto: Univ. of Toronto Press, 1981), I, 329–39.

7. Walter Pater, *Appreciations, with an Essay on Style* (London: Macmillan, 1924), p. 4.

8. Frank Lentricchia, *After the New Criticism* (Chicago: Univ. of Chicago Press, 1980), p. 119. For an attempt to assess its effects on pedagody, see my "Rhetoric, Literature, and Dissociation of Invention," *Journal of Advanced Composition,* forthcoming.

9. I am not arguing here that the Romantic concept of poetry is responsible for the demise of interest in rhetoric in the late nineteenth century, although this case could conceivably be made. Romantic literary theory did prove useful when the academic niche left vacant by the demise of rhetoric needed filling, however. See William Riley Parker, "Where Do English Departments Come From?" *College English,* 38 (February 1962), 339–51.

10. Fred Newton Scott, "The Most Fundamental Differentia of Poetry and Prose," *PMLA,* 19 (1904), pp. 249–69.

11. Jim Kinneavy uses authorial aim as a criterion for discriminating his four modes of discourse from one another. While *Theory of Discourse* is an invaluable scholarly work, its theoretical elegance is marred, I think, by Kinneavy's choice of "aims" as a basis for discriminating kinds of discourse from one another. See Chapter 2 of *A Theory of Discourse* (New York: Norton, 1980), especially pp. 48–50.

12. Hoyt Hudson, "Rhetoric and Poetry," *Quarterly Journal of Speech Education,* 10 (April 1924), 143-54.

13. Herbert Wichelns, "The Literary Criticism of Oratory," in Robert Scott and Bernard Brock, eds., *Methods of Rhetorical Criticism* (New York: Harper and Row, 1972). The essay originally appeared in A. M. Drummond, ed., *Rhetoric and Public Speaking: Essays in Honor of James A. Winans* (New York: Century, 1925). Gordon Bieglow also adopts neo-Romantic formalism to discuss the relation of rhetoric to literature in his "Distinguishing Rhetoric from Poetic Discourse," *Southern Speech Journal,* 19 (December 1953). A. W. Staub and G. P. Mohrmann ostensibly go against the Romantic grain by adopting Aristotle's distinction among kinds of proofs to align rhetoric with *ethos,* philosophy with *logos,* and poetry with *pathos.* They complain that some poems are nevertheless read because of their author's reputation, and solve the riddle by claiming that "not every poem is poetic." See their "Rhetoric and Poetic: A New Critique," *Southern Speech Journal,* 28 (Winter 1962), 111.

14. See E. P. J. Corbett's introduction to his collection of representative pieces of such criticism, entitled *Rhetorical Analyses of Literature* (London: Oxford Univ. Press, 1969). For a survey of more current reader-response theory, see Jane Tompkins, ed., *Reader-Response Criticism* (Baltimore: Johns Hopkins Univ. Press, 1980).

15. Wilbur Samuel Howell, *Poetics, Rhetoric, and Logic: Studies in the Basic Disciplines of Criticism* (Ithaca: Cornell Univ. Press, 1975), pp. 42-43.

16. Kenneth Burke, *Language as Symbolic Action* (Berkeley: Univ. of California Press, 1968), pp. 295-307.

17. Donald Bryant, ed., *Papers in Rhetoric and Poetic* (Iowa City: Univ. of Iowa Press, 1965). Other contributors included Oscar Brockett, Marvin Herrick, and Richard Murphy.

18. C. S. Baldwin, *Ancient Rhetoric and Poetic Interpreted from Representative Works* (New York: Macmillan, 1924), p. 3; Walter Ong, "The Province of Rhetoric and Poetic," *Modern Schoolman,* (January 1942), 48-56; and D. L. Clark, *Rhetoric and Poetic in the Renaissance* (New York: Russell and Russell, 1963), 6-9. The Howell passages are from "Literature as an Enterprise in Communication," *Quarterly Journal of Speech,* 33 (December 1947), 417-26. Reprinted in *Poetics* as Chapter 7. Howell maintains his mimetic distinction throughout the 1975 *Poetics;* see pp. 32-34 and 247 ff.

19. George Kennedy, *Classical Rhetoric and its Christian and Secular Tradition from Ancient to Modern Times* (Chapel Hill: Univ. of North Carolina Press, 1980), pp. 4-5.

20. Stanley Fish, *Is There a Text in This Class?* (Cambridge: Harvard Univ. Press, 1980), p. 369.

21. Murphy makes this comment in the introduction to his *The Rhetorical Tradition and Modern Writing* (New York: Modern Language Association, 1982), p. 3.

Response to "Neo-Romanticism and and the History of Rhetoric"

"Neo-Romanticism and the History of Rhetoric" was primarily a polemic, of course. I wrote it to advance an institutional agenda—the recognition of rhetoric as a legitimate area of scholarship within English studies. The anger that percolates through it reflects the frustration I felt in those days with the way the discipline of English was defined and the way it confined the work its students could legitimately do.

Those of us interested in rhetoric or composition who did our graduate work in the sixties and seventies were forced to treat our interests as peripheral to what nearly everybody considered the primary field of study in English in those days: literary history and criticism. (I distinctly remember sitting in my advisor's office, thinking: "Oh God, not another Chaucer course.") I don't know how others did it, but I did it by adding on speech courses to my graduate work on literature and by persistently writing papers that incorporated what I knew about the history of rhetoric into criticisms of literary texts ("Manley and Rickert were wrong about Chaucer and the rhetoricians and here's why").

Colleagues still chide me about my philistine attitude toward literature. But, I tell them, I earned it.

Of course "Neo-Romanticism" is also a history of the shifting intellectual relations that obtained between rhetoric and literary criticism during the nineteenth and twentieth centuries. Reading it now, I am struck by a fine irony: the history traced in it employs the very tool that I acquired from my graduate training in literary study—close reading of texts. If I were to rewrite the piece today, I would of course have more history to trace. But I would pay less attention to the critical texts and would say a good deal more about the political and institutional ramifications of debates about the relation between rhetoric and literature.

When I was writing "Neo-Romanticism," rhetoric and literature (as disciplines) seemed as incompatible to me as they apparently did to the critics whose work I reviewed. Now I can see at least two reasons for this. First of all, literary studies was conceived and taught in those days as a philosophical endeavor; it was idealist through and through. Literary critics looked for *the* meaning of texts read in isolation from the circumstances of their composition. Indeed, those rhetorical critics who were intent on saddling rhetorical treatises with formalist readings were buying into this idealism, whether they borrowed it from literary criticism or not. But rhetoric is by definition occasional and local in use and material in its effects. So to make its texts fit an idealist mold was a strain, as the debate about it suggests.

Second, within English studies, rhetoric was almost entirely associated with one of its branches — composition. Very few people in English departments realized that both had long cultural and institutional histories. The historical relation of rhetoric and composition to literary studies, either in cultural or institutional terms, wasn't very clear either. And in those days composition was a poor sister indeed, having no discernible theory to give it class and no professors to plump for its status. Any changes in the intellectual relations between rhetoric and literature that have occurred since "Neo-Romanticism" appeared are linked to the rising fortunes of composition as well as to English teachers' rethinking of literary idealism.

Today I would mellow the assertive (if not smart-aleck) tone of the conclusion to "Neo-Romanticism." I would be less hard on rhetoricians who adopted defensive postures toward literary study, because now I understand how difficult it is not to speak the dominant discourse if it is the only game in town. I would be less severe with literary critics for the same reason, and because I admire the ways in which the best of them have begun to dismantle the oppressive institutional structures that literary studies used to inhabit. They are doing this, most of them, with grace and style. But I would nevertheless restate my complaint about their ignorance of the history of rhetoric, and I would still ask that graduate students in English be made acquainted with rhetoric and its history, and for the same reasons. While it is true that literary critics now use the term *rhetoric* with more frequency, I am still not persuaded that they understand it in the same way that rhetoricians do. That is, most literary critics still use a definition of rhetoric that limits it to a theory of tropics.

I must mention a notable exception to this generalization. Stanley Fish wrote me a letter after "Neo-Romanticism" was published, taking exception to my inclusion of his work with that of critics who were, on my presumption, ignorant of the history of rhetoric. He pointed to his articles and books on seventeenth-century texts as examples of his familiarity with rhetoric and its European tradition. Despite Fish's protest, I still maintain that, on the strength of his published work to that time, he belonged in the camp of those literary critics who defined rhetoric very narrowly as a sort of handmaiden to, or informant of, the composition of texts that have since been defined as "literary" (by those very critics, I might add).

Since then, however, Fish has become a full-fledged rhetorician whose work, by the way, ought to be in the rhetorical canon. (Rhetoric still needs a canon for the same reasons that feminism and ethnic studies need a notion of the subject.) Fish has turned his attention to such rhetorical issues as how discursive change comes about, how practice is embedded in and driven by discourse, how force is deployed by means of discourse, the role of precedent in maintaining institutions and their discourses, and the like. That he is still identified by most members of the profession as a literary critic (or as a student of law who ought to get the hell out of English studies) only testifies to the continuing invisibility of rhetoric as an intellectual endeavor as well as to the continued maintenance of the disciplinary barriers to which rhetoric is a primary challenge.

I have less quarrel with rhetoric's disciplinary invisibility than I used to. Politically, our institutional status as nonentities or sports is probably a good thing. We are mistaken for harmless historians or dotty theorists or hardworking composition teachers and are pretty much left alone to do our work. Increasingly, that work is subversive of the academy. A big part of it involves breaking down discipline-specific assumptions about whose texts are more important than whose.

9 : THE HISTORY OF RHETORIC AND THE RHETORIC OF HISTORY

John Schilb
Associated Colleges of the Midwest, Chicago

We need to know what has changed, why it changed, and whether we still wish to live with the results of that change. We must therefore learn our own history. (Murphy 5)

The history of rhetoric is an enigma to English teachers, its texts unread and its evolution misunderstood. (Knoblauch and Brannon 3)

In order to understand what takes place today in many classes in composition, we must understand the history of our field. (Larson 19)

We cannot understand what is happening unless we understand what happened. Furthermore, without a knowledge of history, we have no way of knowing what is genuinely new, what is redundant, what is promising, what has been tried before and found wanting. (Young 3)

Teachers of writing need to know more about the history of rhetoric and the history of rhetorical invention. (D'Angelo 66)

As these quotations from recent works make clear, composition studies is now marked by a strong interest in historical research. Although histories of rhetoric have appeared before, there's a new and fervent impulse to undertake them, which is understandable, considering the profession's new awareness of itself as a profession, rather than an assortment of amateurish practices lacking coherence or intellectual substance. Today, we have more historians of rhetoric because we have more people anxious to legitimize the teaching of writing as a serious affair, and therefore anxious to persuade all writing teachers to think about the contingent nature of their pedagogies so they can revise them for better. Admittedly, this new emphasis of composition studies on historical scholarship isn't an altogether unique event in the academy; it has parallels in contiguous fields. When Fredric Jameson, for example, cries "Always historicize!" (9) at the start of his book *The Political Unconscious,* he expresses the central mission not only of traditional Marxist theorists but also of many literary critics nowadays, who acutely feel the limitations of the New Criticism after its decades-long hegemony. But the budding historical consciousness of writing specialists is especially noteworthy for the momentum it has acquired as part of their drive for respectability.

The recent interest in the history of rhetoric has produced much valuable work, which may indeed help the average composition teacher grow in self-awareness and therefore professional stature. Despite the merits of this scholarship, however, I want to focus on some reservations I've had in reading examples of it. More precisely, I want to suggest that in their zeal to promote historical work in composition studies, and in their excitement over discovering or rediscovering certain documents, a number of scholars aren't engaging in the same kinds of critical reflection that have increasingly characterized the discipline of history during the last few years.[1] And because they really haven't entered into a dialogue with recent theoretical, not historical trends in the discipline of history, their work risks falling short of the sophistication and usefulness they presumably would like it to have. Again, I believe their scholarly efforts have borne fruit; thus, I'm not interested in simply lambasting their work because of what I see as its limits. But I do want to point the limits out, hoping that recognition of them can help composition studies push beyond them while incorporating insights that historians of rhetoric have, in fact, already generated.

Consider, to begin with, the implied definition and status of the word "history" in the quotations I've cited at the beginning of this article. One can easily infer from them that the history of rhetoric is already identifiable—something that lies outside of the human imagination, waiting to be discovered. The quotations don't clearly indicate that "history," in one very important sense of the term, is something *constructed* by historians, and hence open to the kind of study we can accord to human meaning-making activities. While more and more scholars in the discipline of history itself demonstrate awareness that one must distinguish between "history" as an absent referent and "history" as the conjecture and representation for that referent, I don't find in recent histories of rhetoric clear acknowledgment that the authors are composing discourse. Moreover, as the quotations suggest, certain histories of rhetoric virtually ask to be used as warrants for particular teaching practices, even though such foundationalism appears suspect given the loss of metaphysical certitude that many historians have experienced nowadays in their consideration of historical writing as an interpretive act. Although probably the authors of the quotations I've cited would protest that they're not, in fact, oblivious to the issues posed by their being shapers of texts rather than passive recorders of a naked reality, what I miss in reading several recent histories of rhetoric is sustained, explicit recognition that such histories are themselves potential objects of rhetorical study. In short, I think the history of rhetoric needs to address more the rhetoric of history.

Indeed, much historical discourse in composition studies seems determined to avoid metahistorical concerns that scholars working in the discipline of history have felt increasingly compelled to confront. Perhaps the most insistent articulation of these concerns can be found in the writings of Hayden White and Dominick LaCapra. White has busily spun out the implications of history defined as "a verbal structure in the form of a narrative prose discourse that purports to be a model, or icon, of past structures and processes in the interest of explaining what they were by representing them" (*Metahistory* 2). Observing that "historical writing must be analyzed primarily as a kind of prose discourse before its claims to objectivity and truthfulness can be tested," he has called for "subjecting any historical discourse to a rhetorical analysis, so as to disclose the poetical understructure of what is meant to pass for a modest prose representation of reality" (*Tropics* 105). LaCapra has stressed "the idea that rhetoric is a dimension of all language use rather than a separate set of uses of a realm of discourse," and has elaborated the more specific concept "that historiography is itself a tensely mixed mode of language use involving documentary or 'scientific' knowledge and rhetoric in a broader and unavoidably problematic notion of cognition." The chief question for him is "How may the necessary components of a documentary model without which historiography would be unrecognizable be conjoined with rhetorical features in a broader, 'interactive' understanding of historical discourse?" (17, 41, 35). Although White and LaCapra both repeatedly invoke rhetoric, they don't have exactly the same thing in mind. White has basically explored the relationship between figuration (or rather, prefiguration) and narrative structure, whereas LaCapra has focused on "internal contestations of ways texts differ from themselves in their functioning and interaction with contexts," seeing that "texts in variable ways may combine symptomatic, critical, and more 'undecidable' relations to given signifying practices and sociocultural processes" (38). Furthermore, White and LaCapra are unusual among members of the historical profession in their relentless devotion to metahistorical issues. They have, in fact, chided their peers for being insufficiently reflective, and White in particular has been the object of reciprocated critique.[2] But the growing prominence of theorists like these signifies that several members of the profession consider issues of rhetoric inescapable, much as literary critics have had to pay increasing attention to deconstructive critics even if they've ultimately wished to reject or modify their claims. And even many historians who disdain White's and LaCapra's thinking — in the hope that empiricism will someday be vindicated — would admit that the entire discipline of history has endured what, in his own field, the new editor of *The Journal of American History* recently called an "explosion of specialties, methodologies, and points of view" (Thelen 760), so that historical writing increasingly involves conscious choices among compositional alternatives and hence elements of rhetoric.[3]

Perhaps a discipline's willingness to confront the rhetoricity of its discourse does relate inversely to its sense of shared aims. While historians of rhetoric have certainly disagreed with one another — note the ongoing controversy about the validity of classical rhetoric[4] — they share a belief that composition studies has suffered from lack of attention to its past,[5] they hold similar notions of the major figures of the past,[6] they tend to follow the same principles of periodization, they display similar affinities for intellectual history, and they reveal a common desire to see the teaching of writing become more respectable. Perhaps a greater lack of consensus than this is required before many historians of rhetoric will undertake a metahistorical analysis of what they write, with particular attention to textual strategies. Widespread study of the rhetorical activity in histories of rhetoric might depend as well upon an increase in the number of scholars who can actually prepare and write them. Given the belles-lettristic emphasis of most English graduate programs, there really haven't been all that many people trained to engage in histories of rhetoric and critique those written by others. Moreover, perhaps composition specialists need more institutional encouragement to learn what historians are thinking about before they can apply theoretical developments in history to their own work. The recent emphasis on writing across the curriculum programs might greatly facilitate such conversation between fields. Finally, histories of rhetoric might be questioned more commonly if more composition specialists familiarized themselves with post-structuralist thinkers who don't quite fit into any discipline but have formulated insights into a range of them, including history. Jacques Derrida, for example, has attested to a tension he has personally felt between the need to acknowledge material circumstances which have influenced politics and the need to avoid naively lapsing into "the *metaphysical* concept of history," which is "not only linked to linearity, but to an entire *system* of implications (teleology, eschatology, elevating and interiorizing accumulation of meaning, a certain type of traditionality, a certain concept of continuity, of truth, etc.)" (56, 57). And of course, the whole career of Michael Foucault constituted a renunciation of "the historian's history" which "finds its support outside of time and pretends to base its judgments on an apocalyptic objectivity," substituting instead a Nietzschean "genealogy" which "corresponds to the acuity of a glance that distinguishes, separates, and disperses; that

The History of Rhetoric and the Rhetoric of History 241

is capable of liberating divergence and marginal elements—the kind of dissociating view that is capable of decomposing itself, capable of shattering the unity of man's being through which it was thought that he could extend his sovereignty to the events of his past" (87).

To elaborate more concretely my own call for attention to the rhetoricity in histories of rhetoric, I want to single out a passage from a recent collection of articles, *Essays on Classical Rhetoric and Modern Discourse,* and identify what I see as some if not all of the rhetorical activity at work in it. The passage is from the first essay, entitled "The Revival of Rhetoric in America" and written by Robert Connors, Lisa Ede, and Andrea Lunsford (the collection's editors). If I proceed to show in rather microscopic fashion how its textual operations might be tracked, I do so not to hold the authors up to ridicule but to suggest how even those historians of rhetoric most worthy of respect are nevertheless engaged themselves in a construction of discourse, which they as well as their readers ought to ponder. The paragraphs which follow attempt to trace developments in the history of rhetoric during the nineteen-sixties:

> In spite of these harbingers of change, teachers of composition, content in their isolation, continued to emphasize grammatical and stylistic problems rather than rhetorical concerns. Most composition teachers knew of Weaver only through his text, and few were aware of Clark. When Daniel Fogarty's *Roots for a New Rhetoric,* which stressed Aristotle's contributions to contemporary rhetoric, was published in 1959 and lauded in speech departments, only scant attention was paid to it in English. Thus another important contribution to the revitalization of classical rhetoric passed by unheeded. This situation did not last long, however, because by 1960 composition was on the verge of a genuine revolution.
>
> The rediscovery of classical rhetoric in its application to writing pedagogy began in 1962, when P. Albert Duhamel and his colleague Richard E. Hughes published *Rhetoric: Principles and Usage.* This was the first truly popular writing textbook to use classical theory as the informing principle of large sections of its discussion. Hughes and Duhamel said in their preface, "Perhaps the most significant difference between our book and those currently used in composition and rhetoric courses is our attempt to introduce the art of rhetoric as a systematic body of knowledge." For the first time average writing teachers were trying out topical invention and classical argumentative forms—and were finding them effective and useful pedagogical aids. In the previous year, Wayne Booth had published his now famous *The Rhetoric of Fiction,* and suddenly the very word *rhetoric* began to have a new magic to it. The rhetorical revival had begun in earnest.

> The impact of this rhetorical revival on composition studies was confirmed by the 1963 CCCC, the conference that most historians of rhetoric point to as the first gathering of the "modern" profession of composition studies. During that year's meeting, Wayne Booth gave his paper on "The Rhetorical Stance," Francis Christensen delivered his "Generative Rhetoric of the Sentence," and, most important for classical studies, Edward P. J. Corbett spoke on "The Usefulness of Classical Rhetoric." All who attended that convention felt the galvanic charge in the air, the exciting sense of intellectual rebirth. Within the next five years the spirit which had been born at that convention began to transform the teaching of writing. (10)

Rhetoricians could make several observations about this passage. My own thoughts converge on one main question that I believe all historians of rhetoric answer, explicitly or implicitly, knowingly or unknowingly: How might a history of rhetoric be plotted? More specifically, what are the forms that such emplotment can take? Who might be included as the plot's agents? What might be included as the plot's events? Who and what might the plot wind up excluding? What might be the bases of these inclusions and exclusions? Is it possible for whatever plot is chosen to fully cohere? If not, what sorts of disruptions might afflict it? My reading of the passage leads me to suppose that Connors, Ede, and Lunsford *are* engaged in a particular kind of emplotment, and that it deserves study because of its inclusions and exclusions as well as its occasional signs of internal difficulty.

As the title of their chapter indicates, the authors try throughout the essay to trace the fortunes of rhetoric in American higher education: emphasizing how it became important in the eighteenth century, declined in the nineteenth, and was triumphantly brought back to life in the twentieth. In addition to sketching out this three-part pattern, they conflate the destiny of rhetoric in general with the destiny of classical rhetoric in particular. Even though their chapter is called "The Revival of Rhetoric in America," the section from which the passage comes is entitled "The Second Revival of Classical Rhetoric" (8). The "harbingers" mentioned in the first sentence of the passage are efforts made during the fifties to restore "classical tenets of pedagogy" (9), so that when the authors proceed to scold composition teachers for slighting "rhetorical concerns," they imply the two phrases coincide. Similarly, when they note that Fogarty's book "stressed Aristotle's contributions to contemporary rhetoric," they don't then stipulate what "contemporary rhetoric" might mean considered as a term in itself; rather, in a rough chiasmus, they go on to suggest that Fogarty's book stressing *Aristotle's* contributions to *contemporary rhetoric* is *itself* "another important contribution to the revitalization of *classical-rhetoric*" (emphasis mine). It's interesting that Lunsford and Ede characterize Fogarty's book differently at the start of their later essay in the anthology, "On Distinctions between Classical and Modern Rhetoric." There, ironically, they use an image associated with chiasmus in noting that the book "stands at a metaphorical crossroads, affirming the continuing need for a viable rhetoric and sketching in the broad outlines of a 'new' rhetoric that would meet that need" (57). Of course, this self-conscious use of the "crossroads" image doesn't give classical rhetoric the same air of renewed academic priority that it receives in the first essay's reference to Fogarty. Indeed, far from claiming that his book inaugurated a revival of classical rhetoric, Lunsford and Ede's second article laments that it was followed by a mounting series of efforts to demarcate classical rhetoric from modern (57). Yet even without knowledge of this latter piece, a reader would feel entitled to question Connors, Ede, and Lunsford's use of the word "revitalization" toward the end of the first paragraph I've quoted. What can "revitalization" mean if Fogarty's "important contribution to the revitalization of classical rhetoric" went "unheeded" by English departments, presumably the current authors' main constituency? It seems just as possible to say that revitalization couldn't have taken place as long as English departments ignored the writings of Fogarty and similar theorists. I suspect the authors want to posit *some* new life for classical rhetoric that English departments failed to "heed," not failed to *create,* because they associate classical rhetoric with an ultimately irrepressible momentum in history. Such an association looms in the last sentence of the paragraph, which uses the language of causality for narrative drive even if it's fair to contend that a cause–and–effect relationship isn't really at work. Despite the presence of "because" as a linking word, "This situation did not last long" can be said to mean the same thing as "by 1960 composition was on the verge of a genuine revolution." An urge to identify classical rhetoric with an unstoppable appeal becomes even more apparent when one considers that there really isn't much need to have this last sentence at all. If there is no event in the history of rhetoric that the authors deem worth recording for the year 1960, and the start of the next paragraph is therefore going to constitute a leap in the text from 1959 to 1962, why do they bother with the last sentence? Probably because to end the paragraph with the word "unheeded" would emphasize discontinuity or paralysis at just the moment when the authors want to project a sense of classical rhetoric's impending resurgence. Putting readers on the verge of the next paragraph becomes an important *rhetorical* task, which is accomplished by a statement about composition's being "on the verge of a genuine revolution." To be sure, a strategy like this also involves positing a monolithic field named "composition" in which "genuine revolutions" can occur, even though the authors themselves would admit that many teachers of writing still endorse what Fogarty termed "current-traditional rhetoric" (118) despite the theoretical work of him and others who came after him. Indeed, the word "situation" implies a momentary set of circumstances when actually it could be said that current-traditional rhetoric has exerted influence for several decades now. The text assumes, too, that the reader will assent to the Kuhnian resonance of the phrase "genuine revolution" even though the authors don't identify the general definition of "revolution" they have in mind, don't elaborate how a "genuine" revolution differs from a "bogus" one, and don't explain how the word "revolution" might smoothly consort with milder words like "revival" and "rediscovery" that appear elsewhere in the essay.

Even though the authors might concede that the word "revolution" is rather strong, they might have felt able to employ it in a sentence where they also referred to the beginning of the sixties. For certainly the sixties and the concept of revolution fit together in many people's minds, although of course when people think of sixties revolutions, they're more apt to recall political demonstrations in streets than composition exercises in classrooms. Whether or not the authors actually intended to capitalize on the reader's memories of political turbulence in using the word "revolution," it's noteworthy that the social upheaval of the sixties does go unmentioned as they proceed to discuss events during the decade. The word "revolution" remains embedded in discussion of intellectual developments within the academy, not extended to the momentous rhetorical actions which took place outside its walls. References to a larger social context, and materialistic explanations of the academic events which *are* noted, wind up being abjured as the authors note the popularity of the Duhamel and Hughes textbook but don't actually detail why "average writing teachers" decided to try out its ideas; don't mention that many writing teachers probably ignored it; don't point out the possible differences between considering rhetoric "a systematic body of knowledge" and finding its topics and forms "effective and useful pedagogical aids;" don't explain how and for whom the word "rhetoric" had "a new magic"; and don't allude to the "earnest" theorizing about political rhetoric which was soon to characterize the civil rights movement, the New Left, and other social forces.

To my observation that their article excludes a great many social and political circumstances which could pertain to developments in rhetorical theory during the sixties—especially if the term "rhetorical theory" is broadly construed—the authors might reply that they could do only so much within a few pages. They could point to the precedent of Kuhn's *Structure of Scientific Revolutions,* which also brackets a wide range of sociopolitical factors in order to make general remarks about how paradigms within a field change. In his preface, Kuhn apologizes that "except in occasional brief asides, I have said nothing about the role of technological advance or of external social, economic, and intellectual conditions in the development of the sciences" (x). But Kuhn, at least, explicitly signals *that* he's bracketing and *what* he's bracketing. Besides, in the case of Kuhn as well as of the present authors, it seems quite important for a reader to consider how the plot being sketched deemphasizes the conditions that Kuhn identifies in his preface—and how incorporating them into the plot might after its contours or even its very nature.

In reflecting on recent histories of rhetoric as particular kinds of discourse, I've been more and more struck by the fact that scholars in the discipline of history would probably classify almost all of them as intellectual history, and that intellectual historians have felt acutely challenged by other kinds of history over the past decade. As Robert Darnton notes in his essay in intellectual history in the 1980 anthology *The Past Before Us,* "the trend toward self-doubt and beleaguered self-assertion can be found wherever intellectual historians discuss the state of their craft—and the historiographical-methodological discussions have multiplied in the past few years" (327). Yet I simply don't find this kind of phenomenon occurring among the intellectual historians who, in composition studies, labor at the craft of writing histories of rhetoric. Darnton's essay dwells upon what he considers the main challenge to intellectual history in recent years, the tremendous growth of what's been called social history: "Black history, urban history, labor history, the history of women, of criminality, of sexuality, the oppressed, the inarticulate, the marginal—so many lines of inquiry opened up that social history seemed to dominate research on all fronts. The abandoned ally had regained command of the profession" (329). Darnton is far from conceding social history the dominance it's achieved, but he recognizes that its validity has been proven enough for intellectual historians to try incorporating its perspectives into their work. Again, however, I don't see historians of rhetoric engaging in much of an attempt to weave into *their* work the new bodies of scholarship that Darnton cites. What I find instead is a focus on analyzing possible affiliations or lack of affiliations between the canonized texts of what has traditionally been declared the rhetorical tradition, with praise or criticism for how certain insights expressed by these texts get filtered down through teaching materials. There's little explicit recognition that a great variety of sociopolitical factors could and should be taken into account in charting developments in rhetorical theory, and there's little explicit recognition that these developments could be drawn out of the experiences of ordinary people, including ones who've never entered the academy as scholars or students.

An account of rhetorical theory during the sixties might, for example, look considerably different from Connors, Ede, and Lunsford's if it focused on how the New Left tried to distinguish itself from the Old by stressing a rhetoric of participatory democracy and group consensus. Such a history of rhetoric could additionally examine how women of the New Left, increasingly believing that they didn't share the power to speak that its men enjoyed, eventually formed a movement of their own which emphasized consciousness-raising.[7] Still another development which could be probed is the shifting configurations of whites and Blacks within the civil rights struggle, with the Black Power movement ultimately emphasizing the latter's need to articulate their own sense of priorities. And of course, the principles of composition teaching were strongly affected by the establishment during the late sixties and early seventies of open admissions programs, which brought into the academy more and more of "the oppressed, the inarticulate, the marginal" (as they were conventionally defined). It might be objected that events of the kind I've been referring to don't constitute developments in rhetorical *theory* per se, but I'd submit that exclusion of them from accounts of rhetorical theory depends upon a narrow conception of it which God doesn't demand be held—and that if historians of rhetoric paid more attention to these events, such a focus could powerfully transform their understanding of what rhetoric has been and can be. At the very least, historians of rhetoric might put themselves into a better position to grasp the background of teaching practices they're currently well aware of. The challenges posed to conventional modes of authority by political activists in the sixties, and the attention given by feminists then to consciousness-raising, undoubtedly helped prepare the way for many composition teachers' present emphasis on peer critiques, whether they're conscious of this precedent setting or not.

The third paragraph of the Connors, Ede, and Lunsford passage I've quoted describes what the authors obviously consider a climactic moment in their history of rhetoric, and therefore proves especially useful in illuminating the kind of narrative they want to propound. Keeping in mind that the last sentence of the preceding paragraph was "The rhetorical revival had begun in earnest," a reader may be surprised to discover that by the very next sentence, and by the very next year after the publication of the Duhamel and Hughes book, the revival had achieved an "impact" which was "confirmed." The language of triumph doesn't quite jell, either, with the last sentence of the third paragraph. The authors suggest that the revival *hasn't* really gained "impact" in 1963 when they write, "*Within the next five years* the spirit which had been *born* at that convention *began* to transform the teaching of writing" (emphasis mine). Indeed, this sentence closely resembles the last sentence of the preceding paragraph, "The rhetorical revival had begun in earnest," so that the intervening declaration of "impact" seems even more questionable. I can't help getting the impression that the authors are trying to develop a scenario of rhetoric's (and classical rhetoric's) smooth vindication but just can't quite bring it off. The presentation of climax at the heart of the third paragraph is an especially striking maneuver in this regard. In its references to "the first gathering," to "the galvanic charge in the air," to "the exciting sense of intellectual rebirth," to "the spirit which had been born," and to the spirit's ability to "transform" the account greatly elaborates the earlier reference to "magic" by depicting a scene which is downright Pentecostal. While certainly the 1963 CCCC meeting did take place, and while perhaps no one would want to deny that it was exciting and important, the metaphorical framework through which the authors unself-consciously evoke it is at least open to question—especially when one bears in mind that conferences can easily be described in a more political or materialistic vocabulary, whatever their relationship to paradigm change. Many people who lived through the sixties might find it strange that Pentecostal language of this sort was being applied to a meeting of academics, rather than to any of the political demonstrations which endorsed apocalyptic rapture throughout the decade! The authors support the particular image they've chosen with what I, for one, consider an unconvincing declaration that "*All* who attended that convention felt the galvanic charge in the air, the exciting sense of rebirth" (emphasis mine). Do they expect me to believe that they interviewed everyone? Do they expect me to believe that everyone there would have explained the conference in terms of "charge" and "rebirth?" It's possible that they could provide some sort of documentation to warrant an all-inclusive word like "all," but none appears in the paragraph—just as no historians of rhetoric are mentioned, even though it is alleged that "most" of them "point to" the 1963 meeting "as the first gathering of the 'modern' profession of composition studies." I suppose that the use of "all" could simply be accounted for as a mere slip in editing, and that if the authors had caught it, they would have replaced it with a more prudent word like "most" or "many." But then again, one of the latter terms would vitiate the impression of spiritual force that the authors clearly want to convey. "All" seems therefore a rhetorical necessity for them, at least given the particular kind of emplotment they want to have their history of rhetoric follow. It's ironic that in citing the emergence of "modern" rhetoric, a body of knowledge which pays close attention to the various human contingencies operative in symbolic acts, the authors are at this point in their text especially determined to depict history by means of theological metaphors, emphasizing transcendental developments.

As I've indicated, the plot is one of the revival, death, and revival again of classical rhetoric, which is equated with the term rhetoric itself. In its suggestion that the death of the subject is only apparent, that it ultimately springs back to life, the narrative of the essay resembles that of many notable literary works. Note the similar chain of events in Shakespeare's *Much Ado About Nothing* or *The Winter's Tale,* for example. The sheer literariness of the shape that the discourse takes is further affirmed by the essay's closing sentence: "The twentieth-century revival of rhetoric entails a recovery of the classical tradition, with its marriage of a rich and fully articulated theory with an equally efficacious practice" (15). Here, not only is "recovery" stressed, but also "marriage"—a denouement that Shakespeare and countless other artists have favored. Yet, once more in the case of this article, the summative energy of trope doesn't quite obscure certain elements not in harmony with the intended narrative scheme. For one thing, use of the word "marriage" dictates use of a word like "equally," but "articulated" and "efficacious" aren't really parallel as "equally" suggests. Furthermore, it's highly debatable whether the classical tradition of rhetoric was "efficacious" for everybody. The notion of "efficacy" ought to arouse questions such as who held power in the classical world and who didn't, who holds power now and who doesn't, how a kind of world might be created in which everyone enjoyed the same rhetorical leverage. Also, the words "entails" and "recovery" have an ambiguity which a reader might do well to unpack. Does "entails" simply mean "involves" or does it mean "logically demands?" Does "recovery" mean "repetition, albeit with a difference," or does it mean "exact restoration?" With both of these terms, the essay's previous language and general narrative line suggest that the second definition is to be in force, but if such is the authors' goal, I for one think they need to show at greater length why the first definition of each word is to be suppressed. Overall, the "marriage" being cited strikes me as a shotgun wedding.

As I said earlier, my purpose in so intensely examining part of Connors, Ede, and Lunsford's essay isn't to dismiss their endeavor as unworthy. Let me hasten to state more precisely certain negative views toward it I haven't meant to express. First of all, I don't want to give the impression that I find the authors devious. As composers of discourse, they're making rhetorical choices every step of the way, and it's that omnipresence of rhetoric that I've wished to emphasize. I don't believe that they're sly propagandizers; I believe that they're nice civilized writers—who, as such, are inevitably caught up in a rhetorical act. Second, along these lines, I don't want to suggest that a transparent, empirically pure, thoroughly objective, utterly literal history of rhetoric is possible, and that the authors should have therefore written it. If I've raised questions about their metaphors and narrative framework, I haven't done so in the conviction that I myself could write a history of rhetoric that escapes trope and plot. Third, I don't believe that a history of rhetoric is bound to be nothing more than a fiction—that Connors, Ede, and Lunsford should have just surrendered to epistemological skepticism and not written anything at all. My remarks in particular about over-reliance on intellectual history at the expense of social history ought to indicate that I put stock in the chance for referential truth. And I'm perfectly prepared to concede that Connors, Ede, and Lunsford have done more than simply concoct their own fantasies—that contained within their essay is useful knowledge. Rather than call for cynical despair, I'm more interested in seeing historians of rhetoric like these authors examine their discourse with greater self-consciousness, consider alternatives to it, let their text be a dialogue with other such possibilities, and, in general, let themselves enter into a dialogue with the metahistorical reflections to be found now in the discipline of history. Connors, Ede, and Lunsford do exhibit a certain modesty when they observe that "the progress of rhetoric in the late eighteenth and nineteenth centuries" is "a progress for which we as yet have no authoritative history," and when they acknowledge that the essays in the anthology, including their own, "underscore the need for continued historical and theoretical research" (2, 14). I'm basically asking for an extension of the term "research" to cover a sustained re-searching of the textual operations they and other historians of rhetoric undertake.

Finally, I don't think Connors, Ede, and Lunsford are extraordinary among historians of rhetoric in using particular textual strategies that they haven't stood back from and contemplated. Consider, for example, how certain categories formulated by Hayden White can be applied to other histories of rhetoric as well as theirs. In *Metahistory,* White identifies what he calls "levels of conceptualization in the historical work" (5). One of these is "explanation by emplotment" (7-11), and in discussing it he draws upon Northrop Frye's modes of Romance, Tragedy, Comedy, and Satire, suggesting that these terms can be profitably applied to the way historical accounts are constructed. Of Comedy he observes, "The reconciliations which occur at the end . . . are reconciliations of men with men, of men with their world and their society; the condition of society is represented as being purer, saner, and healthier as a result of the conflict among seemingly unalterable elements in the world; these elements are revealed to be, in the long run, harmonizable with one another, unified, at one with themselves and the others" (9). Here I think White has, in effect, described the narrative of Lunsford and Ede's attempt to reconcile ancient and modern rhetoric in their later essay in their anthology. When White characterizes the Romance as "fundamentally a drama of self-identification symbolized by the hero's transcendence of the world of experience, his victory over it, and his final liberation from it" (8), his framework could be applied to C. H. Knoblauch and Lil Brannon's book *Rhetorical Traditions and the Teaching of Writing,* since it charts the emergence of human beings as makers of their own meaning after they've managed to throw off the constraints exalted by the world of ancient rhetoric.

White then proceeds to talk about "explanation by formal argument," deriving from Stephen Pepper "four paradigms of the form that a historical explanation, considered as a discursive argument, may be conceived to take: Formist, Organicist, Mechanistic, and Contextualist" (11–21). Of the Organicist approach, he says the following:

> The Organicist attempts to depict the particulars discerned in the historical field as components of synthetic processes. At the heart of the Organicist strategy is a metaphysical component to the paradigm of the microcosmic-macrocosmic relationship; and the Organicist historian will tend to be governed by the desire to see individual entities as components of processes which aggregate into wholes that are greater than, or qualitatively different from the sum of their parts. (15)

Isn't Frank D'Angelo displaying an Organicist perspective when he declares as his thesis for an essay that "the analytic topoi begin in an undifferentiated state in oral poetic narrative where they are embedded in the narrative continuum, and they emerge historically in stages of increasing abstraction, differentiation, and hierarchic integration" (51). His repeated references to evolution in the same essay recall Hegel, one of White's chief exemplars of the Organicist method.[8] When White goes on to discuss "explanation by ideological implication" (22–29), he notes that:

> anarchists are inclined to idealize a *remote* past of natural-human innocence from which men have fallen into the corrupt "social" state in which they currently find themselves. They, in turn, project this utopia onto what is effectively a nontemporal plane, viewing it as a possibility of human achievement *at any time,* if men will only seize control of their own essential humanity, either by an act of will or by an act of consciousness which destroys the socially provided belief in the legitimacy of the current social establishment. (25)

The History of Rhetoric and the Rhetoric of History 251

Applying this idea to histories of rhetoric, I can't help thinking of how it especially fits James Murphy's remarks that:

> we must understand the principles involved in the programmatic, co-ordinated rhetorical system of teaching literacy explained by Quintilian and used for centuries in Europe and in America until about 1914. Second—a far harder thing rhetorically—we must make a modern adaptation work by convincing ourselves and others that a reexamination is the best plan for the 1980s and beyond.
>
> We will need curricular courage of a high degree, for any realistic effort to recombine the shattered elements of human literacy at the college or university level will entail thinking the unthinkable. Some shocking questions will have to be asked . . . (10)

After introducing explanations by emplotment, formal argument, and ideological explanation, White proceeds to discuss "four basic tropes for the analysis of poetic, or figurative, language: Metaphor, Metonymy, Synecdoche, and Irony," emphasizing how they "permit the characterization of objects in different kinds of indirect, or figurative, discourse" since "they are especially useful for understanding the operations by which the contents of experience which resist description in unambiguous prose representations can be prefiguratively grasped and prepared for conscious apprehension" (31–34). Because, for example, synecdoche is associated with integration of parts in a whole, the trope correlates well with organicist treatments of history like D'Angelo's (36). It's significant that no history of rhetoric is known for offering the kind of discourse which would fit the trope of irony as White defines it, i.e., "a linguistic paradigm of a mode of thought which is radically self-critical with respect not only to a given characterization of the world of experience but also to the very effort to capture adequately the truth of things in language" (37). I'm mainly suggesting that the profession of composition studies would benefit from this type of historical writing—which, I stress again, doesn't necessarily give up on referentiality even though it does openly confront the complex relationship between language and world.[9]

As I've already indicated, Connors, Ede, and Lunsford are not alone in over-emphasizing intellectual lineage. Consider, for example, D'Angelo's statement that "no theory of rhetoric or of invention is a unique creation. Theories of invention evolve from other theories or emerge from older patterns" (66). Surely theories don't evolve or emerge merely from other theories, and surely a history of any phenomenon ought to draw in the wide variety of factors which might have shaped it, be they intellectual or social or political or whatever. I suspect D'Angelo would concede this point and say that he was merely choosing to focus on intellectual lineage in this particular essay. But such a focus supports an overall view of rhetorical thought that consideration of other factors might weaken: the idea that "rhetorical invention, like evolution in general, is progressing toward a goal whose end is nothing less than universal convergence" (68). Greater attention to a range of historical contingencies at work in particular epochs might result more in a vision of Foucauldian discontinuity than one of "universal convergence," or at least might discourage proclamation of the latter. Consider, too, James Kinneavy's observation—contained, along with D'Angelo's, in the Connors, Ede, and Lunsford book—that "the sources of the existentialists and the Marxists are Isocrates, Aristotle, and Cicero" (60). This statement may be true in a sense, but in another sense it greatly overlooks a great many things that could be said to have influenced the shaping of existentialism and Marxism. At the very least, I think it would be good for Kinneavy to explain why it's useful to ignore all these other factors, and I think it's necessary for all historians of rhetoric to think about the notion and validity of the term "sources" in the first place. Consider Sharon Crowley's statement that "Eighteenth- and nineteenth-century discussions of method are grounded in the principles of association psychology" (55). What does the notion of "grounding" here mean? Should it carry the foundationalist connotation that it does? An orthodox Marxist historian would say that Crowley misleadingly traces a phenomenon to the superstructure rather than the base. That point of view might be quarreled with; I mention it simply to indicate that several theories of "grounding" exist in historical and philosophical discourse, so that it's important to analyze an historian's implicit theory of it in conjunction with a range of alternatives. This seems especially the case at the present moment not only because of the insights made possible by social history, but also because of the skepticism toward foundationalist language that has come to affect many disciplines in a poststructuralist era. To put the matter in another way, using Wittgensteinian language: observations like Kinneavy's and Crowley's aren't usually questioned—indeed, are passed over as commonplace—because they are so eminently acceptable in the particular language-game that historians of rhetoric play, a language-game that is actually just one possibility among many. What would a history of rhetoric look like if the language-game played was constituted mostly by statements about sociopolitical circumstances? I'm not absolutely sure, but the possibility exists, and could open up extremely fruitful areas of inquiry.

For me, the most interesting (and frustrating!) playing of an intellectual history language-game occurs in Knoblauch and Brannon's book. I certainly find much to admire in this text; it's wonderfully provocative

The History of Rhetoric and the Rhetoric of History 253

and offers many sound observations for writing teachers to ponder and tanslate into teaching practice. Nevertheless, I'm troubled by what I see as its inclination to slight factors which I think histories of rhetoric should take into account. To be fair, the authors state a third of the way through their book that "our choice to omit biographies and a great mass of other historical as well as scholarly detail depends on our decision to conceive a teacher-reader whose principal interest in this book will be to see relationships between its theoretical information and personal teaching practices, not to learn the intellectual history of the past four centuries" (67). But note the implication that intellectual history is the only kind that should be applied to rhetoric's past, and that any detail added would have contributed to this particular type of discourse. On their very first page the authors write, "Our priority throughout what follows will be the attitudes and values, the beliefs and suppositions that give rise to method, that cause teachers to prefer doing things one way rather than another" (1). While I certainly agree with Knoblauch and Brannon that teachers should understand the philosophical context of their work, I find it difficult to share their apparent presumption here that it's "attitudes and values, beliefs and suppositions" which "give rise to" or "cause" the adoption of methods. Surely a whole panoply of social and instutional forces can operate to influence the methods that teachers choose. And even if such forces could be ignored, the attitudes, values, beliefs, and suppositions that the authors identify are ones largely pertaining just to pedagogy and language. They don't have much to say at all about the political visions that teachers may have of the larger world in which they live, visions which might prove just as influential or even more influential in the case of particular instructors as they use particular teaching methods. Knoblauch and Brannon seem to have doubts on this score themselves when they later write, "It isn't accidental that so many disruptions of time-honored structures and beliefs have occurred in the same 400 years. Beneath them all, and influencing them, revolutions in epistemology and in the methods of acquiring and validating new knowledge have been at work to reconceive the very foundations, dimensions, and aspirations of intellectual inquiry" (23). What is the phrase "beneath them all" doing in conjunction with the phrase "influencing them"? It seems as if the authors can't decide whether they want to claim ideas as the source of social change or as merely influencing factors, so they toss in both theories together. I think it would be more valuable, though, for historians of rhetoric to explicitly examine how the notion of "beneathness" or "grounding" might clash, at least somewhat, with the notion of "influence," rather than meshing with it as smoothly as this sentence suggests it can.

Because they're concerned with emphasizing the discontinuities in ancient and modern philosophical frameworks, Knoblauch and Brannon do bring in a wider range of social elements than other writers I've mentioned. Occasionally, they also suggest that social events and institutions outside the academy or a philosopher's mind can influence what a writing teacher does. Yet I think they also veer toward ahistoricism in places where they attempt to recognize social phenomena as well as intellectual trends, because they're so bent on tying current teaching practices to ancient assumptions as they develop a cultural lag theory of writing instruction. This drift seems most apparent when they write, "Finally, underlying and energizing [note the different terms again] the teaching of grammar and verbal decorum are the same social, ethical, and aesthetic imperatives so powerfully attached to linguistic behavior in antiquity. Students must learn to write properly, whether they actually say anything significant or not, because their teachers, their parents, and perhaps even heavenly forces value the self-discipline, obedience to authority, and above all, good breeding of which polite discourse is the visible sign" (44). Such a declaration seems especially disquieting coming from self-professed devotées of Foucault, for certainly he claims that socializing imperatives have greatly changed since ancient times, and that no smooth transition from "heavenly forces" as ancient reality to "heavenly forces" as present-day metaphor should obscure the discontinuities. One doesn't, of course, have to be a Foucauldian or a Marxist to observe that socializing imperatives are bound to be altered when the world for a student to be socialized into is a late capitalist American economy, not ancient Athens or Rome. The sardonic reference to "heavenly forces" after mention of teachers and parents also obscures how it takes more than just a teacher's or parent's change of heart for worthwhile pedagogy to flourish in a world where *other* people, such as the President of the United States, and a *variety* of *institutions,* such as multinational corporations, want self-discipline, obedience to authority, and good breeding—and push teachers to inculcate these things. To pretend even for a moment that the existence of *these* forces is insignificant as teachers choose (?) their pedagogies is to risk minimizing the classroom changes that Knoblauch and Brannon want to occur. A more detailed history than theirs is necessary if we are to understand teachers' modern "socializing imperatives" and challenge them for the betterment of writing instruction.

 If Knoblauch and Brannon weren't so caught up in tracing purely intellectual affiliations, they might have felt drawn to this more extensive kind of history in writing their book. They might also have felt less inclined to blame teachers as much as they do for poor writing instruction. I find in the book a distressing tendency to blame the victim, which is most prominently displayed when they write, "Writing instructors largely deserve their diminished regard in schools because they have allowed emphatic but unenlightened public pressures, together with their unfamiliarity with the evolving philosophy of their own discipline, to dictate the nature and scope of their work . . ." (42). Even if one were to agree with this statement, as I don't, it contains a host of unexamined asumptions about the power of teachers in relation to "public pressures"—whatever this bland term means—along with other institutions and forces operating in the wider social realm. The book would be even more cogent than it already is if it were to examine these assumptions outright, but to do so would require stepping outside the bounds of intellectual history and engaging in a dialogue with other kinds that historians have recently been engaging in. Certainly Knoblauch and Brannon could have done more with Foucault, a researcher they claim to have influenced them, by using the theory of power he developed in *Discipline and Punish* and *The History of Sexuality,* instead of mostly valuing, as they apparently did, his notion of discontinuity in *The Order of Things* and *The Archaelogy of Knowledge.* Bringing in how various modes of discourse, in the largest sense of the term, intersect to construct all human beings as subjects, including teachers, would probably have led to greater caution about assigning teachers blame.

Knoblauch and Brannon's book, of course, contrasts greatly with Connors, Ede, and Lunsford's anthology in arguing against the continued validity of classical rhetoric. By citing my problems with the historiography practiced by both sets of authors, I've tried here to underscore concerns which I feel could more profitably occupy historians of rhetoric than this debate. Perhaps my assumptions can best be summarized in the words of a recent article, which observes that "for the modern period, connections between thought, language, and reality are thought to be grounded not in an independent, chartable reality but in the nature of the knower instead, and reality is not so much discovered or discoverable as it is constituted by the interplay of thought and language" (47). The quotation, ironically enough, comes from Lunsford and Ede's "On Distinctions between Classical and Modern Rhetoric." As I've suggested, it might be better to think of this as a post-modern rather than a modern period, but putting labels aside, I do think their words aptly convey the premise that I'd like historians of rhetoric to adopt as they look at their own discourse. In publicly scrutinizing the interplay of their own thought and their own language, they would better lead the profession of composition studies to understand the various ways that the reality of the past might be constituted—which in turn just might help the profession constitute a worthwhile reality for the future.

Notes

This essay is a revised and extended version of a paper delivered at the 1985 Conference on College Composition and Communication in Minneapolis, Minnesota.

1. Of course, I'm by no means suggesting that metahistorical reflections are an utterly new phenomenon inside or outside the discipline of history — only that they're currently more in the discipline's core of concerns than was previously the case. For a useful overview of how they were discussed in the past, see Gossman.
2. For a variety of responses to White, see *History and Theory*.
3. Recently I was at a meeting of a committee planning a conference of historians. One of the committee members remarked, "Let's face it, the discipline is intellectually fractured." No one disagreed.
4. The contending positions in this debate are perhaps best exemplified by the Connors, Ede, and Lunsford anthology on the one hand, and by the Knoblauch and Brannon book on the other, as I later suggest.
5. As Nan Johnson has rightly said, "There's so much work to be done" as far as historical research in composition studies is concerned.
6. More precisely, while certainly there have been differing interpretations of the legacies of various canonical figures in the rhetorical tradition, there is basic agreement as to who should be thought of as a canonical figure in the first place.
7. For a valuable history of the relations between the New Left, the civil rights movement, and the women's movement, see Evans.
8. After associating Hegel with Organicism, White does go on to suggest that Hegel shouldn't be identified simply with this approach alone (*Metahistory* 81-131).
9. Much more could be said about the applicability of White's four tropes; here, I simply want to suggest their relevance to histories of rhetoric. For a concentrated, incisive analysis of White's interest in prefiguration, see Downing.

Works Consulted

Connors, Robert J., Lisa S. Ede, and Andrea A. Lunsford. "The Revival of Rhetoric in America." In *Essays on Classical Rhetoric and Modern Discourse*. Ed. Connors, Ede, and Lunsford. 1-15. Carbondale: Southern Illinois Univ. Press, 1985.

Crowley, Sharon. "Invention in Nineteenth-Century Rhetoric." *College Composition and Communication* 36 (1985): 51-60.

D'Angelo, Frank J. "The Evolution of the Analytic Topoi: A Speculative Inquiry." In Connors, Ede, and Lunsford, 50-68.

Darnton, Robert. "Intellectual and Cultural History." In *The Past Before Us: Contemporary Historical Writing in the United States*. Ed. Michael Kammen, 327-49. Ithaca: Cornell Univ. Press, 1980.

Derrida, Jacques. *Positions*. Trans. Alan Bass. Chicago: Univ. of Chicago Press, 1981.

Downing, David B. "'Radical Historicity' and Common Sense: On the Poetics of Human Nature." *Pre/Text* 3 (1982): 185-210.
Evans, Sara. *Personal Politics: The Roots of Women's Liberation in the Civil Rights Movement and the New Left.* New York: Knopf, 1979.
Fogarty, Daniel, S.J. *Roots for a New Rhetoric.* New York: Russell and Russell, 1959.
Foucault, Michel. *The Archaeology of Knowledge.* Trans. A. M. Sheridan Smith. New York: Pantheon, 1972.
———. *Discipline and Punish: The Birth of the Prison.* Trans. Alan Sheridan. New York: Pantheon, 1978.
———. *The History of Sexuality, Volume 1: An Introduction.* Trans. Robert Hurley. New York: Random House, 1978.
———. "Nietzsche, Genealogy, History." In *The Foucault Reader.* Trans. Donald F. Bouchard and Sherry Simon. Ed. Paul Rabinow, 76-100.
———. *The Order of Things: An Archaelogy of the Human Sciences.* Trans. Alan Sheridan Smith. New York: Random House, 1970.
Gossman, Lionel. "History and Literature: Reproduction or Signification." In *The Writing of History: Literary Form and Historical Understanding.* Ed. Robert H. Canary and Henry Kozick, 3-39. Madison: Univ. of Wisconsin Press, 1978.
History and Theory XIX, Beiheft 19 (1980).
Jameson, Fredric. *The Political Unconscious: Narrative as a Socially Symbolic Act.* Ithaca: Cornell UP, 1981.
Kinneavy, James L. "Translating Theory into Practice in Teaching Composition: A Historical View and a Contemporary View." Connors, Ede, and Lunsford, 69-81.
Knoblauch, C.H. and Lil Brannon. *Rhetorical Traditions and the Teaching of Writing.* Upper Montclair: Boynton/Cook, 1984.
Kuhn, Thomas S. *The Structure of Scientific Revolutions.* 2nd ed. Chicago: Univ. of Chicago Press, 1970.
LaCapra, Dominick. *History and Criticism.* Ithaca: Cornell Univ. Press, 1985.
Larson, Richard L. "Editor's Note." *College Composition and Communication* 36 (1985): 19.
Lunsford, Andrea A. and Lisa S. Ede. "On Distinctions between Classical and Modern Rhetoric." Connors, Ede, and Lunsford, 37-49.
Murphy, James J. "Rhetorical History as a Guide to the Salvation of American Reading and Writing: A Plea for Curricular Courage." In *The Rhetorical Tradition and Modern Writing.* Ed. Murphy, 3-12. New York: MLA, 1982.
Thelen, David. "Note from the Editor." *Journal of American History* 72 (1985): 760-61.
White, Hayden. *Metahistory: The Historical Imagination in Nineteenth-Century Europe.* 1973. Baltimore: Johns Hopkins Univ. Press, 1975.
———. *Tropics of Discourse: Essays in Cultural Criticism.* 1978. Baltimore: Johns Hopkins Univ. Press, 1985.
Wittgenstein, Ludwig. *Philosophical Investigations.* Trans. G. E. M. Anscombe. 3rd ed. New York: Macmillan, n.d.

Young, Richard. "Invention: A Topographical Survey." In *Teaching Composition: 10 Bibliographical Essays*. Ed. Gary Tate, 1-43. Fort Worth: Texas Christian Univ. Press, 1976.

Postscript

In a sense, I already wrote a postscript to "The History of Rhetoric and the Rhetoric of History": an article entitled "Differences, Displacements, and Disruptions: Toward Revisionary Histories of Rhetoric," which appeared in the Spring/Summer 1987 issue of *PRE/TEXT*. In the later article, I noted that the earlier one had basically accused current histories of rhetoric of "(1) a failure to acknowledge that such histories are themselves works of rhetoric, reflective of particular compositional choices, with alternative master-tropes and narratives available, and (2) a failure to move beyond intellectual history to consider a variety of sociopolitical factors and incorporate marginalized groups" (30-31). I noted as well that my criticisms had reflected my continuing interests in deconstruction and social conditions. Yet I went on to observe that the earlier article had concealed a tension I felt between these interests. I admitted that I was still uncertain about how "to produce a history of rhetoric sensitive both to the possible self-subversiveness of discourse and to the plight of various people in an extra-textual world" (31). Nevertheless, I used the later article to test a way for histories of rhetoric to link deconstruction and social awareness. Inspired by Barbara Johnson's more socially attuned reworking of the ideas of her mentor, the archdeconstructionist Paul de Man, I suggested that:

> a revisionary history of rhetoric would try to make a difference in composition studies by keeping heavily in mind (1) the attention that deconstruction gives to how reality is mediated through texts, and especially to how texts can in some sense differ from themselves; (2) the attention that various modes of social criticism give to societal differences, such as those based on gender, race, and class; (3) the ways that these two emphases might converge; (4) the ways that the differences between them can illuminate their respective merits and weaknesses; and (5) the ways that a simultaneous awareness of deconstruction and social criticism can eventually help make a difference in society. (32)

Many years later, I find myself still endorsing the above aims. I realize, however, that other people in composition studies may find my clash of interests laughably outdated. After all, has not deconstruction finally received its comeuppance as a paralytic formalism? And does not composition now dwell on the social construction of knowledge? My answer to both questions is "Well, not quite."

True, now only J. Hillis Miller seems to prefer deconstruction outright over other schools of literary criticism. Even Jacques Derrida is bent on demonstrating that he always keeps worldly politics in mind. Many have argued, however, that deconstruction originally did have a social outlook, which it lost when critics like Miller appropriated it from Derrida and reduced it to a technology of American literary studies. Whatever the merits of this claim, at present several literary scholars are finding deconstructive techniques useful even as they seek to transcend formalism. In Ralph Cohen's words, they are "incorporating deconstructive practices" though "abandoning deconstructive ends" (xii). For example, the New Historicists follow deconstruction when they show that certain discourses boasting referential truth depend on unstable tropes, although these critics move beyond deconstruction's emphasis on supposedly intrinsic properties of language to consider in a more Foucauldian vein the ways that institutions manipulate words. Furthermore, students of de Man and Derrida like Johnson and Gayatri Spivak continue to demonstrate the value of deconstructive concepts for analysis of the global scene. In particular, they show that deconstruction's concern for the interplay of margin and center illuminates the relations of various notions, races, and cultures.

Composition studies can also learn much from closely examining the instabilities of discourse—including its own. Unlike literary studies, it can hardly claim to be surfeited with this approach. While deconstruction has preoccupied literary studies since the early seventies, composition studies has barely acknowledged it, let alone worked through its implications. Only two books about it exist in the field, Jasper Neel's *Plato, Derrida, and Writing* and Sharon Crowley's *A Teacher's Introduction to Deconstruction,* both of them products of the late eighties. If composition studies began to apply deconstructive techniques more extensively to its own scholarship, it would start to overcome one of its persistent flaws: widespread empiricism. Although its books and articles certainly provoke disagreement, too often they are written as if their textual performances basically circulate raw data. Even today, few composition scholars extensively probe the rhetoric of rhetorical histories, or of composition research, or of suggestions for teaching writing. Stephen North's book *The Making of Knowledge in Composition* and most issues of *PRE/TEXT* are exceptions that prove the rule. By tracing the interplay of their own narratives and metaphors, composition scholars might see how their institutional commitments pressure them not only to adopt certain rhetorical devices, but also to declare their work unified, transparent, and objective despite its textual dynamics. As Crowley emphasizes, they can also consider how various forms of institutional authority—especially, of course, their own teaching—attempt to regulate their students' writing.

Again, to comprehend adequately this field or any other human project, more than a deconstructive approach remains necessary. Although deconstruction can identify nuances of form, it does risk degenerating into linguistics-based despair unless it considers how particular social conditions produce, infuse, and get modified by the textual details it notices. Also, as I suggested in my later article, those who would use deconstruction should be determinedly animated by the goal of social reconstruction, not simply identifying semantic difficulty for its own sake.

Many scholars in composition studies may feel that its "social turn" has acknowledged these broader issues of context. Certainly the field no longer views text or writer as isolated entities, considering instead how they emerge from and negotiate various nexuses of social conditions. And in the years since I wrote my article calling for more attention to "sociopolitical circumstances," scholars in composition and rhetoric have increasingly attended to variables like gender, race, and class. For example, Ede and Lunsford have gone on to demonstrate a consciously feminist perspective in their study of collaboration *Singular Texts/Plural Authors,* and Connors has been researching the role of women in the history of rhetoric as well as the traditionally low-class status of composition teachers ("Overwork/Underpay").

Still, as with deconstruction, it is significant that feminism, Marxism, and other schools of radical criticism have only begun to influence composition many years after entering literary studies. The lateness of their arrival in composition suggests the primacy of the field's service ethos over its populist sympathies. Often writing instructors treat culturally diverse students more sensitively than their colleagues do, yet just as often they ultimately press students to comply with existing disciplinary structures. This commitment to institutional orthodoxy has determined the main form that composition's "social turn" has taken. Privileging neo-Pragmatists like Stanley Fish, Richard Rorty, and Kenneth Bruffee who scorn radical challenges to the academy, the field has recharacterized existing disciplines as "discourse communities" whose rituals and commonplaces students need to master. Even as composition scholars begin to develop a wider frame of reference, questioning the distribution of power in the academy and the world outside it, they need to consider the ways it still threatens to reduce their sense of "the social."

In looking again at "The History of Rhetoric and the Rhetoric of

History," I am struck by another feature of the article: its two voices. I was both determined to expose a trend that bothered me and scared to alienate the scholars that exemplified it. Consequently, the article alternates strong criticism with attempts at soothing possibly ruffled feelings. In fact, Victor Vitanza's only suggestion about it as editor was that I should cut the apologies. Frankly, I retained them because this was one of my first published articles in a field that I hoped would accept me. The resulting shifts of tone remind me now, however, of a situation that all composition scholars face. Since the field is still relatively small, they are apt to meet people they have chided in their writing, and may even find themselves wanting to strike up a friendship with them. Therefore, often they brood over whom to single out, and what tone to use, when they criticize aspects of composition in their writing. This matter partly involves their deciding whether they can deal with their targets' responses upon actually meeting them. Of course, composition scholars may worry less about arguing with one another in print now that distinctly different visions of the field have emerged. Leftist and moderate notions of social constructionism are at odds; both challenge the enduring cognitivist emphasis of institutions like Carnegie-Mellon; and the whole field now buzzes over the supposed conflict of "theory" and "practice." In my article, I suggested that "a discipline's willingness to confront the rhetoricity of its discourse does relate inversely to its sense of shared aims." Because whatever consensus this field enjoyed has begun to erode, perhaps the rhetorical features of its scholarship will now be more publicly debated.

Still, I wonder if I would have criticized Sharon Crowley if I had known that we would become good friends and that on many an occasion she would mock me for what I had said about her. I was already on friendly terms with Lil Brannon when I wrote the article; however, maybe I would have eased my criticism of her book if I had known that someday in the Palmer House lobby she would tease me by warning someone whose work I had just praised, "Oh, be careful around him! Before you know it, you'll wind up exposed in *PRE/TEXT!*"

WORKS CITED

Cohen, Ralph, ed. *The Future of Literary Theory.* New York: Routledge, 1989.
Connors, Robert J. "Overwork/Underpay: The Labor and Status of Composition Teachers Since 1880." *Rhetoric Review* 9 (1990): 108–25.
Crowley, Sharon. *A Teacher's Introduction to Deconstruction.* Urbana: NCTE, 1989.
Ede, Lisa, and Andrea Lunsford. *Singular Texts/Plural Authors: Perspectives*

on *Collaborative Writing.* Urbana: Southern Illinois Univ. Press, 1990.

Neel, Jasper. *Plato, Derrida, and Writing.* Urbana: Southern Illinois Univ. Press, 1988.

North, Stephen N. *The Making of Knowledge in Composition: Portrait of an Emerging Field.* Upper Montclair: Boynton/Cook, 1987.

Schilb, John. "Differences, Displacements, and Disruptions: Toward Revisionary Histories of Rhetoric." *PRE/TEXT* 8 (1987): 29–44.

10 : TOWARD A SOPHISTIC HISTORIOGRAPHY

Susan C. Jarratt
Miami University

INTRODUCTION

While most histories of rhetoric begin with the sophists, I'd like to suggest that a revision of rhetorical *historiography* must begin with them as well. The point of starting with the sophists is not to privilege their originary or ontological status vis a vis "rhetoric" as a discipline—the "fact" that they invented a self-conscious practice of public discourse—but rather to identify the sophists with an explicitly historical mode of thought and to delineate its features toward the description of a twentieth-century practice of rhetorical history.[1]

The overlap of rhetoric and history in the work of the first sophists derives from the speculations of certain pre-Socratic philosophers who represent what Havelock calls the "biological-historical" view of human existence and institutions, a view which takes historical contingency as the crucial defining feature of the species (*LT* 30–31). These fifth-century B.C. Greek anthropologists—Anaximander, Xenophanes, Anaxagoras, Archelaus—understood not only physiology but also cultural mores as changing products of evolutionary process (*LT* 104f). Theirs is a basically diachronic understanding of human existence and stands in opposition to the ahistorical, "religious-metaphysical" orientation arising out of the universalist tendencies of Pythagoras and Parmenides and finding its fullest expression in Plato. The war between rhetoric and philosophy is a version of that opposition: between the temporal and the eternal, the contingent and the universal.

Of special interest to the sophists was the range of group behaviors they took note of in traveling among the Greek city/states (Guthrie 55). They understood that any discourse seeking to effect action or shape knowledge must take into account those differences. Not only was it essential to judge the circumstances obtaining at the moment of an oration, its *kairos,* but even more essential was the orator/alien's understanding of the local *nomoi:* community-specific customs and laws. The sophists translated the natural scientists' observations about the temporality of human existence into a coherent body of commentary on the use of discourse in the function of the social order: that is, they concentrated on the power of language in shaping human group behavior explicitly within the limits of time and space. Sophistic rhetoric, then, as an instrument of social action in the *polis* was bound to the flux.

Given this definition of the sophists as "historicist" (Streuver 11), it's possible to describe a historiography for rhetoric loosely based on certain features of their thought and practice. I intend for this historiography to indicate a direction for the future of rhetorical history in the twentieth century: it is a historiography in the subjunctive mode.[2] Rather than critiquing extensively or categorizing current histories of rhetoric (Schilb "History"; Vitanza "Historiographies"), some of which already contain strains of what is here styled sophistic rhetorical history, I instead look to the works of the sophists themselves as a creative analog for a particular kind of historical practice. Though the sophists didn't write "histories" as we understand the genre today, in certain of their fragments and attributions historical representation plays a significant part.[3] They created a discursive practice preceding the hardening of generic categories like "history" but always pervaded by an awareness of the historical. Thus both a general sophistic attitude toward history and specific examples of sophistic historical representation will provide the elements of a revised historiography for rhetoric.

The practice of a sophistic historiography entails:

1. a redefinition and consequent expansion of the materials and subject matters of rhetorical history, resulting in what today would be styled multi-disciplinarity—historical investigations on the margins of traditionally conceived disciplines;

2. the denial of progressive continuity: a conscious attempt to disrupt the metaphor of a complete and full chain of events with a *telos* in the revival of rhetoric in the twentieth century; and,

3. the employment of two pre-logical language *techné*, antithesis and parataxis, creating narratives distinguished by multiple or open causality, the indeterminacies of which are then resolved through the self-conscious use of probable arguments.

The resulting narratives will set aside "the history of rhetoric" in favor of "rhetorical histories"—provisional, culturally relevant "fictions of factual representation" (White *Tropics*).

The Expansion of Materials and Sites of Rhetorical Activity

Traditional histories of rhetoric could be defined as those histories having taken as their subject matter chiefly documents explicitly calling themselves "rhetorics": that is, pedagogical treatises concerned with the composition and delivery of persuasive orations (Kennedy; Howell).[4] This selection is based on a narrow definition of rhetoric as the teaching and performance of an opinion-based discourse for use in the social sphere as distinct from the poetic and the philosophical or scientific. The thought and practice of the sophists themselves, however, was never so narrowly defined. They were interested in a whole group of intellectual materials and social actions, the common feature of which was language use. It might be argued that Plato and Aristotle as well exhibited such a range of interests, but the difference is that, for the sophists, all other subjects were subsumed under the rhetorical. In their works, rhetoric permeated every topic: natural science and "epistemology" (Protagoras B1-2; Gorgias, *On Nature* B1-5; Prodicus B3-4; Antiphon B66c), social and political theory (Protagoras C1; Thrasymachus B6a; Antiphon B129-151), aesthetic response and psychology (Protagoras B1; Gorgias, *Enconium to Helen* B11; Antiphon B123), law (Protagoras B6; Gorgias B11a; Antiphon B1-66), religion and ethics (Protagoras A23, B4; Gorgias A28), as well as language theory and pedagogy (Protagoras A 5, 21, 26; Gorgias B14).[5] Sophistic "rhetoric" collided and interbred with literature, science, and philosophy before such interests were bracketed by Aristotle as disciplines. Just as the sophists engaged in a wide range of eclectic intellectual and social activities before the constraints of Platonic/Aristotelian metaphysics and epistemology cordoned off investigations of human mental and physical behavior, so can they serve today as a point of reference for the formation of a comprehensive historical practice unfettered by strict disciplinary boundaries, a practice of history neither exclusively "intellectual" nor "social" (Schilb "History") nor even strictly "factual" in differentiation from the fictional (White *Tropics*). The revisionary historian today will work with an expanded range of materials: not only the pedagogical treatises summarized in traditional histories, but any literary artifact as it operates to shape knowledge and effect social action. The *identification* of materials at an active site becomes as much the work of the revisionary historian as her commentary on them.

There are several forces in play in the academic scene which have circumscribed the province of histories of rhetoric over the last few decades. The disciplinary structure of the universities and presses oftentimes puts a historian of "rhetoric," today lacking a strong deciplinary identity, in competition with scholars in overlapping disciplines of more stability or prestige. George Kennedy, for example, writing classical history of rhetoric, must compete with the ponderous philological productions typical in classical scholarship. Likewise, Wilbur Samuel Howell works within the generally atheoretical, positivist conventions of European intellectual history. The problem of overlap works in reverse as well. The general academic prejudice against rhetoric—a long-term effect of Platonic censure—has at times forced scholars in other disciplines to diminish the significance of rhetoric or simply redefine rhetorical materials as they appear in their histories. Havelock in *Liberal Temper,* for example, elaborates a sophistic "theory and practice of communication" (216), which includes an "epistemology of public opinion" along with a "theory of popular cognition and decision" (220). Though all of those descriptions easily fall within the purview of "rhetoric" broadly defined, Havelock mentions the term only briefly and in a pejorative context (206).[6] Two recent books on the sophists by Guthrie (1971) and Kerferd (1981) are the first extensive and favorable treatments in classics since Hegel and Grote in the last century.

In departments of English, the hegemony of literary studies has shaped the recent practice of history of rhetoric in several ways. The notion of history of rhetoric as a history of writing instruction has evolved naturally out of the recent revolution in writing pedagogy. Such an approach serves a genuine desire to know something about forgotten teachers and their ways while at the same time satisfying conventional disciplinary requirements for transforming "composition" into a distinct and legitimate area of study—it can be shown to have a history. But it's a definition with draw-backs, as well, for both composition and literature. Literary scholars, under such an arrangment, can keep the new co-habitant of the "English" department from usurping already well-staked turf (Harkin). But at the same time this narrow definition of rhetoric also keeps in place an equally narrow view of "literature" (Eagleton).

The movement from a disciplinary "history of rhetoric" to a postdisciplinary rhetorical historiography demands an expansion of the field of study. A shattering of categories like "literature," while potentially politically troublesome, must become an essential feature of a revised rhetorical historiography. "Rhetoric" at its most fruitful has historically functioned as a meta-discipline through which a whole spectrum of language uses and their outcomes as social action can be refracted for analysis and combination. In terms of physical evidence and pedagogical practice, the point is most radically to reconsider the notion of a canon. The rhetorician has from the beginning been a generalist. The goal for the historian in an age of vast and highly specialized knowledge should become neither the mastery of a limited body of texts nor the impossible task of knowing everything and ordering it, but rather an agility in moving between disciplines, standing back from them with the critical perspective characteristic of both history and rhetoric (Streuver 197f.) for the purpose of illuminating meaningful connections, disjunctions, overlaps, or exclusions. The choice of texts for any particular history will become an expression of *ethos*—an idiosyncratic, charismatic assertion of the relevance of a particular combination of materials. Already rhetorical historians are beginning to venture outside the most limited version of what constitutes "rhetoric" and into other areas. Berlin and Covino have taken on traditionally literary figures Emerson and De Quincey; LeFevre includes Freud and Kant in a study of invention; Campbell and Bazerman have begun rhetorical investigations of scientific discourse with studies of Darwin and contemporary physicists. Striking examples of the direction rhetorical histories could take are pointed by Foucault's studies of sexuality, prisons and punishment; G. E. R. Lloyd's investigations of linguistic structures, science, and folklore in ancient Greece; and the work of Michel Serres.

While the general historicism of the first sophists suggests an attitude toward history, two texts from the period will provide a model for the practice of rhetorical historiography. In both Gorgias' *Encomium of Helen* and the Great Speech of "Protagoras" in Plato's dialogue[7] a multiplicity of subjects comprehended under rhetoric are interwoven into an historical narrative. *Helen,* an argument seeking to deny her responsibility in starting the Trojan War, offers speculation on morals, the psychology of reception, the relation between sense impressions and language; Protagoras' retelling of the Prometheus myth in response to Socrates' question about teaching virtue takes into consideration the origin and development of the species, language, pedagogy, and social philosophy. It could be argued that such discourses are irrelevant to the modern situation because of the differences in genre. The encomium and the parable, though both contain elements common to history, have histories of their own as genres. I would respond that a recuperation of literary sub-genres congruent to history as a strict empirical science would not be a fruitless enterprise for rhetorical historians, for whom an expansion of materials may suggest a concomitant reconsideration of generic categories.[8]

Perhaps an even more troublesome problem for the contemporary historian in accepting these two discourses as models for history writing is their mythic status: the raw material for both histories is what we would today take to be exclusively "literary" or "fictional." But in both discourses what is more significant than establishing irrefutable facts is the choice of an historical incident for its usefulness in the reconstruction and interpretation of culturally meaningful and instructive pasts. The opportunities for speculation provided by the narrative situation in each case—on the power of *logos* in *Helen* and on the role of language in our evolution as a species in *Protagoras*—supersedes the establishment of the "factual" status of the materials themselves as a goal for the discourse. I'm certainly not suggesting that rhetorical historians fabricate a past that never existed but rather that a view of history as merely uncovering lost "facts" doesn't take fully enough into account the inevitably literary or mythic quality of any historical reconstruction and its relevance to the present. The use of these sophistic historical arguments as analogs for a contemporary historical practice is intended to encourage an increased self-consciousness about that process of reconstruction as it functions to open for investigation fruitful questions about belief, purpose and self-definition rather than answer questions of "fact."

THE DISRUPTION OF PROGRESSIVE CONTINUITY

In each sophistic discourse, the retelling of a well-known story throws into question existing versions. Gorgias casts doubt on Helen's responsibility for the Trojan War; Protagoras' Prometheus stands in sharp contrast to earlier characterizations. Whereas both Hesiod's and Aeschylus' narratives culminate in the conflict between the Titan and Zeus, the sophist downplays that outcome and focuses on the god's concern for the fate of the human species. Each sophistic discourse disrupts a stable historical narrative and subverts the teleology of its analogs. Gorgias' retelling of the abduction of Helen explicitly throws into question the moral censure of her behavior:

> Helen [is] a woman about whom the testimony of inspired poets has become univocal and unanimous as had the ill omen of her name, which has become a reminder of misfortunes. For my part . . . I wish to free the accused of blame and, having reproved her detractors as prevaricators and proved the truth, to free her from their ignorance. (Sprague B114)

In so doing, the sophistic historian disrupts the continuity of the given historical narrative which uses Helen to take the blame for what could be re-seen as a petty and destructive adventure launched by a few ill-advised toughs with disastrous consequences for the whole society. In terms of the broader issue of cultural values, holding Helen responsible for the archaic war reflected and reinforced the fatalism (and misogyny) of the period. By pulling out that crucial link in the chain of events leading to the war, Gorgias opened up the causal chain, not only implicitly calling into question the historical reasons for her condemnation but, more important, introducing new issues of significance in the present as a consequence: questions about the relations or similarities between love and force, language and love, language and force. In the fledgling Athenian democracy, the power of persuasive speech was a new and potent force which Gorgias' discourse aimed to investigate. Through breaking the tight, uni-directional causal chain — of consciously refusing to tell history as a continuous, complete narrative leading to a pre-understood end — the sophist was able to throw into new light a range of facts and causes for the purpose of a more general consideration. Streuver associates sophistic rhetoric with a historical practice which continually redefines rather than affirms a pre-existing definition. Havelock links the sophists with a school of historical writers including first-century A.D. Diodorus Siculus who attempted encyclopedic projects — histories which didn't lend themselves to strong thematic structure (*LT* 73).

The issues of continuity and teleology are complicated in the case of Protagoras' Promethean myth by the fact that it's ultimately Plato's discourse. Havelock's sensitive reading of the story in three stages offers a convincing method for extracting what can be verified as the sophistic elements in the narrative through comparison with other sources. In the first stage of "Protagoras" story, the brothers Prometheus and Epimetheus are assigned the task of distributing faculties to the various creatures at the time of creation. Epimetheus thoughtlessly gives away all the qualities of physical strength and protection, so his fore-sightful brother steals fire and, more important, the technological skill needed to use it for humans. The second stage of the story finds humans building cities, using language, tilling the soil, but still in danger of extinction by wild beasts and war among themselves. At this moment, Zeus intervenes in the evolutionary development, bestowing divine gifts of justice and respect equally distributed among humans, though technical skill is not. Havelock argues that the third stage can be read as Plato's co-opting of what began as an anthropological account of human development for a defence of in-born excellence as the basis of an aristocratic political order (*LT* 87-94). Though there is no way of knowing how the historical Protagoras would have carried on the story, his well-known agnosticism makes it is reasonably certain that his account would not have included the intercession of a divine force. Though Havelock sees in Protagoras' portion of the story an evolutionary continuity leading to a justification for a democratic political structure, that very use of the Prometheus myth, I would argue, represents a "revision" of the other versions — Hesiod's, Aeschylus', and Plato's — in each of which human creation and development is delimited by and culminates in the authority of Zeus.[9]

The point for a modern rhetorical historiography is the disruption of the conventional expectation that a history be a complete, replete, full, and logically consistent narrative record. The ancient idea of the Great Chain of Being, much older even than its eighteenth-century revival, is still a contending epistemological metaphor in the twentieth century. While the positivism of the nineteenth century removed the necessity for a transcendent source for the order, the desire for "data" which fill in a pre-formulated hypothesis remains strong. Not only is the chain full, but it has direction. For historical practice, the model dictates the location of every datum on a ladder advancing up to or down from a certain culminating point.

The point of breaking the chain, of resisting the impulse to fit historical materials into a neat, continuous line from beginning to end especially for rhetorical historians is to achieve a kind of critical distance which allows for re-vision. Rather than attempting to trace a line of thought from A to B, the rhetorical historian will seek to re-group and redefine. The point is to expose an increasing *complexity* of evidence or data, to resist the simplification which covers over subtleties, to exploit complexity toward the goal of greater explanatory power. The revisionary historian of rhetoric will look not for superficial similarities which group themselves quickly into "species" but will persist in confounding categories by looking longer and discovering finer and finer shades of difference—more and more varieties. She will see the sophist in Plato, Augustine, and Bacon; the hidden Platonist in Nietzsche.

There are several candidates for metaphors to replace the chain or ladder. Foucault argues in "The Discourse on Language" for the replacement of continuities with "events and series" combined through a theory of "discontinuous systematization" (230-31). He represents this process figuratively as cutting a "slice" or finding a "staging post" (232)— metaphors similar to White's figuration of "Contextualist" historical arguments as those which "incline more toward synchronic representations of segments or sections of the process, cuts made across the grain of time as it were" (*Metahistory* 19). The problem is describing a historical practice which denies both "mechanically causal links and an ideal necessity" among events (Foucault, "Discourse" 231). Nietzsche offers the notion of "genealogy" in contrast to history as a solution—a concept which receives its most powerful articulation in Darwin's evolutionary theory. Though Foucault, in reading Nietzsche on history, discredits "evolution" as an attempt to "map the destiny of a people" ("Nietzsche" 146), Darwin's reading of natural history exactly parallels Foucault's description of a proper historical practice: "to follow the complex course of descent is to maintain passing events in their proper dispersion; it is to identify the accidents, the minute deviations—or conversely, the complete reversals—the errors, the false appraisals, and the faulty calculations that gave birth to those things that continue to exist and have value for us" ("Nietzsche" 146).[10] Stephen Jay Gould's pedestrian metaphor for Darwinian historiography—the bush—offers a strong contender to replace the ladder as a way of re-seeing events both within their complex relations diachronically and in series through time. Any one of the multitude of possible revisionary reconstructions will follow a "circuitous path running like a labyrinth, branch to branch, from the base of the bush to a lineage now surviving at its top" (Gould 61).

The differences in outcome between a traditional or continuous history and a discontinuous alternative can be observed among the current treatments of the sophists themselves. On the ladder view, the first sophists' stylistic innovations provided the raw materials for Plato's dialectic and later Aristotle's logic of non-contradiction. Their emotional appeals and arguments from probability were systematized and legitimized by Aristotle's *Art*. In short, they are significant as a link between the oral society of the archaic period and the literate flowering in the fourth century B.C. These explanations are recognizable as commonplaces of traditional histories of rhetoric (Guthrie; Kennedy; Havelock *Literate Revolution*). But reconsidered as a branch of a bush, the sophists become the practitioners of a rhetoric which represents an independent and legitimate alternative response to the particular environment of the fifth-century B.C. Greek city-states—materialist, anthropological, "historical," "liberal," pragmatic (Enos; Havelock *Liberal Temper*). They become a source for analysis of a number of subsequent historical moments, such as Renaissance humanism (Streuver) and the "post-literate" media age of the late twentieth-century America (Corcoran).

What has led to such revisions and what emerges as a feature of a number of contemporary historiographical theories is the necessity for overturning givens: those sequences of event which have through repetition evolved from "truth" into truism. This impulse toward iconoclasm is variously described by Nietzsche as "critical history" (67), by Foucault as reversal (229), by White as the ironic mode (*Metahistory* 433). It is an expectation that "one can already be pretty sure that the stresses will not fall where we expect, and that taboos are not always to be found where we imagine them to be" (Foucault, "Discourse" 232). The sophists employed a verbal *techné* instrumental in effecting that critical, revisionary turn: antithesis. The stylistic device of setting in sequence opposing grammatical and lexical structures operates at a deeper level of narrative construction and causal linkage as an instrument of rhetorical historical practice.

Antithesis and Parataxis:
History in the Tragic-Comic Mode

The first two features of revisionary history—the broad range of materials and the denial of progressive continuity—complicate issues of "logical" structure and causal connection in historical narrative. Method becomes crucial and problematic under a reconsidered project of history.

Here the legacy of the sophists is quite specific at the level of syntax. Their discursive practice suggests a two-stage process of historical composition—a tragic dissolution consonant with the iconclastic movement of critical or ironic historiography followed by a "comic" reconstruction. Of the two syntactic structures therein employed, antithesis creates an openness to the multiplicity of possible causal relations; then parataxis demands the employment of probable arguments in the reconstitution of provisional historical narratives.

Antithesis Under a traditional historiography, the sophist's antithetical pairings are interpreted in two ways. First, they're seen as a manipulative device for eliciting emotional effects in oratorical performance: the antithetical style creates "a tintinnabulation of rhyming words and echoing rhythms" with hypnotic effect on listening crowds (Kennedy 29). Second, in the development of logic, antithesis becomes a precursor to Socratic definition and, eventually, to an Aristotelian logic of non-contradiction, both of which work because they *exclude* one of the two options (Kerferd; Guthrie). Even in Solmsen's lengthy, serious treatment of the sophists' "intellectual experiments" (83–125), the assumption of a split between form and content leads to a generally suspicious attitude toward antithesis defined as a pre-logical stylistic device. For example, he describes Thucydides' use of the *techné* as an "idiosyncracy" (110), an "addiction" (84), something he's "not above" (84).

But other historians have introduced possibilities for interpreting antithesis extending beyond those traditional explanations. Finley's analysis of Thucydides' style acknowledges a more significant conceptual role for the *techné*. In arguing for a chronology of influence, Finley traces an increasing sophistication in its use from Homer to the earliest prose writers through Sophocles and Euripides and finally to the sophists. Though Finley discredits Gorgias as pressing antithesis to its "illogical conclusion" (112), he sees its use by others as fostering an expanding capacity for more complex generalization (109). Untersteiner goes further, describing the introduction of paired opposites as a Gorgian "tragic" sense of knowledge (101–161) Under this revisionist view, antithesis is not a spurious trick for clouding the minds of the listeners but rather works to awaken in them an awareness of the multiplicity of possible truths.[11] In Gorgias the antithetical style, because of the attitude toward causality it fosters, becomes a grammatical structure with implications for a historiographical method. Pairs of words or phrases in opposition set up alternative chains of causality and lead to a syntax expressing a multiplicity of probable connections between events rather than a single necessary cause. The sophistic historian will not "confine reality within a dogmatic scheme but allow it to rage in all its contradictions, in all its tragic intensity" (Untersteiner xvi). The sophists were less concerned with the "scientific" project of establishing specific events in a tight causal sequence than with exploring the possibilities for interpreting past events for present needs (Poulakos).

Gorgias' own revision of the story of Helen of Troy exemplifies the function of antithesis in the establishment of complex causal relations. In the speech, he aims to "set forth the causes through which it was likely that Helen's voyage to Troy should take place" (Sprague 51). What follows is an antithetical quartet of possible causes for the abduction: it was *either* fate *or* physical force *or* persuasion *or* love. But rather than excluding three causes in favor of one, setting up a necessary chain of causal relation, Gorgias focuses the discussion on the interplay among causes, the interrelation of the four. In this case, Gorgias insists upon an indeterminacy of situation in order to speculate on the power of *logos*—a force coming to be seen in the mid-fifth-century Greek *polis* as rivaling the fate of the gods or even physical violence in its power. Because of the gap between the reality of deeds—past, present, and future—and the words which represent them, any persuasion has an element of deception (Rosenmeyer; de Romilly). Thus Helen "against her will, might have come under the influence of speech, just as if ravished by the force of the mighty" (52). Though *logos* lacks the power of fate, it takes the same form, "constraining the soul . . . both to believe the things said and to approve the things done." The parallel between verbal persuasion and the desire created by a pleasing visual impression works as a third means of exploring the psychology of *logos* (Segal). At one point, Gorgias playfully suggests the scheme of a sophistic historiography, implicitly challenging the conventions of factual, continuous history, historical time, and simple cause/effect relations:

> Who it was and why and how he sailed away, taking Helen as his love, I shall not say. To tell the knowing what they know shows it is right but brings no delight. Having now gone beyond the time once set for my speech, I shall go on to the beginning of my future speech, and I shall set forth the causes through which it was likely that Helen's voyage to Troy should take place. (Sprague B115)

The importance of pleasure in the telling and the reference to the future indicate purposes for Gorgias' history. At the end of the speech, none of the four is identified as the single, or even primary cause. Antitheses have evolved into complex interrelations.

Thus Gorgias' "encomium" is capable of interpretation in terms of a historiographical method. Laying out a number of causes for a past event is taken as the occasion for exploring issues of vital importance for the present and future. In Gorgias' hands history becomes not the search for the true, but an opening up of questions; an enterprise not so much of reaching conclusions but of uncovering possible contradictions. Antithesis as more than a mere stylistic gesture disrupts previous complacent givens without, in this case, offering a clear resolution.

Parataxis While the example of Gorgias as rhetorical historian corresponds to the descriptions of critical history cited earlier, the lack of resolution fails to signal a directive for action. Removing the blame from Helen entails a reconsideration of values, but the rhetorical historian both then and now has a strong obligation to action in a social and pedagogical world. A second syntactic structure characteristic of sophistic discourse balances the analytic effect of antithesis with a synthetic gesture which, nonetheless, remains flexible—free from the tighter bonds of a "logical" alternative. The loose association of clauses without hierarchical connectives or embedding is, under traditional explanations, a language behavior typical of primitive story-telling: a less sophisticated organization than its opposite, hypotaxis, the highest expression of which is Aristotelian propositional logic. But again extended beyond the level of mere style, parataxis can suggest a kind of historical practice complementary to the dissolvent impulse of antithesis alone.

The discourse of the character "Protagoras" illustrates the role of parataxis in historical argument: through the narrative *techné* he moves beyond the critical to the constructive (Untersteiner 57–62). While antithesis functioned to overthrow a commonplace about a historical character within the encomium, parataxis arises from a different *ethos*. In the dialogue, Socrates plays the critical role, trying to ruffle the wise old sophist with his hard-edged dialectic.[12] For his part, "Protagoras" demonstrates his ability to read the character and needs of his audience in choosing the form of his discourse. As an old man among young men, he chooses an entertaining narrative over dry argumentation as the most effective way of showing that civic responsibility can indeed be taught, Socrates' objections to the contrary. "Once upon a time," he begins, "there were gods only, and no mortal creatures" (§320d). Though he uses the familiar formula of the story-teller, the effect of this myth is not the hypnotic mystification to which Plato objected in the oral poetry of his fathers (Havelock *Preface*) but rather myth as "externalized thought" (Untersteiner 58): a pleasing, human and thus provisional way of composing an explanation of a human condition through time. Further evidence of the intellectual as opposed to purely aesthetic content of this sophistic history occurs as "Protagoras" blurs the line between *mythos* and *logos,* spinning off moral arguments from straight-forward narrative. These are not the repeated maxims and lessons of customary behavior learned through the oral tradition, but rather *new* solutions to the problems of social organization posed by democracy. The transition from story to its application demonstrates its use. After Zeus has distributed the qualities of justice and mutual respect to early humans equally, they are able to form cities:

> And this is the reason, Socrates, why the Athenians, and mankind in general, when the question relates to excellence in carpentry or any other mechanical art, allow but a few to share in their deliberations. And when anyone else interferes, then as you say, they object if he be not of the few; which, as I reply, is very natural. But when they meet to deliberate about political excellence or virtue, which proceeds only by way of justice and self-control, they are patient enough of any man who speaks of them, as is also natural, because they think that every man ought to share in this sort of virtue, and that states could not exist if this were other wise. I have explained to you, Socrates, the reason of this phenomenon. (322d–323a)

Though this defence of democracy as a happy moment in the evolution of humans challenges the conservative belief in in-born excellence at the foundation of both the older warrior-culture and of Plato's utopian aristocracy, the effect of the discourse is less critical than constructive. As the spokesman for democratic decision-making, Plato's "Protagoras" recommends specific pedagogical practices as natural extensions of his historical narrative: a literary study following on the socialization by the family which inculcates civic virtues (§325–27). While Gorgias' "history" successfully opened a number of speculations through antithesis, "Protagoras" passes over any potentially disruptive moment of his discourse in favor of a resolution leading to specific action. But the resolution provided by paratactic discourse differs from traditional history in that it is always open for reformulation: the continuity of the narrative represents only a contingent stability.

The repeated movement from the tragic critique provided by antithesis to the comic reformulation of parataxis was essential for the sophists. Though they are at worst characterized as skeptics and idle bickerers, in fact, they and their students did the political and legal work of the *polis*. In most disciplines the space between theory and practice allows for a wider separation between critical and constructive purposes. But rhetoric, because of its commitment to action, must be able to move from critique to reconstruction. The historical discourses of Gorgias and Protagoras, as well as their lives as teachers and diplomats, illustrate that movement.[13]

Arrangement in Tragic/Comic Rhetorical History The displacement of the "logical" structure of traditional history in favor of "narrative"[14] structure of rhetorical history changes dramatically the status of arrangement. A reconsideration of arrangement is best approached through a graphic analogy. Imagine parataxis as *linear* in its structure and aural effect while hypotaxis is essentially *visual*. This analogy overturns the typical representation of inferential logic as "linear" based on the sentence as an equation. The alternative way to figure the difference takes as crucial the fact that in a propositional equation, the end is prefigured from the beginning—the whole structure is built in a vertical form, "hypo" suggesting an organization "from under."[15] The hypotactic discourse seems to exist as a complete, two-dimensional visual construct — as Platonic *eide* (appearance) or Aristotelian *theoria* (vision)—before its verbal performance; whereas discourse structured paratactically creates the effect of evolving in time, through sound striking the ears, minds, bodies of its listeners in a total experience which leads to action. The claim is not that hypotactic discourse does *not* affect the total auditor, but rather pretends not to—it obscures or ignores its own existence on the paratactic level of effect while discrediting any "logical" content of the paratactic alternative.

Antithesis allows for laying out options; parataxis provides for their loose coordination in a narrative with a social rather than epistemological purpose, strictly defined. The difference between sophistic historiography and a deconstructive practice is that parataxis follows or is interwoven with antithetical dissolution. The tragic opening up is resutured in a consciously constructed story: a temporary comic resolution.[16] This concept of arrangement is not Plato's organic form, growing from inside; it is rather a human invention. The story-teller plays with his material like Frankenstein with body parts. With both antithesis and parataxis, the point is not exposing or discovering the unknown, but rearranging the known. Invention is collapsed with arrangement as a single rhetorical canon. Traditional histories of rhetoric, bound by convention, derive their force and appeal from their logical presentation. Sophistic histories, on the other hand, could introduce into twentieth-century scholarship an alternative "method" of discourse in the most literal sense of finding a new path—specifically in asserting the validity of narrative as a vehicle for the serious tasks of knowledge creation, storage, and use on a more self-conscious level than the modes of emplotment White finds in the "restricted" historical art of the nineteenth century (*Metahistory* 9).[17] A sophistic method works by exposing and exploring a range of possibilities for knowledge and action and implicitly theorizing the process of their acceptance by the community less on the basis of logical validity and more on the force of their "rhetorical," that is, persuasive and aesthetic, appeal.[18] Rearrangement is revaluation. In sophistic history the pretense to distanced objectivity is overshadowed by an open acknowledgement of a value orientation: any realignment is made for a purpose.[19]

Rhetorical histories move along a continuum toward literary performance and away from objective collection of empirical data, which have themselves currently become subjects of analysis as discursive performances (Bazerman). Such histories are frankly imaginative reconstructions, instruments of *psychogogia* granted assent through their reception by the whole person who reads or hears them—not just on "cognitive" or "rational" grounds—and adopted because they serve social needs for the cultures out of which they arise. They self-consciously and without false modesty argue their theses, holding them up for applause and revision.

Conclusions

One primary objection to be anticipated to the historical practice outlined here comes out of the metaphysical/philosophical tradition: that such histories would neglect objective evidence and lack logical validity—the objection launched against the sophists by Plato. The goal for a rhetorical historiography would be not completely to renounce the "logical" or "factual," but to stop relying on their supremacy over their supposed opposites, to investigate a range of alternatives between those illusory poles. Both the categories of "fact" and "logic" have been undergoing severe critique since the beginning of the century with Peircian semiotics and Saussurean linguistics. Seizing a timely moment in academic history to take the lead in the generation of various forms of post-logical, post-disciplinary academic discourse would be an ideal role for historians of *rhetoric*. Several significant strands in philosophy and literary theory are pointing in such a direction (Eagleton; Lentricchia). What is absent thusfar is a general *practice* which takes seriously into account the insights of the theoretical developments of the last century.

Another possible objection to encouraging cross-disciplinary histories written from a variety of critical stances is the danger of a naive pluralism, a kind of theory-drift under which a particular historian fails to engage seriously enough with any one discourse tradition to understand it fully or apply it accurately (Schilb "Bricolage"). Rhetoric has always been open to the charge from philosophy of lack of system, but that feature is its virtue as well as its short-coming and is related to the special relation "rhetoric" itself signifies between theory and practice (Eagleton 207). While one check for misuse or misunderstanding will be the dialogue among historians from different positions, the more crucial test of any rhetorical history will come from the uses to which its insights are put in the classroom (Phelps) and beyond. That link provides the very definition of rhetoric's critical capacity.

For the present, what would a sophistic historiography promise? Among many possibilities, it could lead to a finer and fuller elaboration of the historical crossings of knowledge and discourse and of the social with the intellectual, a continuing exploration of "scientific" discourse as it evolved out of natural philosophy and magic, a more focused investigation of the points of contact between aesthetic, poetic and rhetoric in theory and between "literature" and non-belletristic discourse forms in practice. More fundamentally, a sophistic historiography would free the writers of histories in rhetoric from the restrictions that bind other disciplines and from the insularity of academic discourse in general, allowing its practitioners to engage, like the first sophists, in genuinely "rhetorical" acts — writing and speaking which make real changes in the world.

NOTES

1. Nancy S. Streuver's elaboration of the relation between sophistic rhetoric and history in the Italian Humanists informs the following discussion. Another source for that connection is Eric A. Havelock, who associates the sophist Protagoras with one of three histoical historical myths arising out of early Greek political thought (*The Liberal Temper in Greek Politics,* especially Chs. I–IV).

2. In borrowing this notion from Streuver (145), I'm shifting the emphasis. Whereas she's interested in the potential for critical distance inherent in the grammatical subjunctive, I exploit its predictive and prescriptive force, gesturing toward what could, would, and even should happen in the field.

3. The birth of the genre "history" contemporaneous with the first sophists offers another site at which to investigate the conjunction of the two strands. See Finley on the development of sophistic style in Thucydides.

4. The category "traditional" is neither exclusive (e.g., Howell's discussion of Locke in *Eighteenth-Century British Logic and Rhetoric*) nor pejorative, but rather is used to describe a particular historical practice arising in response to the needs of the field at a particular moment in its own history.

5. References are to Sprague's edition of Diels-Kranz, *Die Fragmente der Vorsokratiker.*

6. The title of Streuver's study, *The Language of History in the Renaissance,* by omitting reference either to the sophists or rhetoric, suggests the possible operation of a similar disciplinary prejudice in comparative literature.

7. Both Havelock (*LT* 157f.) and Guthrie (265–66) takes the Great Speech as an accurate reflection of the historical Protagoras' views.

8. White employs literary categories as "modes of emplotment" in the analysis of various forms of historical composition (*Metahistory* 7–11).

9. Aeschylus' *Prometheus Bound,* written during the stirrings of democratic sentiment in the mid-fifth century, contains a long description of human development along the same lines as Protagoras' and poses the strongest challenge to a divine *telos* as a grounds for autocracy, though Prometheus seems to be defeated by Zeus in the end. The two lost plays in the trilogy might have provided a more revolutionary challenge to the Hesiodic view of Prometheus.

10. Though White sees Darwinian historiography as rudely mechanistic ("Fictions of Factual Representation"), in line with his reputation for contributing to the materialistic determinism of late-nineteenth-century thought, Darwin's own text, *The Origin of Species,* reveals qualities of ambiguity, indeterminacy, and openness in the narrative form which demand a reconsideration of such a categorization.

11. Havelock associates changes in syntactic structures with evolution in thought (*Literate Revolution,* Ch. 11, especially 246, 253, 256).

12. Vlastos outlines short-comings in Socrates' argument and defends Protagoras' strong moral position in the dialogue.

13. Though the two most complete productions of Gorgias and Protagoras have been offered as a composite of sophistic historiography, both moments are realized within the works of Protagoras. His famous agnosticism, the man-as-measure doctrine, and the title *Contradictory Arguments* all suggest the critical impulse.

14. Fisher's recent work on narrative as argument incorporates an opposition between rationality and narrativity, though he keeps in place an essentially Aristotelian logic of coherence, consistency, and fidelity as criteria for evaluating narrative arguments.

15. The Jakobsonian distinction between the metaphoric and metonymic poles is a clear analog to the relation between hypotaxis and parataxis. What is particularly suggestive about Jakobson and Halle's original discussion of the terms is the observation that most metalanguage about symbol systems concerns the metaphoric mode, whereas metonymy "easily defies interpretation" (95). White's reduction of metonymy to a structure ruled by deterministic causality (*Metahistory* 35-36) misses the complexity of the metonymic and the depth of difference between the two registers.

16. This formulation fits White's definition of emplotment by Comedy – "the temporary triumph of man over his world by the prospect of occasional *reconciliations* of forces at play in the social and natural worlds" [emphasis in original] – but not his view of Tragedy as law-governed (*Metahistory* 9). Untersteiner's understanding of Gorgian epistemology is the source of my use of the tragic (140f.).

17. Among rhetorical historians today, Vitanza makes the most striking and successful attempt to use the antithetical style of the first sophists to achieve "tragic" dissolution, but he defines the "comic" in terms of parody rather than reconciliation or reconstruction ("Critical Sub/Versions"). At moments, Streuver uses antithesis for the disruptive effective in a "comic" narrative (e.g., "unique" and "ounity," 143). A heavy irony within *this* essay is the extent to which it conforms to the conventional logic of academic prose while calling for change. Outside the parameters of disciplinary rhetoric, French feminists Cixous and

Iragaray are experimenting with narrative alternatives to hypotaxis in intellectual argument.

18. Fisher advances narrative argument as a theory which seeks to account for how people come to adopt the *stories* that guide their behavior.

19. In its political interest, this "aesthetic" history differs from White's interpretation of Nietzsche's concept of myth (*Metahistory* 372). In advocating dialectical movement between forms, different styles of historiography for various historical needs (72), and the value of history in the service of life (116), it follows Nietzsche.

WORKS CITED

Bazerman, Charles. "Physicists Reading Physics: Schema-Laden Purposes and Purpose-Laden Schema." *Written Communication* 2 (1985): 3–23.

Berlin, James A. *Writing Instruction in Nineteenth-Century American Colleges.* Carbondale: Southern Illinois Univ. Press, 1982.

Campbell, Joseph Angus. "The Polemical Mr. Darwin." *Quarterly Journal of Speech* 61 (1975): 375–90.

Corcoran, Paul. *Political Language and Rhetoric.* Austin: U of Texas P, 1981.

Covino, William. "Thomas De Quincey In a Revisionist History of Rhetoric." *PRE/TEXT* 4 (1983): 121–37.

De Romilly, Jacqueline. *Magic and Rhetoric in Ancient Greece.* Harvard Univ. Press, 1975.

Eagleton, Terry. *Literary Theory. An Introduction.* Minneapolis: Univ. of Minnesota Press, 1983.

Enos, Richard Leo. "Rhetorical Theory and Sophistic Composition: A Reconstruction." Report of the 1985 National Endowment for the Humanities Summer Stipend.

Finley, John H., Jr. *Three Essays on Thucydides.* Cambridge: Harvard Univ. Press, 1967.

Fisher, Walter R. "Narrative as a Human Communication Paradigm: The Case of Public Moral Argument." *Communication Monographs* 51 (1974): 1–22.

Foucault, Michel. *The Archaeology of Knowledge and The Discourse on Language.* Trans. A. M. Sheridan Smith. New York: Pantheon, 1972.

———. *Discipline and Punish. The Birth of the Prison.* Trans. Alan Sheridan. New York: Pantheon, 1977.

———. "Nietzsche, Genealogy, History." In *Language, Counter-memory, Practice.* Ithaca: Cornell Univ. Press, 1977.

Gould, Stephen Jay. "Bushes and Ladders in Human Evolution." In *Ever Since Darwin. Reflections in Natural History.* New York: Norton, 1977.

Guthrie, W. K. C. *The Sophists.* Cambridge Univ. Press, 1971.

Harkin, Patricia. "Reifying Writing: The Politics of Disciplines. Paper. Mid-West Modern Language Association. Chicago, 1986.

Havelock, Eric. A., *The Liberal Temper in Greek Politics.* New Haven: Yale, 1957.

———. *The Literate Revolution in Greece and Its Cultural Consequences.* Princeton Univ. Press, 1982.

———. *Preface to Plato.* Harvard Univ. Press, 1962.

Howell, Wilbur Samuel. *Eighteenth-Century British Logic and Rhetoric,* Princeton Univ. Press, 1971.
Jakobson, Roman and Morris Halle. *Fundamentals of Language.* 2nd ed. The Hague: Mouton, 1971.
Kennedy, George A. *Classical Rhetoric and Its Christian and Secular Tradition from Ancient to Modern Times.* Chapel Hill: Univ. of N. Carolina Press, 1980.
Kerferd, G. B. *The Sophistic Movement.* Cambridge Univ. Press, 1981.
LeFevre, Karen Burke. *Invention as a Social Act.* Carbondale: So. Illinois Univ. Press, 1987.
Lentricchia, Frank. *Criticism and Social Change.* Chicago Univ. Press, 1983.
Lloyd, G. E. R. *Magic, Reason and Experience. Studies in the Origins and Development of Greek Science.* Cambridge Univ. Press, 1979.
Nietzsche, Friedrich. "On the Uses and Disadvantages of History for Life." *Untimely Meditations.* Trans. R. J. Hollingdale, Cambridge Univ. Press, 1983.
Phelps, Louise Wetherbee. "The Domain of Composition." *Rhetoric Review* 4 (1986): 182-95.
Poulakos, John. "Rhetoric, the Sophists, and the Possible." *Communication Monographs* 51 (1984): 215-25.
Rosenmeyer, Thomas G. "Gorgias, Aeschylus, and *Apate.*" *American Journal of Philology* 76 (1955) 225-60.
Schilb, John. "The History of Rhetoric and the Rhetoric of History." *PRE/TEXT* 7 (1986): 11-34.
———. "When Bricolage Becomes Theory: The Hazards of Ignoring Ideology." Paper presented at Mid-West Modern Language Association. Chicago, 1986.
Segal, Charles P. "Gorgias and the Psychology of the Logos." *Harvard Studies in Classical Philology* 66 (1962): 99-155.
Serres, Michel. *Hermes. Literature, Science, Philosophy.* Ed. Josué V. Harari and David F. Bell. Baltimore: The Johns Hopkins Univ. Press, 1982.
Solmsen, Friedrich. *Intellectual Experiments of the Greek Enlightenment.* Princeton Univ. Press, 1975.
Sprague, Rosamund, ed. *The Older Sophists. A Complete Translation by Several Hands of the Fragments in* Die Fragmente Der Vorsokratiker, *ed.* Diels-Kranz. Columbia: Univ. of S. Carolina Press, 1972.
Streuver, Nancy S. *The Language of History in the Renaissance. Rhetoric and Historical Consciousness in Florentine Humanism.* Princeton Univ. Press, 1970.
Untersteiner, Mario. *The Sophists.* Trans. Kathleen Freeman. Oxford: Basil Blackwell, 1954.
Vitanza, Victor J. "Critical Sub/Versions of the History of Philosophical Rhetoric." *Rhetoric Review* 6.1 (1987): 41-66.
———. "Historiographies of Rhetoric: Traditional, Revisionary, and Sub/Versive." Paper presented at Conference on College Composition and Communication. Atlanta, 1987. [This brief ms., in much greater development now, is included in this issue of *P/T.*]

Vlastos, Gregory, ed. *Plato. Protagoras.* Trans. Benjamin Jowett, revised by Martin Ostwald. Indianapolis: Bobbs-Merrill, 1956. (References are to Stephanus pages.)

White, Hayden. "Fictions of Factual Representation." *Tropics of Discourse. Essays in Cultural Criticism.* Baltimore: The Johns Hopkins Univ. Press, 1978.

———. *Metahistory. The Historical Imagination in Nineteenth-Century Europe.* Baltimore: The Johns Hopkins Univ. Press, 1973.

In an altered form, this essay appears as a chapter in the author's book *Rereading the Sophists: Classical Rhetoric Refigured* (Carbondale: Southern Illinois Univ. Press, 1991).

AFTERWORD

It's a rare opportunity to be able to return to a published text, to talk back to it and its readers, saying I did mean that, I didn't really mean that, now I mean this instead. Some of my first responses are to the style: it seems tortured, painfully qualified, the adverbs in strange positions, as though by their odd placement they could forestall objections. The style seems excessively enthymematic, coming from within a closed conversation, expecting lots of knowledge from the reader. It seems forced out in heavy chunks. Given this "masonic" style, the irony I note seems even more striking: while I recommend a break, or rather a slipping away, from the tighter constraints of "logic," my own prose remains securely walled up. My only defense is feminist/sophistic: I embody contradictions. In Denise Riley's rewriting of Sojourner Truth, "ain't I a fluctuating identity?"

In a way, almost everything I've written since this essay has been an "Afterword" to it: a growing group of comrades continue to write and speak on historiographical questions, so actively that I find it difficult to keep my published statements updated with my latest thoughts. My most detailed response to this essay has just been submitted to yet another *PRE/TEXT* volume, this one on ethics and historiography. That essay explores the biggest change in my thinking since the earlier article was written: a movement toward feminism, specifically socialist feminism. In rereading "Toward a Sophistic Historiography," happily, I find many ideas compatible with my current thinking, but I would now recast them in a different vocabulary. Besides the names of those excluded from a tradition of male-authored European rhetoric, I would fill in terms like "ideology" and "overdetermination." The main focus of the piece, though, finding and supporting an explicitly historical mode of thought and a disruptive historiographical practice, I would defend as thoroughly feminist. But concerns about typologies make me less eager to declare myself under a particular banner such as "revisionary." These concerns come from two places. At the Writing Histories of Rhetoric conference in Arlington (October 1989) participants were styled "traditional," "revisionary," or "subversive" historians. Though the categories were, of course, not meant to be restrictive but only heuristic, they seemed to suggest a progress toward the third category as the most daring, the most disruptive, the most exciting. Adrienne Rich's beautiful, self-reflective essay "'When We Dead Awaken': Writing as Revision" offers a feminist orientation for the label "revisionist," one easy for me to embrace, but putting people and their scholarship in sets of categories with a certain telos seems to cut off conversation fast.

Recently feminist theorists have also called into question typologies; the categories radical/essentialist, liberal, poststructuralist have appeared in a number of recent histories (e.g., Chris Weedon's *Poststructuralist Theory and Feminist Practice*). They call forth the same narrative telos. The first stage is most naive and fundamentalist, the second a bit more sophisticated, but the third is really where it's at. The problem here is similar: reducing and ignoring the complexity of early feminist work, especially under the first category. While I do hope my essay has had some effect on the way histories of rhetoric have been written, I might not offer it so confidently as "revisionist" at this particular historical moment (January 1991).

Using a phrase from Nancy Streuver, I say that I write in the subjunctive mode, aiming to influence people to do history in a certain way. As I return to the three general suggestions I offered, I think mostly of areas of scholarship I now know about but didn't then and of the direction of scholarship since 1986. First came an idea about expanding disciplinary boundaries in history writing. There's a (now) obvious connection here with new historicism and its method of cross-cultural montage. New historicism certainly fits with what I had in mind, especially the personal and charismatic focus of the new historicist on the representive anecdote. But I think sophistic historiography gets past the complaint that new historicism lacks a political dimension. A sophistic historiography foregrounds a present and future oriented agenda. But another problem with new historicism might be shared by my proposal: depth of understanding in a certain historical period or area. The advantage to moving into a period or field from outside is the outsider's ability to see things the insider can't see. Feminist historiography looks into the margins for women and others left out of the picture. But without the specialist's knowledge it's possible to miss things — big important things. The feminist concept of being bilingual and bicultural enters here: the sophistic historian in rhetoric must know what the specialist knows, but see it from the outside. This is a long and difficult process and should be taken into account by departments in judging the work of young scholars in the history of rhetoric. The supportive context provided by journals like *PRE/TEXT, Rhetoric Review, RSQ,* and others creates the possibility for such exploratory work. And as the field ages, I would hope that we can make our work more available to specialists in various fields. Just as feminist work is moving into some mainstream journals, I think historians in rhetoric should try to publish our work in disciplinary journals as well as for each other.

As for the dissolution of disciplinary boundaries in the academy, as far as I can see there hasn't been a great deal of progress. Though composition and rhetoric seem to have a finger-hold, and even a ledge to stand on, in many "English" departments, faculty from both sides of a composition/literature divide still resist integration in many places. Students and teachers either do one thing, or the other, or both — but they don't yet define themselves in more comprehensive terms as suggested by Gayatri Spivak ("cultural politics"), Steven Mailloux (simply "rhetoric"), Terry Eagleton ("political criticism"), and recently James Berlin, who argued at Indiana University at Pennsylvania for a description of English studies as "reading and writing practices." Cultural studies seems a promising direction, advocated by John Trimbur and others, and I hope more historians in rhetoric pursue it.

On the second issue I raise — discontinuity — I'm still committed to breaking apart linear narratives. Rereading my advocacy of the "bush" as an alternative to the ladder as a metaphor for historical development made me laugh. The gendered connotations of those two metaphors never occurred to me before, but now . . . how can I avoid drawing attention to them, with an off-stage (ob-scene) gesture. Yes! Let's write histories like bushes! Talk about writing the body! I still like the idea of humble, above ground, lateral growth of the bush. I'm not ready yet to go underground and embrace the rhizome — sounds gritty and suffocating. I would have to argue with Gould, though, about tracing the bush from bottom to top, reinscribing a heirarchy back into his alternative metaphor. I would make more of the genres of encomium, parable, and others — myth, fairy tale, allegory — and more strongly advocate in general the creative rewriting of history, especially feminist history, in multiple genres. I don't think these are the only kinds of histories we need: some of us will continue to prosaically plod along, doing exposition or conventionally argued theory, but these texts can support and create a space for more inventive discourses. Multiplicity is crucial. That's why I can argue so vehemently with what Victor says, much of which I disagree with violently, but appreciate his way of saying it. Here's my rewriting of Voltaire: I disagree with what you say, but will defend, certainly *not* to the death, because I refuse to subscribe to such a masculinist heroic ethic, but at least to the point of a good argument, your *way* of saying it!

This brings me to the final category: my discussion of antithesis and parataxis. I'm still excited about the priority of arrangement over invention, about the potential for developing the rhetorical implications of narrative, and the importance of challenging the structures of thought and value kept in place by conventional logic. But after working with Cixous and *écriture féminine* (and with the help of many commentators on my work), I think now that what I'm advocating is not completely "other" to hypotactic logic. I advocate arguments themselves "logical" in fundamental ways but which challenge the conclusions and the patterns of Aristotelian systems, including his informal logic. The ideological importance of contradiction has emerged in numerous places, and feminist critiques of "rationality" and "good reason," thankfully, abound.

The vocabulary of contradiction, resistance, overdetermination is absent from this piece. But my summing up the work of rhetoric as a continuing movement from critique to reconstruction is exactly what feminist theory and politics is about: critique is essential, but political action always demands some element of Spivak's now-famous strategic essentialism. I think the sophists suggest such a practice and a pedagogy. We in rhetoric, and particularly through history, could continue in that vein by practicing more "popular" discourse. The sophists were public intellectuals — granted, in a much different context. But there is such a desperate need, in this time of war, for a vigorous, prolific critique of "rhetoric" as we receive it and for a reunderstanding of critical discourse outside the demeaning and misguided label of "political correctness." I don't know if anyone reading my original essay would make that connection, but that's what I see as it's most important potential use now.

Afterword

Around 1980

David Bartholomae
University of Pittsburgh

As editors of the Pittsburgh Series in Composition, Literacy, and Culture, Jean Carr and I were pleased at the thought of bringing together under one cover a series of articles from a somewhat legendary journal whose issues, particularly the early ones, were lost, hard to find, not in most university libraries. In this sense, *PRE/TEXT: The First Decade* is designed to bring the journal to a wider audience. The book provides a representative look at the work of an "underground" journal, one that played a key role in a key moment in the development of composition as a discipline. In the eighties, both the area and the journal came out from underground to achieve a precarious and somewhat ironic status as an established, recognizable, certified, official part of the profession of English studies. *PRE/TEXT,* the book, completes the ironic journey (making the disreputable journal that much more reputable); it is one more attempt to establish the importance of a journal known for being, in its editor's terms, "subversive," "avant-garde," "disruptive," "abnormal."

We also hope that the book will be read as a historical document, as a way to think back on the eighties and to think about the journal, and journals, and the role they played. We hope the book will be read by those who were there in the eighties, reading the journals, going to conferences, running programs. We also hope, of course, that the book will be read by people who were *not* there in the profession in the eighties—either not there in the eighties or not "in" composition and rhetoric. We hope the book will not simply be read as an anthology, but as a way of investigating the roles an "alternative" journal played (or might have played) in the disciplinary formation of composition studies. At a time when composition studies is becoming more and more respectable, we hope it can be read as a reminder that the area, at its most productive, has always been a place where people went to get away from the limits of the usual ways of doing things.

If, as we hope, the book will be read as a piece of history (or pieces of history), then it might be useful if I gave some sense of context, of what the standard professional journals looked like and what professional talk sounded like around 1980 when *PRE/TEXT* first made its intervention into the ways things were said and done. I am going to try to do this in as straightforward a manner as possible. The lists below are representative but not complete. They are meant to give a quick index to the "normal," a baseline against which *P/T* can be read as a counterstatement.

• The 1980s, the beginning of the Reagan era. Here is a sampling of what you would have found in *CCC* (the official journal of the Conference on College Composition and Communication), in *College English* (the journal of the College Section of the National Council of Teachers of English) and *Freshman English News* (itself a long-standing alternative journal). In *Freshman English News:*

> James Berlin and Robert Inkster, "Current Traditional Rhetoric: Paradigm and Practice"
> Richard Koch, "Polarity and the Composing Process"
> W. Ross Winterowd and Barbara Crane, "Eureka! An Assignment: Heuristics in Theory and Practice"
> Richard Graves and Harry Soloman, "New Graduate Courses in Rhetoric and Composition: A National Survey"
> Jasper Neel, "A Dramatic Essay Not on the Teaching of Poesy"
> Lisa Ede, "That Composing Process: What we Know/What we Tell our Students"
> Richard Gebhardt, "The Writing Process: Core of the Writing Program"

In *CCC:*

> Linda Flower and John Hayes, "The Cognition of Discovery"
> Lee Odell, "The Process of Writing and the Process of Learning"
> C. H. Knoblauch, "Intentionality in the Writing Process: A Case Study"
> David Bartholomae, "The Study of Error"
> Andrea Lunsford, "The Content of Basic Writers' Essays"
> Marilyn Sternglass, "Sentence-Combining and the Reading of Sentences"
> Sondra Perl, "Understanding Composing"
> Nancy Sommers, "Revision Strategies"
> Mike Rose, "A Cognitivist Analysis of Writer's Block"

In *College English:*

> John Gage, "Philosophies of Style"
> Lawrence Green, "Enthymemic Invention and Structural Prediction"

Charles Bazerman, "A Relationship Between Reading and Writing: The Conversational Model"
Barry Kroll, "Developmental Perspectives and the Teaching of Composition"
David Hamilton, "Interdisciplinary Writing"
Ann Raimes, "Writing and Learning Across the Curriculum"
Gerald Graff, "The Politics of Composition"
James Berlin, "Richard Whately and Current-Traditional Rhetoric"
Lee Odell and Charles Cooper, "Procedures for Evaluating Writing"
Ann Ruggles Gere, "Writing Composition: Toward a Theory of Evaluation"
William Covino et al., "Graduate Education in Rhetoric: Attitudes and Implications"

• In 1980, Louise Rosenblatt received the NCTE David H. Russell Award for Distinguished Research in the Teaching of English for her book, *The Reader, the Text, the Poem.*

• In 1980, the following books were advertised in *CCC, CE,* and *FEN: The Writer's Options: College Sentence Combining,* Daiker, Kerek, and Morenberg; *Practical Stylist* (5th ed.), Sheridan Baker; *Modern Rhetoric* (4th ed.), Brooks and Warren; *Forming/Thinking/Writing,* Ann Berthoff; *Process and Thought in Composition,* Frank D'Angelo; *Writing Well,* Donald Hall; *Random House Handbook,* Frederick Crews; *Writing with a Purpose* (7th ed.), James McCrimmon; *Four Worlds of Writing,* Lauer, Lunsford, Emig, and Montague; *The Practice of Writing,* Scholes and Comley; *Problem-Solving Strategies for Writers,* Linda Flower; *Errors and Expectations,* Mina Shaughnessy; *Eight Approaches to the Teaching of Composition,* Donovan and McClelland.

• And the following books were advertised in *Critical Inquiry* and *PMLA: Renaissance Self-Fashioning,* Stephen Greenblatt; *Is There a Text in This Class,* Stanley Fish; *Writing and Difference,* Jacques Derrida; *Madwoman in the Attic,* Gilbert and Gubar; *Criticism in the Wilderness,* Geoffrey Hartman; *The Genesis of Secrecy,* Frank Kermode; *Metaphors We Live By,* Lakoff and Johnson; *Reader-Response Criticism,* Jane Tompkins, ed.; *After the New Criticism,* Frank Lentricchia; *Power/Knowledge: Selected Interviews and Other Writings,* Michel Foucault; *Problems in Culture and Materialism,* Raymond Williams.

• The 1980 CCCC meeting (in Washington, D.C.) had as its theme, "Writing: The Person and the Process." Lynn Troyka was the program chair. James Britton, James Kinneavy, and Maxine Kumin were advertised as featured speakers. Kinneavy had published *A Theory of Discourse* in 1971; the Norton paperback edition was issued in 1980. Britton (and colleagues) had published *The Development of Writing Abilities (11-18)* in 1975. The American paperback edition was released in 1977. Both Britton and Kinneavy had achieved a special status as icons, figures representing not only the best that could be done in the field but the kind of character (saintly, to the insiders) that distinguished people in composition from those elsewhere. Maxine Kumin, in a sense, had nothing to do with CCCC but was there in a familiar CCCC gesture; she was the "creative" artist who gave a proper respectability to the proceedings, brought to Washington in a perhaps reflex gesture to composition's old nervous relationship with the English department.

While the title of the meeting defined writing as both "person" and "process," 1980 (as you can see from the articles in the journals) was an important year in the establishment of "process" as a key word in composition. (1980 was the publication date for Lee Gregg and Erwin Steinberg's *Cognitive Processes in Writing*.)

Our special feature of the meeting was a series of "primers," sessions designed as "introductory mini-courses" for people "who have not had the time or resources to look into some of the newest ideas in the field." There were "primers" on: Descriptive Grammars; Speech Act Theory and Rhetoric; Concepts in Cognitive Psychology As They Apply to the Writing Process; Psycholinguistic Reading Theories for Teachers of Writing; The "Case" Approach to Composition Teaching.

There was a postconvention workshop on research in composition featuring Rosemary Hake, Janet Emig, Linda Flower, and Richard Young. Victor Vitanza spoke in a session on "Roots of the Invention Process in Rhetorical Theory." His talk was titled "'Invention' and 'Discovery': A Study in Contrasts." Ann Ruggles Gere was the chair of his session; on the panel with him were Jim Raymond ("Critical Reading: The Inverse of Invention") and Joanne Cockelreas ("Composition and Experiential Perception: A Space-time Heuristic"). Jim Berlin spoke at a session titled "Nineteenth-Century Rhetoric." The title of his paper was "The Rhetorics of Romanticism." With him on the panel were Nan Johnson, Ed Corbett, and Win Horner. Sharon Bassett gave a talk on E. D. Hirsch's *Philosophy of Composition* titled "Towards a Servile Rhetoric." The other speakers at her session were Lisa Ede (who spoke on Chaim Perlman) and Andrea Lunsford (who spoke on Frank D'Angelo).

It is worth noting that the 1980 conference was the first to require all potential speakers to submit proposals in order to be considered for the program. This was a PRE/TEXT-like move by the program chair (or both were responding similarly to counter the order of things in composition). Lynn Troyka, teaching at a two-year college, changed the way the program was formed in order to insure greater representation. This was partly a response to the sudden growth of the organization (850 attended the 1970 CCCC meeting; 2,402 attended the 1980 meeting; and 3,607 the 1990 meeting). This growth is really quite remarkable—unmatched, I believe, by any other professional organization in the humanities. While it was popular in the early eighties to continue to refer to the CCCC convention as a kind of town meeting, a cozy get-together on friendly turf for those beleaguered by the professionalism and careerism of MLA, the 1980 meeting marked (ironically) the transition in CCCC from small meeting to big, from casual to professional, from cozy to unrelenting. The change in the routes of access to the program was an attempt to break the hold of the old boy (and girl) network, and to formalize that break. (In the nineties the proposal review process was itself accused of serving special interests in the profession and has undergone several changes, including a move to blind review.)

• The period around 1980 saw a proliferation of special postdoctoral seminars, some of them sponsored by the National Endowment for the Humanities. The purpose of the seminars was to provide opportunities for faculty at out-of-the-way places to catch up on research at the schools where things were happening. This form of special education had a particular valence for composition studies, because the people in charge of programs in 1980 (I was one of them) had been produced by graduate programs (many of them) that included no training in composition and rhetoric—that is, the new crop of experts in the field had been given little formal disciplinary preparation. There were few graduate programs with areas in composition and rhetoric. And there was little coordination between programs. The very "idea" of graduate study in composition was under review, as you can tell by the surveys reported in the journals and by one of the sessions at the 1980 meeting, a "how-to" session called "Doctoral Programs in Rhetoric," chaired by Edward P. J. Corbett and Richard Larson and featuring James Kinneavy ("Essentials of a Program"), Ross Winterowd ("The Contexts of a Program") and Richard Young ("Designing a Program"). The respondent was Janice Lauer. (All these figures played a central role in developing the kinds of graduate programs now taken for granted in composition and rhetoric.) And so these seminars functioned as a kind of quick introduction to the knowledge and methods one needed in order to profess expertise in the field.

In 1980, these were the seminars you could choose from, at least according to the ads in *CCC, CE,* and *FEN:*

At Carnegie Mellon University, "Studying the Composing Process" (with Richard Young)

At the University of Detroit, "Current Theories of Composition" (with Ross Winterowd, James Kinneavy, Frank O'Hare, Janice Lauer, Richard Young, and Edward P. J. Corbett)

At Purdue University, "Current Theories of Teaching Composition" (with Corbett, Kinneavy, Lauer, O'Hare, Young, Winterowd, and Walter Ong)

In the Smokey Mountains, "The Writing Process: A Seminar on Teaching Writing" (with Kinneavy)

At Texas A&M University, "Writing As Process" (with Corbett and Cowan)

At the University of Massachusetts in Boston, "Philosophy and the Composing Process" (with Ann E. Berthoff)

At the University of Pittsburgh, "Teaching Writing: Theories and Practices" (with William E. Coles, Jr.)

As Victor Vitanza indicates in his "Retrospective," the seminar phenomenon had immediate bearing on the history of *PRE/TEXT*. In the 1978-79 academic year, the editor and the first editorial board of the journal were all part of a group at CMU, most of them there for a nine-month seminar offered by Richard Young, some as adjunct faculty who had been in the English department at CMU, but whose status was uncertain given the changes in the direction of the department (toward a new combination of rhetoric and cognitive science) initiated by Young, its new chair.

Young and the seminar, as Victor says, provided the "conditions for the possibilities of *P/T*." As I have heard the story told, the editorial board began as a group who gathered at an office at CMU, all feeling a bit unreal, the way you do when you are cut off from your home, your family, your department, your training, its expectations, the profession, its centers. The group had traveled to Pittsburgh, perhaps to find a way (to use Victor's phrase) to put their feet in the door of the profession — not simply to get jobs or standing (since many of them had that already), but to open up a space for interests that seemed shut out of the rooms they had been chosen, and prepared, to occupy. The seminar was (and was not) the space where this alternative conversation might take place — that is, while there was the official work of the seminar to read and to talk about, the group also met to read material *not* assigned in the seminar. The group met in Sharon Bassett's apartment; the first items on the alternative reading list were Walter Benjamin's "The Work of Art in the Age of Mechanical Reproduction" and Jacques Derrida's "Structure, Sign and Play in the Discourses of the Human Sciences," works that were being read and talked about in alternative reading groups all around the periphery of English studies. The reading group was a gesture simultaneously away from and back to English; it made the CMU seminar both safer and more dangerous.

This is one way of imagining the context for *P/T.* There was a group of people who wanted to identify with each other and to identify with the field defined as "composition and rhetoric," and so they needed to go someplace to read what they wouldn't normally read. And while they were reading what they wouldn't normally read, they wanted, at the same time, to find a way of reading and thinking about another body of excluded work that seemed powerful and important (and to belong elsewhere, like the work of Benjamin and Derrida). The Benjamin/Derrida reading group seriously questioned the reigning assumptions of the "new rhetoric" that was emerging as a challenge to the old field of composition. A simple way to put it is this: the "new rhetoric," the "process" movement that marked the emerging consensus in composition and rhetoric, the turn to cognitive science, all were based on a theory of mind that was necessarily erased (bracketed) by the arguments of Derrida and Benjamin.

One way of reading the table of contents of *PRE/TEXT* the book, then, is as the continuing work of an alternative reading/writing group, a group that wanted to read both in *and* out of the "official" reading list at the advance of the field (to be both with and against the avantgarde). Kameen's wonderful opening essay, "Rewording the Rhetoric of Composition," could be seen as a way of working out the argument against not simply Frank D'Angelo or Richard Young or Linda Flower but the emerging new alternative (and exciting, and, as it was said, "paradigm breaking") consensus on the composing process, the curriculum, culture, and the mind. (It is worth noting that Paul Kameen's essay was written, in part, for an NEH seminar—Ann Berthoff's in Boston. Ann Berthoff spent much of the eighties opposing the new consensus, or any consensus, providing ways for people to meet in an alternative mode at the CCCC convention for example, leading the charge against those she deemed as the "positivists," lamenting the directions taken by composition and its professionals.)

It may be hard now, in 1993, to read Kameen's essay as subversive: it is mildly stated, scholarly, careful, and thoughtful. Perhaps the best way to account for the force of its entry into the field (and, in a sense, its integrity) is to note that Kameen was at CMU when he published his essay in *P/T,* an essay written to find a way to speak from outside the discourse identified with CMU, with Richard Young and Linda Flower, among others. It is also worth noting the way that the essay speaks at once of Coles and D'Angelo, of Coleridge and Heidegger, and of textbooks for composition courses. This was in no way a "normal" or predictable or easy combination (not in the eighties and certainly not today, in the nineties, when textbooks, powerful instruments in the production of reading and writing in America, still remain politely ignored and unread). The combination of Heidegger and textbooks, Coleridge and Perelman and Jacqueline Berke would have been read as an unserious (or unseemly, even parodic) mix of high and low.

The material in Kameen's essay was not normal, nor was the style of his argument. At a time when the "report" (the presentation of new knowledge) had the greatest intellectual cachet, Kameen took as his work a "rewording"—a working on the key terms and the discursive order of his field, a kind of philosophical work that was not synthetic, not historical, not polemical, and not merely a translation (for "practitioners") of Big Books and Big Ideas. It was an attempt to imagine and enact that it would mean to think simultaneously outside and inside not only the old order of English but the new.

This was a writing, in other words, that marked a striking alternative to the essays you see in the pages of *CCC, CE,* and *FEN,* essays not all of which (but many of which) worked primarily to identify the writer with a particular line of research or teaching. There was little to gain in the 1980s by doing one's work through Coleridge or by taking a particular care with footnotes, or by worrying over the meanings and derivations of key terms, terms like *vitalism* and *problem solving, imagination* and *audience.* I'm not entirely convinced that *PRE/TEXT* provided a place for writers whose work would otherwise have been ignored. Most (all?) of the authors in this collection were also publishing in the journals. *PRE/TEXT* did, however, allow for a kind of writing that would *not* be published anywhere else, a prose that was speculative, skeptical, self-indulgent, experimental, sometimes mixing genres, almost always taking seriously the catch-phrase of the process movement, that writing was a way of knowing.

From Kameen's essay, it is easy for me to trace a line through the remaining essays in the collection, each of them, in a sense, a rewording of the rhetoric of composition, each of them written with an eye toward the writing as method, as part of the problem of doing the work of an intellectual not entirely happy with his or her location in a field. Bizzell, in an essay that produced a significant counterswing away from "science" in composition research, returned to the key terms of the "process movement" in composition. Bazerman turned attention to the rhetoric of science and to writing outside of the composition classroom. Phelps, Covino, Halloran, Swearingen, Crowley, Schilb, and Jarratt wrote histories designed to intervene in the present, to reword or challenge both the foundations and the discourse of composition, to unsettle composition's new status as a settled field of knowledge and practice.

I should add, however, that in spite of my willingness to confirm the editors' conviction of the journal's eccentricity, what I most remember was a journal that was dauntingly, relentlessly scholarly. There was a spirit of P. T. Barnum, most often from the editor and in the marginalia, but at the same time, *P/T* was a journal of high seriousness. *PRE/TEXT* was distinguished from the other journals by the length of the essays, the range and depth of allusions, the obvious ways it paid homage to a European philosophical tradition. Its manner of using and addressing authority and tradition is unlike Kinneavy's (the first chapter alone of *A Theory of Discourse* has a bibliography with 117 entries, ranging from Bain to Chomsky to Malinowski and Ransom; there is a wonderful brief exercise in comparing citations in *A Theory* and in *PRE/TEXT*), but it was, at the same time, "traditional" in the degree to which it placed the problems of "composition" in traditions of thought and teaching.

In fact, the seriousness was a part of what made people mad or nervous, since it seemed to give in to what was still referred to as the value system of the old professors of literature. Or, to put it another way, the journal was (or seemed) unreadable to many who had been prepared to read pieces that were more practical, more "democratic," more rooted in the business of composition, readers who were (and with good reason) skeptical of the gesture to high culture and who needed to know how to teach the research paper or handle the paper load. You don't want to think about this simply — it was not just that PRE/TEXT was for intellectuals and *CCC,* say, was for practitioners. There are other ways to phrase this — you could say that *P/T* chose to work in the terms of the academic elite, citing sources, like Heidegger, that carried greater cultural capital in the academy and the English department than the research paper. You could say that *P/T* made a choice about how it would direct/constitute an intellectual investment in rhetoric that ran counter to other serious, alternative versions of what it meant to do work in English.

There was a point around 1980, then, when the undercurrent or oversound of professional talk in composition was interrupted and then accompanied by the work appearing in *PRE/TEXT.* The journal played a significant role in the formation of the profession and in the careers of professionals. Now that it has turned into a book, and from a university press no less, now that its writers are middle-aged establishment types, what might we say of its future? And what might we say about the role of the journals at this stage in the development of the field?

While I don't have time to do it here, it would be interesting to pursue the last question more generally, to look at the roles journals have played in developments in the discipline. I recently had the pleasure of reading a dissertation by Richard E. Miller that included a history of the film studies journal *Screen* and its companion publication, *Screen Education,* both sponsored by the British Society for Education in Film and Television, an organization important to the development of cultural studies in Britain and the United States. For *Screen* and *Screen Education,* the questions that shaped the development of the journals grew out of debate over the relationships between theory and pedagogy and over the degree to which a desire for "radical" critique might be realized in teaching and writing.

In 1976, four of the editors of *Screen* resigned from the editorial board and argued, in "Why We Have Resigned from the Board of *Screen*," that: (1) "*Screen* is unnecessarily obscure and inaccesible" (the immediate source of the problem was the journal's preoccupation with Lacan); (2) "The politico-cultural analysis that has increasingly come to underpin *Screen*'s whole theoretical effort is intellectually unsound and unproductive"; and (3) "*Screen* has no serious interest in educational matters."[1] In 1982, *Screen Education* was merged into *Screen*. The new journal was titled *Screen Incorporating Screen Education* and its mission was "the business of radical writing on film, television and (to a lesser extent) education." According to Miller, at this point "the story is all but complete, with pedagogy quietly receding into the background once disciplinary legitimation has been realized."[2]

In 1975, the editors of *Screen Education* (the "practical" half of the original pair of journals) asked a sociologist, Nell Keddie, to read through recent issues and to report on what she saw as the relationship between the journal, the discipline, and the academy. Her conclusion was that the journal, in relation to the discipline, seemed poised between "low academic status on the one hand and . . . a commitment to the status quo on the other."[3] The writing in the journal, she said, participated in the very processes of reification it presumed to question and counter. It created a special class of film analysts, distant from those film viewers they presumed to serve. Within the institution, "if Film Studies achieves subject status it will occupy a separate box on the timetable and so occupy time and space within the school day; it will be entitled to a budget; it will recognized by public examples; expert teachers will be in a position to make esoteric assessments of pupils' progress, and syllabuses will be constructed which will largely define what counts as Film Studies for years to come."[4] The journal, she concluded, exhibits the contradictions inherent in its position, expressing a radical social philosophy within an educational system committed to traditional liberal values. A journal, in this argument, cannot not be normal.

Similarly, in the book which gave me my title, *Around 1981: Academic Feminist Literary Theory,* Jane Gallop looks back over the entry of feminism into American university discourse (in 1981, for example, there were special "feminist" issues of *Critical Inquiry* and *Yale French Studies*). She said:

> Between 1975 and 1983 the mainstream of academic feminist criticism implicitly defined its enterprise in a way that fit the literary academy. Cooptation or strategy? We may not be able simply to decide what motivated this fit. But we live in the legacy of that period; we benefit from it. It allows us not only radically to call its terms — "women" and "literature" — into question but to be heard through an institution's channels of transmission when we do so. . . . Now that we are comfortable enough to ask these questions and be heard, let us use this position not to accuse each other of being too academic or elitist or reformist but to articulate these questions with the institution in which we work and through which we interact with society.[5]

As I think back over the period of the eighties, I think of composition as one of several places (film studies and women's studies are two others) where English as a field was being reimagined and renegotiated. Within composition, *PRE/TEXT* provided a place where part of that renegotiation was carried out in writing. I find myself sympathetic to Gallop's desire to make our present the site of our work rather than to lament how far we have fallen (or to value only the new), and so I like to think of *PRE/TEXT*'s acquired status as potentially strategic rather than evidence of cooptation.

At the end of his preface, Victor wrote, "During the past decade, *P/T* added those writers and thinkers (as Robert Connors has said) for whom there was no place in the field." (As I've said, I don't think this was quite true. If you look at the cast of characters in our table of contents, you can find many of them also present around 1980 in the journals.) "Today, however, many of these people have gone on to be major voices, in great part, because of *P/T*." (Maybe — but why quibble. I'm happy to grant Victor his pride in his achievement.) "Given the language game of avant-garde art, the language game of the future anterior, these major voices must drop out of *P/T*, and in their place new-but-yet-unknown voices (both music and noise) must be found and then heard."

It is a compelling argument. Who would go on record denying a place for the yet unknown to speak? I hope, however, that the editor will not give in completely to his sense of the need to provide a place for the always new (or the forever young), not simply because I would like to hear more from the people I have read in *P/T*, and in the manner that *P/T* allows, but because I think one role the journal can play at this point in the history of the profession is to allow those who identify with its history and its work to continue to explore their relationship to the field and its knowledge, to the institutions within which we work, and (as Jim Berlin hopes) to social and political life not only locally but in the world.

I hope the journal can be a place (as, I think, it has been) where those who define themselves, by writing, as both "in" and "out of" the field can test the limits of that in-between place, doing a kind of writing that stands against the desire to finally know the field and its work, to know it for sure, to enforce that knowledge, to be correct. This desire for knowledge and correctness—represented in Victor's anecdote by the person who said, "for the health of our discipline and field, we should exclude anyone who wants to talk about Foucault"—this desire, says Victor, is what *P/T* "will stand *against*." But, he reminds us, "against" means both "contra to" and "along side." It is important also to know (not just listen to) the ways work with Foucault might be said to be unhealthy. I take this as a strong and wise editorial policy—and carefully put, since many would identify *PRE/TEXT* as a journal simply *for* Foucault, or as a journal simply *against* expressive writing (which, in a recent special issue, it was also "for"). This is not just pluralism (the journal that will take all sides) but, as I read it, a principled statement of what it means to be committed to critical inquiry. This was the strength of the journal in its first decade. I'm looking forward to the second.

Notes

I am grateful to Steve Carr and Steve Sutherland for their help in the preparation of this essay.

1. Richard Miller, "Representing the People: Theoretical and Pedagogical Disjunctions in the Academy," Ph.D. diss., University of Pittsburgh, 1992, p. 160.

2. *Ibid.*, p. 152.

3. Nell Keddie, "What Are the Criteria for Relevance?" *Screen Education* 15 (Summer 1975), 10.

4. *Ibid.*, p. 4.

5. Jane Gallop, *Around 1981: Academic Feminist Literary Theory* (New York: Routledge, 1992), p. 243.

Afterword

A Pretext for Rhetoric: Dancing 'Round the Revolution

Steven Mailloux
University of California, Irvine

I

In his Prospective, James Berlin briefly comments on the strategic uses of rhetoric in the Persian Gulf War. His analysis brings to mind a prophetic slip of the tongue I heard during the congressional debates. Senator Patrick Leahy of Vermont was arguing vigorously against the immediate use of military force and for continued sanctions against Iraq: "If we determine that it is in the national interest, we can make the financial sacrifices, and we can rotate tropes, uh, troops to keep them fresh."[1]

II

Even more telling was the rhetorical commentary in the Senate chaplain's opening prayer: "[A]ware of the power of words to conceal as well as illuminate, to deceive as well as inform, to confuse as well as clarify, to kill as well as edify, grant to the Senators in their debate cool heads, warm hearts and economy of language."[2]

III

In the fragments that follow I will rotate the tropes of some *P/T* essays, move them around in a rhetorical dance to show how they are kept fresh to conceal and illuminate, deceive and inform, confuse and clarify. This rotation of tropes, this turning of turns will be both playful and serious. Like *P/T* in its first ten years.

IV

Both Victor Vitanza and James Berlin talk prospectively about the subversiveness of *P/T*. And this seems quite appropriate given the traditional view of the journal's topic. Yes, rhetoric can be subversive, but Vitanza and Berlin actually mean rather different things in invoking the notion. Indeed, we might begin marking this difference by citing two contrasting (or maybe complementary) takes on rhetoric, contemporary perspectives that could be troped as ludic poststructuralism and ideology critique.[3] It is precisely the battle or dance between these rhetorical perspectives that makes the prospects of *P/T* so promising and this volume's essays so interesting. Quite often the introductions, essays, and afterwords stage these two sides of contemporary rhetoric. Its indeterminate linguistic side and its interventionist political side. The play of signs and the war of words. The Dance and the Revolution.

V

Vitanza notes how *P/T* has continually "stood in playful . . . juxtaposition to the discipline of rhetoric and composition," but it has been playfulness with a political purpose: "*P/T* has been dedicated to those people and ideas that have been, heretofore, 'excluded.' . . . So that they might be 'included'—thereby ever widening and dispersing the field of rhetorics and possible audiences." It was a battle with conservatism. But scrupulous rhetorical historian that he is, Vitanza admit *P/T*'s desires and its achievements were not always congruent: "Much that is in *P/T,* by today's standards and perhaps those of the eighties, is conservative, or is written in normal discourse, for a normal audience, and for an (apparently) normal field." Still the disciplinary battle was carried on, with playfulness as a weapon: "it was so easy to be outlandish and to upset particular members of the field. . . . Perhaps that is what *P/T* has been about. If rhetoric can conserve, it can also upset stasis."

VI

Rhetoric: "the power of words . . . to kill and edify."[4] As an academic discipline: "the discipline of rhetoric is conservative while denying the possibilities of being (perpetually, laughingly) revolutionary. If it does speak of revolution or of change, it speaks seriously" (Vitanza's Prospective). Beyond and within the academy: "The central role of rhetoric in human affairs has never been more apparent. When the Bush administration denied rhetoric in the name of truth, freedom, democracy, and the American Way, it reminded us that all terms are rhetorical, especially such apparently transparent ones as these. These designations themselves are finally terrains of ideological battle in a quest to determine who will decide what their meanings will be" (Berlin's Prospective). Rhetoric: "the political effectivity of trope and argument in culture."[5]

VII

Nietzsche: "What is truth? a mobile army of metaphors, metonyms, anthropormorphisms, in short, a sum of human relations which were poetically and rhetorically heightened, transferred, and adorned, and after long use seem solid, canonical, and binding to a nation."[6] If we agree with Nietzsche here, then can't we say that to rotate the tropes is precisely to rotate the troops?

VIII

... war, battle, troops, tropes, arguments, rhetoric ... A caution: "Somewhere between overqualified scepticism to the point of silence and barbaric self-importance perhaps we can create a few spaces for talk as opposed to lines drawn in the sand, standoffs, shoot-outs, and other martial metaphors that in this era of desert storms and canon blasting we can hardly encourage" (C. Jan Swearingen's "Afterplay"). Yes, rhetoric does involve cooperation as well as competition.[7] ... rhetoric, persuasion, identification, cooperation, dancing together ...

IX

In "The Dance of Discourse" Louise Phelps borrows some metaphors from modern physics to argue for a different model of discursive structure in compositional rhetoric. (Her definition of the latter: "the theory of communication through written symbols that was implicit in earlier composition teaching and is now being explicitly formulated and revised in theoretical studies and empirical research" [n. 1].) The "continual cosmic dance of energy" becomes Phelps's trope for dealing with "written discourse as a communication event, the dance of discourse." For her, "structural features laid down in the text must organize the dance of cognitive energies between writer and reader so as to constitute the complete discourse event." Or again: "discourse is essentially dance, event, or pattern of symbolic energies in which the discourser participates, ordered or structured with the aid of cues laid down by the writer in the text for himself and the reader." Such formulations tend to slip back into the very separation of subject from object, active reader from pre-existent text, which in other places Phelps argues convincingly against. Comments more consistent with a transactive (rather than interactive) troping of the discourse event include: "Discourse structure emerges from the dance of discourse as one thing or another—the progress of a metaphor, the clashing of positive and negative lines of force, alternating voices in a conversation—by virtue of the attention of the dancer."[8] Neither structure nor reader are isolatable from each other in terms of pre-given "cues" constraining the reading event — whether that reading is the author's during revision or her audience's during a later public reception. Discourse structure is less a pre-given constraint on reading than a tropological result of the reader's interpretive argument during the discourse event.

X

Such formulations are often met with a question: Does the theory implied here risk letting the dance of discourse get out of control and allow reading to fall into interpretive relativism? Certainly the issue of relativism — interpretive, ethical, and political — variously defined and variously criticized — is a significant topic in several essays in this volume, and the connection between philosophical relativism and political anarchy dances around the pages of many verbal battles in *P/T*'s history. In an early dialogue on the merits of American and French cooking, for example, one interlocutor accuses the other of "philosophical relativism" in defending cultural difference. The debate continues:

ME: This is not philosophy. It's a discussion of food.
CH: Yes, so you say, but I fear all this talk about food is a pretext to talk about something else as well, with a hidden analogy here and there.

And later:

CH: Jello and tuna together *is* anarchy.
ME: ... That's a good word, *anarchy*.[9]

XI

In "Thomas DeQuincey in a Revisionist History of Rhetoric," William Covino plays out one set of implications of this "good word" for rhetorical theory. In DeQuincey's writings, Covino argues, "rhetoric is the art of wondering: 'to hang upon one's own thoughts as an object of conscious interest, to play with them, to watch and pursue them through a maze of inversions, evolutions, and harlequin changes.'" Covino advocates an "intellectual play of discourse resisting closure" and argues that rhetoric "involves a tension between convention and invention, mechanic and organic, closure and wonder" and that "one becomes a rhetorical animal through involvement in the process of intellectual play." Covino suggests some social consequences for this anarchic view of rhetoric, which opposes the contemporary dedication "to communicative efficiency and the necessity of public business," but such consequences seem far removed from the more deliberate political interventions advocated by other contributors to the volume. This distance is nicely marked by Covino's quotation from DeQuincy: "Where conviction begins, the field of Rhetoric ends."

XII

Something like "conviction" clearly pervades most of the rhetorical work in the pages of these essays. In fact, ideological conviction or political commitment is often explicitly cited as a motive for that work. At the very least, there appears to be a political turn within the rhetorical turn. Note how many of the essays take up rhetorical politics or political rhetoric; and among those that don't do so, note how many are followed by an afterword that deals with or gestures toward the neglected link between rhetoric and politics.

XIII

It is also noteworthy — though not surprising in a volume with rhetoric as its pretext — that several of the essays analyze the guiding metaphors in the theory or project they are examining. In "Rewording the Rhetoric of Composition," Paul Kameen notes rightly that each category of composition textbook is "both created and bounded by certain metaphoric conceptions of the 'universe of discourse' within which writing can take place," and he is especially sensitive to the "particular metaphors that function as analogies for the writing process." I find myself applauding his critiques of all those composition tropes I don't find useful — until, of course, he comes close to rejecting *my* favorite trope of use: "Language is not a tool to express something else with; it is what is expressed." Well, yes and no: Language certainly isn't a tool for simply expressing some nonlinguistic, pre-existent idea or thought — which is Kameen's main point; but can't one piece of language be used as a tool to express (translate) another piece? But then again perhaps there's no disagreement here — at least about some kind of usefulness for the trope of language-use. For later Kameen writes that language "both creates and bounds the field of our discourse" and in that sense it is "an instrument rather than a record of creative thought."

XIV

But another essay does clearly take to rhetorical task the instrumentalist trope. In "The Rhetor as Eiron: Plato's Defense of Dialogue," Jan Swearingen attempts a vigorous defense of Plato's criticisms of sophistic rhetoric and writes: "An instrumentalist view of language and linguistic interactions is one which posits that language is used to do something, to effect a change in thinking or in other human beings. Primacy is given to the efficaciousness of a given utterance, over and above its ultimate truth or meaning. The sophistic emphasis on *techne,* a craft or technique, was one of the sources of their instrumentalist conception of language, and the one which Plato singles out more than any other for scrutiny." It is a function of how much I am in the grips of the instrumentalist trope, of how much it is using me as much as I am using it, that I can only see the instrumentalist view. That is, not only do I not agree with Swearingen's Platonic critique of instrumentalism; her formulation of the rejected view—"language is used to do something, to effect a change in thinking or in other human beings"—strikes me as a convincing definition of rhetoric as such. She rejects as a dangerous stance toward language a definition that I see as a quite useful definition of rhetoric itself.

XV

A neo-sophist might suggest that Swearingen is simply begging the question in her critique of sophistic instrumentalism here. She uses a Platonic distinction to claim that for the sophists "primacy is given to the efficaciousness of a given utterance, over and above its ultimate truth or meaning." But it is precisely the sophistic claim that there is no absolute or "ultimate truth." It's rhetoric all the way down (or up). Thus, the Platonic objections to instrumentalism are convincing only if you already agree with the Platonic distinctions.

XVI

Not surprisingly the Greek Sophists are often invoked in debates over relativism and anarchy. But recently, defining sophistic teachings has become almost as controversial as defining rhetorical theory more generally.

XVII

For Kameen, the sophists made the dangerous mistake of separating form and content: "Like Plato, Coleridge recommends that systems which depend on radical form-content distinctions be 'resigned, as their proper trade, to the sophists.'" Similarly, for Swearingen, the problem is the sophistic separation of technique from truth, of instrument from foundation. As Gadamer tells the story: "Rhetorical theory was a long prepared-for result of a controversy that represented the breaking into Greek culture of an intoxicating and frightening new art of speaking and a new idea of education itself: that of the Sophists. At that time an uncanny skill in standing everything on its head, the Sicilian art of oratory, flowed in on the strait-laced but easily influenced youths of Athens. Now it became paramountly necessary to teach this new power (this great ruler, as Gorgias had called oratory) its proper limits—to discipline it. From Protagoras to Isocrates, the masters of rhetoric claimed not only to teach speaking, but also the formation of a civic consciousness that bore the promise of political success. But *it was Plato who first created the foundations* out of which a new and all-shattering art of speaking . . . could find its limits and legitimate place."[10]

XVIII

In "Cognition, Convention, and Certainty," Patricia Bizzell makes use of the instrumentalist trope and combines it with an anti-foundationalist historicism that, to this neo-sophist, convincingly answers the charge of relativism without relying on Platonic or any other foundationalism. She points out that the trope of language use does not necessarily mean treating language as a neutral instrument or a transparent medium. Like Hubert Dreyfus, she argues that language-use is regular but not rule governed, and like Stanley Fish she connects the regularity of language-use to the membership in diverse interpretive or discourse communities. She notes that "Language-using is connected not only to the immediate situation but to the larger society, too, in the form of conventions for construing reality." And finally she emphasizes the "ethical and political dimensions" of socializing our students "into the academic discourse community." Does making students aware of the contingent nature of their discourse communities lead them to embrace a dangerous relativism of values? Like Richard Rorty, Bizzell answers that such relativism in the cultural conversation is impossible: to be in history within a discourse community does not mean that a member can say just any old thing; rather such a rhetor is enabled and constrained by the conversation she is in. "For the goal of discovering Truth, Rorty substitutes the goal of continuing conversation, but this will not be a dangerously relativistic goal because always conditioned by and having to answer to an historical framework."[11]

XIX

As Stanley Fish has written, "one could say without too much exaggeration that modern anti-foundationalism is old sophism writ analytic. . . . The rehabilitation by anti-foundationalism of the claims of situation, history, politics, and convention in opposition to the more commonly successful claims of logic, brute fact empiricism, the natural, and the necessary marks one more chapter in the long history of the quarrel between philosophy and rhetoric, between the external and the temporal, between God's view and point of view."[12] What needs to be added here is that the foundationalist/anti-foundationalist conflict is being (indeed has always been) fought out within the rhetorical tradition itself, and that the Sophists' teachings are one of the recurrent pretexts for rhetorical theory's staging of the conflict. The present set of essays participate in that staging with the the anti-sophistic arguments of Swearingen's Plato and Kameen's Coleridge juxtaposed to the revisionary readings of the Sophists in Susan Jarratt's "Toward a Sophistic Historiography."

XX

For those of us advocating a more political definition of rhetoric and a more politicized use of rhetorical theory, many of Jarratt's observations about the Sophists are especially helpful for focusing attention on the historical connections between rhetoric and politics. "Though [the Sophists] are at worst characterized as skeptics and idel bickerers, in fact, they and their students did the political and legal work of the *polis*." Jarratt's reading of the Sophists and her argument that "rhetoric, with its commitment to action, . . . must be able to move from critique to reconstruction" should be read in conjunction with Michael Halloran's powerful plea for a new rhetorical studies, a "rhetoric of citizenship," which addresses "students as political beings, as members of a body politic in which they have a responsibility to form judgments and influence the judgments of others on public issues" (at the end of his "Rhetoric in the American College Curriculum: The Decline of Public Discourse").

XXI

These calls for rhetorical intervention in public discourse seem especially urgent in the nineties, when the martial tropes start taking such turns as the following: Worried about the "many small [academic] skirmishes" over canon revision, curriculum reform, and "the supplanting of esthetic by political responses to literature," George Will writes that "in this low-visibility, high-intensity war, Lynne Cheney [chair of the National Endowment for the Humanities] is secretary of domestic defense. The foreign adversaries her husband, Dick, must keep at bay are less dangerous, in the long run, than the domestic forces with which she must deal. Those forces are fighting against the conservation of the common culture that is the nation's social cement."[13]

XXII

GROUCHO: Now that you're Secretary of War, what kind of an army do you think we ought to have?
CHICO: Well, I'll tell ya what I think. I think we should have a standing army.
GROUCHO: Why should we have a standing army?
CHICO: Because then we save money on chairs.

—from the Marx Brothers' *Duck Soup* (1933), a political satire reportedly banned in Italy by Mussolini.[14]

XXIII

Revolution: radical change, coup d'etat, uprising, rebellion, overthrow, reversal, debacle, cataclysm.

Revolution: turning, spinning, gyration, revolving, cycle, rotation, whirl, wheel, pirouette.[15]

Dance: whirl of bodies, revolution of figures, rotation of tropes.

XXIV

In explaining her rhetorical borrowings from modern physics, Phelps notes two principles of its epistemology: "The first is the basic event-nature of the universe in which objects (as structures or forms) are constituted interactively from the energy of flux (i.e., structure *is* process). The second principle is the identity of the dancer with the dance: the significance of perspective to all knowledge, and thus the participation of the observer in the reality of the observed." Phelps uses these principles to elaborate her suggestive trope of discourse as dance, which in effect deconstructs the process vs. product opposition that continues to structure much thinking about both writing and reading.

XXV

Something of the same thing is accomplished though differently by Charles Bazerman in "The Writing of Scientific Non-Fiction," which complements Phelps's piece in ways I am only beginning to understand. Whereas Phelps uses the tropes of science to reconceptualize composition, Bazerman uses the concepts of composition to reunderstand science. For Phelps, discourse structure is redefined as participatory practice; for Bazerman, scientific practice is represented as rhetorically structured. Phelps's afterword notes how "new gestalts have become salient, bringing into focus cultural and political understandings of discourse as activity," while Bazerman's "Afterthoughts" rejects as least one old political way of troping his rhetorical task: He no longer sees himself as walking a narrow line "between the marauding bands of radical relativists and what they claimed were the entrenched forces of positivistic domination." Instead, he sees himself walking (why couldn't he have said "dancing"?) along "a broad and familiar path, passing through many locales, and intersecting with many other roads." And on his journey in science studies he has discovered that the "legend of a fearsome positivistic phalanx is a legend only, fostered by a small number of interested parties on both sides of a line they have mutually constructed."

308 *Steven Mailloux*

XXVI

Another one of these rhetorically constructed lines — within and between disciplines — is examined in Sharon Crowley's "Neo-Romanticism and the History of Rhetoric." Her story about poetics and rhetoric will surprise only those literary critics and theorists — and they may be legion — who still ignore the rhetorical return within contemporary critical theory and who continue to be willfully ignorant of recent composition research and theorizing.

XXVII

Someone familiar with both sides of the poetics/rhetoric line is John Schilb. In "The History of Rhetoric and the Rhetoric of History," he suggests how disciplinary boundaries between history and rhetoric are usefully crossed, and then in his "Postscript" he performs a similar operation on the lines between literary and composition studies. The "Postscript" also reiterates the tension I have alluded to throughout these fragments: between ludic poststructuralism and ideology critique, between (in Schilb's terms) "deconstruction and social awareness," between attention to the "self-subversiveness of discourse" and sensitivity to the "plight of various peoples" in structures of domination and exploitation. Schilb joins others in trying to integrate the two perspectives though he makes his own preference clear: "Although deconstruction can identify nuances of form, it does risk degenerating into linguistics-based despair unless it considers how particular social conditions produce, infuse, and get modified by the textual details it notices."

XXVIII

With apologies to Lennon and McCartney:

> You say you want a revolution,
> Well, you know,
> We all want to change the world.
> You tell me that it's evolution,
> Well, you know,
> We all want to change the world.
> But when you talk about de[con]struction,
> Don't you know that you can count me out.
> — from "Revolution" (1968), more or less.

XXIX

I wish I could quote in full here several paragraphs from Schilb's incisive discussion of "revolution" and its use as a term in historical discourse.

I will content myself with appropriating one sentence and give it a wider application than it initially had in Schilb's essay but one I believe is consistent with the arguments he makes elsewhere: In reading disciplinary histories, we should be more aware of how the "word 'revolution' remains embedded in discussion of intellectual developments within the academy [and is] not extended to the momentous [and sometimes not so momentous] rhetorical actions which took place outside its walls."

XXX

A newspaper headline: "Proms Test Dance Democracy."
The article begins: "The students were in formal dress Friday night for Corcoran High School's Senior Ball, but when the king and queen took the floor, they weren't about to sway to some worn-out love song. Instead, they danced to the ball's official song: "Let's chill." The song, by the black artist Guy, wasn't everybody's idea of the perfect romantic tune. But it did symbolize a key to holding a successful prom in an urban high school: It must be a model of cultural and ethnic diversity."[16]

XXXI

The inaugural issue of *P/T* announced that "The editors have made it their standing [dancing?] policy . . . to be less receptive to conventional academic articles with clearly stated theses that involve no risk and that especially lead to a sense of closure and that have as their main goal to analyze the logic of theories and finally to prove or refute them. The editorial board will be more receptive, instead, to the kind of open-ended speculative discourse found in exploratory articles, progress reports, and working papers. Hence the title and term 'pre/text.'"[17] With this pretext for the unconventional in place, the first issue concluded with some cooking recipes and rhetorical meditations. My favorite bit is not the (in)famous: "Jello and tuna together *is* anarchy," but rather the equally symptomatic comment on Julia Child's postscript "On Playing with Your Food": "What we really need to do in the first place perhaps is not to forbid *free play* in cooking. Play, as Julia sees it, is simply to enjoy speculating about new possibilities in every method and each raw material. She says that true cooks love to set one flavor against another in the imagination. She says they do not follow recipes slavishly, but invent from them, play with them, in other words. Recipes are only a pretext for cooking, don't you agree? . . . What she says about playing with food applies to virtually everything — writing, making love, running, dancing, whatever."[18]

XXXII

The editor of "Rhetoric, Cookery, and Recipes" notes at the beginning of his introduction: "Each of us, I'm sure, has a personal explanation of how we came to be interested in rhetoric. For me, it was in part while reading for a philosophy course and coming across and being especially upset at Socrates' attack on Gorgias and rhetoric. Actually, it would be more accurate to say that it was Socrates' attack on cookery that really most upset me at this time. Such a noble art and activity was grossly and unfairly being misrepresented in the dialogue, and I guess I responded personally because my family, specifically my maternal grandparents, were from a long line of very proud Sicilian cooks."[19]

XXXIII

Here's a story about the origin of rhetoric in ancient Sicily. In Syracuse around 465 B.C., Corax invented rhetorical theory to maintain his influence in the new republic after the tyrannies of Gelon and Hieron. The revolution that changed the state came about in direct response to the tyrants' authoritarian savagery. Perhaps fearing the power of words, Gelon and Hieron had forbidden the Syracusans to speak and ordered them instead to use their hands, feet, and eyes to communicate without sound. Thus, the story goes, the invention of a silent dancing preceded the overthrow of the tyrants, which in turn led to the establishment of a democratic republic and the beginning of rhetorical theory.[20]

XXXIV

Rhetoric: "our field—which I broadly define as anyone interested in language and (mis)communication" (Vitanza's Prospective).

XXXV

Roman, my then-eight-year-old son, once asked me about the meaning of my "Marx and Lennon" T-shirt with its pictures of Groucho and John. I first tried to explain something about Karl Marx and Communism, V. I. Lenin and Soviet history, and the political significance of the phrase "Marx and Lenin." Then I went on about the Marx Brothers, the Beatles, and plays on words. When I concluded my mini-lecture, my son turned to me and said, "I just have one question. Why did a comedian start the Russian Revolution?"

NOTES

1. Unfortunately, the *Congressional Record* does not record the slip I thought I heard during the live television coverage of the debate. See *Congressional Record,* 137, no. 6 (10 January 1991), p. S105.

2. Rev. Richard C. Halverson, "Prayer," *Congressional Record,* 137, no. 6 (10 January 1991), p. S97.

3. My distinction here looks like (and partially borrows from) one pos-

ited by Teresa Ebert—between "ludic postmodernism" and "resistance postmodernism"—but I am also contesting her too easy assignment of the "rhetorical" to the ludic side of the opposition. See her "Writing in the Political: Resistance Postmodernism," unpublished ms (1990), quoted in Mas'ud Zavarzadeh, *Seeing Films Politically* (Albany: State University of New York Press, 1991), pp. 32-33.

4. Halverson, *Congressional Record,* p. S97.

5. Steven Mailloux, *Rhetorical Power* (Ithaca: Cornell University Press, 1989), p. xii.

6. "On Truth and Lying in an Extra-Moral Sense," in *Friedrich Nietzsche on Rhetoric and Language,* ed. and trans. Sander L. Gilman, Carole Blair, and David J. Parent (New York: Oxford University Press, 1989), p. 250.

7. Kenneth Burke, "Rhetoric and Poetics," in his *Language as Symbolic Action* (Berkeley and Los Angeles: University of California Press, 1966), p. 296.

8. And note her afterword's comment that "the concept of the 'dance' here applies to all transactions over and through text." For discussion of the transactive metaphor, see Mailloux, "The Turns of Reader-Response Criticism," in *Conversations: Contemporary Critical Theory and the Teaching of Literature,* ed. Charles Moran and Elizabeth F. Penfield (Urbana: National Council of Teachers of English, 1990), pp. 41-42.

9. Victor Vitanza, "A Dialogue Concerning Tuna and Strawberry Jello," *Pre/Text* 1 (Spring-Fall 1980): 208.

10. Hans-Georg Gadamer, "On the Scope and Function of Hermeneutical Reflection," trans. G. B. Hess and R. E. Palmer, in Gadamer, *Philosophical Hermeneutics,* ed. David E. Linge (Berkeley and Los Angeles: University of California Press, 1976), p. 22, emphasis added.

11. Much has been written recently about the conservative tendencies of Rorty's liberalism and its use of the trope of egalitarian conversation. For an attempt to give the trope a more Foucauldian twist, see my *Rhetorical Power,* pp. 146-47.

12. "Anti-Foundationalism, Theory Hope, and the Teaching of Composition," in Fish, *Doing What Comes Naturally: Change, Rhetoric, and the Practice of Theory in Literary and Legal Studies* (Durham, N.C.: Duke University Press, 1989), p. 347. This would be the appropriate place to take up Fish's critique of Bizzell and othes who attempt to make practical use of anti-foundationalism. It would be especially appropriate here to confront Fish's claim that "revolution and reform can take no particular warrant from anti-foundationalism, and to think otherwise is once again to make the mistake of making anti-foundationalism into a foundation" (p. 351). (Un)fortunately, I must use the excuse of space limitations and seem to dance around Fish's point by simply citing relevant discussions elsewhere. See my *Rhetorical Power,* ch. 6, and Cornel West, *The Evasion of Philosophy: A Genealogy of Pragmatism* (Madison: University of Wisconsin Press, 1989). Also see Bizzell, "Foundationalism and Anti-Foundationalism in Composition Studies," *Pre/Text* 7 (Spring-Summer 1986): 37-56.

13. George F. Will, "Literary Politics," *Newsweek,* 22 April 1991, p. 72. I am grateful (that doesn't seem the right word) to David Downing for first bringing this article to my attention.

14. Groucho Marx, *The Groucho Phile* (Indianapolis: Bobbs-Merrill, 1976), p. 107

15. Thanks to my handy *Roget's College Thesaurus* (New York: New American Library, 1962), pp. 312, 315.

16. Paul Riede, "Proms Test Dance Democracy," Syracuse *Post-Standard,* 18 May 1991, p. A-1 (paragraphing modified).

17. "Foreword," *Pre/Text* 1 (Spring-Fall 1980): 5-6.

18. Victor Vitanza, "A Dialogue Concerning Tuna and Strawberry Jello," *Pre/Text* 1 (Spring-Fall 1980): 208, 210.

19. Victor Vitanza, "Sunday Dinners and Rhetoric: A Personal Reminiscence," *Pre/Text* 1 (Spring-Fall 1980): 205.

20. "Prolegomena Artis Rhetoricae," in *Prolegomenon Sylloge,* ed. Hugo Rabe (Leipzig: Teubner, 1931), pp. 24-25. I am very grateful to Karen Bassi and Jeffrey Carnes for their help in translating this Greek text by an anonymous Christian author of the fourth or fifth century. See D. A. G. Hinks, "Tisias and Corax and the Invention of Rhetoric," *Classical Quarterly* 34 (1940): 67; Stanley Wilcox, "Corax and the *Prolegomena,*" *American Journal of Philosophy* 59 (1943): 15-16; and Vincent Farenga, "Periphrasis on the Origin of Rhetoric," *MLN* 94 (1979): 1033-55.

Contents of *PRE/TEXT,* Volumes 1–10
Notes on Contributors

CONTENTS OF *PRE/TEXT,* Volumes 1-10

VOLUME 1, nos. 1-2 (1980), featuring articles on Paul Feyerabend

Tom Cook and Ron Seamon, *"Ein Feyerabenteur* or, Who Is Feyerabend and Where Can He Go from Here/Rhetoric and Skepticism in Feyerabend's Philosophy of Science"

Walter B. Weimer, "For and Against method: Reflections on Feyerabend and the Foibles of Philosophy"

With additional articles by:

Sharon Bassett, "A Problem in Interpretation: Arnold, Hirsch, and the Making of Texts"

Carl B. Holmberg, "A Heuristic Matrix Theory of Rhetorical Figures"

E. Fred Carlisle, "Literature, Science, and Language"

Paul Kameen, "Rewording the Rhetoric of Composition"

James P. Zappen, "Carl R. Rogers and Political Rhetoric"

Sharon Bassett, "Freudian Psychoanalysis: A Rhetorical Situation?" (review/article)

"Editorial Preface 2: 'Rhetoric, Cookery, and Recipes'"

VOLUME 2, nos. 1-2 (1981), special issue on Michael Polanyi, edited by Sam Watson,

Harry Prosch, "Polanyi and Rhetoric"

William H. Poteat, "Further Polanyian Meditations"

Robin Hodgkin, "Making Sense and the Means for Doing So"

With additional articles by:

James A. Reither, "Some Ideas of Michael Polanyi and Some Implications for Teaching Writing"

Diane Sautter, "Tacit and Explicit Tulips"

Rembert Herbert, "Into the Tacit Dimension: Reflections on Michael Polanyi's *Personal Knowledge*"

William E. Goding, "Polanyi and Peak: A Short Semantic Symphony"

Robert L. Scott, "The Tacit Dimension and Rhetoric: What It Means to Be Persuading and Persuaded"

James L. Wiser, "Michael Polanyi and the Problem of Toleration"

Lloyd D. Rue, "Reconstructing the Conditions for Cultural Coherence"

Dale W. Cannon, "The 'Primitive'/'Civilized' Opposition and the Modern Notions of Objectivity: A Linkage"

Sam Watson, "Breakfast in the Tacit Tradition: Preface 3"

With nine pages of photographs of Michael Polanyi

VOLUME 3, no. 1 (1982), begins as a quarterly

Peter Schofer and Donald Rice, "The Rhetoric of Displacement and Condensation"
Carolyn R. Miller, "Public Knowledge in Science and Society" (review/article)
Louise Wetherbee Phelps, "The Dance of Discourse: A Dynamic, Relativistic View of Structure"

VOLUME 3, no. 2 (1982)

Frank D'Angelo, "Rhetoric and Cognition: Toward a Metatheory of Discourse"
Michael McGuire, "Some Problems with Rhetorical Example"
Gerard Hauser and Carole Blair, "Rhetorical Antecedents to the Public"

VOLUME 3, no. 3 (1982)

David B. Downing, "'Radical Historicity' and Common Sense: On the Poetics of Human Nature"
Patricia Bizzell, "Cognition, Convention, and Certainty: What We Need to Know About Writing"
S. Michael Halloran, "Rhetoric in the American College Curriculum: The Decline of Public Discourse"

VOLUME 3, no. 4 (1982)

C. Jan Swearingen, "The Rhetor as *Eiron:* Plato's Defense of Dialogue"
Peter Elbow, "Preface 4: The Doubting Game and the Believing Game."

VOLUME 4, no. 1 (1983)

Brian G. Caraher, "*Allegories of Reading:* Positing a Rhetoric of Romanticism; or, Paul de Man's Critique of Pure Figural Anteriority" (review/article)
Martin Steinmann, Jr., "Learning, Inscrutability, and Rhetoric: Paolo Valesio's *Novantiqua*" (review/article)
W. Ross Winterowd, "Post-Structuralism and Composition"
W. Ross Winterowd, "Dear Peter Elbow"

VOLUME 4, no. 2 (1983)

William Covino, "Thomas De Quincey in a Revisionist History of Rhetoric"
Floyd Merrell, "How General Should/Can Rhetoric Be?- (review/article)
Tilly Warnock, "Preface 5: The Dreadful Has Already Happened, or, What is a Rhetorician's Role in an English Department?"

VOLUME 4, nos. 3-4 (1983), special issue on Paul Ricoeur, edited by Louise Wetherbee Phelps

Charles Regan, "Hermeneutics and the Semantics of Action"
Mary Gerhart, "Genre as Praxis: An Inquiry"
Stephen William Foster, "Deconstructing a Text on North Africa: Ricoeur and Post-Structuralism

With additional articles by:
Louise Wetherbee Phelps, "Possibilities for a Post-Critical Rhetoric: A Parasitical Preface 6"

Robert D. Sweeney and Louise Wetherbee Phelps, "Rhetorical Themes in the Work of Paul Ricoeur: A Bibliographical Introduction"
Bill Deloach, "On First Looking into Ricoeur's Interpretation Theory: A Beginner's Guide"
C. Jan Swearingen, "Between Intention and Inscription: Toward a Dialogical Rhetoric"
Stuart L. Charmé, "Paul Ricoeur as Teacher: A Reminiscence"
Leonard Lawlor, "Event and Repeatability: Ricoeur and Derrida in Debate"

VOLUME 5, no. 1 (1984)

Paul Ricoeur, "Toward a 'Post-Critical' Rhetoric?"
Sharon Crowley, "Pre/face, No. 7: Neo-Romanticism and the History of Rhetoric"
Charles Bazerman, "The Writing of Scientific Non-fiction"

VOLUME 5, no. 2 (1984), special issue on Chaim Perelman

Robert L. Scott, "Chaim Perelman: Persona and Accommodation in *The New Rhetoric*"
Marie J. Secor, "Perelman's *Loci* in Literary Argument"
Charles W. Kneupper, "The Tyranny of Logic and the Freedom of Argumentation"

VOLUME 5, nos. 3-4 (1984)

Jim W. Corder, "A New Introduction to Psychoanalysis, Taken As a Version of Modern Rhetoric"
James S. Baumlin, "Decorum, *Kairos,* and the 'New' Rhetoric"
Sharon Crowley, "On Post-Structuralism and Compositionists"
Charles W. Kneupper, "Rhetoric As Epistemic: A Conversation with Richard A. Cherwitz"
"A Rhetor's Miscellany"

VOLUME 6, nos. 1-2 (1985)

James P. Zappen, "Historical Perspectives on the Philosophy and the Rhetoric of Science: Sources for a Pluralistic Rhetoric"
Brian G. Caraher, "A Grammar of Actions and Attitudes: Unfolding a Humanist Theory of Literary Studies (review of Charles Altieri's *Act and Quality*)
Richard Leo Enos and Elizabeth Odoroff, "The Orality of the 'Paragraph' in Greek Literature"
R. J. Reddick, "The Grammar of Logic" (review of Beauzée's article on grammar, originally published in Diderot's *Encyclopédie*)
Ralph Flores, "The Rhetoric of the Buddha: Selfless Selves, The Theatre of Persuasion"

VOLUME 6, nos. 3-4 (1985), special double issue on Kenneth Burke

Reviews:
Hank Lazer, "Thinking of Kenneth Burke" (KB at Univ. of Alabama)
Michael Feehan, "Three Days and Three Terms" (KB at Univ. of Texas at Arlington)

Victor J. Vitanza, "A Mal-Lingering Thought (Tragic-Comedic) About KB's Visit" (KB at UTA)
Gregory S. Jay, "Burke Re-Marx" (South Atlantic MLA panel on KB and Marx)
Gerald A. Hauser, "An Afternoon with Burke and Cowley" (KB at The Pennsylvania State Univ.)
Kenneth Burke and Malcom Cowley, "A Conversation" (KB at Penn State)
Tilly Warnock, "Anecdotes on Accessibility: KB in Wyoming" (KB at the Wyoming conference on Freshman and Sophomore Literature)

Articles:
Paul Jay, "Kenneth Burke: A Man of Letters"
Denise M. Bostdorff and Phillip K. Tompkins, "Musical Form and Rhetorical Form: Kenneth Burke's *Dial* Reviews as Counterpart to *Counter-Statement*"
Don M. Burks, "Dramatic Irony, Collaboration, and Kenneth Burke's Theory of Form"
Bob Heath, "Kenneth Burke's Perspective on Perspectives"

Photographs/Sculpture:
Don and Virginia Burks, "KB at Home and Bust of KB"

Notes:
Lewis Baker, "Some Manuscript Collections Containing Kenneth Burke Materials"
Charles W. Mann, "The KB Collection: The Penn State Library"

Statement/Counter-Statement:
Michael Feehan, "Oscillation as Assimilation: Burke's Latest Self-Revisions"
Kenneth Burke, "In Haste"

A pre/text:
Lewis Baker, from "A Biography of Kenneth Burke (in progress)"

VOLUME 7, nos. 1-2 (1986)

John Schilb, "The History of Rhetoric and the Rhetoric of History"
Patricia Bizzell, "Foundationalism and Anti-Foundationalism in Composition Studies"
Susan Wells, "Richards, Burke and the Relations between Rhetoric and Poetics"
James R. Bennett, "PRE/FACE 9: Critical Pluralism and Democracy"
Barry Brummett, "Richard Cherwitz in the Prison House of Lanauge" (a response to inter/view with Cherwitz in vol. 5, nos. 3-4)
"A Rhetor's Miscellany"

VOLUME 7, nos. 3-4 (1986), special double issue on Orality and Literacy, edited by C. Jan Swearingen

Eric A. Havelock, "Orality, Literacy, and Star Wars"
Robert McIlvaine, "Response to Eric A. Havelock"

Discussion following Havelock Lecture:
C. Jan Swearingen, "Literate Rhetors and Their Illiterate Audiences: The Orality of Early Literacy"

Thomas J. Farrell, "A Defense for Requiring Standard English"
Beth Daniell, "Against the Great Leap Theory of Literacy"
John Baugh, "Response and Discussion"
Eric A. Havelock "After Words: A Post Script"

VOLUME 8, nos. 1-2 (1987), special double issue on Historiography and the Histories of Rhetorics I: Revisionary Histories

Susan C. Jarratt, "Toward a Sophistic Historiography"
John Schilb, "Differences, Displacements, and Disruptions: Toward Revisionary Histories of Rhetoric"
James A. Berlin, "Revisionary History: The Dialectical Method"
Victor J. Vitanza, "'Notes' Towards Historiographies of Rhetorics; or the Rhetorics of the Histories of Rhetorics: Traditional, Revisionary, and Sub/Versive"
"Colloquy"

VOLUME 8, nos. 3-4 (1987), special double issue on Cultural Criticism and the Teaching of Writing

Sharon Crowley, "Derrida, Deconstruction, and Our Scene of Teaching"
Luanne T. Frank, "Criticism and the Meaning of Writing"
Lynn Worsham, "The Question Concerning Invention: Hermeneutics and the Genesis of Writing"

With Additional Essays by:
Edward P. J. Corbett, "Rhetoric's Past and Future (an inter/view)"
William A. Covino, "Takin' It to the Streets"
Earl Croasmun, "Response to Cherwitz and Brummett"

VOLUME 9, nos. 1-2 (1988)

Steve Whitson, "The Phaedrus Complex"
Rex Olson, "Derrida (f)or Us? Composition and the Taking of Text"
Ann E. Berthoff, with John Schilb, Patricia Harkin, and C. Jan Swearingen, "How Philosophy Can Help Us" (a polylog)

VOLUME 9, nos. 2-3 (1988)

Thomas S. Frentz, "Resurrecting the Feminine in *The Name of The Rose*"
Takis Poulakos, "Towards a Cultural Understanding of Classical Epideictic Oratory"
Alan G. Gross, "Discourse on Method: The Rhetorical Analysis of Scientific Texts"
Thomas E. Porter, review/article on T. Maranhao, *Therapeutic Discourse and Socratic Dialogue*
Sharon Crowley, Lorie Goodman Batson, Theresa Enos, and Anne Rosenthal, "Women in the Profession (of Composition)" (a polylog)

VOLUME 10, nos. 1-2 (1989)

Paul Jude Beauvais, "Sartre's Pleas and the Purposes of Writing"
James J. Sosnoski, "The Psycho-Politics of Error"

Patricia Harkin, "Bringing Lore to Light"
Dilip Gaonkar, Susan C. Jarratt, Henry Johnstone, Jr., Takis Poulakos, Jane Sutton, and Victor J. Vitanza, a polylog on Presocratic fragments

VOLUME 10, nos. 3-4 (1989), special issue on Barbara Herrnstein Smith's *Contingencies of Value*

Patricia Harkin and James J. Sosnoski, "Barbara Herrnstein Smith: A Contemporary Sophist"
Barbara Herrnstein Smith, "A Conversation" (inter/view)
Charles Eric Reeves, "*Measure for Measure:* 'Judging' and 'Meting' in the Academic Community"
Colleen R. Lamos, "Playing to Win"
Joseph Valente, "Coming to Judgment"
Morse Peckham, "Valuing"
Barbara Herrnstein Smith, "Selected Bibliography"

Notes on Contributors

DAVID BARTHOLOMAE is Professor of English at the University of Pittsburgh.

CHARLES BAZERMAN is Professor of Literature, Communication and Culture at the Georgia Institute of Technology.

JAMES A. BERLIN is Professor of English at Purdue University.

PATRICIA BIZZELL is Professor of English at the College of the Holy Cross in Worcester, Mass.

WILLIAM COVINO is Associate Professor and Associate Head of the Department of English at the University of Illinois, Chicago.

SHARON CROWLEY is Professor of English at the University of Iowa.

S. MICHAEL HALLORAN is Associate Dean and Professor in the Department of Language, Literature, and Communication at Rensselaer Polytechnic Institute in Troy, New York.

SUSAN C. JARRATT is Director of College Composition and Professor of English at Texas Christian University.

PAUL KAMEEN is Professor of English and Head of the Writing Workshop at the University of Pittsburgh.

STEVEN MAILLOUX is Professor of English at the University of California, Irvine.

LOUISE WETHERBEE PHELPS is Professor in the Writing Program at Syracuse University.

JOHN SCHILB is Assistant Professor of English at the University of Maryland, College Park.

C. JAN SWEARINGEN is Professor of English at the University of Texas, Arlington.

VICTOR J. VITANZA is Associate Professor of English and Director of the Center for Rhetorical and Critical Theory at the University of Texas, Arlington.

Pittsburgh Series in Composition, Literacy, and Culture

ACADEMIC DISCOURSE AND CRITICAL CONSCIOUSNESS
    Patricia Bizzell

EATING ON THE STREET: TEACHING LITERACY IN A MULTICULTURAL SOCIETY
    David Schaafsma

FRAGMENTS OF RATIONALITY: POSTMODERNITY AND THE SUBJECT OF COMPOSITION
    Lester Faigley

THE INSISTENCE OF THE LETTER
    Bill Green, Editor

KNOWLEDGE, CULTURE, AND POWER: INTERNATIONAL PERSPECTIVES ON LITERACY AS POLICY AND PRACTICE
    Peter Freebody and Anthony R. Welch, Editors

LITERACY ONLINE: THE PROMISE (AND PERIL) OF READING AND WRITING WITH COMPUTERS
    Myron C. Tuman, Editor

THE POWERS OF LITERACY: A GENRE APPROACH TO TEACHING WRITING
    Bill Cope and Mary Kalantzis, Editors

PRE/TEXT: THE FIRST DECADE
    Victor Vitanza, Editor

WORD PERFECT: LITERACY IN THE COMPUTER AGE
    Myron C. Tuman

WRITING SCIENCE: LITERACY AND DISCURSIVE POWER
    M. A. K. Halliday and J. R. Martin